John Momson

EVERYMAN, I will go with thee,

and be thy guide,

In thy most need to go by thy side

JEAN FRANÇOIS MARIE AROUET DE VOLTAIRE

Born in Paris in 1694. Educated at the Jesuit Collège Louis le Grand. His provocative writings necessitated frequent changes of residence, and he lived in England, 1726–9, in Germany, 1751–3, and on the shores of the Lake of Geneva from 1754 till the year of his death. He died in 1778.

VOLTAIRE

The Age of Louis XIV

TRANSLATED BY
MARTYN P. POLLACK

PREFACE BY
F. C. GREEN, M.A., PH.D.
Professor of French Literature in the
University of Edinburgh

DENT: LONDON
EVERYMAN'S LIBRARY
DUTTON: NEW YORK

© *Preface, J. M. Dent & Sons Ltd, 1961*
All rights reserved
Made in Great Britain
at the
Aldine Press · Letchworth · Herts
for
J. M. DENT & SONS LTD
Aldine House · Bedford Street · London
First included in Everyman's Library 1926
Last reprinted 1969

NO. 780

SBN: 460 00780 7

PREFACE

FRANÇOIS-MARIE AROUET, born in Paris in 1694, did not begin to call himself De Voltaire until 1722. By then he was well known to men of letters, to the theatre-going public and to the secret police. He enjoyed two educations; one at the Jesuit College of Louis-le-Grand, the other in the *salon* of the notorious Duc de Vendôme, Grand Prior of the Order of the Knights Templars. In the former he acquired a taste for the humanities and a contempt for orthodox religion; in the latter he frequented the society of *libertins* or freethinkers like the epicurean poets, Chaulieu and La Fare.

Voltaire's father, who was family lawyer to some of the noblest houses in France, decided to remove his son from this dangerous *milieu* and, in 1713, sent him to Holland in the suite of the diplomat Châteauneuf. A romantic love-affair led to his speedy return and the youth was articled to a colleague of his father's. Here Voltaire picked up enough law to provide him later with ammunition in his campaign against the antiquated legal system of the *ancien régime*. His talent for satiric verse attracted the unfavourable attention of the Regent, who exiled the young satirist to Sully-en-Loire, where he remained for a time as guest of the Duc de Sully, a former *habitué* of the Temple. Here he enjoyed himself, composing a tragedy, *Œdipe*, and an epic, *La Henriade*, published in 1723. The Regent, the least vindictive of men, allowed him to return with a paternal warning. But in 1717 Arouet was imprisoned for a satirical poem which he had not written, and to this experience, which lasted eleven months, we owe a spirited little poem humorously describing the manner of his arrest and entitled *La Bastille*.

Meanwhile the Comédie-Française was rehearsing his tragedy *Œdipe*, produced with great success a month after the author's release from jail. The Regent gave him a pension and a medal. The play put Voltaire in the first rank of living dramatists. Yet, viewing it in perspective, one can already discover why its author was never to share the immortality of Corneille or Racine. *Œdipe*, like nearly every tragedy composed by Voltaire, is 'une pièce à thèse', a vehicle for his anticlericalism.

For some years Voltaire worked at *La Henriade*, an epic dealing with the religious civil wars under Henri IV and long regarded as his chief title to fame. Ambitious, impetuous, determined to surmount the social handicap imposed upon him by his lack of nobility, Voltaire frequented the *salons*, where he soon became known for his audacity and deadly wit. At the Opéra he had words with the young chevalier de Rohan-Chabot, who twitted him upon his new name De Voltaire, inviting the riposte: 'Mon nom, je le commence et vous finissez le vôtre.' The chevalier's revenge was to entice his enemy downstairs from a dinner with the Duc de Sully and to have him soundly thrashed by six lackeys. In a fury his victim called out his aggressor, who could not, however, cross swords with a commoner. To save Voltaire from the wrath of the Rohan family, the authorities, at the request of his relatives, had him secretly conveyed to Calais *en route* for England. This was in 1726, and the affair left its mark on Voltaire. From that moment he was a *mécontent*, a brilliant and merciless critic of authority. That he was not an intransigent enemy of the social order is clear from subsequent events. But he was an angry and embittered man whose *amour-propre* could only be soothed by fame and royal favour. In this frame of mind Voltaire acquired his first impressions of England.

Here he was well known, thanks to *La Henriade*, and the second edition, published in London and dedicated to Queen Anne, was a huge success. The English did much to smooth Voltaire's ruffled pride. In the excitement of meeting Bolingbroke again, of being introduced to Pope, Gay and Swift, of seeing Shakespeare acted at Drury Lane, the exile almost forgot his troubles. But he was resolved to go back to Paris and by sheer force of his talents to extort an *amende honorable*. His boast to young Rohan-Chabot had to be fulfilled.

Very quietly, early in 1729, Voltaire returned to France bringing with him the manuscripts of three important works. In 1730 he published *Brutus*, a tragedy without a love interest designed to show the superiority of the French (or Voltairian) genius over that of Shakespeare and the English. Its preface was a discourse on tragedy in which

Voltaire praised the energy and vitality, but condemned the uncouth irregularities of our drama. His own role was clearly indicated. Tragedy must no longer consist of long dialogues about love: it must have action. Whilst retaining the classic structure of French tragedy, Voltaire will make it more picturesque, more topical, more national and more exciting. Impressed by the spectacular appeal of Shakespeare's historical tragedies, he cursed the French practice of allowing spectators on the stage, which was not abolished until 1759. Nevertheless, with *Zaïre* (1732) Voltaire scored a dazzling success. This fine tragedy, with its interwoven themes of jealous love and religious tolerance, is situated in the Jerusalem of the seventh Crusade. It was followed in 1734, 1735 and 1736 by three more historical plays: *Adélaïde du Guesclin*, a national tragedy set in the reign of Charles VII, *La Mort de César* and *Alzire*, with an exotic setting in sixteenth-century Peru.

It is, therefore, perhaps significant that 1731 marked the début of Voltaire the historian with his *Histoire de Charles XII*, which was a revelation in the art of writing history. The author's brilliant imagination, his sense of the dramatic and the independence of his judgment put him in a class by himself. Since Charles XII had only been dead for thirteen years, Voltaire was able to consult not only documents but living sources of information either personally or by correspondence. And the amendments contained in later editions of his work show that he could profit from the criticisms of rival historians.

The famous *Lettres philosophiques*, published secretly and anonymously in 1734, reveal a less impartial attitude to facts. In these impressions of his sojourn in England, Voltaire described and analysed the Anglo-Saxon point of view in regard to religion, politics, science, philosophy and drama. In every case, save that of drama, the author held up England as a desirable model to his compatriots and by contrast showed them the gulf which divided Frenchmen from the religious tolerance, the political freedom, the economic solidity, the philosophic and scientific enlightenment of these islanders. He told them about the achievements of Newton, Bacon and Locke and smiled in pity at that fumbling amateur Descartes. He pointed the way to a new method of thought, the empirical Newtonian method without which no progress was possible. The book, following on Bayle's *Dictionnaire critique*, exercised a profound and disturbing influence on French thought. Essentially, it is a plea for religious tolerance and intellectual freedom but, in advocating these and other liberties, Voltaire harboured no sinister designs against the existing regime. He was in no sense a political revolutionary.

In 1733 Voltaire was presented to Madame du Châtelet, a lady possessed of strong scientific curiosity whose influence over him lasted fifteen years. As her guest at Cirey in Champagne he continued his dramatic work, cultivated the sciences and wrote his philosophic poems, notably the series entitled *Discours en vers sur l'homme* (1734–7). During the first half of his sojourn at Cirey Voltaire contented himself with general propaganda: he was still a candidate for a seat in the Académie Française. Privately he was busy with *La Pucelle*, an obscene and impious mock epic poem on Joan of Arc. Madame du Châtelet made him promise to leave it in manuscript, but copies passed from hand to hand. His *Siècle de Louis XIV* was now on the stocks and Voltaire was on excellent terms with the abbé Dubos, the *secrétaire perpétuel* of the Academy, asking his advice on historical points.

In 1741 *Mahomet, ou le Fanatisme* was staged in Lille, and the ferocity of its tone aroused murmurs of surprise and protest. This tragedy is a vivid illustration of the effects of religious fanaticism. A son (Séide) kills his father, induced thereto by his blind adoration for the hypocritical Mahomet. In a private letter to Frederick of Prussia, who had adopted Voltaire as his professor, the latter disclosed that his Séide is the type of regicide like Ravaillac, the assassin of Henri IV, who is used by a religious sect for its sinister political ends. But publicly, in a humble letter to the Academy, he professed his adoration for the Christian religion. A final passionate appeal to his old headmaster, le Père Tournemine, removed the last obstacle, and in April 1746 Voltaire was elected to the Académie Française.

This year marks a turning point in the movement of French thought and also in the career of Voltaire. He was fifty-two and had achieved several of his ambitions. As historiographer royal and *gentilhomme de la chambre* he was no longer a *roturier* but a noble. At the suggestion of his friend D'Argenson, now in charge of Foreign Affairs, Voltaire was sent on a diplomatic mission to Berlin, where he acquitted himself with credit. But he was still an object of suspicion to the Church; and the court, whilst admiring his dramatic talents, distrusted his political views. For four years, until the death of Madame du Châtelet in 1750, Voltaire tried desperately to please and flatter the king, but only succeeded in offending him by his lack of tact and familiarity. An indiscreetly phrased madrigal to Mme de Pompadour irritated Louis XV and, by reflex, angered his mistress, whose friendship for Voltaire turned into active hostility. Leaving the court in disgust, he relieved his feelings by writing *Zadig*, the first of the brilliant philosophic tales which today constitute his chief title to universal fame. In narrating the comic misadventures of his intelligent hero at the court of the oriental monarch Moabdar, a disillusioned Voltaire suggests that nowhere is the role which chance plays in life more strikingly illustrated than in the career of a courtier.

Yet in June 1750 he turned a serious ear to the pressing and flattering invitations of Frederick of Prussia, who acceded to all his conditions. For a time all was beautiful. But one day he learned from a compatriot that Frederick had no intention of keeping him longer than suited his convenience—a year at the outside, he was alleged to have said, adding: 'When you have squeezed the orange you throw away the peel.' Probably the king was tired of Voltaire's quarrels with Maupertuis, the French scientist who was president of his Academy of Sciences. Moreover, having intervened anonymously in these controversies, Frederick had received some nasty knocks from his honoured guest. After some typical experiences with the Prussian secret police, who thought he was carrying off certain French poems written by the King, Voltaire and his niece managed to get out of the country. He finally took up residence at Ferney, in French territory, but suggestively close to the Swiss frontier. Voltaire now had few illusions about absolute monarchs though eventually he made up his differences with Frederick.

It was at Berlin that Voltaire completed and, in 1751, published a work which had occupied him for some twenty years: *Le Siècle de Louis XIV*. As originally planned it was to have culminated in a history of the arts, 'my sole objective'. To this section he proposed to devote six chapters. These were reduced to two in the final plan whilst the five closing chapters were allocated to ecclesiastical affairs. The whole work, moreover, was greatly expanded by the addition of ten chapters. Otherwise Voltaire did not alter his grand design, which was, as he said, to depict not the achievements of a single man but of the human mind in the most enlightened age the world had seen. He thus enlarged the traditional concept of history to embrace aspects of civilization ignored by his predecessors—literature, philosophy, science, the arts and crafts, industry and commerce, the central government, the administration of justice and taxation. Finally, in language which surprises the reader by its restraint, he discussed the tragic persecution of the Huguenots which Voltaire obviously considered much more disastrous to the nation than the heresies of the Jansenists and Quietists. He did not neglect what his predecessors regarded as the staples of history: two-thirds of his book are devoted to the wars, treaties and foreign affairs of the period. But this unpromising material acquired under his pen a new interest and meaning, to the delight of a public inured to the pedestrian eloquence of the traditional histories.

In Voltaire the age of Louis XIV found its ideal historian. His early impressions and admirations were formed in the brilliant society of *Le Temple* to which as a schoolboy he was introduced by his godfather, the abbé de Châteauneuf. And until the publication of his history, Voltaire was in constant touch with survivors of the old regime from the Duchesse du Maine down to the humblest of the royal servants. By these living records he checked the information gleaned from memoirs and other documents. As a result, his pages convey an impression of actuality not to be found in histories with a longer perspective. This is of course partly due to Voltaire's incomparable narrative style. Observe, for instance, how lucidly he describes in his transparent idiom the chaotic events of the *Fronde* or the complicated situations which led to the great campaigns of Louis XIV. The great figures of the age are portrayed with a detachment unusual in Voltaire. One senses his dislike of Mazarin and Louvois but he does full justice to their talents and services, and he paid tribute to the administrative genius of Colbert when it was the fashion to disparage that great statesman. His sympathetic portrait of Mme de Maintenon reflects the same independence of judgment which is nowhere more evident, however, than in his balanced appreciation of Louis XIV. There is no attempt to gloss over the king's faults: the arrogance in victory, reluctance to delegate authority, the wars he undertook too lightly, the folly of his policy towards the Protestants. But these are eclipsed by the great deeds and noble qualities so admirably illustrated in Voltaire's history. There are no finer pages than those which describe the splendid fortitude displayed by the king during the shattering bereavements and military disasters which darkened the closing days of his reign. But Voltaire shows us also a more human Louis XIV: sensible, hardworking, loyal and generous to his friends, affable though always dignified, considerate and just to his subordinates and, in his private life, an excellent father.

For years Voltaire had been working on a general history of world civilization. This *Essai sur les mœurs et l'esprit des nations*, as it was eventually entitled, appeared in 1756 and included *Le Siècle de Louis XIV*, which forms logically the final 'chapter' of the larger history. In the *Essai*, however, Voltaire thrusts purely political history well into the background and sketches a vast panorama of Christian civilization in Europe from Charlemagne to Louis XIV preceded by eight chapters on the *mœurs*, religions and laws of China, India, Persia and Arabia. In conceiving this brilliantly original programme, Voltaire really founded modern history. But the *Essai*, though it makes fascinating reading, is marred throughout by the author's intransigent hatred of Christianity which distorts his whole outlook.

Meanwhile Voltaire's attitude to life had undergone a change which is reflected in the *Essai* and in his philosophic poems. *Le Poème sur le désastre de Lisbonne*, inspired by the earthquake of 1756, is an attack on the comfortable optimism of Pope and Leibnitz. This note of disillusionment attains its climax in the novel *Candide*, a malicious parody of the Leibnitzian idea that everything is for the best in the best of all possible worlds. *Candide* is a savage indictment of human ferocity and stupidity which shows us little of the finer side of man. But it is not entirely pessimistic. There is such a thing as progress, slow though it may be. Meanwhile, like Candide, we must 'cultivate our garden', i.e. devote ourselves with all our might to the job in hand. In that way, Voltaire implies, the average man can best serve the community; by example rather than by schemes for universal reform. We must not rely on Providence. God exists but it is clear from the existence of evil that He is not concerned with our petty doings. We are the mice in the ship's hold: the captain has other things to think about. So far as our world is concerned, *Sa Majesté le Hasard* is in command.

From Ferney, Voltaire took an active part in the great battle now engaged between the *philosophes* or intellectual reformers and the defenders of tradition who were represented largely by the Church and the *Parlements* or High Courts of Justice. So far he had been merely a brilliant man of letters: now he came forward as the defender of the oppressed. In March 1762 the fanatical *Parlement* of Toulouse had condemned and executed a Protestant, Jean Calas, accused on flimsy evidence of having murdered his son who was about to turn Catholic. With his usual incredible energy, Voltaire collected information from every source and instituted an inquiry which, after many delays, led to a retrial and to the posthumous rehabilitation of Calas. Voltaire took advantage of the general excitement to publish his *Traité sur la Tolérance* (1763) one of his finest works. The Calas case was followed by many others in which he successfully intervened, thus showing up the obsolete and barbarous nature of French legal procedure which had never been publicly exposed. The Church was not responsible for this state of affairs but Voltaire made it the scapegoat for all he detested in the social system of his time.

From 1760 until the death of Voltaire in 1778 a stream of subversive writings issued anonymously from Ferney. The most notable of these is the *Dictionnaire philosophique* (1764) a brilliantly written, devastating commentary on every conceivable subject connected with religion, morality and current beliefs. The battle between the *philosophes* and the defenders of orthodoxy was now in full swing and the Crown had revived the death penalty for impious writings. To distract attention Voltaire went through the doubtful comedy of taking communion at Easter 1768, to the indignation of Protestants and Catholics alike. Besides, no one cried more loudly for *lettres de cachet* against his critics than Voltaire. This was another of his favourite tricks for diverting suspicion.

When all France took to the new science of political economy, arguing bitterly over the respective merits of commerce and agriculture, Voltaire intervened with two tales: *Jeannot et Colin* (1764) and *L'Homme aux quarante écus* (1768). In sharp contrast to the theorizings of the physiocrats, he proposed several practical reforms. As a big landowner who had introduced modern methods into his own estates, Voltaire spoke with authority in language clear and amusing enough to disconcert his pedantic opponents. With his amazing versatility he could explain and animate the dreariest topic. His activity was stupefying. In addition to plays, poems, novels, pamphlets, he found time to write to correspondents all over Europe. His correspondence contains some twelve thousand letters. Moreover, as he used to say, he was the *maître d'hôtel de l'Europe*.

At the age of eighty-three Voltaire decided to revisit his beloved Paris, which he had not seen for twenty-eight years. Despite his great age, he had just composed a tragedy, *Irène*, which was to be performed at the Comédie-Française. His arrival in the capital on 10th February 1778 was the occasion of frenzied celebrations. All Paris flocked to the Rue de Baune where Mme Denis, the great man's niece, kept her *salon*. Benjamin Franklin brought his grandson to receive the patriarch's blessing and the Académie sent a delegation to welcome its illustrious member, whose condition seriously alarmed his physician, the famous Dr Tronchin. Meanwhile Voltaire felt well enough to visit the theatre where his *Irène* was being played (30th March). First he went to the Académie Française, where honours were showered upon him: he called on the great minister, Turgot, and finally proceeded to the theatre, where his bust was placed on the stage whilst the whole company smothered it with wreaths. Tronchin wanted to get his patient out of Paris before he was killed by kindness. At the end of April Voltaire paid another visit to the Académie Française, but a fortnight later he fell seriously ill, and died on 30th May 1778. As the local clergy refused to grant Christian burial, Voltaire's nephew, the abbé Mignot, smuggled the corpse out of Paris and interred it provisionally at Scellières on the road to Ferney.

F. C. GREEN.

1961.

SELECT BIBLIOGRAPHY

DRAMATIC WORKS. *Œdipe*, 1718; *Artémire*, 1720; *Mariamne*, 1724; *Zaïre*, 1732; *Samson* (opera), 1732; *L'Enfant prodigue*, 1736; *Mahomet, ou le Fanatisme*, 1742; *Mérope*, 1743; *Sémiramis*, 1748; *Nanine*, 1749; *Oreste*, 1750; *L'Orphelin de la Chine*, 1755; *Tancrède*, 1760; *L'Ecossaise*, 1760; *Le Dépositaire*, 1722; *Irène*, 1778; *Agathoclès*, 1779 (performed on the anniversary of the poet's death). Other dramas and operas.

POEMS. *La Bastille*, 1717; *La Henriade* (fraudulently published as *La Ligue*, 1723-4), 1728; *Mort de Mlle Lecouvreur*, 1730; *Temple du Goût* (prose and verse), 1733; *Le Mondain*, 1736; *Discours sur l'homme* (*Épîtres sur le Bonheur*, 1738-9); *Sur les Événements de 1744*; *Fontenoi*, 1745; *Temple de la Gloire*, 1745; *La Pucelle d'Orléans*, 1755 (some of the *Chants* had been in circulation since 1735), in twenty *Chants*, 1762; a supplemental one, *La Capilotade*, appeared separately in 1760; *Sur le désastre de Lisbonne*, 1756; *Sur la Loi Naturelle*, 1756; *La Vanité*, *Le Pauvre Diable*, *Le Russe à Paris*, 1760; *Contes de Guillaume Vadé* (with prose, 1764); *La Guerre Civile de Génève* (burlesque poem), 1768; *Les Trois Empereurs en Sorbonne*, 1768; *Épître à Borleau*, 1759; *Les Systèmes, Les Cabales*, 1772; *La Tactique*, 1773; and others.

PROSE TALES. *Le Monde comme il va* (or *Babouc*), 1764; *Zadig*, 1748 (published in 1747 as *Memnon, Histoire orientale*); *Memnon, ou la Sagesse Humaine*, 1749; *Micromégas*, 1750; *L'Histoire d'un Bon Bramin*, 1759; *Candide*, 1759; *Le Blanc et Le Noir*, 1764; *Jeannot et Colin*, 1764; *L'Homme aux Quarante Ecus*, 1767; *L'Ingénu*, 1767; *La Princesse de Babylone*, 1768; *Histoire de Jenny*, 1769; *Lettres d'Amabed*, 1769; *Le Taureau Blanc*, 1774; *Les Oreilles du Comte de Chesterfield*, 1774; and others.

HISTORICAL WORKS. *Histoire de Charles XII*, 1731; *Siècle de Louis XIV*, 1751; enlarged edition, 1753 (two chapters had been printed and suppressed in 1739); *Abrégé de l'Histoire Universelle*, vols. i and ii, 1753; vol. iii, 1754; complete edition, 1756 (fragments had appeared in 1745); *Annales de l'Empire*, 1753; *Précis du Siècle de Louis XV*, published in part 1755 and 1763, with additional chapters, 1769; *Essai sur l'Histoire générale et sur les Mœurs et l'Esprit des Nations depuis Charlemagne jusqu'à nos jours*, various vols., 1756, including vol. vii of the *Siècle de Louis XIV* (some chapters had appeared in the *Mercure* in 1745-6); *Histoire de Russie sous Pierre le Grand:* first part, 1759; second part, 1763; *La Philosophie de l'Histoire*, 1765 (later the 'Discours préliminaire' to the *Essai sur les Mœurs*); *La Défense de mon Oncle* (in reply to an adverse criticism on the above work), 1767; *Le Pyrrhonisme de l'Histoire*, 1768; *Fragments sur l'Histoire générale* (Pyrrhonism and Tolerance), 1773.

WORKS ON PHILOSOPHY AND RELIGION. *Épître philosophique à Uranie*, 1732; *Lettres sur les Anglais* (twenty-four letters), 1733, 1734 (also published as *Lettres philosophiques*); *Traité de Métaphysique*, 1734; *Éléments de la Philosophie de Newton*, 1738; *Métaphysique de Newton*, 1740; Articles for the *Encyclopédie*, 1757; *Dictionnaire philosophique portatif*, 1764; *Catéchisme de l'Honnête Homme*, 1763; *Le Philosophe ignorant*, 1766; *La Raison par Alphabet* (new edition of the *Dictionnaire philosophique*), 1769; *Lettres de Memmius*, 1771; *Questions sur l'Encyclopédie par des Amateurs*, 1770–2; *Lettres chinoises, indiennes, et tartares par un Bénédictin*, 1776; *Mémoires pour servir à la vie de M. Voltaire* (printed 1784); and others.

CRITICAL WORKS. *Essai sur la Poésie*, 1726; *Utile Examen des Épîtres de J. J. Rousseau*, 1736; *Lettres sur la 'Nouvelle Héloïse'*, 1761; *Appel à toutes les Nations de l'Europe des Jugements d'un écrivain anglais* (later known as *Du Théâtre anglais*), 1761; *Éloge de M. de Crébillon*, 1762; *Idées républicaines* (in the *Contrat Social*), 1762; *Théâtre de Corneille* (with translation of Shakespeare's *Julius Cæsar*), 1764; *Examen important de Milord Bolingbroke*, 1767; *Commentaire Historique sur les Œuvres de l'auteur de la Henriade*, 1776; *Éloge et Pensées de Pascal* (corrected and enlarged edition), 1776; *Commentaire sur l'Esprit des Lois de Montesquieu*, 1777; and others.

MISCELLANEOUS WRITINGS. *Épîtres aux Manes de Genonville*, 1729; *Épître des Vous et des Tu*, 1732; *Sur la Calomnie*, 1733; *Anecdotes sur Pierre le Grand*, 1748; *Mensonges imprimés* (on Richelieu's Will), 1749; *Des Embellissements de Paris*, 1750; *Remerciement sincère à un Homme charitable*, 1750; *Diatribe du Doctor Akakia*, 1752; *Les Quand*, 1760; Writings for the rehabilitation of Jean Calas, who had been unjustly executed, 1762; *Traité sur la Tolérance à l'occasion de la Mort de Jean Calas*, 1763; *Le Sentiment des citoyens* (attack on Rousseau), 1764; *Discours aux Welches*, 1764; *Les Anciens et les Modernes, ou la Toilette de Mme de Pompadour*, 1765; *Commentaires sur le livre des délits et des peines*, 1766; *Le Cri des nations* (against Papal domination), 1769; *De la Paix Perpétuelle* (on fanaticism and tolerance), 1769; *La Méprise d'Arras* (on another judicial mistake), 1771; *Éloge de Louis XV*; *de la Mort de Louis XV et de la Fatalité*, 1774; and other works.

For the most complete edition of Voltaire's enormous correspondence, see that ed. by T. Besterman, Geneva, 1953–60.

CHIEF GENERAL EDITIONS OF WORKS, Ed. Beaumarchais, etc., 70 vols., 8°, 1784; 92 vols., 12°, 1785–90; Beuchot, 70 vols., 1828, etc; Ed. du Siècle, 8 vols., 1867–70; Moland, 50 vols., 1877–83; with 'Table générale et analytique', by Charles Pierrot, 1885; Selections have been published, and separate volumes of letters.

BIBLIOGRAPHY. G. Bengesco, 1882–90.

BIOGRAPHY AND CRITICISM. Condorcet, 1787; G. Desnoireterres, *Voltaire et la Société Française au XVIIIme Siècle*, 1871–6; Longchamp et Wagnière, *Mémoires sur Voltaire, et ses ouvrages*, 1825; Bersot, *Études sur le XVIIIme Siècle*, 1855; A. Pierron, *Voltaire et ses Maîtres*, 1866; Maynard, *Voltaire; sa vie et ses œuvres*, 1867; D. F. Strauss, 1870; J. Morley, 1872, 1886; James Paston, 2 vols., 1881; G. Maugras, *Voltaire et Jean Jacques Rousseau*, 1886; E. Faguet, 1895; E. Champion, *Voltaire: Études Critiques*, 1897; L. Crouslé, 1899; G. Lanson, 1907; and in Sainte-Beuve, *Causeries du Lundi*, vol. ii; Brunetière, *Études critiques*, vols. i, iii, iv; S. G. Tallentyre, 1903; R. Aldington, 1925; André Maurois, Eng. trans., 1932; H. N. Brailsford, 1935; Alfred Noyes, 1936; N. L. Torrey, *The Spirit of Voltaire*, 1938; M. M. H. Barr, *Voltaire in America, 1744–1806*, 1940; I. O. Wade, *Voltaire and Mme du Châtelet*, 1941; M. T. Maestro, *Voltaire and Beccaria as Reformers of Criminal Law*, 1942; K. O'Flaherty, *Voltaire, Myth and Reality*, 1945; T. W. Russell, *Voltaire, Dryden, and Heroic Tragedy*, 1946; I. O. Wade, *Voltaire and Candide*, 1959; H. T. Mason, *Pierre Bayle and Voltaire*, 1963; W. Durant, *The Age of Voltaire*, 1966.

CONTENTS

CHAPTER I

INTRODUCTION

It is not merely the life of Louis XIV. that we propose to write; we have a wider aim in view. We shall endeavour to depict for posterity, not the actions of a single man, but the spirit of men in the most enlightened age the world has ever seen.

Every age has produced its heroes and statesmen; every nation has experienced revolutions; every history is the same to one who wishes merely to remember facts. But the thinking man, and what is still rarer, the man of taste, numbers only four ages in the history of the world; four happy ages when the arts were brought to perfection and which, marking an era of the greatness of the human mind, are an example to posterity.

The first of these ages, to which true glory belongs, is that of Philip and Alexander, or rather of Pericles, Demosthenes, Aristotle, Plato, Apelles, Phidias, Praxiteles; and this honour was confined within the limits of Greece, the rest of the known world being in a barbarous state.

The second age is that of Cæsar and Augustus, distinguished moreover by the names of Lucretius, Cicero, Livy, Virgil, Horace, Ovid, Varro and Vitruvius.

The third is that which followed the taking of Constantinople by Mahomet II. The reader may remember that the spectacle was then witnessed of a family of mere citizens in Italy accomplishing what should have been undertaken by the kings of Europe. The scholars whom the Turks had driven from Greece were summoned by the Medici to Florence; it was the hour of Italy's glory. The fine arts had already taken on new life there; and the Italians honoured them with the name of virtue as the early Greeks had characterised them with the name of wisdom. Everything

1

conduced to perfection. The arts, for ever transplanted from Greece to Italy, fell on favourable ground, where they flourished immediately. France, England, Germany and Spain, in their turn, desired the possession of these fruits; but either they never reached these countries or they degenerated too quickly.

Francis I. encouraged scholars who were scholars and nothing else: he had architects, but neither a Michael Angelo nor a Palladio; it was in vain that he endeavoured to found Schools of Painting, for the Italian painters whom he employed made no French disciples. A few epigrams and fables made up the whole of our poetry. Rabelais was the only prose writer in fashion in the age of Henry II.

In a word, the Italians alone possessed everything, if one except music, which had not yet been brought to perfection, and experimental philosophy, equally unknown everywhere, and which Galileo at length brought to men's knowledge.

The fourth age is that which we call the age of Louis XIV.; and it is perhaps of the four the one which most nearly approaches perfection. Enriched with the discoveries of the other three it accomplished in certain departments more than the three together. All the arts, it is true, did not progress further than they did under the Medici, under Augustus or under Alexander; but human reason in general was brought to perfection.

Rational philosophy only came to light in this period; and it is true to say that from the last years of Cardinal Richelieu to those which followed the death of Louis XIV., a general revolution took place in our arts, minds and customs, as in our government, which will serve as an eternal token of the true glory of our country. This beneficent influence was not merely confined to France; it passed over into England, and inspired a profitable rivalry in that intellectual and fearless nation; it imported good taste into Germany, and the sciences into Russia; it even revived Italy, who had begun to languish, and Europe has owed both her manners and the social spirit to the court of Louis XIV.

It must not be assumed that these four ages were exempt from misfortunes and crimes. The attainment of perfection in those arts practised by peaceful citizens does not prevent princes from being ambitious, the people from being mutinous, nor priests and monks from becoming sometimes turbulent and crafty. All ages resemble one another in respect of the criminal folly of mankind, but I only know of these four ages so distinguished by great attainments.

Prior to the age which I call that of Louis XIV., and which began almost with the founding of the *Académie française*, the Italians looked upon all those north of the Alps as barbarians; it must be confessed that to a certain extent the French deserved the insult. Their fathers joined the romantic courtesy of the Moors to Gothic coarseness. They practised scarcely any of the fine arts, which proves that the useful arts were neglected; for when one has perfected the necessary things, one soon discovers the beautiful and agreeable; and it is not to be wondered at that painting, sculpture, poetry, oratory and philosophy were almost unknown to a nation which, while possessing ports on the Atlantic Ocean and the Mediterranean, yet had no fleet, and which, though inordinately fond of luxury, had but a few coarse manufactures.

The Jews, the Genoese, the Venetians, the Portuguese, the Flemish, the Dutch, the English, in turn carried on the trade of France, who was ignorant of its first principles. When Louis XIII. ascended the throne he did not possess a ship; Paris did not contain four hundred thousand inhabitants, and could not boast of four fine buildings; the other towns of the kingdom resembled those market towns one sees south of the Loire. The whole of the nobility, scattered over the country in their moat-surrounded castles, oppressed the people, who were engaged in tilling the land. The great highways were well-nigh impassable; the towns were without police, the state without money, and the government nearly always without credit among foreign nations. The fact must not be concealed that after the decadence of Charlemagne's descendants France had continued more or less in this state of weakness simply because she had hardly ever enjoyed good government.

If a state is to be powerful, either the people must enjoy a liberty based on its laws, or the sovereign power must be affirmed without contradiction. In France, the people were enslaved until the time of Philip Augustus; the nobles were tyrants until the time of Louis XI., and the kings continually engaged in upholding their authority over that of their vassals had neither the time to think of the welfare of their subjects nor the power to make them happy.

Louis XI. did a great deal for the royal power, but nothing

for the happiness and glory of the nation. Francis I. inaugurated commerce, navigation, letters and the arts; but he did not succeed in making them take root in France, and they all perished with him. Henri-Quatre was about to redeem France from the calamities and barbarity into which she had been plunged by twenty years of dissension, when he was assassinated in his capital, in the midst of the people to whom he was on the point of bringing prosperity. Cardinal Richelieu, occupied with the humbling of the House of Austria, Calvinism and the nobles, did not possess a sufficiently secure position to reform the nation; but at least he inaugurated the auspicious work.

Thus for nine hundred years the genius of France had almost continually been cramped under a gothic government, in the midst of partitions and civil wars, having neither laws nor fixed customs, and changing every two centuries a language ever uncouth; her nobles undisciplined and acquainted solely with war and idleness; her clergy living in disorder and ignorance; and her people without trade, sunk in their misery.

The French also had no share in the great discoveries and wonderful inventions of other nations; printing, gunpowder, glassmaking, telescopes, the proportional compass, pneumatic machines, the true system of the universe—in such things they had no concern; they were engaged in tournaments while the Portuguese and Spaniards discovered and conquered new worlds to the east and west. Charles V. was already lavishing on Europe the treasures of Mexico before a few subjects of Francis I. discovered the uncultivated regions of Canada; but even from the slight accomplishments of the French at the beginning of the sixteenth century, one could see what they are capable of when they are led.

We propose to show what they became under Louis XIV.

Do not let the reader expect here, more than in the description of earlier centuries, minute details of wars, of attacks on towns taken and retaken by force of arms, surrendered and given back by treaties. A thousand events interesting to contemporaries are lost to the eyes of posterity and disappear, leaving only to view great happenings that have fixed the destiny of empires. Every event that occurs is not worth recording. In this history we shall confine ourselves to that which deserves the attention of all time, which paints the spirit and the customs of men, which may serve for instruction and to counsel the love of virtue, of the arts and of the fatherland.

The state of France and the other European States before the birth of Louis XIV. has already been described: [1] we shall here relate the great political and military events of his reign. The internal government of the kingdom, the most important matter for the people at large, will be treated separately. To the private life of Louis XIV., to the peculiarities of his court and of his reign, a large part will be devoted. Other chapters will deal with the arts, the sciences, and the progress of the human mind in this age. Finally, we shall speak of the Church, which has been joined to the government for so long a period, sometimes disturbing it, at other times invigorating it, and which, established for the teaching of morality, often surrenders herself to politics and the passions of mankind.

CHAPTER II

EUROPEAN STATES BEFORE LOUIS XIV

ALREADY for a long time one could regard Christian Europe (except Russia) as a sort of great republic divided into several states, some monarchical, others of a mixed character; the former aristocratic, the latter popular, but all in harmony with each other, all having the same substratum of religion, although divided into various sects; all possessing the same principles of public and political law, unknown in other parts of the world. In obedience to these principles the European nations do not make their prisoners slaves, they respect their enemies' ambassadors, they agree as to the pre-eminence and rights of certain princes, such as the Emperor, kings and other lesser potentates, and, above all, they are at one on the wise policy of maintaining among themselves so far as possible an equal balance of power, ceaselessly carrying on negotiations, even in wartime, and sending each to the other ambassadors or less honourable spies, who can acquaint every court with the designs of any one of them, give in a moment the alarm to Europe, and

[1] In Voltaire's *Essay on Customs* (Essai sur les Mœurs).

defend the weakest from invasions which the strongest is always ready to attempt.

Since the time of Charles V. the balance inclined to the side of the House of Austria. Towards the year 1630 this powerful House was mistress of Spain, Portugal, and the treasures of America; the Netherlands, the Milanese States, the Kingdom of Naples, Bohemia, Hungary, even Germany (one may say) had become her patrimony; and since so many states had become united under a single head of this House, it is credible that all Europe would at last have been subdued.

GERMANY

The German Empire is France's most powerful neighbour: it has a greater expanse, is not so rich in bullion perhaps, but more prolific in vigorous men inured to hard labour. The German nation is ruled in almost the same manner as France under the first kings of the House of Capet, who were the chiefs often ill-obeyed of a few great vassals and a large number of petty ones. To-day, sixty free towns, known as imperial towns, nearly as many secular sovereigns, nearly forty ecclesiastical princes, either abbots or bishops, nine electors, among whom to-day one can count four kings, and finally the Emperor, the chief of these potentates, form this great Germanic body, which, thanks to German stolidity, has survived until the present day, with almost as much order as there was formerly confusion in the French government.

Each member of the Empire has his rights, his privileges, his duties; and the hardly acquired knowledge of so many laws, often disputed, has given rise to what is known in Germany as *the Study of Public Law*, for which the German nation is famed.

By himself the Emperor would be no more powerful and rich than a Venetian doge, for Germany, being divided into towns and principalities, allows the head of so many states only a highly-honoured pre-eminence, without possessions, without money, and consequently without power.

He does not possess a single village in virtue of being Emperor. Nevertheless, this dignity, often as empty as it was supreme, had become so powerful in the hands of the Austrians, that it was often feared that they would transform what was a republic of princes into an absolute monarchy.

Two parties at that time divided Christian Europe, as they still do to-day, and especially Germany.

The first is that of the Catholics, more or less subjected to the Pope; the second is that of the enemies of the spiritual and temporal rule of the Pope and the Catholic prelates. The adherents of this party are called by the general name of Protestants, although they are made up of Lutherans, Calvinists, and others, who hate one another almost as much as they hate Rome. In Germany, Saxony, part of Branden-burg, the Palatinate, part of Bohemia, Hungary, the States of the House of Brunswick, Würtemberg and Hesse, observe the Lutheran religion, which is known as *evangelistic*. All the imperial free towns have embraced this sect, which seemed more suitable than the Catholic religion to people who were jealous of their liberty.

The Calvinists, scattered among the strongest party, the Lutherans, form only a moderate party; the Catholics com-pose the rest of the Empire and with the House of Austria as their head were undoubtedly the most powerful.

Not only Germany, but all the Christian States were still bleeding from the wounds they had received in numerous religious wars, a madness peculiar to Christians and unknown to pagans, the unfortunate result of a dogmatic spirit so long introduced into all classes of society. Few indeed are the points of difference which have resulted in civil war; and foreign nations (perhaps our own descendants) will find it hard to understand how our fathers were at one another's throats for so many years whilst at the same time preaching forbearance.

I have in a former work pointed out how Ferdinand was about to transform the German aristocracy into an absolute monarchy, and how he was on the point of being dethroned by Gustavus Adolphus. His son Ferdinand III. who inherited his policy, and like him directed wars from the shelter of his study, reigned during the minority of Louis XIV.

Germany was far from being at that time so flourishing as she afterwards became; luxury was a thing unknown, and the comforts of life were very rare even among the greatest nobles. It was not until 1686 that they were intro-duced by French refugees who set up their manufactures there. This fertile and populous country lacked trade and money: the seriousness of their customs and the peculiar sluggishness of the Germans debarred them from those pleasures and agreeable arts which Italian acuteness had cultivated for so many years, and which French industry from that time began to bring to perfection. The Germans, rich at home, were poor abroad; and this poverty, added to the difficulty of mobilising so many different peoples under the same standard at such short notice, rendered it almost impossible, as to-day, for them to carry on war for any length of time against their neighbours. Hence the French have nearly always made war on imperial soil against the Emperors. The difference of government and of national genius seems to render the French more adapted for attack and the Germans for defence.

Spain

Spain, ruled by the elder branch of the House of Austria, had, after the death of Charles V., inspired more terror than the German nation. The Kings of Spain were immeasurably more powerful and rich. The mines of Mexico and Potosi apparently supplied whatever was necessary to buy the freedom of Europe. This generation saw the scheme of a monarchy, or rather of a universal superiority over Christian Europe, begun by Charles V., and continued by Philip II.

The greatness of Spain under Philip III. was nothing more than that of a vast body without substance, having more fame than power.

Philip IV., heir to his father's weakness, lost Portugal by carelessness, Roussillon through the weakness of his forces, and Catalonia by the abuse of despotism. Such kings could not for long be successful in their wars against France. If they gained certain advantages from the divisions and mistakes of their enemies, they lost them by their own incapacity. Moreover, they governed a people whose privileges allowed them to be disloyal; the Castilians had the right of not fighting outside their own country; the Aragonese ceaselessly contested their liberty against the Royal Council, and the Catalonians, who regarded their kings as their enemies, would not suffer them even to raise troops in their provinces.

Nevertheless, united with the empire, Spain was a formidable factor in the balance of Europe.

Portugal

Portugal at this time again became a separate kingdom; John, Duke of Braganza, a prince commonly thought weak, had snatched this province from a king weaker than himself. The Portuguese cultivated commerce out of necessity as Spain neglected it out of pride; in 1641 they leagued themselves with France and Holland against Spain. This revolution in Portugal was worth more to France than the winning of the most decisive victories. The French ministry, which had contributed nothing to the event, reaped without effort the greatest advantage that one can have over an enemy, that of seeing her attacked by an irreconcilable power.

Portugal, shaking off the yoke of Spain, expanding her trade and increasing her power, recalls to mind the case of Holland, who enjoyed the same advantages in quite a different way.

The United Provinces

This small state, consisting of seven united provinces, a country abounding in pasture land but barren of grain, unhealthy, and almost swamped by the sea, had presented for nearly fifty years an almost unique example in the world of what love of liberty and indefatigable labour can accomplish. These far from wealthy people, numerically small, far less disciplined in war than the poorest Spanish troops, and who as yet counted for nothing in Europe, withstood the whole forces of their master and tyrant Philip II., evaded the schemes of various princes who wished to aid them in order to subdue them, and laid the foundations of a power that we have witnessed counterbalance the might of Spain herself. Despair, engendered by tyranny, first armed them; liberty exalted their courage and the princes of the House of Orange made them into excellent soldiers. Scarcely had they conquered their masters than they established a form of government which so far as it is possible maintains equality, the most natural right of men.

This state of so peculiar a nature was from its commencement closely allied with France: interest united them, they had the same enemies, and the great Henri-Quatre and Louis XIII. had been the allies and protectors of Holland.

England

England, much more powerful, assumed the supremacy of the seas and claimed to set a balance among the states of Europe; but Charles I., who had reigned since 1625, far from being able to support the weight of this balance already felt the sceptre slipping from his grasp; he had wished to make his power independent of the laws of England and to change the religion of Scotland. Too obstinate to abandon his designs and too weak to execute them, a good husband, a good master, a good father, an honest man, but an ill-advised monarch, he became involved in a civil war, which, as we have shown elsewhere, at length caused him to lose his throne and his life on the scaffold in the course of an almost unprecedented revolution.

This civil war, begun during the minority of Louis XIV., prevented England for a time from interesting herself in the concerns of her neighbours; she lost alike her prosperity and her reputation; her trade was suspended; and other nations believed her to be buried beneath her own ruins, until suddenly she became more formidable than ever under the sway of Cromwell, who ruled her, the Bible in one hand and a sword in the other, wearing the mask of religion on his face, and disguising in his government the crimes of a usurper under the qualities of a great king.

Rome

This balance, which England had long flattered herself she had preserved among kings by her power, the court of Rome endeavoured to maintain by her policy. Italy was divided as to-day into several sovereignties; that which the Pope possesses is large enough to make him respected as a prince and too small to make him formidable. The nature of his government does not tend to populate the country, which has indeed little money and trade; his spiritual authority, always somewhat involved with the temporal, is destroyed and abhorred by one-half of Christendom; and if by the other half he is regarded as a father, he has children who sometimes oppose him with both reason and success. The rule of France has been to regard him as a sacred but over-reaching person, whose feet one must kiss, but whose hands one must sometimes bind. In all Catholic countries one may still see traces of the steps taken by the court of Rome towards a universal monarchy. All princes of the Catholic religion on their accession send to the Pope embassies of obedience, as they are called. Every crowned head has a cardinal in Rome who takes the name of protector. All bishoprics receive their bulls from the Pope, and in these bulls he addresses them as if he conferred such dignities by his power alone. All Italian, Spanish and Flemish bishops are pronounced bishops by divine permission and *that of the Holy See*. About the year 1682, many French prelates rejected this formula, unknown to earlier centuries; and in our time, in 1754, we have seen a bishop (Stuart Fitz-James, Bishop of Soissons) brave enough to omit it in a decree which deserves to be handed down to posterity; a decree, or rather a unique instruction, wherein it is expressly stated what no pontiff had yet dared to say, that all men, even unbelievers, are our brothers.

In fine, the Pope has preserved certain prerogatives in all Catholic countries which he certainly would not now obtain had time not previously given them to him. There is no kingdom in which there are not many benefices under his nomination, and as tribute he receives the first-year revenues of the consistorial benefices.

The monks, whose superiors are resident at Rome, are still the immediate subjects of the Pope, and are scattered throughout every state. Custom, which is all-powerful, and which is the cause of the world being ruled by abuses as well as by laws, has sometimes prevented princes from entirely removing danger, especially when it was related to matters considered as sacred. To take an oath to anyone but one's sovereign is a crime of high treason in the layman; it is an act of religion in the monk. The difficulty of knowing to what extent such a foreign sovereignty should be obeyed, the ease of allowing oneself to be won over, the pleasure of throwing off a natural yoke in order to accept one chosen by oneself, the spirit of disorder, the evil of the times, have only too often prompted whole religious orders to serve Rome against their own country.

The enlightened spirit that has prevailed in France for the last century and which has been diffused among nearly all classes has been the best remedy for this evil. Good books on this matter are of real service to kings and peoples, and one of the great changes thus brought about in our customs under Louis XIV. is the conviction which the monks are beginning to have, that they are subjects of the king before being servants of the Pope.

Jurisdiction, that essential mark of sovereignty, still rests with the Roman pontiff. In spite of all the liberties of the Gallic Church, even France permits a final right of appeal to the Pope in certain ecclesiastical cases.

If one wishes to annul a marriage, to marry one's cousin or one's niece, to be released from one's vows, it is still to Rome and not to one's bishop that application must be made; to Rome where favours are bought and individuals from every country obtain dispensations at varying prices.

The right to confer these advantages, regarded by many people as the result of the most intolerable abuses, and by others as the relics of the most sacred rights, is always cunningly maintained. Rome looks after her credit with as much policy as the Roman republic employed in conquering half the known world.

Never did a court know better how to conduct itself in conformity with men and with the times. The popes are nearly always Italians grown old in the conduct of affairs, free from any blinding passions; their council is formed of cardinals of similar characters, all emboldened with the same spirit. From this council mandates are issued that extend to China and America; in this respect it embraces the whole world, and it could sometimes be said of it what a foreigner once said of the Roman senate: "I have seen a Council of Kings." The majority of our writers have justifiably cried out against the ambition of this court, but I do not know of one of them who has done sufficient justice to its prudence. I know of no nation that could have maintained so long in Europe so many prerogatives that were continually being challenged; any other court would have lost them, either by pride or weakness, by over-eagerness or indolence, but Rome, rarely failing to employ at the appropriate moment now firmness and now tact, has kept everything that was humanly possible for her to keep. We see her raging under the hand of Charles V., violent towards Henri III. of France, by turns the enemy and friend of Henri IV., cunning with Louis XIII., openly opposed to Louis XIV. at the time when he was to be feared, and often the secret enemy of the Emperors whom she distrusted more than the Turkish Sultans.

Rome retains to-day a few rights, many pretensions, a statecraft and patience, which is all that is left of her ancient power which six centuries ago attempted to bring the empire, nay all Europe, under the tiara.

Naples is an extant example of that right which the popes once seized with such ingenuity and magnificence, that of creating and bestowing kingdoms; but the King of Spain, the possessor of that state, left to the Roman court only the honour and the danger of having too powerful a vassal.

For the rest, the papal state was enjoying a prosperous peace, which had only been broken by the little war of which I have spoken elsewhere between the Cardinals Barberini, the nephews of Pope Urban VIII., and the Duke of Parma.

The Rest of Italy

The other provinces of Italy were occupied with various interests. Venice feared the Turks and the emperor; she was hard put to defend her mainland states from the claims of Germany and from the invasion of the Sultan. She was no longer that Venice once the mistress of the world's trade, who a hundred and fifty years before had aroused the envy of so many kings. The wisdom of her government remained, but the loss of her enormous trade deprived her of nearly all her power, and the city of Venice thus remained by reason of her situation invincible, but by reason of her decadence unable to make fresh conquests.

The State of Florence was enjoying peace and prosperity under the rule of the Medici; literature, the arts, and polite manners, which the Medici had created, still flourished. Tuscany, at that time, was to Italy what Athens had been to Greece.

Savoy, torn by civil war and overrun by French and Spanish troops, was at length completely united on the side of France, and contributed towards the weakening of the Austrian power in Italy.

The Swiss preserved as they do to-day their liberty without attempting to oppress others. They hired their forces to neighbours richer than themselves; they were poor, they were unacquainted with the sciences and arts which luxury had created, but they were prudent and happy.

THE NORTHERN STATES

The northern European states, Poland, Sweden, Denmark and Russia, were like the other powers continually suspicious of one another or openly at war. One might witness in Poland then as to-day the customs and government of the Goths and Franks—an elective king, nobles sharing his power, an enslaved people, weak infantry and a cavalry recruited from the nobles, no fortified towns and practically no trade. These people were attacked now by the Swedes or Russians, now by the Turks. The Swedes, constitutionally a still freer nation, admitting even peasants to the states-general, but at that time more under the subjection of their kings than Poland, were victorious nearly everywhere; Denmark, at one time formidable to Sweden, was now no longer so to any state; and her real greatness only commenced under her two kings, Frederick III. and Frederick IV.

Russia was still in a state of barbarism.

THE TURKS

The Turks were no longer what they had been under the Selims, the Mahomets and the Solymans; effeminacy corrupted the seraglio, but did not banish cruelty. The Sultans were at one and the same time the most despotic of rulers in their seraglio and the least assured of their thrones and their lives. Osman and Ibrahim met their death by strangulation. Mustapha was twice deposed. Shaken by these shocks, the Turkish Empire was, moreover, attacked by the Persians; but, when the Persians allowed her breathing space and palace revolutions were at an end, that empire became formidable to Christendom; for, from the mouth of the Dnieper as far as the Venetian States, Russia, Hungary, Greece and the islands of the Mediterranean became in turn the prey of the Turkish forces; and from the year 1644 onwards they steadily prosecuted a war in Candia which was disastrous to the Christians. Such were the state of affairs, the forces and the aims of the chief European nations at the time of the death of Louis XIII., King of France.

The Situation in France

France, allied to Sweden, Holland, Savoy and Portugal, and possessing the goodwill of other neutral countries, was waging a war against the Empire and Spain, ruinous to both sides and disastrous to the House of Austria. It resembled many other wars that have been waged for centuries by Christian princes, in which millions of men are sacrificed and provinces laid waste in order finally to obtain a few small frontier towns whose possession is rarely worth the cost of conquest.

Louis XIII.'s generals had taken Roussillon. The Catalonians were about to go over to the side of France, the protectress of the liberty for which they fought against their own kings; but these triumphs did not prevent our enemies from taking Corbie in 1636 and advancing as far as Pontoise. Half the inhabitants of Paris had fled from fear, and Cardinal Richelieu, deep in his vast schemes for the humbling of the Austrian power, had been reduced to taxing the gates of Paris for each one to provide a lackey to go to the war and drive the enemy back from the gates of the capital. The French had thus done much damage to the Spaniards and Germans, and had suffered no less themselves.

The Forces of France after the Death of Louis XIII. and the Manners of the Time.

The wars had produced famous generals such as Gustavus Adolphus, Wallenstein, the Duke of Weimar, Piccolomini, Jean de Vert, the Marshal of Guébriant, the Princes of Orange and the Count d'Harcourt. Certain ministers of state had been no less conspicuous. The chancellor Oxenstiern, the Count-Duke of Olivares, and above all, Cardinal Richelieu, had attracted the attention of Europe. No century has lacked famous statesmen and warriors, for politics and warfare seem unhappily to be the two most natural professions to man, and he must always be either bargaining or fighting. The most fortunate is considered the greatest, and public opinion often ascribes to merit the happy chances of fortune.

War was not then waged as we have seen it waged in the time of Louis XIV.: armies were not so numerous; after the siege of Metz, for instance, by Charles V., no general found himself at the head of fifty thousand men; towns were besieged and defended with fewer cannon than are used to-day, and the art of fortification was still in its infancy. Pikes and arquebuses were used, and the sword which has become useless in our time was employed a great deal. The old international rule of declaring war by a herald was still in use. Louis XIII. was the last to observe this custom, when in 1635 he sent a herald-at-arms to Brussels to declare war upon Spain.

It is common knowledge that nothing was more usual at that time than to see priests in command of armies; the Cardinal Infant of Spain, the Cardinal of Savoy, Richelieu, La Valette, Sourdis, Archbishop of Bordeaux, Cardinal Theodore Trivulzio, commandant of the Spanish cavalry, had all donned the cuirass and fought in person. A Bishop of Mende had been many times an army commissary. The popes sometimes threatened these warrior priests with excommunication. Pope Urban VIII., when vexed with France, told Cardinal de la Valette that he would deprive him of his cardinal's hat if he did not lay down his arms; but once reconciled to France he overwhelmed him with benedictions.

Ambassadors, no less ministers of peace than ecclesiastics, made no difficulty about serving in the armies of allied powers, in whose service they were employed. Charnace, sent from France into Holland, commanded a regiment there in 1637, and later even the ambassador, d'Estrades, became a colonel in their service.

France had only about 80,000 foot-soldiers available in all. The navy, neglected for centuries, was restored a little by Cardinal Richelieu, but ruined again by Mazarin. Louis XIII. had only about 45,000,000 livres of ordinary revenue; but money was at 26 livres to the mark; these 45,000,000 would amount to about 85,000,000 to-day, when the arbitrary value of the silver mark has risen to as much as 49½ livres, and that of pure silver to 54 livres 17 sous; a value that public interest and justice alike demand should never be changed.

Commerce, to-day spread widely abroad, was then in very few hands. The policing of the kingdom was wholly neglected, a sure proof of a far from prosperous administration. Cardinal Richelieu, mindful of his own greatness, which was itself bound up with that of the state, had begun to make

France formidable abroad, but had not yet been able to bring prosperity to her at home. The great highways were neither kept in repair nor policed, and they were infested with brigands; the streets of Paris, narrow, badly paved and covered with filth, were overrun with thieves. The parliamentary registers show that the city watch was at that time reduced to forty-five badly paid men, who, to crown all, totally neglected their work.

Since the death of Francis II. France had been continually torn by civil wars or factions. The yoke had never been borne easily and voluntarily. The nobles had been bred up in the midst of conspiracies; such was indeed the art of the court, as since it has been that of pleasing the sovereign.

This spirit of discord and faction spread from the court to the smaller towns, and pervaded every community in the kingdom; everything was disputed, because there was nothing fixed, and even in the parishes of Paris the people were continually coming to blows; processions fought one another for the honour of their respective banners. More than once the canons of Notre-Dame were seen at grips with their brethren of the Sainte-Chapelle; members of parliament and of the chambers of accounts fought each other for pride of place in Notre-Dame on the day that Louis XIII. placed his kingdom under the protection of the Virgin Mary.

Practically every commune in the kingdom was armed, practically every person was inspired by the passion for duelling. This gothic barbarism, sanctioned once by kings themselves, and become a part of the national character, contributed to the depopulation of the country as much as civil or foreign wars. It is not too much to say that in the course of twenty years, ten of which had been troubled by war, more French gentlemen were killed at the hands of their own countrymen than at the hands of their enemies.

We shall say nothing here with regard to the cultivation of the arts and sciences; that part of the history of our customs will be found in its proper place. We shall merely remark that the French nation was steeped in ignorance, not excepting those who held that they were not of the people.

People consulted astrologers, and, what is more, believed them. Every memoir of that period, from President de Thou's History onward, is prodigal of prophecies. The serious and austere Duke de Sully solemnly describes those which were made to Henri IV. This credulity, the most infallible sign of ignorance, was so universal that care was taken to have an astrologer hidden near the bedchamber of Anne of Austria at the birth of Louis XIV.

What is hardly credible, but which is nevertheless vouched for by the abbé, Vittorio Siri, a very well-informed contemporary writer, is that Louis XIII. was surnamed the *Just* from his infancy, because he was born under the sign of Libra.

The same ignorance which popularised the absurd phantom of judicial astrology gave credit to the belief in possession by the devil and sorcery; it was made a point of religion, and there was scarcely a priest who did not exorcise devils. The courts of justice, presided over by magistrates who ought to have been more enlightened than the vulgar herd, were occupied in judging sorcerers. The memory of Cardinal Richelieu will always be stained by the death of the celebrated curé of Loudun, Urbain Grandier, who was condemned to the stake as a magician, by a decree of the council. One is shocked that the minister and judges should have had the ignorance to believe in the devils of Loudun, or the barbarity to have condemned an innocent man to the flames. Posterity will always remember with amazement that the Maréchale d'Ancre was burnt as a sorceress in the Place de la Grève.

One may still see in a copy of some registers of *Le Châtelet* the record of a trial begun in 1610, concerning a horse who had been laboriously trained by his master to perform very much like a modern circus animal; it was proposed to burn both master and horse.

We have said enough here to show in a general way the customs and the spirit of the age preceding that of Louis XIV.

This lack of enlightenment in all classes of society favoured superstitious practices even in the most upright which brought disgrace upon religion. The Calvinists, confusing the rational Catholic religion with the abuses emanating from it, became only the more determined in their hatred of our church.

As was typical of all the reformers, they opposed to our popular superstitions, often intimately allied to debauchery, a fierce austerity and harsh manners; thus the partisan spirit tore and debased France; and the social spirit that to-day makes this nation so renowned and so attractive was entirely unknown. There were no houses where men of ability might gather together for the purpose of communicating knowledge, no academies, no regular theatres. In short, customs, laws, the arts, society, religion, peace and war, were as nothing to what they afterwards became in the century known as the *Age of Louis XIV*.

CHAPTER III

MINORITY OF LOUIS XIV. FRENCH VICTORIES UNDER THE GREAT CONDÉ, THEN DUKE D'ENGHIEN

CARDINAL RICHELIEU and Louis XIII. had but recently died, the one respected and hated, the other already forgotten. They had bequeathed to France, unsettled as she was at the time, hatred for the very name of minister, and but little respect for the throne. In his will Louis XIII. ordered a Council of Regency to be set up. The king, ill-obeyed during his lifetime, trusted to be better obeyed after his death; but the first step of his widow, Anne of Austria, was to have his orders cancelled by a decree of the Parliament of Paris. This body, long hostile to the court, which had hardly preserved under Louis XIII. the freedom of making remonstrances, now annulled the testament of its king as easily as it would have judged the case of a simple citizen. Anne of Austria applied to this body for an unlimited regency, because Marie de' Medici had made use of the same tribunal after the death of Henri IV.; and the precedent had been given by Marie de' Medici, because every other way would have been lengthy and uncertain, whereas parliament surrounded by her guards could not resist her wishes, and a decree ratified by parliament and the peers seemed to assure a right that would be indisputable.

The custom of conferring the regency on the mothers of kings seemed to the French at that time as fundamental a law as that which debars women from the throne. The parliament of Paris having twice settled this question, that is to say, having by its sole authority and decree ratified this claim of the king's mother, appeared indeed to have conferred the regency; it looked upon itself not without some show of truth as the guardian of kings, and every councillor saw in himself a portion of the sovereign power. By the

same decree, Gaston, Duke of Orleans, the young uncle of
the king, was given the empty title of Lieutenant-General
of the kingdom under the absolute regency.

Anne of Austria was first of all obliged to continue the
war against her brother, Philip IV., King of Spain, for
whom she had a great affection. It is difficult to say precisely
why this war was carried on; nothing was demanded from
Spain, not even Navarre, which should have been the patrimony of the kings of France. Fighting had been going on
since 1635, because Cardinal Richelieu had so desired; it
would seem that he had desired it in order to make himself
indispensable. He had formed a league with Sweden and
Duke Bernard of Saxe-Weimar, a noted condottiere, against
the Emperor. He also attacked the Austro-Spanish branch
of the Empire, comprising the ten provinces known under
the general name of Flanders, and had divided with the
Dutch, then our allies, that part of Flanders which is
never conquered.

The seat of war was on the Flanders side; the Spanish
troops marched over the frontiers of Hainault to the number
of 26,000 under the leadership of an old and experienced
general, Don Francisco de Melo; they laid waste the frontiers
of Champagne, attacked Rocroi, and thought to advance
swiftly up to the gates of Paris, as they had done eight
years before. The death of Louis XIII., the feebleness of a
minority, raised their hopes; and when they saw that they
were only opposed by an army of inferior numbers, commanded by a youth of twenty years, their hopes were transformed into certainty. This inexperienced youth, whom they
scorned, was Louis de Bourbon, then Duke d'Enghien,
known afterwards as the great Condé. The majority of great
captains have become so by degrees, but this prince was a
born general; the art of war seemed in him to be a natural
instinct; he and the Swede, Torstensson, stand alone in Europe
as having possessed at the age of twenty the genius that
can outrival experience.

The Duke d'Enghien had received with the news of the
death of Louis XIII. orders not to risk a battle on any account.
Marshal de l'Hospital, who was attached to his suite as
counsellor and guide, seconded these timid orders by his own
cautiousness. The prince had faith neither in the marshal
nor in the court; he confided his schemes only to Gassion,
a field-marshal, who was worthy of being consulted by him;

together they compelled the marshal to agree that a battle was necessary.

(19 May, 1643) It is noteworthy that the prince, having seen that everything was in order on the evening before the battle, slept so soundly that he had to be wakened for the fight. The same story is told of Alexander. It is natural that a youth worn out with making of preparations for so great a day should fall fast asleep; but it is also natural that one with such a genius for war should remain unruffled in the midst of action, and should be sufficiently calm to sleep soundly on the eve of battle. The prince won the battle by his own efforts. He perceived at one glance a danger and its remedy, and his activity, free from haste, carried him at the right moment to all parts of the field. It was he who at the head of the cavalry attacked the Spanish infantry hitherto invincible—as strong and as firmly knit as the celebrated phalanx of old, and which opened out with a celerity unknown to the phalanx in order to allow the discharge of eighteen cannons that were concealed in its midst. The prince surrounded and attacked it three times. Immediately he was victorious he stopped the slaughter. The Spanish officers threw themselves on their knees in order to find in him a shelter from the fury of the victorious soldiery. The Duke d'Enghien was at as much pains to spare them as he had lately been to vanquish them.

The old Count de Fuentes, who commanded the Spanish infantry, died covered with wounds. Condé, on being informed of this, said that "he would have wished to die like that, if he had not been victorious."

The respect that Europe entertained for Spanish arms was now transferred to the French, who had not for a hundred years gained so notable a victory; for the desperate battle of Marignan, contested rather than won by Francis I. against the Swiss, was as much the work of bands of swarthy Germans as of French troops. The battles of Pavia and Saint-Quentin were still stains on France's escutcheon. Henri IV. was unfortunate enough to gain memorable victories only against his own country. Under Louis XIII. Marshal de Guébriant had obtained some slight successes, but they were invariably balanced by losses. The great battles that shake nations and remain for ever memorable in the minds of men, were fought during this period by no one except Gustavus Adolphus.

The Battle of Rocroi consequently marked an epoch in the glory of France, and consequently in that of Condé. He knew how to win and how to profit from his victory. His letters to the court made them resolve upon the siege of Thionville, which Richelieu had not dared to undertake, and by the time his messengers had returned all was prepared for this expedition.

The Prince de Condé marched across the enemy's country, eluded the vigilance of General Beck, and at length on 8 August, 1643, took Thionville. Thence he hastened to lay siege to Sierck and made it surrender. He drove the Germans across the Rhine, crossed after them, and hastened to make good the losses and set-backs the French had sustained on those frontiers since the death of the Marshal de Guébriant. He found Freiburg taken and General Merci beneath its walls with an army even superior to his. Condé had under his command two marshals of France, Grammont and Turenne, the latter having been promoted but a few months before, after serving successfully in Piedmont against the Spanish. He there laid the foundations of the great reputation he afterwards enjoyed. With these two generals, the prince attacked the camp of Merci, entrenched as it was on two heights (31 August, 1644). The engagement was renewed three times on three separate days. It is said that the Duke d'Enghien hurled his baton into the enemy's trenches, and advanced to recover it sword in hand at the head of Conti's regiment. Such daring deeds were perhaps necessary in order to lead troops to such difficult attacks. This Battle of Freiburg, more bloody than decisive, was the second victory gained by Condé. Merci decamped four days later. The surrender of Philippsburg and Mayence provided the proof and the fruits of this victory.

The Duke d'Enghien returned to Paris, received the acclamations of the people and asked for recompense from the court, leaving his army under the command of the Prince Marshal de Turenne. But this general, able as he was already, was beaten at Marienthal in April 1645. The prince hurried back to the army, again took over command, and enjoyed the glory not only of once more commanding Turenne, but of avenging his defeat. He attacked Merci on the plains of Nördlingen, and there, on 3 August, 1645, gained a complete victory. Marshal de Grammont was taken, but General Glen, who was in command under Merci, was made prisoner, and

Merci was among the fallen. Respected as one of the greatest of leaders, he was buried near the field of battle, his tombstone bearing the words: "STA, VIATOR; HEROEM CALCAS": "Stop, traveller; you tread a hero's bones." This battle was the crowning point of Condé's glory. It also made the reputation of Turenne, who to his credit rendered powerful help to the prince in winning a victory by which he might have been humiliated. Perhaps he was never greater than in thus serving the man whose rival and conqueror he afterwards became.

At that time the name of the Duke d'Enghien eclipsed all others. (7 October, 1646) He next besieged Dunkirk in sight of the Spanish army, and was the first to win that town for France.

So many successes and services, looked upon with suspicion rather than rewarded at court, made him feared by the ministry as much as by his enemies. He was withdrawn from the scene of his victories and of his glory, and sent into Catalonia with inferior, ill-paid troops; he besieged Lerida, but was compelled to raise the siege (1647). Certain writers accuse him of idle display in having opened the attack with the music of violins. They evidently did not know that this was the custom in Spain.

The unsettled state of affairs soon compelled the court to recall Condé to Flanders. The Archduke Leopold, brother of the Emperor Ferdinand III., was besieging Lens in Artois. Condé, once again at the head of troops who had always been victorious under him, advanced immediately upon him. This was the third occasion on which he had given battle with inferior numbers. His only words to his men were: "My friends, remember Rocroi, Freiburg and Nördlingen."

(10 August, 1648) He himself rescued Marshal de Grammont, who was thrown back on the left wing, and took General Beck prisoner. The archduke and Count de Fuensaldaña saved themselves with difficulty. The Imperial and Spanish troops which formed the army were scattered, and they lost more than a hundred standards and thirty-eight pieces of cannon, a very considerable number for those times. Five thousand prisoners were taken, three thousand of the enemy were killed, and the remainder deserted; the archduke was left without an army. Those who really wish to derive profit from this work may note that not since the foundation of the monarchy had the French won so many

*B 780

battles in succession, glorious alike for their leadership as for their display of courage.

While the Prince de Condé was thus counting the years of his youth by his victories, and the Duke of Orleans, brother of Louis XIII., had also upheld the reputation of a son of Henry IV. and that of France by the capture of Gravelines (July 1644), Courtrai and Mardick (November 1644), the Viscount Turenne had taken Landau, expelled the Spaniards from Trèves and reinstated the Elector.

(November 1647) With the aid of the Swedes he won the battles of Lavingen and Sondershausen, and compelled the Duke of Bavaria to evacuate his states at the age of nearly eighty years. (1645) The Count d'Harcourt took Balaguer and beat the Spaniards. They lost Porto-Longone in Italy. (1646) Twenty French vessels and an equal number of galleys, which comprised nearly the whole of the navy as re-established by Richelieu, beat the Spanish fleet off the coast of Italy.

This was not all; the French armies had also invaded Lorraine and made war on Duke Charles IV., a warlike prince, but vacillating, foolhardy and unfortunate, who found himself both deprived of his state by France and kept prisoner by the Spaniards. The allies of France pressed hard on the Austrian power on the south and north. The Duke d'Albuquerque, the Portuguese general, won the Battle of Badajoz against Spain in May of 1644. Torstensson challenged the imperial troops near Tabor (March 1645) and won a complete victory. The Prince of Orange, at the head of the Dutch, penetrated as far as Brabant.

Beaten on all sides, the King of Spain saw Roussillon and Catalonia fall into the hands of the French. Naples revolting against him had recently gone over to the Duke of Guise, the last prince of that branch of a house so prolific in eminent and dangerous men. The latter, considered merely a daring adventurer, because success did not come his way, at last had the glory of taking a ship single-handed into the midst of the Spanish fleet, and of defending Naples with no other support but that of his own courage.

In view of the numerous misfortunes that fell upon the House of Austria, of the many victories gained by the French and seconded by the successes of their allies, one would expect Vienna and Madrid to be only waiting the moment to open their doors, and the Emperor and the King of Spain to have lost practically all their states. Nevertheless, five years of glory troubled by scarcely a reverse produced very few real advantages, much bloodshed, and no revolution. If there were one to be feared, it was in France, who was near to ruin in the midst of her apparent prosperity.

CHAPTER IV

CIVIL WAR

ANNE OF AUSTRIA, now become absolute regent, had made Cardinal Mazarin France's master and her own. He had such dominion over her as a clever man may well have over a woman born with sufficient weakness to be ruled and sufficient obstinacy to persist in her choice.

One reads in certain memoirs of that period that the queen placed her confidence in Mazarin only after the complete failure of Potier, Bishop of Beauvais, whom she had first chosen as her minister. This bishop is represented as being an incompetent man; it is probable that he was, and that the queen only used him for a certain time as a lay figure, in order not to alarm the nation by the immediate choice of another cardinal, who was moreover a foreigner.

But it is unbelievable that Potier inaugurated his ministry by declaring to the Dutch "that they would have to become Catholics if they wished to remain the allies of France." He would have had to make the same stipulation to the Swedes. This absurdity is related by nearly all historians, because they have read it in the memoirs of courtiers and *frondeurs*. There are only too many facts in these memoirs that are either corrupted by prejudice or based upon popular rumour. What is obviously puerile should not be quoted, just as what is obviously absurd cannot be believed. All goes to show that for a long time, perhaps even during the life of Louis XIII., the queen had decided in her own mind upon Cardinal Mazarin as her minister; indeed, it cannot be doubted when one has read the Memoirs of La Porte, first gentleman of the bedchamber to Anne of Austria. Subordinates who are witnesses of the inner working of the court, know things of which parliaments and even the leaders of parties are unaware or do no more than suspect.

At first Mazarin used his power with moderation. One must have lived a long time with a minister to portray his character, to say what degree of courage or weakness he possessed, how far he was either prudent or crafty. Accordingly, we will merely say what Mazarin did, without attempting to guess what he was. At the outset of his greatness, he affected as much simplicity as Richelieu had previously displayed haughtiness. Far from surrounding himself with guards and travelling with royal pomp, he was accompanied at first by the most unpretending suite; where his predecessor had displayed an unbending arrogance, he revealed an affability of nature sometimes approaching to weakness. The queen was eager that her regency and her person should be loved by court and people alike, and she succeeded in both. Gaston, Duke of Orleans, brother of Louis XIII., and the Prince de Condé upheld her power, and had no other rivalry but that of how best to serve the state.

Taxes were needed for the maintenance of the war against Spain and the Emperor. Since the death of the great Henry IV., France's exchequer had been as badly managed as that of Spain and Germany. The administration of taxes was in a state of chaos; ignorance was extreme; brigandage was at its height, although not directed to such large ends as it is to-day. The national debt was one-eighth of what it is now; there were no armies of two hundred thousand men to keep up, no immense subsidies to pay, no naval war to maintain. In the first years of the regency state revenues amounted to nearly seventy-five million livres of the period. Had the ministry practised economy all would have been right; but in 1646 and 1647 new means of raising revenue became necessary. The comptroller at that time was a Siennese peasant, by name Particelli Emeri, whose mind was even lower than his birth, and whose pomp and dissoluteness aroused the whole country's indignation. This man invented burdensome and ridiculous expedients. He created the posts of controllers of faggots, jurors for the selling of hay, king's councillors to act as criers of wine; he also sold letters of nobility. Paris municipal stocks at that time amounted only to close upon eleven millions. A few quarters were re-divided among the *rentiers*, custom duties were increased; posts were created for masters of petitions, and pay to the extent of eighty thousand crowns was withheld from the magistrates.

It is easy to conjecture how the minds of men were stirred

up against the two Italians, both of whom had come penniless to France, and who had enriched themselves at the expense of the nation over which they had so great a hold. The parliament of Paris, the masters of petitions, the other courts, the *rentiers*—all rebelled. In vain did Mazarin deprive his favourite, Emeri, of the comptrollership and dismiss him to one of his estates; indignation was felt that this man should still possess estates in France, and Cardinal Mazarin was regarded with detestation, although at that very time he was concluding the great work of the peace of Münster; for it should be noted that that famous treaty and the barricades belong to the same year, 1648.

The civil wars began in Paris as they had begun in London, over the question of a little money.

(1647) The parliament of Paris, possessing as it did the right of inspecting the decrees of taxes, vehemently opposed the new edicts and gained the confidence of the people by the continued opposition with which it harassed the ministry.

Revolution did not come at once; men's minds are provoked and become bold only by degrees. The populace may at once rush to arms and choose a leader, as they did at Naples; but magistrates and statesmen proceed with more caution and at first observe a certain decorum, so far as a partisan spirit allows them.

Cardinal Mazarin had thought that by skilfully dividing the magistracy he could prevent all disturbance; but they met his subtlety with inflexibility. He kept back four years' pay from all the higher courts, meanwhile granting them exemption from the *paulette*, that is to say, exempting them from payment of the tax devised by Paulet under Henri IV., which secured to them the ownership of their offices. This remission was not wrong, but he allowed parliament to keep their four years' pay, thinking thus to appease its members. Parliament, however, scorned a favour which exposed it to the reproach of preferring its own interest to that of other bodies in the state.

(1648) The offer accordingly did not prevent it from issuing its decree of union with the other courts of justice. Mazarin, who had never been able to pronounce French properly, said that the *arrêt d'ognon* (i.e. the "onion" decree) was unlawful, and having had it annulled by the council, this word "onion" alone was sufficient to make him ridiculous; and as one does not submit to those one despises, parliament became still more venturesome.

It boldly demanded the dismissal of all the commissaries, regarded by the people as extortioners, and the abolition of the new type of magistracy, which had been established under Louis XIII. without the usual apparatus of legal formulary; such a project pleased the nation as much as it annoyed the court. It claimed that in accordance with ancient laws no citizen should be imprisoned without the proper judges being informed of the fact within twenty-four hours; nothing appeared more just.

Parliament did more; it abolished (14 May, 1648) the commissaries by a decree, ordering the local king's attorneys to take proceedings against them.

Thus hatred of the minister, aided by ardour for the public welfare, threatened the court with a revolution. The queen gave way; she offered to dismiss the commissaries, asking only that she might be allowed to retain three: this demand was refused.

(20 August, 1648) While these troubles were brewing, the Prince de Condé won the famous victory of Lens, the crowning point of his glory. The king, who was then only ten years of age, exclaimed: *"Parliament will be very grieved at this."* These words were sufficient to show that the court at that time looked upon the parliament of Paris as merely a body of rebels.

The cardinal and his courtiers gave it indeed no other name. The more that members of parliament had to complain of being treated like rebels, the more they resisted.

Queen and cardinal determined to remove three of the most obstinate magistrates in parliament, Novion Blanc-ménil, Chief Justice, as he was called; Charton, President of a Chamber of Common Pleas, and Broussel, formerly Clerk Councillor of the grand chamber.

They were not themselves the party leaders, but their tools. Charton, a very narrow-minded man, was known by the nickname of President *Je dis ça* ("That's what I say") because he always began and ended his speeches with these words. Broussel had only his white locks to commend him, his hatred of the ministry, and the reputation of always raising his voice against the court on whatever subject was brought up. His colleagues thought little of him, but the populace idolised him.

Instead of removing them quietly in the silence of the night, the cardinal thought to overawe the people by arresting them in broad daylight, while the *Te Deum* was being sung in Notre-Dame for the victory of Lens, and the Swiss guards were bearing in the seventy-three standards taken from the enemy. It was precisely this that caused the rising of the whole kingdom. Charton escaped, Blancménil was taken without any trouble, but with Broussel matters were very different. A solitary old serving-woman seeing her master forced into a carriage by Comminges, a lieutenant of the lifeguards, stirs up the people; they surround the carriage and break it open, but the French Guards come to the rescue, and the prisoner is escorted on the road to Sedan. So far from intimidating the people, his abduction irritates and encourages them. Shops are closed, and the large iron chains that were at that time stretched at the entrance to the principal streets are hung up; some barricades are erected, and four hundred thousand voices cry *Liberty and Broussel*.

It is difficult to reconcile all the details given by the Cardinal de Retz, Mme. de Motteville, the Solicitor-General, Talon, and many others, but all agree on the principal points.

During the night that followed the riot, the queen called up about two thousand troops quartered some leagues from Paris to defend the king's palace. Chancellor Segnier was already on his way to parliament, preceded by a lieutenant and several archers, for the purpose of annulling all decrees and even, it was said, of suspending parliament itself. But on the same night, the rebels had assembled at the house of the Coadjutor of Paris, so well known as the Cardinal de Retz, and everything was arranged for putting the city under arms.

The people stop the chancellor's carriage and overturn it. He barely makes his escape with his daughter, the Duchess de Sulli, who, against his will, had wished to accompany him; upon this he retires in confusion into the Hôtel de Luines, hustled and insulted by the crowd. The civil lieutenant comes to fetch him away in his carriage and conveys him to the Palais-Royal, escorted by two companies of Swiss troops and a squad of gendarmes; the people fire on them, and several are killed; the Duchess de Sulli herself is wounded in the arm (26 August, 1648). Two hundred barricades spring up in a moment, and they are thrust forward to within a hundred yards of the Palais-Royal. Having seen several of their number fall, the whole of the troops retreat and gaze passively on the actions of the people. Parliament marches in a body on foot to the queen, passes the barricades, which are lowered before it, and again demands the release of its imprisoned members. The queen is compelled to give them up, and by so doing encourages the rebels to fresh outrages.

Cardinal de Retz boasted that he had by himself armed all Paris on that *day of the barricades*, the second of its kind. This singular man was the first bishop in France to make civil war without having religion as a pretext. He has described himself in his Memoirs with an impetuosity of genius but with unequal power, which exactly reflect his behaviour. He was a man who, in the midst of debauchery and still languid from its shameful consequences, preached to the people and caused them to idolise him. He breathed the air of faction and conspiracy: at the age of twenty-three he had been the leading spirit of a plot against Richelieu's life; he it was who was responsible for the barricades; he involved parliament in cabals and the people in riots. His excessive vanity caused him to undertake daring crimes, so that he should be talked about. It was this same vanity which made him repeat so often: "I am descended from a Florentine house as old as that of the greatest princes"; he, whose ancestors had been tradesmen, like so many of his fellow-countrymen.

What seems really astonishing is that parliament should have been carried away by him and should have raised the standard of revolt against the court, even before securing the support of any prince.

For a long time that body had been regarded quite differently by the court and by the people. If one believed the voice of all the ministers and the court itself, the parliament of Paris was a court of justice set up for hearing the cases of its citizens; it held this prerogative solely by the will of the king, it had no pre-eminence over the other parliaments of the kingdom, except that of seniority and a wider juris-diction; it was only the court of peers, because the court resided at Paris; it had no more right to frame remonstrances than other bodies, and the right itself was one of mere favour; it had succeeded the parliaments that had formerly repre-sented the French nation, but it had inherited nothing from those ancient assemblies but its name; as indisputable proof of this the states-general were actually substituted in

place of the national assemblies, and the parliament of Paris
resembled the parliaments held by our former kings no more
than a consul of Smyrna or Aleppo resembles a Roman
consul.

This simple error in name was made the pretext for the
ambitious claims of a body of lawyers who, having all
bought their offices, thought to take the places of the conquerors of the Gauls and of the nobles who held fiefs under
the crown. This body had at all times abused the power
that is necessarily assumed by a primary tribunal always
resident in the capital. It had dared to formulate a decree
against Charles VII. and banish him from the kingdom; it
had initiated a criminal lawsuit against Henry III.; it had
continually resisted the king so far as lay in its power; and
now, during the minority of Louis XIV., under the most easy-
going of governments and the most indulgent of queens,
it was attempting to make civil war on its prince, thus
imitating the contemporary English parliament which was
holding its king a prisoner, and which later struck off his
head. Such were the opinions and sentiments of the cabinet.

But the citizens of Paris and all who were connected with
the law looked upon parliament as an august body which
had distributed justice with honourable disinterestedness,
whose only aim was the welfare of the state (an aim that it
had pursued to its own peril), whose ambition was confined
to the glory of curbing the ambition of favourites, and
which kept a middle path between king and people; moreover, without an examination into the origin of its rights and
power, they were assumed respectively to be in the highest
degree sacred and indisputable. When it upheld the people's
cause against the hated ministers, it was called *the father of
the state*, and little distinction was made between the right
that gives crowns to kings and that which gives to parliament
the power of restricting their desires.

It was impossible to find a just mean between these two
extremes; for, after all, there was no recognised law other
than that of opportunity and of time. Parliament was
nothing under a vigorous government: it was everything
under a feeble king; and one could apply to it the words of
M. de Guéméné when parliament under Louis XIII. complained of having been preceded by the deputies of the
nobility: "Gentlemen, you will no doubt take your revenge
during the minority."

We do not propose to repeat here all that has been written about these dissensions, and copy out whole books in order to present to our readers a multitude of details once valuable and important, but now almost forgotten; we must rather show what characterised the spirit of the nation, and say less of what is common to all civil wars than of what especially distinguished that of the Fronde. An archbishop and a parliament of Paris, two authorities set up among men with the sole object of maintaining peace, began the disturbances; the people thereafter thought their wildest excesses justified. The queen could not appear in public without being insulted; she was invariably called *Dame Anne*, and if any title were added it was an opprobrious one. The people frenziedly accused her of having sacrificed the country to her affection for Mazarin; and what was more insufferable, she heard on every side songs and loose jokes, the outward signs of coarseness and malice, which seemed eager to perpetuate the suspicions concerning her own honour.

Mme. de Motteville, with her noble and sincere simplicity, said: " These insults horrified the queen and she pitied from her heart the self-deceived Parisians."

On 6 January, 1649, she fled from Paris with her children, her minister, the Duke of Orleans, brother of Louis XIII., to Saint-Germain, where practically the whole court slept on straw. She was obliged to pawn the crown jewels.

The king was often in want of the necessities of life. His household pages were dismissed, for he could not provide them with food. At that time even the aunt of Louis XIV., a daughter of Henri-Quatre, and the wife of the King of England, now a refugee in Paris, was reduced to extreme poverty; and her daughter, afterwards married to the brother of Louis XIV., remained in bed, not being able to afford a fire: meanwhile the people of Paris, blind with frenzy, paid no attention to the sufferings of so many royal personages.

Anne of Austria, whose wit, charm and kindliness had been so praised, had known little but misfortune in France. Long treated as a criminal by her husband, and persecuted by Cardinal Richelieu, she had seen her papers seized at Val-de-Grace; she had been obliged to sign in full council a confession of guilt towards her husband, the king. When she gave birth to Louis XIV., her husband refused to embrace her, as was the custom, and the slight so altered her health as to put her life in danger. Finally, during her regency, after having heaped favours on all who petitioned her, she found herself driven from the capital by a fickle and angry people. Both she and her sister-in-law, the Queen of England, are memorable examples of what changes of fortune crowned heads may be called upon to bear; and her mother-in-law, Marie de' Medici, had been still more unfortunate.

With tears in her eyes the queen begged the Prince de Condé to act as protector to the king. The victor of Rocroi, of Freiburg, of Lens and of Nördlingen could not belie so many past services; he was flattered at the honour of defending a court, which he thought ungrateful, against the Fronde who were seeking his support.

Parliament had thus to battle with the great Condé, and did not flinch from carrying on the struggle.

The Prince de Conti, younger brother of the great Condé, and as jealous of him as he was incapable of equalling him, the Duke de Longueville, the Duke of Beaufort, and the Duke de Bouillon, spurred on by the mischief-making mind of the coadjutor, and all alike avid of novelty, thinking to build their greatness on the ruin of the state and make the blind actions of parliament serve their own particular ends, came and offered parliament their services. In the grand chamber the generals of an army were appointed, though the army was as yet non-existent. Everyone was taxed to raise troops. Twenty councillors had been created by Cardinal Richelieu with new charges. Their colleagues, with a meanness of spirit of which every community is capable, seemed to vent their hatred of Richelieu upon them; they heaped insults upon them and refused to regard them as members of parliament; each one was now compelled to give fifteen thousand livres towards the expenses of the war and thus buy the indulgence of their colleagues.

The grand chamber, those of enquiries and of petitions, the chamber of accounts, the court of relief, which had clamoured so loudly against slight but necessary taxes and especially against an increase in the tariff, which amounted only to two hundred thousand livres, now contributed a sum of nearly ten millions in present-day currency for the object of raising rebellion in the country. They issued a decree which authorised the seizure of all money belonging to partisans of the court, and they obtained 1,200,000 livres in present-day value. Twelve thousand men were raised by act of parliament (15 February, 1649); every court-yard gate provided a man and a horse. This cavalry was called *the cavalry of the court-yard gates*. The coadjutor had a regiment of his own, known as *the regiment of Corinth*, the coadjutor being titular Archbishop of Corinth.

Except for the names of the King of France, of the great Condé, and of Paris, the capital city, this war of the Fronde would have been as ridiculous as that of the Barberini; no one knew why he was under arms. The Prince de Condé besieged a hundred thousand citizens with eight thousand soldiers. The Parisians sallied into the fields dressed out with feathers and ribands, and their evolutions were a standing jest among regular soldiers. They fled on encountering two hundred men of the royal army. Everything was turned into jest; the regiment of Corinth having been beaten by a handful of men, their defeat was known as *the first of Corinthians*. The twenty councillors who had each provided fifteen thousand livres received no other honour than that of being called the fifteen-twenties.

The Duke of Beaufort-Vendôme, grandson of Henri IV., the idol of the people, whom at the bidding of others he stirred up to rebellion, was a popular prince, but of limited intelligence: he was made the public butt of jests by the court, and even by the Fronde. He was always referred to as *the king of the markets*. A shot having raised a contusion on his arm, he remarked that it was only a confusion. The Duchess of Nemours relates in her Memoirs that the Prince de Condé presented to the queen a hunchbacked dwarf in full armour. "Here," he said, "is the generalissimo of the Parisian army." By this he intended his brother, the Prince de Conti, who was indeed a hunchback, and whom the Parisians had chosen as their general. However, Condé himself was afterwards the general of the same troops; and Madame de Nemours adds that he used to say that the whole war was only worth recording in comic verse. He also used to call it the war of the chamber-pots.

The Parisian troops who sallied out of Paris, only to return always beaten, were received with hoots and peals of laughter. These slight repulses were countered by nothing more substantial than couplets and epigrams. Taverns and other houses of revelry were the tents where councils of war were held, to the accompaniment of jesting, songs and the most dissolute gaiety. Such unbridled licence obtained that one night the chief officers of the Fronde happening to meet the

Holy Sacrament as it was being conveyed through the streets to a man suspected of belonging to the Mazarin party, they turned the priests back, striking them with the flat of their swords.

To top all, the coadjutor, as Archbishop of Paris, was seen to take his seat in parliament with a dagger in his pocket, the handle being visible, and the cry went up: *"There's the breviary of our Archbishop."*

A herald-at-arms, attended by a gentleman-in-waiting of the king's chamber, came to the gate of Saint-Antoine to make certain proposals. (1649) Parliament would not consent to receive him, but it admitted into the grand chamber a messenger from the Archduke Leopold, who was then at war with France.

In the midst of these disorders the nobles assembled in a body at the monastery of the Augustines, appointed officials, and held regular public sittings. One would have thought that they were going to reform France and convoke the states-general; but the great question simply concerned the permission given by the queen to Mme. de Pons to be seated on a stool at royal audiences; perhaps there was never a more obvious proof of the levity of mind for which the French were long reproached.

The civil strife which devastated England at precisely the same time serves to bring out clearly the characteristics of the two nations. The English displayed in their civil disturbances as it were a sullen fury and a reasoned frenzy; sanguinary battles were fought; the sword was the deciding factor, and scaffolds were erected for the vanquished; their king, taken on the field of battle, was brought before a court of justice, was charged with having misused the royal power, and was condemned to be beheaded: on 9 February, 1649, he was executed in public with the same order and show of justice as would have been accorded to an ordinary criminal, while London, in the midst of these awful disturbances, scarcely felt the calamities of civil war.

The French, on the contrary, rioted for a whim with laughter on their lips; women were at the head of factions; love made and unmade plots. The Duchess de Longueville persuaded Turenne, but lately made a marshal of France, to stir up the army he commanded to revolt against the king. It was the same army that the celebrated Duke of Saxe-Weimar had mustered. It was commanded, after the death of the Duke of Weimar, by Count d'Erlach, who came of an ancient family in the canton of Berne. Count d'Erlach gave this army to France and with it, as a result, Alsace. The Viscount de Turenne endeavoured to win him over; Alsace would have perished for Louis XIV., but he was mmovable; he held the Weimar troops true to their oath of allegiance. He was even charged by Cardinal Mazarin to arrest the viscount. Disloyal through lack of resolution, that great man was forced to flee from the army which he commanded, in order to please a woman who slighted his passion; from being a general of the King of France he became a lieutenant under Don Estevan de Gamara, and was beaten with him at Rethel by the Marshal du Plessis-Praslin.

The letter of the Marshal d'Hocquincourt to the Duchess de Montbazon is well known: Peronne belongs to the fairest of the fair: as also are the verses composed by the Duke de La Rochefoucauld for the Duchess de Longueville, on receiving, at the Battle of Saint-Antoine, a musket shot that temporarily deprived him of his sight.

> Pour mériter son cœur, pour plaire à ses beaux yeux,
> J'ai fait la guerre aux rois; je l'aurais faite aux dieux.

In the Memoirs of Mademoiselle there is a letter of Gaston, Duke of Orleans, her father, addressed as follows:

"To Mesdames the countesses, camp marshals of my daughter's army opposed to Mazarin."

The war ended and began again several times; there was not a man who did not frequently change sides. After bringing back the court to Paris in triumph, the Prince de Condé allowed himself the pleasure of disdaining it after having defended it; and finding he was not rewarded as he considered his fame and services demanded, he was the first to turn Mazarin to ridicule, defy the queen, and insult the government which he despised. It is said that in a letter he once addressed the cardinal as *"illustrissimo Signor Faquino."* He said to him one day: *"Adieu, Mars."* He encouraged a certain Marquis de Jarsai to make a declaration of love to the queen, and took it ill that she dared to be offended. He allied himself with his brother, the Prince de Conti, and the Duke de Longueville, who abandoned the Fronde party. The Duke of Beaufort's secret party at the beginning of the regency had been known as that of *"the importants"*: Condé's was known as the *"party of the petits-maîtres,"* because they wished to become masters of the state. The only traces left to-day of all these troubles are the names of *petit-maître*, applied nowadays to conceited and ill-bred youths, and of *frodeurs*, used to designate the critics of the government.

Each party resorted to methods as abject as they were odious. Joli, councillor at the Châtelet, afterwards secretary to the Cardinal de Retz, had the idea of making a wound in his arm and then discharging a pistol in his carriage, to make believe that the court had attempted to assassinate him.

Some days later, in order to divide the party of the Prince de Condé from the Frondeurs and make them irreconcilable, shots were fired at the carriages of the great Condé, and one of his footmen was killed: this was called a *joliade renforcée* (as going one better than Joli). Who perpetrated this singular outrage? Was it Cardinal Mazarin's party? They were strongly suspected of it. Cardinal de Retz, the Duke of Beaufort, and the venerable Broussel were accused of the deed in parliament, but cleared themselves.

All parties came into collision with each other, made treaties and betrayed each other in turn. Every man of note, or who wished to be so, purposed building his fortune on the public ruin, yet the public welfare was on the lips of everyone. Gaston was jealous of the great Condé's fame and of Mazarin's authority. Condé neither liked nor esteemed them. The coadjutor of the Archbishopric of Paris was eager to become a cardinal on the queen's nomination, and therefore devoted his services to her in order to obtain a foreign title which gave him no authority but great prestige. Such was then the force of prejudice that the Prince de Conti, the great Condé's brother, also desired to add the cardinal's hat to his prince's crown; and such too the power of intrigue that an abbé, possessing neither birth nor merit, contended for this Roman hat with the prince. Neither of them obtained it; the prince because he finally came to despise it, La Rivière because his ambition was openly jeered at; but the coadjutor obtained it as a reward for having abandoned the Prince de Condé to the resentment of the queen.

This resentment had no other foundation than the petty wranglings of self-interest between Condé and Mazarin. Condé could be accused of no treason against the state; nevertheless, he was arrested in the Louvre together with his brother, the Prince de Conti, and his brother-in-law, the Duke de Longueville, without any legal formality, and solely because he was feared by Mazarin (18 January, 1650). This step was undoubtedly contrary to all laws; but laws were alike unrecognised by every party.

In order to become master of these princes the cardinal resorted to a deception that is known as statecraft. The Frondeurs were accused of having attempted to assassinate the Prince de Condé; Mazarin gave him to understand that it was a question of arresting one of the conspirators and of deceiving the Frondeurs; and that it was the duty of his highness to sign the order to the gendarmes of the guard to hold themselves in readiness near the Louvre. The great Condé himself signed the order for his own imprisonment. Never has it been better demonstrated how often statecraft consists of lying and that ability is shown by unmasking the liar.

One reads in the Life of the Duchess de Longueville that the queen-mother retired into her small private chapel whilst the princes were being arrested, and that there she and her eleven-year-old son, the king, fell on their knees and devoutly prayed for the successful result of the expedition. Had Mazarin done this, it would have been an outrageous mummery. In Anne of Austria it was to be attributed but to the common frailty of women. With them, piety is closely allied with love, with politics and even with cruelty; only great women are above such littlenesses.

If he had only been willing to please, the Prince de Condé could have ruled the state; but he was content to be admired. The people of Paris, who had erected barricades for the sake of an almost imbecile councillor-clerk, lit triumphant bonfires when the defender and hero of France was conveyed to the dungeon of Vincennes.

The imprisonment of the three princes shows, moreover, how men are deceived as to the course of events, for it was thought likely to calm down the factions, yet it was the very thing which again roused them to action. Condé's exiled mother remained at Paris in spite of the court and brought her petition before parliament (1650). His wife after a thousand perils found refuge in the city of Bordeaux, and there, with the aid of the Duke de Bouillon and the Duke de La Rochefoucauld, she raised the city and armed Spain.

All France demanded the release of the great Condé. Had he appeared then, the court was lost. Gourville, who from being a mere valet to the Duke de La Rochefoucauld had with his fearless and cautious character become a man of importance, conceived a sure means of releasing the princes from their imprisonment at Vincennes. One of the conspirators was foolish enough to confess himself to a priest of the Fronde. The ill-starred priest informed the coadjutor, at that time the persecutor of the great Condé, and thus the venture failed owing to the disclosure of a confession, a common occurrence in the civil wars.

In the curious but little-known Memoirs of the statecouncillor Lenet one sees how in that period of unbridled licence, disturbance, lawbreaking, and even of impiety, the priests still had great power over men's minds. He relates that in Burgundy the dean of the Sainte-Chapelle, an adherent of the Prince de Condé, offered as the utmost of his assistance to order all preachers to speak from the pulpit in his favour, and all priests to do what they could for him in the confessional.

As demonstrating still better the manners of the time he records that when the great Condé's wife sought shelter at Bordeaux, the Dukes de Bouillon and de La Rochefoucauld marched before her at the head of a crowd of young noblemen, shouting: *Vive Condé !* adding an obscene expression for Mazarin, and begging her to join her voice to theirs.

(13 February, 1651) One year later the same Frondeurs who had sold Condé and the princes to the timid vengeance of Mazarin, forced the queen to open the doors of their prison and to banish her first minister from the kingdom. Mazarin himself went to Hâvre, where they were confined, and on restoring them to liberty was received by them with the contempt that he could only have expected; he then immediately withdrew to Liège. Condé re-entered Paris amidst the acclamations of the same people who had hated him so bitterly. His presence renewed the secret party cliques, disturbances and murders.

The country remained in this disturbed state for some years. The government was drawn almost continuously from weak and vacillating parties: it seemed bound to fall; but the rebels were never united, and this saved the court. The coadjutor, sometimes the friend, sometimes the enemy of Condé, stirred up against him a section of parliament and of the people; he had the temerity to serve the queen at the same time that he opposed the prince, and to wound her deeply by forcing her to remove Mazarin still further, and he now retired to Cologne. The queen, owing to a paradox only too common during weak governmental régimes, was compelled at once to accept his services and submit to his affronts, and actually to nominate the coadjutor to a cardinalship, the very man who was responsible for the barricades, and who had forced the royal family to flee from the capital and later to besiege it.

CHAPTER V

CONTINUATION OF THE CIVIL WAR TO THE END OF THE REBELLION IN 1653

AT length the Prince de Condé resolved upon a war which he should have begun at the time of the Fronde, if he had wished to make himself master of the state, or which he would never have begun at all if he had been a patriot. He left Paris to raise insurrections in Guienne, Poitou and Anjou, and begged the help of Spain against France, he who had been the greatest scourge of the Spaniards.

Nothing shows more clearly the folly of the times and the lack of arrangement which characterised all enterprises, than what now happened to this prince. The queen dispatched a courier from Paris to him with proposals urging him to return and make peace. The courier blundered, and instead of going to Angerville, where the prince was, arrived at Augerville. The message came too late. Condé said that had he received it sooner, he would have accepted the peace proposals; but that, as he was already so far from Paris, it was not worth while to return. Thus through the error of a courier and the sheer caprice of the prince, France was again plunged into civil war.

(December 1651) Cardinal Mazarin, who had ruled the court from his exile in Cologne, now re-entered the country, not so much like a minister coming to resume his duties, as a sovereign retaking possession of his states; he was accompanied by a small army of seven thousand men, raised at his own expense, that is to say with the nation's money which he had appropriated to his own use.

The king is said to have made a proclamation at that time that the cardinal had really raised these troops with his own money; this cannot but contradict the statement of those who have declared that on his first retirement from the kingdom Mazarin was in a state of poverty. He gave the command of his small army to Marshal d'Hocquincourt. All the officers wore green scarves, which was the colour of the cardinal's livery. Each party had at that time its special scarf; the king's was white and that of the Prince de Condé, cream. It was astonishing that Cardinal Mazarin, who up till then had affected such humility, should have had the audacity to have his livery worn by a whole army, just as though he belonged to a different party from that of his master; but he could not resist the vanity: it was exactly what the Marshal d'Ancre had done and what had contributed not a little to his ruin. The same temerity brought good fortune to Cardinal Mazarin; the queen approved of it. The king, now of age, together with his brother, went before him.

(December 1651) At the first news of his return, Gaston of Orleans, brother of Louis XIII., who had demanded the cardinal's banishment, had raised troops in Paris without well knowing to what use to put them. Parliament again began to issue decrees; it banished Mazarin and fixed a price on his head. The archives had to be searched to find out what price should be put on the head of an enemy of the kingdom. It was discovered that under Charles IX. a decree was issued promising fifty thousand crowns to anyone who should take Admiral Coligni dead or alive. It was quite seriously thought that all was done in order when the same price was fixed for the assassination of a cardinal and chief minister.

The proscription did not tempt anyone to earn the fifty thousand crowns, which after all would never have been paid. With any other nation and at any other period such a decree would have discovered the necessary assassins; but its only result was to call forth fresh jests. Blot and Marigni, wits who infused a spirit of gaiety into the midst of these disturbances, had Paris plastered with a division of the hundred and fifty thousand livres: so much for anyone who cut off the cardinal's nose, so much for an ear, so much for an eye, etc. This ridicule was the sole result of the proscription of the minister's person, but his belongings and library were sold by a second decree; the money was reserved to pay the assassin, but was squandered by the trustees, as was all money raised at that time. For his part, the cardinal employed neither poison nor assassination against his enemies; and notwithstanding the bitterness and folly of so many parties and enmities, fewer great crimes were committed, the party chiefs were less cruel, and the people less frenzied, than at the time of the Ligue, for it was not a war of religion.

(December 1651) The topsy-turvy spirit of the time so completely dominated the whole parliament of Paris that after having solemnly authorised an assassination which was merely scoffed at, it issued a decree ordering several councillors to repair to the frontier for the purpose of spying upon Mazarin's army, that is to say, upon the royal army.

Two councillors were foolish enough to break down with the aid of some peasants the bridges over which the cardinal was to pass; one of them, named Bitat, was taken prisoner by the king's troops, but was indulgently released and made fun of by all parties.

(6 August, 1652) The king, now of age, suspended the parliament of Paris and transferred it to Pontoise. Fourteen members attached to the court obeyed; the rest resisted. There were thus two parliaments who completed the confusion by thundering decrees at one another, as in the time of Henri IV. and Charles VI. At the very moment that this body was proceeding to such extremes against the king's minister, it declared the Prince de Condé guilty of high treason, whose only fault was to have taken up arms against the minister; moreover, by an abrupt change of face on a par with its previous actions, it ordered the newly-raised troops of Gaston, Duke of Orleans, to march against Mazarin, while at the same time forbidding the appropriation of any public revenues for the purpose of paying them.

Nothing else could be expected from a body of magistrates out of their natural sphere, who, knowing nothing of their rights or real power, and equally unacquainted with political affairs and the art of war, held uproarious meetings, and took courses which had not been so much as thought of the day before, and at which parliament itself was afterwards astonished.

The Parliament of Bordeaux was then on the side of the Prince de Condé, but its proceedings were rather more consistent since being further from the court it was less disturbed by opposing factions. The whole of France was concerned with more important affairs.

Condé, in league with the Spanish, was in the field against the king; and Turenne, abandoning the Spanish with whom

he had been defeated at Rethel, had recently made his
peace with the court and was in command of the royal army.
Neither of the two parties was able to afford a large army,
owing to the impoverishment of their finances; but small
armies did not the less decide the fate of the state. At times
a hundred thousand men can with difficulty capture a couple
of towns; at others a battle between seven or eight thousand
may overturn or establish a throne.

Bred in adversity, Louis XIV. travelled from province to
province with his mother, his brother and Cardinal Mazarin,
accompanied by but few more troops than he afterwards
possessed in times of peace as a bodyguard. Five or six thousand men, some sent from Spain, others raised by Condé's
adherents, pursued him into the heart of his kingdom.

Meanwhile, the Prince de Condé rapidly advanced from
Bordeaux to Montauban, took various towns, and everywhere increased the number of his party.

All the hopes of the court were centred in Marshal de
Turenne. The royal army was close to Gien on the Loire;
that of the Prince de Condé some leagues distant under the
command of the Duke of Nemours and the Duke of Beaufort.
The discord between these two generals was destined to be
fatal to the prince's party. The Duke of Beaufort was incapable of the least command: the Duke of Nemours was
considered a brave and likeable man, rather than an able
soldier. Together the two ruined their army. The rank and
file knew that the great Condé was a hundred leagues away
and gave themselves up for lost. In the middle of the night,
however, a courier appeared before the main guard in the
forest of Orleans. The sentinels recognised in the courier
the Prince de Condé himself, who after a thousand adventures
and in disguise had come from Agen to put himself at the
head of his army.

His presence did much, his unexpected arrival still more.
He well knew that the sudden and unlooked-for excites the
minds of men, and he determined to make instant use of
the confidence and fearlessness that his coming inspired. The
great talent of this prince in warfare consisted in adopting
in a moment the most daring plans and executing them with
no less order and promptitude.

(7 April, 1652) The royal army was divided into two bodies.
Condé fell upon the one at Blenau under the command
of Marshal d'Hocquincourt, and the enemy was scattered

as soon as attacked. There was no time to warn Turenne. Cardinal Mazarin in alarm hastened in the middle of the night to Gien to awaken the king from sleep and acquaint him with the news. His little court was in consternation; it was proposed that the king should fly and make his way secretly to Bourges. The victorious Prince de Condé marched on Gien; gloom and fear were intensified. Turenne reassured everyone by his resolution and saved the court by his adroitness; with the few troops that remained to him he manœuvred so successfully, and availed himself so well of ground and weather, that he prevented Condé from following up his advantage. It was difficult to say who had covered himself with greater glory—the victorious Condé, or Turenne, who had snatched from him the fruits of victory. It is true that in this battle of Blenau, long famous in France, not four hundred men were killed; but the Prince de Condé was none the less within an ace of capturing the whole of the royal family and of having within his hands his special enemy, Cardinal Mazarin.

There can hardly have been a smaller combat accompanied by more imminent danger and with greater interests at stake.

Condé, who did not expect to surprise Turenne as he had d'Hocquincourt, advanced with his army towards Paris; he was eager to enter that city to revel in his glory and enjoy the friendly dispositions of a deluded people. Admiration for this latest battle, whose details they exaggerated, the hatred for Mazarin, the name and presence of the great Condé, seemed at first to make him absolute master of the capital; but at heart all men thought differently; each party was subdivided into factions, as always happens in times of disturbance. The coadjutor, now become Cardinal de Retz, was apparently reconciled to the court, who feared him and whom he defied, but he was no longer the master of the people and no longer played the chief rôle. He ruled the Duke of Orleans and was opposed to Condé. Parliament wavered between the court, the Duke of Orleans, and the prince; although everyone agreed in decrying Mazarin, everyone secretly looked after his own particular interest; the people were like a stormy sea, whose waves are driven hither and thither by a hundred contrary winds. The shrine of Sainte Geneviève was carried through the streets of Paris to secure the expulsion of the cardinal minister, and the populace doubted not that this saint would perform the miracle in the same way as she brings rain.

There was nothing to be seen but negotiations between party chiefs, deputations of parliament, assemblies of the chambers, rebellion among the people and soldiers in the field. Guards were posted at monastery gates. The prince had summoned the Spanish to his aid. Charles IV., that Duke of Lorraine who had been driven from his estates and retained naught but an army of eight thousand men, which he hired out every year to the King of Spain, approached Paris, accompanied by this army. Cardinal Mazarin offered him more money to turn back than the Prince de Condé had given him to come. The Duke of Lorraine accordingly soon quitted France, laying waste the country through which he passed, and carrying away money from both parties.

Condé remained at Paris, his power diminishing day by day and his army growing ever weaker. Turenne now led the king and his court towards the capital. The king at the age of fifteen years witnessed (July 1652) the Battle of Saint-Antoine from the heights of Charonne, where the two generals accomplished so much with so few troops that the reputation of each which seemed to have reached its zenith was enhanced.

The Prince de Condé with a small number of the noblemen of his party, followed by a few soldiers, held their own and repulsed the advance of the royal army. The Duke of Orleans, uncertain as to which side he should take, remained in his palace of Luxembourg. Cardinal de Retz likewise shut himself up in his archbishop's residence. Parliament awaited the result of the battle in order to issue a decree. The weeping queen lay prostrate in a Carmelite chapel. The people, now fearful alike of the king's troops and those of the prince, had closed the gates of the city and allowed no one to enter or leave, whilst all that was greatest in France was shedding its blood in fierce combat in the suburbs. It was there that the Duke de La Rochefoucauld, famed for his courage as for his wit, received a blow over the eyes which temporarily caused him to lose his sight. One of Cardinal Mazarin's nephews was killed there, and the people considered themselves avenged. Continuous files of young noblemen, either killed or wounded, were to be seen being carried to the gate of Saint-Antoine, which remained shut against them.

At length Mademoiselle, the daughter of the Duke of Orleans, took the side of Condé, whom her father dared not support, opened the gates to the wounded, and had the temerity to order the cannon of the Bastille to be fired on the king's troops. The royal army fell back; Condé achieved nothing but glory; but Mademoiselle by her violent action forfeited for ever the favour of her cousin, the king, and Cardinal Mazarin, who was aware of Mademoiselle's extreme desire to marry a crowned head, made the remark: "*That cannon-shot has just killed her husband.*"

The majority of our historians display to their readers little more than such fights and prodigies of courage and policy; but to one who knows what scandalous methods it was necessary to employ, into what a state of misery the common people were necessarily plunged, and to what sordid actions men were reduced, the glory of those heroes appears to deserve rather pity than admiration. The evidence of Gourville, a gentleman in attendance upon Monsieur le Prince, is sufficient to judge by. He confesses that in order to obtain money for his master he himself stole some from a receiver's office, and that he imprisoned a postmaster in his house until he extorted a ransom from him: moreover he describes these violent acts as if they were common occurrences.

A pound of bread in Paris was then worth twenty-four sous. The people suffered, there was not sufficient alms to go round, and in several provinces famine prevailed.

There can have been few more distressing incidents than the following, which happened during the Bordeaux campaign. A nobleman was captured by the royal troops and executed; whereupon the Duke de La Rochefoucauld had a nobleman of the king's party hanged by way of reprisal; and yet de La Rochefoucauld was considered a philosopher. Such horrors were soon forgotten amidst the momentous affairs of the party chiefs.

But at the same time can there have been few things more ridiculous than the sight of the great Condé kissing the shrine of Sainte Geneviève in a procession, rubbing his rosary against it, and displaying it to the people, thus plainly proving by such mummery that heroes often show off in order to win the favour of the mob?

Decency and propriety were alike unknown in conduct and word. Omer Talon relates that he heard councillors in discussion call the cardinal and chief minister a *scoundrel*. A councillor named Quatre-Sous rudely insulted the great Condé at a parliamentary sitting. Blows were exchanged within the sanctuary of the courts of justice.

Fighting had taken place in 1644 in Notre-Dame for a place which the presidents of inquiries disputed with the dean of the grand chamber.

In 1645 certain women of the people were admitted to that part of the court reserved for the gentlemen of the king, and begged on their knees that parliament would revoke the taxes.

Disorder of every kind thus prevailed from 1644 to 1653, at first without causing open disturbance, but at the end of that period riots were continually breaking out from one end of the kingdom to another.

(1652) The great Condé so far forgot himself as to box the ears of the Count de Rieux, son of the Prince d'Elbeuf, at the house of the Duke of Orleans; it was not the way to regain the hearts of the Parisians. The Count de Rieux returned the box on the ears to the conqueror of Rocroi, Freiburg, Nördlingen and Lens, and the curious episode came to nothing; Monsieur committed the son of the Duke d'Elbeuf to the Bastille for a few days, and nothing more was said about it.

The quarrel between the Duke of Beaufort and his brother-in-law the Duke of Nemours was, however, serious. They challenged each other to a duel, each engaging four seconds. The Duke of Nemours was killed by the Duke of Beaufort; and the Marquis de Villars, surnamed *Orondate*, who had acted as Nemours' second, killed his opponent, Héricourt, who was entirely unknown to him. It is only just to say that no ill-will was shown. Duels were frequent, theft was common, and profligacy was carried to the point of public shamelessness; but a certain gaiety of spirit always permeated these disorders and rendered them less odious.

The bloody and useless battle of Saint-Antoine over, the king could not enter Paris and the prince could not long remain there. Popular feeling and the fact that they believed him to be responsible for the murders of several citizens had made him hateful to the people. Nevertheless he still controlled a party in parliament. On 20 July, 1652, that body, no longer intimidated by a fugitive court which had practically been chased from the capital, and urged on by the parties of the Duke of Orleans and the prince, issued a decree proclaiming the Duke of Orleans lieutenant-general of the kingdom, although the king was of age; it was the same title which had been given to the Duke of Mayenne at the time of the Ligue. The Prince de Condé was appointed generalissimo of the armies. The two parliaments of Paris and Pontoise, disputing as they did each other's authority, issuing contradictory decrees, and thereby earning the contempt of the people, were at one in demanding the expulsion of Mazarin, to such an extent did hatred of this minister seem the essential duty of Frenchmen.

At that time there was no party which was not weak; that of the court was as much so as the others; they all alike lacked money and troops; factions multiplied; fighting had produced on either side nothing but losses and regrets. The court found itself again compelled to sacrifice Mazarin, whom everyone named as the source of trouble, but who was in reality only the pretext.

On 12 August, 1652, he left the kingdom for the second time; to add to his shame the king was obliged to make a public declaration in which he dismissed his minister, at the same time eulogising his services and deploring his exile.

The King of England, Charles I., had just lost his head on the scaffold, because at the beginning of the disturbances he had delivered the life of his friend, Strafford, into the hands of parliament: Louis XIV., on the contrary, became the peaceful master of his kingdom by permitting Mazarin's exile. Thus the same weakness yielded very different results. By delivering up his favourite the King of England emboldened a people who longed for war and hated their kings; Louis XIV., or rather the queen-mother, by dismissing the cardinal removed every pretext of revolt from a people who were tired of war and loved monarchy.

(20 October, 1652) The cardinal had scarcely departed on his way to Bouillon, his new retreat, when the citizens of Paris on their own initiative sent a deputation to the king entreating him to return to his capital. He entered it: and so peaceful was everything that it was difficult to imagine that confusion had reigned there but a few days before. Gaston of Orleans, unfortunate in his undertakings which he never succeeded in carrying to a finish, was banished to Blois, where he passed the remainder of his life in repentance: he was the second son of Henri-Quatre to die with but little glory. Cardinal de Retz, as foolhardy as he was dauntless, was arrested in the Louvre, and after being conducted from prison to prison, led for a long time a wandering life, which was at length ended in retirement, where he acquired virtues

which his great courage had not known during the tumult of his public career.

Some of the councillors who had most abused their office paid for their misdeeds by exile; the others hid themselves within the precincts of the magistracy and a few were held to their duty by an annual gratuity of five hundred crowns, which Fouquet, attorney-general and comptroller of the treasury, secretly gave to them.

The Prince de Condé, however, forsaken by nearly all his supporters in France, and poorly aided by the Spanish, continued to wage an unsuccessful war on the frontiers of Champagne. In Bordeaux the factions were still rampant, but were soon suppressed.

The tranquillity of the kingdom was the result of the banishment of Cardinal Mazarin. Scarcely, however, had he been expelled by the universal outcry of the French people and by royal declaration than the king had him recalled. He was astonished to re-enter Paris on 3 February, 1653, with all his power and without disturbance. Louis XIV. received him as a father and the people as a master. He was entertained at the Hôtel-de-Ville amid the acclamations of the citizens; he flung money to the populace; but it is said that in the exultation of so auspicious a change he remarked with contempt on the fickleness or rather the folly of the Parisians. The chief members of parliament, after putting a price on his head, as on that of a notorious brigand, were almost unanimous in requesting the honour of his protection; and the same parliament a short time afterwards sentenced the Prince de Condé to death by default (27 March, 1653). It was a common change of policy in such times and all the more humiliating in that they were sentencing to death one with whom for a long time they had been partners in guilt. It was to be observed that the cardinal who urged this condemnation of Condé married one of his nieces to Condé's brother, the Prince de Conti (22 February, 1654); and was but a proof that the minister's power was to be limitless.

The king united the two parliaments of Paris and Pontoise, and forbade the sitting of the chambers. Parliament attempted to remonstrate, but one councillor was imprisoned and several others were exiled; parliament was silenced; great changes were already taking place.

CHAPTER VI

THE STATE OF FRANCE UNTIL THE DEATH OF CARDINAL MAZARIN IN 1661

WHILE the state had thus been riven at home it had been attacked and weakened abroad. All the fruits of the battles of Rocroi, Lens and Nördlingen were lost. In 1651 the important town of Dunkirk was retaken by the Spaniards; they drove the French out of Barcelona and recaptured Casal in Italy.

Nevertheless, in spite of the disorders of a civil war and the burden of a foreign one, Mazarin had been sufficiently adroit and fortunate to conclude the celebrated peace of Westphalia, by which the Emperor and the Empire sold the sovereignty of Alsace to the king and crown of France for three million livres in to-day's currency. (1648) By this treaty, destined to become the basis of all future treaties, a new electorate was created for the House of Bavaria. The rights of all princes and imperial cities and the privileges of the smallest German noblemen were ratified. The Emperor's power was restricted within narrow limits, and France combined with Sweden to become the legislators of the Empire. France's glory was at least partly due to Swedish arms. Gustavus Adolphus had begun to shake the foundations of the Empire. His generals had still farther extended their conquests under the rule of his daughter, Christina. One of them, Wrangel, was about to enter Austria. The Count of Königsmarck was master of half the city of Prague, and was besieging the other half when peace was concluded. Thus in order to crush the Emperor, it cost France little more than a million a year given to Sweden.

Sweden thus obtained greater benefit from these treaties than did France; she received Pomerania, a considerable number of towns and cash, and she forced the Emperor to allow livings which belonged to Roman Catholics to pass into Lutheran hands. Rome cried out against such impiety and declared that the cause of God was betrayed, but the Protestants boasted that they had hallowed the work of peace by plundering the Papists. Interest alone was the mainspring of every action.

Spain did not participate in this peace, and with good

reason; for, observing that France was plunged in civil war, she hoped to profit by the divisions of her neighbour. The disbanded German troops became a fresh support to the Spaniards. After the peace of Münster the Emperor sent over nearly thirty thousand men to Flanders during a period of four years. It was an obvious violation of the treaties; but it is thus that they are usually carried out.

At the beginning of the negotiations of Westphalia the Spanish ministers were shrewd enough to make a separate peace with Holland. The Spanish monarchy was now only too happy to have no longer as enemies, indeed to acknowledge as sovereigns, those whom for so long she had treated as rebels unworthy of pardon. The republicans increased their wealth and strengthened both their greatness and their security by treating with Spain and at the same time avoiding a break with France.

(1653) They were so powerful that in the war they subsequently fought against England, a hundred ships of the line put to sea under their flag: and the result was often in doubt between the English admiral, Blake, and the Dutch, Van Tromp, who became on sea what Condé and Turenne were on land. At that time France did not possess ten ships of fifty guns in seaworthy condition; her navy was indeed steadily diminishing.

Louis XIV. thus found himself in 1653 absolute master of a kingdom still shaken from the blows it had received, every branch of administration in disorder, but full of resources, having no ally save Savoy for an offensive war, but also having no foreign enemy but Spain, who was in still worse plight than France. Those who had taken part in the civil war were by now crushed, excepting the Prince de Condé and some of his partisans, one or two of whom had remained faithful to him through bonds of friendship and true sincerity—such as the Count de Coligni and Bouteville —and the others, because the court was not willing to buy them at their price.

Condé, now general of the Spanish forces, was unable to raise the strength of regiments which he had himself enfeebled by the massacre of their infantry in the battles of Rocroi and Lens. He was fighting with fresh troops, over whom he had not the supreme command, against old French regiments who under him had learnt the art of victory and who were commanded by Turenne.

Turenne and Condé were fated to be always victorious when they fought together at the head of Frenchmen and to be beaten when they commanded the Spanish. When Turenne, from being a general of the King of France, became the lieutenant of a Spanish general, he was hard put to it to save the remnants of the Spanish army at the Battle of Rethel; the Prince de Condé was now to have the same fortune before Arras. On 25 August, 1654, he was besieging that town with the archduke. Turenne attacked them in their camp and forced their lines; the archduke's troops were put to flight, and Condé, with two regiments of French and of Lorraine, sustained the attacks of Turenne single-handed; while the archduke fled from the field he beat the Marshal d'Hocquincourt, repulsed the Marshal de La Ferté, and retired victorious, covering the retreat of the defeated Spanish. The King of Spain wrote him these words with his own hand: "I learn that all was lost and that you have saved all."

It is difficult to say what decides the issue of battles, but it is certain that Condé was one of the greatest generals that have ever lived, and that the archduke and his council refused in this battle to carry out a single one of his proposals.

With Arras saved, the lines forced, and the archduke put to flight, Turenne was covered with glory; but it was to be noted that in a letter written in the name of the king to parliament on this victory, the success of the whole campaign was attributed to Cardinal Mazarin and Turenne's name was not even mentioned. The cardinal had indeed been with the king at some leagues from Arras. He had even entered the camp at the siege of Stenai, which Turenne had taken before relieving Arras. Councils of war had been held in his presence, and on these grounds he attributed to himself the honour of victory; such vanity inspired ridicule which not all the dignity of the ministry could efface.

The king was not present at the Battle of Arras, although no outward circumstances prevented him; he had been in the trenches at the siege of Stenai; but Cardinal Mazarin did not wish him again to expose his person, on which both the peace of the state and the power of the minister seemed to depend.

Mazarin on the one side, the absolute master of France and the young king, and Don Luis de Haro on the other, who ruled Spain and Philip IV., continued to carry on the war in the name of their masters, in a desultory manner.

As yet the name of Louis XIV. was not known to the world, and the King of Spain was a mere nonentity. At that time but one crowned head in Europe was surrounded by personal glory: Christina, Queen of Sweden, governed by herself, and upheld the honour of the throne, which was perished, withered or unknown in other states.

Charles II., King of England, a fugitive in France with his mother and brother, had there to reflect on his misfortunes and his hopes. A simple citizen had subjugated England, Scotland and Ireland. Cromwell, that usurper who proved himself worthy to rule, had assumed the name of Protector, not that of King, since the English knew how far the rights of their kings should reach, but were ignorant of the limits of a Protector's power.

He strengthened his power by knowing the right moment to restrain it; he did not encroach on privileges of which the people were jealous; he forbore to quarter soldiers in the city of London; he levied no taxes that could give cause for complaint; offended none by excessive pomp, allowed himself no pleasures, heaped up no riches, and took care that justice should be observed with a relentless impartiality that made no distinction between great and small.

The brother of Pantaleon Sa, the Portuguese ambassador in England, believing that his lawlessness would go unpunished because his brother's person was sacred, insulted the citizens of London and had one of them killed in revenge for their resistance; he was condemned to be hanged. Cromwell, who could have pardoned him, allowed him to be executed and afterwards signed a treaty with the ambassador.

Never had trade been so unrestricted and flourishing, never had England been so rich. Her victorious fleets made her name respected on every sea; whilst Mazarin, solely occupied in making himself powerful and rich, allowed justice, trade, the navy and even the treasury to languish in France. Ruler of France, as Cromwell was of England after a civil war, he could have done for the country what Cromwell had done for his, but he was a foreigner, and the soul of Mazarin lacked not only the coarseness of Cromwell's, but also its greatness. The European nations, who had without exception despised the alliance of England under James I. and Charles I., now solicited it under the Protector. Christina herself, though she had execrated the murder of Charles I., now entered into an alliance with a tyrant whom she admired.

Mazarin and Don Luis de Haro vied with each other in allying themselves with the Protector. For some time he enjoyed the satisfaction of being courted by the two most powerful kingdoms of Christendom.

The Spanish minister offered to help him in taking Calais; Mazarin suggested besieging Dunkirk and offered to hand over that town to him on its capture. Cromwell had to choose between the keys of France and those of Flanders. He was also greatly importuned by Condé; but he was very unwilling to negotiate with a prince who possessed nothing but his name, and who was without a party in France or power in Spain.

The Protector decided in favour of France, but without making definite treaties or agreeing to share future conquests in advance; he wished to make his usurpation famous by greater undertakings. His scheme was to snatch Mexico from the Spanish; but they were warned in time. Cromwell's admirals, however, captured Jamaica from them in May of 1655, an island which the English still hold and which secured their trade in the New World. It was not until after the Jamaica expedition that Cromwell signed a treaty with the King of France, and he still made no mention of Dunkirk. The Protector negotiated on an equal footing with the King of France, and forced him to address him as brother in his letters. (8 November, 1655) His secretary signed before the French plenipotentiary on the draft treaty which remained in England; but he showed himself his superior by forcing the King of France to expel from the country Charles II. and the Duke of York, a grandson of Henri IV., to whom France owed shelter. A greater sacrifice of honour to interest could not be made.

While Mazarin was making this treaty, Charles II. asked for one of his nieces in marriage. The parlous state of his affairs which forced him to this step brought upon him a refusal. The cardinal has ever been suspected of having wished to marry this lady, whom he refused to the King of England, to the son of Cromwell. It is certain at any rate that on seeing that the road of Charles lay once more open to the throne he was eager to push forward the marriage, but was refused in his turn.

The mother of the two princes, and the daughter of Henri-Quatre, Henrietta, remained in France without resources, and was reduced to the necessity of imploring the cardinal to obtain from Cromwell at least the payment of her jointure. It was the last and most bitter humiliation for her to have to ask for subsistence from one who had shed her husband's blood upon the scaffold. Mazarin made some feeble representations in England on the queen's behalf and informed her that he had obtained nothing. Mortified at having besought the pity of Cromwell, she remained at Paris in poverty, while her children joined the armies of Condé and Don John of Austria to learn the art of warfare against France—the country that had abandoned them.

Driven from France, Charles I.'s children took refuge in Spain. In every court, especially that of Rome, Spanish officials clamoured in speech and document against a cardinal who, they said, had sacrificed laws divine and human, honour and religion alike, to the murderer of a king, and who had driven Charles II. and the Duke of York, cousins of Louis XIV., from France in order to please their father's executioner. The one reply made to the outcries of the Spanish was the production of the offers which they themselves had made to the Protector.

The war was still being carried on in Flanders with varying success. Turenne, besieging Valenciennes with Marshal de La Ferté, met with a similar reverse to that which Condé had sustained before Arras. Condé, supported by Don John of Austria, worthier to fight by his side than was the archduke, broke the lines of Marshal de La Ferté, took him prisoner and relieved Valenciennes. Turenne did what Condé had done after a similar defeat. (17 July, 1656) He saved the defeated army and everywhere presented a front to the enemy; a month afterwards he even attacked and captured the little town of La Capelle; it was perhaps the first time that a defeated army had dared to undertake a siege.

This celebrated march of Turenne, before taking La Capelle, was eclipsed by a still finer march of the Prince de Condé in April 1657. Turenne had hardly besieged Cambrai, when Condé with two thousand cavalry cut through the besieging army, and beating down all opposition forced his way into the town. The citizens fell on their knees before their deliverer. In such manner did these two men opposed to each other display the resources of their genius. They were admired as much in defeat as in victory, for their good deeds as well as for the errors which they always knew how to redeem. Their military gifts stopped in turn the progress

*c 780

of France and Spain, but the financial chaos in the two countries was a still greater obstacle to their success.

The alliance with Cromwell finally gave France a definite superiority: on the one side Admiral Blake set off to burn the Spanish galleons off the Canary Islands, and caused them to lose the only treasures with which the war could be carried on; on the other, twenty English ships proceeded to blockade the port of Dunkirk, and six thousand veterans who had fought in the English revolution reinforced the army of Turenne.

Dunkirk, the most important town in Flanders, was thus besieged by sea and land. Condé and Don John of Austria, collecting all their forces, advanced to relieve it. The eyes of Europe were upon them. Cardinal Mazarin conducted Louis XIV. close to the theatre of war without allowing him actually to enter it, although he was nearly twenty years of age. The king remained therefore at Calais. It was there that Cromwell sent him a pompous embassy at the head of which was his son-in-law, Lord Falconbridge. The king sent to him the Duke de Créqui and Mancini, Duke de Nevers, nephew of the cardinal, accompanied by two hundred noblemen. Mancini presented a letter to the Protector from the cardinal. The letter is certainly remarkable: in it Mazarin said "that he regretted he was unable to pay in person the respect due to the greatest man in the world." It was thus that he spoke to the murderer of the son-in-law of Henry IV. and the uncle of his master, Louis XIV.

Meanwhile the Prince Marshal de Turenne attacked the Spanish army, or rather the Flemish army, hard by the Dunes. It was commanded by Don John of Austria, the son of Philip IV. and an actress, who became the brother-in-law of Louis XIV. two years afterwards. The Prince de Condé was in the army, but not in command, and the victory of Turenne was therefore easy. Six thousand English contributed to the victory which was complete (14 June, 1658). The two English princes, who were later to become kings, saw their fortunes still further wane in the ascendant of Cromwell.

The genius of the great Condé could do nothing against the superior French and English troops. The Spanish army was annihilated, and Dunkirk surrendered soon after. The king hastened with his minister to see the garrison pass out. The cardinal would not allow Louis XIV. to appear either as warrior or as king; he had no money to distribute among the soldiers; he was barely waited upon; when he was with the army he took his meals with Mazarin or Marshal de Turenne. This neglect of the royal dignity was not in Louis XIV. the result of contempt for pomp, but was due to the mismanagement of his affairs and to the care that the cardinal took to reserve all the splendour and authority for himself.

Louis entered Dunkirk, only to hand it over to Lord Lee, Cromwell's ambassador. Mazarin tried to see if by some artifice he could evade the treaty and avoid surrendering the town; but Lockhart threatened and English firmness prevailed over Italian cunning.

It has been asserted by some that the cardinal, who appropriated to himself the glory of the Battle of Arras, tried to persuade Turenne to cede to him the honours of the Battle of the Dunes. It is said that Du Bec-Crépin, Count de Moret, was sent by the minister to propose that the general should write a letter in which it would appear that the cardinal had himself planned the whole scheme of operations. Turenne received these suggestions with contempt and refused to give an avowal which would have been shameful to a general of an army and ridiculous for a churchman. Mazarin, who had the foolishness to suggest this, had also the foolishness to remain on bad terms with Turenne until his death.

In the midst of this initial triumph the king fell ill at Calais, and for several days lay at death's door. Immediately all the courtiers turned towards his brother, Monsieur. Mazarin showered praises, adulation and promises on Marshal du Plessis - Praslin, the former tutor of this young prince and his favourite, the Count de Guiche. A cabal was formed at Paris bold enough to write to Calais against the cardinal. He made preparations for quitting the kingdom and for securing the safety of his immense riches. A quack named d'Abbeville cured the king with an emetic wine which the court physicians looked upon as a poison. This honest fellow seated himself on the king's bed and said: "The lad is very ill, but he will not die." As soon as he was convalescent, the cardinal banished all those who had plotted against him.

(13 September, 1658) A few months afterwards Cromwell died at the age of fifty-five in the midst of plans for the establishment of his power and his country's glory. He had humbled Holland, imposed the conditions of a treaty upon

Portugal, conquered Spain and compelled France to seek his alliance. But a short while before his death, on hearing with what high-handedness his admirals had borne themselves at Lisbon, he had said: "I desire the English Republic to be as much respected as was the Roman Republic in ancient times." The physicians told him that he was dying. I do not know if it is true that in that moment he assumed the air of a seer and prophet, answering that God would perform a miracle on his behalf. His secretary, Thurlow, affirms that he said to them: *"Nature is more powerful than physicians."* These are not the words of prophecy, but of strict common sense. It may be that knowing that the physicians were not infallible he wished in case he recovered to have the glory of having prophesied his recovery, and thus make his person more revered by the people, though even then it was held as something sacred.

He was buried as a legitimate monarch and left behind him in Europe the reputation of a fearless man, at times fanatical, at others crafty—a usurper who knew how to rule.

Sir William Temple claims that before his death Cromwell had wished to form an alliance with Spain against France, and gain possession of Calais with the help of the Spanish, as he had obtained Dunkirk at the hands of the French. Nothing was more in accordance with his character and policy. By thus despoiling two nations one after the other, who were equally hated by his country, he would have made himself the idol of the English nation. Death terminated his vast designs, his tyranny, and the greatness of England.

It should be noted that the French court went into mourning for Cromwell, and that Mademoiselle was the only person who did not pay this respect to the memory of the murderer of one who was a king and related to her by ties of blood.

We have seen that Richard Cromwell succeeded peaceably and unopposed to his father's Protectorate, just as a Prince of Wales would have succeeded a King of England. Richard plainly showed that the fate of a nation often depends on the character of a single man. His nature was very different from that of Oliver Cromwell, possessing all the mildness of the civic virtues and none of that stern fearlessness which sacrifices all to its own interest. Had he been willing to put to death three or four important officers in the army, who were opposed to his accession, he could have preserved intact the heritage of his father's labours. He preferred to resign the government than to reign by assassination; he lived in private life, indeed, forgotten, until the age of ninety, in a country of which he had been for a few days the ruler. He travelled in France after resigning the Protectorate; it is said that at Montpellier the Prince de Conti, brother of the great Condé, was one day conversing with him, not knowing who he was, and said: "Oliver Cromwell was a great man, but his son Richard is a pitiable character, who was unable to enjoy the fruits of his father's crimes." Nevertheless, Richard enjoyed a happiness which his father had never known.

Some time before, France witnessed a still more memorable example of contempt for a crown. Christina, Queen of Sweden, came to Paris. She was regarded with admiration as a young queen who, at twenty-seven years of age, had renounced a throne of which she was worthy in order to live at peace and in tranquillity. It is to the shame of Protestant writers that they have dared to say without the least foundation that she only abdicated the crown because she could no longer keep it. She had made this resolution when she was twenty years of age, and for seven years had allowed it to mature. This resolution, so far removed from commonly accepted ideas and so long reflected, might well have closed the mouths of those who reproached her for fickleness and an unwilling abdication. The one reproach annulled the other; but there will never be lacking petty minds to attack the great.

One has only to read the letters of this queen to understand her exceptional character. In a letter she wrote to Chanut, once French ambassador at her court, she says: "I have ruled without pomp, I abdicate with ease. Thereafter, have no fears for me; my welfare is not controlled by the power of fortune." She wrote to the Prince de Condé: "I consider myself as much honoured by your esteem as by the crown that I have worn. If on abandoning it you judge me less worthy of it, I will admit that the tranquillity I have so much desired has cost me dear; nevertheless, I shall not repent of having bought it at the price of a crown, and I will never dishonour with mean regrets an action which seemed to me so glorious; if it should happen that you condemn my action my whole excuse will be that I should not have renounced the gifts which fortune gave me, had I believed them necessary to my happiness, and that I should have aspired to the empire of the world, if I had been so sure of succeeding or of dying in the attempt, as the great Condé would have been."

Such was the mind of this singular person; such was her command of our language which she but rarely spoke. She knew eight languages, and had been the pupil and friend of Descartes, who actually died in her palace at Stockholm, though he had been unable to secure even a pension in France, where his works were banned for the only good things they contained.

She had attracted to Sweden everyone who could enlighten that country, and the disappointment at finding not one of her own subjects amongst them had sickened her of reigning over a nation of soldiers. She decided it was better to live with men of thought than to rule over men who had neither culture nor genius. She had cultivated all the arts in a country where they were still unknown. Her intention was now to retire to Italy, the home of the arts. She came to France only to pass through it, since the arts were only beginning to spring up there. Her instinct guided her to Rome. With this view she renounced the Lutheran for the Catholic faith; indifferent to either, she made no scruple of conforming in appearance to the sentiments of the people among whom she desired to live. She had left her kingdom in 1654, and the ceremony of her renunciation had been publicly performed at Innsbruck. She gained the approbation of the French court, although there was not to be found there a single woman whose intellect was equal to hers. The king saw her and paid her great honours; but he hardly spoke to her. Brought up in ignorance, his natural good sense made him bashful.

Most of the ladies and courtiers noticed nothing about this philosophical queen save that she was not coiffured in the French fashion and that she danced poorly. The wise found nothing to censure but the murder of her equerry Monaldeschi, who was assassinated by her orders at Fontaine-bleau during a second visit. In whatever way he had offended her since she had abdicated the throne, she should have demanded justice and not performed it. It was not a queen punishing a subject; it was a woman putting an end to a love affair by a murder; it was an Italian procuring another's murder by the order of a Swede and in a palace of a king of France. No person should be put to death except by law. In Sweden, Christina would not have had the right of ordering

the death of anyone, and what would have been a crime at
Stockholm was certainly not authorised at Fontainebleau.
Those who have justified the action deserve to find themselves
the servants of such masters. This shameless and cruel deed
sullied the philosophy of Christina which had led her to give
up a throne. In England and in all countries which know
the reign of law, she would have been punished; but France
shut her eyes to this outrage to the king's authority, to the
rights of nations and to humanity.

After the death of Cromwell and the deposition of his
son, England was given over for a year to lawlessness and
disorder. Charles Gustavus, into whose hands Christina had
resigned the Kingdom of Sweden, made himself feared in the
North and in Germany. Emperor Ferdinand III. had died
in 1657; his son Leopold, seventeen years of age, already
King of Hungary and of Bohemia, had not been elected King
of the Romans while his father was alive. Mazarin determined
to try and make Louis XIV. Emperor. It was a fantastic
scheme; the electors would either have to be coerced or
bribed. France was not strong enough to seize the Empire
nor rich enough to buy it; accordingly the preliminary
overtures made at Frankfort by Marshal de Grammont and
Lyonne were dismissed as soon as proposed. Leopold was
elected. All that the policy of Mazarin could accomplish
was to make an alliance with the German princes for the
observance of the treaties of Münster, and to limit the
Emperor's authority over the Empire (August 1658).

The Battle of the Dunes and the glory of her arms made
France powerful abroad, especially in the reduced state of
the other nations; but home affairs were in a bad state; her
finances were exhausted, and peace was badly wanted.

Nations under Christian monarchies scarcely ever interest
themselves in the wars of their rulers. Mercenary armies
raised by the orders of a minister, and commanded by a
general who blindly obeys him, fight several ruinous campaigns, without the kings in whose name they are fighting
having either the hope or even the intention of seizing each
other's heritage. The victorious nation never profits from the
spoils of the conquered; it pays for everything; it suffers as
much when its armies are successful as when they are beaten;
and peace is almost as necessary after the greatest victory
as when the enemy has captured its frontier towns.

Two things were requisite for the cardinal to crown his

ministry with success; to make peace and to secure the tranquillity of the state by the king's marriage. The plots that arose during the king's illness showed him that an heir to the throne was an essential complement to the greatness of the minister. These considerations determined him to marry Louis XIV. promptly. There was a choice of two matches: the daughter of the King of Spain and the Princess of Savoy. The king had lost his heart to another; he was passionately in love with Mdlle. Mancini, one of the cardinal's nieces; naturally of a sensitive disposition and yet obstinate in his whims, passionate by nature and yet inexperienced, he might have decided to marry his mistress.

Mme. de Motteville, the favourite of the queen-mother, whose Memoirs have a convincing air of truth, asserts that Mazarin was tempted to encourage the king's passion and place his niece on the throne. He had already married another of his nieces to the Prince de Conti, and one to the Duke de Mercœur; the one with whom Louis XIV. was in love had been asked in marriage by the King of England. These were all reasons which might justify his ambition. He cleverly sounded the queen-mother. "I am greatly afraid," he told her, "that the king is very eager to marry my niece." The queen, who saw through the minister, understood that he desired what he pretended to fear. She replied to him with the pride of a princess of the blood of Austria, the daughter, the wife and the mother of kings, and with the bitterness inspired by a minister who for some time had feigned to be no longer dependent on her: "If the king were capable of such infamy," she said, "I should place myself with my second son at the head of the whole nation against the king and against you."

It is said that Mazarin never forgave this reply of the queen, but he took the wise course of thinking as she did, he attributed it to himself as an honourable duty to thwart the passion of Louis XIV. His power stood in no need of support from a queen of his own kin. He even feared the character of his niece, and thought to strengthen still further the power of his ministry by avoiding the dangerous glory of exalting his house too high.

As early as 1656 he had sent Lyonne to Spain to sue for peace and to ask for the Infanta; but Don Luis de Haro, convinced that however weak Spain might be, France was not less so, had rejected the offers of the cardinal. The

Infanta, a daughter by the first marriage, was intended for the young Leopold. The King of Spain, Philip IV., had at that time but one son by his second marriage, and it was feared that the sickly infant would not survive. It was desirable that the Infanta, who would possibly be the heiress to so many states, should take her possessions to the House of Austria, and not to that of an enemy; but at length, Philip IV. having had another son, Don Philip Prosper, and his wife being again with child, the danger of giving the Infanta to the King of France seemed to be less, and the Battle of the Dunes made peace imperative.

Spain promised the Infanta, and asked for a suspension of hostilities. Mazarin and Don Luis met on the frontiers of Spain and France, on the Île des Faisans (1659). Although the marriage of a King of France and a general peace were the objects of their conference, nevertheless more than a month was passed in settling difficulties of precedence and in making preparations for the ceremonies.

The cardinals dubbed themselves the equals of kings and superior to other sovereigns. France with greater justification claimed pre-eminence over the other powers: however, Don Luis de Haro secured an equal footing with Mazarin and Spain treated with France as an equal.

The conference lasted four months. Mazarin and Don Luis employed all their diplomacy; the cardinal excelled in finesse, Don Luis in procrastination. The latter spoke very seldom a word, the former was continually prevaricating. The forte of the Italian minister was to surprise; that of the Spaniard to prevent himself from being surprised. He is said to have thus described the cardinal: "As a diplomat he has one great defect; he is continually endeavouring to deceive." Such is the vicissitude of human affairs that of this famous treaty of the Pyrenees not so much as two articles exist to-day. The King of France kept Roussillon, which he would have preserved even if there had been no peace; but with regard to Flanders the Spanish monarchy has retained no portion. France was at that time bound to friendship with Portugal; she is so no longer; all has been changed. But if Don Luis de Haro said that Cardinal Mazarin was an adept at deceit, it has since been said that he was an adept at foretelling the future. He had long contemplated the alliance of the ruling houses of France and Spain, as witness that famous letter of his written during the negotiations of

Münster: "If the most Christian king, by marrying the Infanta, could have the Netherlands and Franche-Comté as a dowry, we could then aspire to the Spanish succession, whatever renunciation might have to be made to the Infanta; and this expectation would not be so very remote seeing that there is only the life of the prince, her brother, that could hinder its realisation." This prince was Balthasar, who died in 1649.

The cardinal was evidently mistaken in thinking that the Netherlands and Franche-Comté could be given away in marriage to the Infanta. Not a single town was stipulated for her dowry. On the contrary several important towns which had been captured, such as Saint-Omer, Ypres, Menin, Oudenarde and others, were surrendered to the Spanish monarchy. A few were retained. The cardinal, however, was in no wise mistaken in thinking that the surrender would one day prove fruitless; but those who ascribe to him the honour of this prophecy are making him foresee that the Prince, Don Balthasar, would die in 1649; that later the three children of the second marriage would be carried off in the cradle; that Charles, the fifth of all the male children, would die without issue, and that this Austrian king would one day make a will in favour of a grandson of Louis XIV. In a word, Mazarin foresaw the value of these renunciations in case the male line of Philip IV. should die out, and after more than fifty years foreign events have justified him.

Maria Theresa, who might have had for dowry the towns surrendered by France, brought by her marriage contract no more than five hundred thousand gold crowns; it cost the king more than that to go and receive her on the frontier. These five hundred thousand crowns, at that time worth two million five hundred thousand livres, were the subject of much wrangling between the two ministers, and in the end France received no more than a hundred thousand francs.

So far from this marriage bringing any other immediate and substantial advantage, the Infanta surrendered all rights she may ever have possessed in any of her father's territories; and Louis XIV. ratified this renunciation in the most solemn manner, having it registered subsequently by parliament.

Such renunciations and dowries of five hundred thousand crowns seemed to be the usual terms for marriages between the Spanish Infantas and the Kings of France. Anne of Austria, daughter of Philip III., had been married to Louis

XIII. on such conditions; and when Isabella, daughter of Henri-Quatre, was given to Philip IV., King of Spain, not more than five hundred thousand gold crowns were demanded for her dowry, and even that sum was never paid; indeed, it appeared that there was no advantage to either side in these great marriages; kings' daughters were married to kings and hardly received so much as a wedding present.

The Duke of Lorraine, Charles IV., of whom both Spain and France had much to complain, or rather who had much to complain of them, was included in the treaty, but as an unfortunate prince, who was penalised because he was unable to make himself feared. France restored to him his estates, but razed Nancy to the ground and forbade him to raise troops. Don Luis de Haro compelled Cardinal Mazarin to receive the Prince de Condé into his favour by threatening to leave him as sovereign ruler over Rocroi, Catelet and other towns of which he was in possession. Thus France gained at one and the same time these towns and the great Condé. He lost his post of grand-master of the king's household, which was given to his son, and returned with practically naught save his glory.

Charles II., titular King of England, and yet more unfortunate than the Duke of Lorraine, came to the Pyrenees, where the peace was being concluded, and besought the aid of Don Luis and Mazarin. Surely, he thought, their masters and his own cousins by marriage who were now leagued together would at last venture to avenge a cause common to all sovereigns, especially since Cromwell was now no more; but he could not so much as obtain an interview either with Mazarin or with Don Luis. Lockhart, the ambassador of the English Republic, was at Saint-Jean-de-Luz; he still commanded respect even after the Protector's death, and the two ministers, fearing to offend this Englishman, refused to see Charles II. They believed his restoration impossible and thought that all English factions, however divided amongst themselves, were at one on the principle of never again acknowledging a monarch. They were both mistaken; a few months afterwards fortune brought about what these two ministers might have had the glory of undertaking. Charles was recalled to his throne by the English people without a single European monarch having either attempted to prevent the father's murder or aid the restoration of the son. He was received on the plains of Dover by twenty

thousand citizens who fell on their knees before him. Old
men, who were there, have told me that nearly everyone was
in tears. Perhaps there has never been a more moving sight,
nor a more sudden revolution. (June 1660) The change was
made in much less time than was taken to conclude the treaty
of the Pyrenees; and Charles II. was already in peaceful
possession of the throne of England before Louis XIV. had
yet been married by proxy.

(August 1660) At length Mazarin returned to Paris,
bringing the king and the new queen. A father who married
his son without allowing him to have the control of his own
affairs would not have acted otherwise than Mazarin; he
returned more powerful and more jealous than ever of his
power and even of his honours. He demanded and obtained
that parliament should send deputies to address him. Such a
step was without precedent under the monarchy; but it was
not too great a compensation for the injury that parliament
had done him. He no longer gave his hand to princes of the
blood of third rank as heretofore. He who had treated Don
Luis de Haro as an equal intended to regard the great Condé
as an inferior. He travelled consequently with royal pomp,
having in addition to his guards a troop of musketeers,
which to-day is known as the second company of the King's
Musketeers. There was no longer free access to his person;
if there were any courtier foolish enough to ask a favour of
the king, he was lost. The queen-mother, so long the stubborn
defender of Mazarin against France, was disregarded now
that he had no need of her. Her son, the king, brought up
in blind obedience to the minister, was unable to shake
himself free from the yoke which she had imposed upon him
as well as upon herself; she had a high opinion of her handi-
work, and while Mazarin lived, Louis XIV. did not yet dare
to reign.

A minister may be excused the harm he does when the
helm of state is twisted in his hands by the force of tempests,
but in times of calm he is to blame for all the good that he
omits to do.

Mazarin only served his own interests and those that concerned his family. Eight years of absolute and undisturbed
power from his last return to the time of his death were
marked by not a single glorious or useful achievement; for
the College of the Four Nations was only founded by the
provisions of his will.

He administered the treasury like the steward of a bank-rupt nobleman. The king sometimes asked Fouquet for money, who replied: "Sire, there is no money in your majesty's coffers, but M. le Cardinal will lend you some." Mazarin's wealth amounted to about two hundred millions in present-day money. Several memoirs state that he amassed a part of his wealth by methods beneath the dignity of his position. It is related, though never proved, that he shared the profits of their cruises with pirateer owners; the Dutch suspected him of doing so, and they would never have suspected Richelieu.

It is said that he was overcome with remorse as he lay dying, although outwardly he exhibited courage. At any rate, he was anxious about his property and made it over by deed of gift in its entirety to the king, believing that the king would return it to him. He was not mistaken; the king returned his gift at the end of three days. At length, on 9 March, 1661, he died: the king alone seemed to mourn him, for that prince had already learnt the art of counterfeit. The yoke had begun to gall, he was eager to reign. Never-theless he was desirous of showing some emotion at a death which placed him in possession of his throne. Accordingly both he and the court went into mourning for the cardinal —an unusual honour and one which Henry IV. had paid to the memory of Gabrielle d'Estrées.

We shall not enquire here whether Cardinal Mazarin were a great minister or not; it is for his actions to speak, and for posterity to judge. The vulgar sometimes assume a prodi-gious breadth of intellect and a genius not far removed from the divine in those who have governed empires with some success. Statesmen are not made by a superior acute-ness of mind but by their character. Men of however little common sense rarely fail to perceive their own interests, and on this point a citizen of Amsterdam or Berne knows as much as any Sejanus, Ximenes, Buckingham, Richelieu or Mazarin: but our conduct and undertakings depend solely on the temper of our mind; our success depends upon our fortune.

For example, had a genius such as Pope Alexander VI. or his son Borgia wished to take Rochelle, he would have invited the principal leaders into his camp under a sacred oath and would have made away with them. Mazarin would have taken two or three years longer to enter the town by cor-rupting and spreading dissension among the citizens; Don

Luis de Haro would not have risked the undertaking. Richelieu built a dyke across the water in imitation of Alexander and entered Rochelle as a conqueror; but a higher tide or a little more vigilance on the part of the English would have saved Rochelle and made the conduct of Richelieu appear merely foolhardy.

Men's characters may be judged by their actions. One may be quite sure that the mind of Richelieu breathed pride and revenge, and that Mazarin was prudent, cunning and eager for wealth. But in order to know to what extent a minister has greatness of mind, one must either often hear him speak or read what he has written. What may be daily seen among the ranks of courtiers is not unknown among great statesmen; he who has the greatest mind fails, and the one who has most patience, strength, and craft in his character succeeds.

In reading the letters of Cardinal Mazarin and the Memoirs of Cardinal de Retz it is easy to see that Retz was the greater genius. Yet Mazarin was all-powerful and Retz overthrown.

To sum up, it is very true that often all that is necessary for the making of a powerful minister is the possession of a mediocre mind, common sense and good fortune; but the dominant passion of a good minister must ever be the love of public welfare. The great statesman always leaves behind him great monuments useful to his country. The monument which immortalises Cardinal Mazarin is the acquisition of Alsace. He gained possession of this province for France at the time when France had risen against him, and by a singular trick of fate he served the kingdom better when he was persecuted by it, than when he found himself undisturbed in the enjoyment of absolute power.

CHAPTER VII

LOUIS XIV. GOVERNS BY HIMSELF. HE FORCES THE SPANISH
HAPSBURGS TO GIVE PRECEDENCE TO HIM EVERYWHERE,
AND THE COURT OF ROME TO GRANT HIM SATISFACTION.
HE BUYS DUNKIRK: RENDERS ASSISTANCE TO THE
EMPEROR, TO PORTUGAL, TO THE STATES-GENERAL AND
MAKES HIS KINGDOM FLOURISHING AND FORMIDABLE

NEVER were there so many intrigues and expectations in any
court as while Cardinal Mazarin lay dying. Women with any
pretence of beauty flattered themselves that they would
rule a prince of twenty-two, whom love had already so far
beguiled as to make him offer his crown to his mistress.
Youthful courtiers saw visions of a new reign of favourites.
Each minister hoped for the premier place. Not one of them
thought that a king brought up in seclusion from affairs of
state would dare to take the burden of government upon his
own shoulders. Mazarin had prolonged the monarch's childhood so long as he could. It was only quite lately that he had
instructed him in public affairs and only because the king
had so desired.

It was so little expected that their sovereign would take
up the government himself, that of all those who had hitherto
worked with the first minister there was not one who asked
the king when he would require his services. They all
enquired, "To whom shall we address ourselves?" and
Louis XIV. replied, "*To me.*" They were still more surprised
to see him persevere in his resolution. He had already tested
his forces and secretly examined his talent for ruling: his
resolution once taken, he kept it to the last moment of his
life. He fixed the limits of the power of each minister, requiring
them to render a full account to him at stated times, giving
them the confidence necessary to the credit of their office,
and keeping a watch on them to prevent their abusing it.

Mme. de Motteville informs us that the renown of
Charles II., King of England, who was said to govern by
himself, aroused the envy of Louis XIV. If such was the
case he greatly surpassed his rival and deserved throughout
his life what was said of Charles during the first years of
his reign. He began by putting his revenues in order, disorganised as they were by prolonged peculation. Discipline

was restored among the troops as was order in finance. Magnificence and propriety distinguished his court. Pleasure itself put on splendour and grandeur. All the arts were encouraged, and all dedicated to the glory of the king and of France.

This is not the place to depict him in his private life nor in the inner working of his government; we shall deal with these matters in their places. It suffices to say that his people, who had not known a real king since the death of Henri-Quatre, and who detested the rule of a first minister, were filled with admiration and hope when they saw Louis XIV. accomplish at twenty-two years of age what Henri had done at fifty. Had Henri IV. had a first minister, he would have been lost, because hatred of one particular man would have stirred up twenty factions too powerful to be suppressed. Had Louis XIII. not had one, his mind, enervated by a poor and feeble body, would have sunk under the burden of government. Louis XIV. took no risk either in retaining or discarding a first minister. Not the least trace remained of the old factions; there was now but a master and his subjects in France. From the first he showed that he aspired to every kind of glory and that he wished to be as respected abroad as he was absolute at home.

The ancient royal houses of Europe preserve an entire equality among themselves, as is quite natural; but the kings of France have always claimed a precedence due to the antiquity of their line and of their kingdom; and if they have given way to the emperors it is because men are seldom bold enough to oppose a long-established usage. The head of the German republic, an elective prince and possessing little real power of his own, takes precedence without contradiction over all sovereigns, on account of the title of Cæsar and as being the inheritor of Charlemagne. At that time his German chancellor did not even treat the other kings as majesties. Kings of France might dispute precedence with the Emperors since France had founded the real Empire of the West, of which the name alone exists in Germany. They had not only the superiority of a hereditary crown as opposed to an elective dignity, but the advantage of being descended from an uninterrupted line of sovereigns who ruled over a great monarchy several centuries before any other great royal house that still possesses a crown had attained any eminence. The French wished at least to precede the other powers of

Europe. They cited in their favour the appellation of *très
chrétien*, to which the kings of Spain replied with the title
of *Catholic*; and since Charles V. had held a King of France
prisoner in Madrid, Spanish arrogance was more than ever
averse to forfeiting such precedence. The English and the
Swedes, who to-day adopt neither of these titles, acknowledge
as little as may be this superiority.

It was at Rome that these pretensions were formerly
debated. The Popes, who bestowed states by means of bulls,
thought themselves to have a still stronger right to determine
distinctions among the crowned heads. This court, where
everything is done with ceremony, was the tribunal before
which such vanities of greatness were judged. When she was
more powerful than Spain, France had always held the
supremacy there, but after the reign of Charles V. Spain
neglected no opportunity of behaving as an equal.

The dispute remained undecided; a step higher or lower
in a procession, a chair placed near the altar or opposite the
pulpit, such trivialities were accounted triumphs and established claims to pre-eminence. The fantastic point of honour
was as keen in this matter among crowned heads as was the
rage for duelling among private gentlemen.

(1661) It happened that on the arrival of a Swedish
ambassador in London, a dispute arose between Count
d'Estrades, the French ambassador, and the Baron de
Watteville, the Spanish ambassador, as to who should take
precedence. The Spaniard with more money and a larger
suite had won over the English populace; he began by
killing the horses drawing the French carriages, and soon the
company of the Count d'Estrades, wounded and scattered,
was forced to let the Spaniards pass on with drawn swords
as in triumph.

When Louis XIV. learnt of this outrage he recalled his
ambassador from Madrid, dismissed the Spanish ambassador,
broke off the conferences which were still being held in
Flanders with regard to boundaries, and sent word to his
father-in-law, Philip IV., that if he did not acknowledge the
supremacy of the French crown and make amends for this
outrage by a solemn satisfaction, war would be begun afresh.
Philip IV. had no desire to plunge his country into a new
war on account of an ambassador's precedence; and he sent
Count de Fuentes to declare to the king at Fontainebleau in
the presence of all the foreign ministers at that time in France

(24 March, 1662) that "in future Spanish ministers would not enter the lists against the French." This was not a definite acknowledgment of the pre-eminence of the French king, but it was a plain enough avowal of the weakness of Spain. That court, still proud in its poverty, murmured at such a humiliation. Since then, several Spanish ministers have renewed their former claims: they obtained an equal footing at Nimeguen; but Louis XIV. then acquired by his firmness a real supremacy in Europe by showing how much he was to be feared.

Hardly had he come out of this little affair with such a display of greatness than he showed still more in a matter where his glory seemed less interested. The youthful Frenchmen who had taken part in the wars waged so long in Italy against Spain had given the wary and jealous Italians the impression that France was an impetuous nation. Italy regarded all the nations by whom she was invaded as barbarians, and the French as barbarians who differed only from the rest in being gayer and also more dangerous, since while they introduced pleasures into their houses they also introduced contempt, and added insult to licentiousness. They were feared everywhere, above all at Rome.

The Duke de Créqui, ambassador to the Pope, had disgusted the Romans by his arrogance; his servants, carrying as usual their master's faults to an extreme, perpetrated in Rome outrages similar to those committed by the undisciplined youths of Paris, who used to make it a point of honour every night to attack the watch who were on guard in the city.

Some of the lackeys of the Duke de Créqui bethought themselves to charge, sword in hand, a squad of Corsicans (the bodyguard of the Pope who see to the execution of justice). The whole company of Corsicans was bitterly offended, and secretly stirred up by Don Mario Chigi, brother of Pope Alexander VII., who hated the Duke de Créqui, they armed themselves and proceeded to attack the ambassador's residence (20 August, 1662). They fired on the coach of his wife, who was returning to the palace; and succeeded in killing one of her pages and wounding several servants. The Duke de Créqui left Rome, accusing the Pope's relations and the Pope himself of having countenanced the murders. The Pope delayed making reparations as long as he could, believing that one has only to temporise with the French and all is forgotten. Finally, at the end of four months, he had a Corsican and a guard hanged, and the governor expelled from Rome who was suspected of having authorised the outrage; but he was astounded to learn that Louis threatened to lay siege to Rome, that he was already marching troops into Italy and that the Marshal du Plessis-Praslin had been appointed to command them. The affair had become a quarrel between one nation and another, and the king was determined that his country should be respected. Before making the reparation demanded, the Pope implored the mediation of all Catholic princes; he did his best to stir them up against Louis XIV., but circumstances were unfavourable to him. The empire was being attacked by the Turks, and Spain was hampered by an unsuccessful war with Portugal.

The Roman court only succeeded in irritating Louis without being able to do him real damage. The Parliament of Provence subpœnaed the Pope and seized the County of Avignon. In former times such outrages would have been followed by excommunications from Rome, but they were now useless weapons and had become ridiculous; the Pope had perforce to give way; he was obliged to banish his own brother from Rome, to send his nephew, Cardinal Chigi, as legate *a latere* to give satisfaction to the king, to break up the Corsican guard and to erect a pyramid in Rome, bearing an inscription relating both the insult and the reparation. Cardinal Chigi was the first legate of the Roman court ever sent to ask for pardon. Heretofore the legates had come to impose laws and prescribe the tenths. The king had no desire to be recompensed for an insult by an hour's ceremony, or some equally short-lived memorial, for he allowed the pyramid to be pulled down a few years later; accordingly he forced the Court of Rome to promise the surrender of Castro and Ronciglione to the Duke of Parma, and to compensate the Duke of Modena for his claims on Comacchio; he thus reaped from the insult the substantial honour of becoming the protector of the Italian princes.

Whilst upholding his dignity he did not forget to increase his power. (27 October, 1662) The state of his finances wisely administered by Colbert enabled him to buy Dunkirk and Mardick from the King of England for five million livres, at twenty-six livres ten sous to the mark. Poor, but prodigal, Charles II. had the shame of selling what had been bought at the price of English blood. His chancellor, Hyde, accused of having either advised or sanctioned this misdeed, was afterwards banished by the English parliament, which often punishes the faults of favourites and sometimes even sits in judgment on its kings.

(1663) Louis set thirty thousand men to work on the fortifying of Dunkirk, both by land and sea. Between the town and fortress he constructed a harbour large enough to contain thirty ships of war, so that the English had scarcely sold this town than it became a source of dread to them.

(30 August, 1663) Some time afterwards Louis forced the Duke of Lorraine to surrender the stronghold of Marsal to him. The unfortunate Charles IV., famous as a warrior, but feeble, vacillating and imprudent as a prince, had just concluded a treaty by which he promised Lorraine to France after his death, on condition that Louis should allow him to raise a million on the state that he was giving up, and that princes of the blood of Lorraine should be esteemed princes of the blood of France. This treaty, ratified to no purpose by the parliament of Paris, served only to produce fresh inconstancies on the part of the Duke of Lorraine, who was only too glad afterwards to surrender Marsal and to throw himself on the clemency of the king.

Louis extended his territories even in time of peace and held himself always in readiness for war, fortifying his frontiers, keeping his troops well-disciplined, adding to their number, and holding frequent reviews.

The Turks were at this time very formidable to Europe; they were attacking both the Emperor of Germany and the Venetians. Since the time of Francis I. the policy of France has always been to ally herself with the Turkish Sultans, not only for the benefits of trade but to prevent the House of Austria from becoming too powerful. Nevertheless, a Christian king could not refuse help to the Emperor in real danger; and it was to the interest of France that the Turks should harass Hungary, but not that they should invade her: in a word, her treaties with the Empire made it her duty to take this honourable step. Louis therefore sent six thousand men into Hungary under the command of the Count of Coligni, the sole survivor of that house of Coligni so famous in our civil wars, and who deserves perhaps for his courage and honesty as great a fame as that of the admiral. Friendship had attached him to the great Condé and not all the offers of Cardinal Mazarin had been able to persuade him to betray his friend.

He had under him the flower of the French nobility, among them La Feuillade, young, enterprising and eager for glory and fortune. (1664) These French troops went to serve under General Montecuculi in Hungary, who was then engaged against the grand-vizier Kiuperli or Kouprogli, and who later, when fighting against France, equalled the reputation of Turenne. A great battle was fought between the Turks and the Emperor's army at Saint-Gothard on the banks of the Raab. The French performed prodigies of valour; even the Germans, who were by no means friendly towards them, were compelled to do them this justice; but it is unjust to the Germans to say, as may be read in many books, that the French alone had the honour of this victory.

While openly throwing his weight on the side of the Emperor and adding lustre to the French arms, the king directed his policy towards supporting Portugal secretly against Spain. By the treaty of the Pyrenees Mazarin had formally deserted the Portuguese; but Spain had broken several of the smaller provisions of the peace. France now broke out boldly and decisively; Marshal de Schomberg, a foreigner and a Huguenot, marched into Portugal with four thousand French soldiers, whom he paid with money from Louis XIV., but pretended to do so in the name of the King of Portugal. These four thousand French soldiers joined with the Portuguese troops, and obtained a complete victory at Villa-Viciosa (17 June, 1665) which established the House of Braganza on the throne. Louis XIV. was thus already regarded as a warlike and diplomatic prince, and Europe feared him even before he had yet made war.

It was by his diplomacy that he evaded his promise to unite the few vessels he then possessed to the Dutch fleet. He had allied himself with Holland in 1662. About that time, that republic renewed the war with England on the absurd and idle pretext of respecting the national flag, the real issue being the question of trade in the Indies. Louis was delighted to see these two maritime powers launch year by year fleets of more than a hundred vessels, which mutually destroyed one another in some of the most stubborn fights that have ever taken place, the net result of which was the weakening of both powers. One fight lasted three whole days (11, 12 and 13 June, 1666). It was in these engagements that the Dutchman, Ruyter, gained the reputation of being the greatest seaman that had ever lived. It was he who burnt the finest English ships within harbour, but four leagues from London. He made Holland supreme on the seas, the sovereignty of which had hitherto been held by the English, and in which Louis XIV. had as yet no part. For many years the supremacy of the sea had been divided between these two nations. The art of building ships and of utilising them for trade and war was properly understood by them alone. During the ministry of Richelieu, France thought herself to be powerful at sea, because out of about sixty men-of-war lying in her ports, nearly thirty were seaworthy and one carried seventy cannon. Under Mazarin, the few vessels she possessed were bought from Holland. Sailors, officers and materials for their construction and equipment were alike lacking. With incredible activity Louis set about re-establishing the navy and providing France with everything she lacked; but in 1664 and 1665, whilst the English and the Dutch were overrunning the seas with nearly three hundred large ships of war, he had as yet but fifteen or sixteen vessels of the poorest class, which the Duke of Beaufort was employing against the Barbary pirates; and when the Netherland States urged Louis XIV. to join his fleet to theirs, only a single fireship could be found in the port of Brest, which he was ashamed to send, but it was necessary to do this at their repeated requests. With all speed Louis XIV. hastened to remove this ignominy.

(1665) He rendered more material and creditable aid to the Netherlands with his land forces, sending six thousand French to defend them against Christopher Bernard Van Galen, Bishop of Münster, a warrior prelate and their implacable enemy, who had been bribed by England to lay waste Holland; but he made them pay dearly for this help and treated them like a powerful man who sells his protection to wealthy merchants. Colbert charged them not only with the soldiers' pay, but even with the expenses of sending an ambassador to England to conclude peace with Charles II. Never was help given with so bad a grace or received with so little gratitude. Having thus accustomed his troops to war and made fresh officers on the fields of Hungary, Holland and Portugal, the king, respected and revenged in Rome, found himself with not a single ruler to fear. With England ravaged by the plague, and London reduced to ashes by a conflagration unjustly attributed to the Catholics, with the perpetual extravagance and poverty of Charles II., as perilous to the state as plague and fire, France had no cause of fear so far as England was concerned. The Emperor was hardly yet recovered from the exhaustion of a war against the Turks. The King of Spain, Philip IV., whose kingdom was as feeble as himself, lay dying and Louis XIV. remained the sole powerful and formidable monarch. He was young, rich, well-served, blindly obeyed, and eager to distinguish himself by foreign conquest.

CHAPTER VIII

THE CONQUEST OF FLANDERS

AN opportunity soon presented itself to a king who sought one. His father-in-law, Philip IV., died in 1665; by his first wife, the sister of Louis XIII., he had had the Princess Maria Theresa, who married her cousin, Louis XIV.; a marriage by which the Spanish monarchy was at length united to the House of Bourbon, so long its enemy. From his second marriage with Maria Anna of Austria, Charles II. was born, a weak and sickly child, the heir to the throne, and the sole survivor of three male children, two of whom had died at an early age. Louis XIV. claimed that Flanders, Brabant and Franche-Comté, provinces of the Spanish kingdom, should, according to the laws of those provinces, revert to his wife in spite of her renunciation. Could the pleas of kings be judged according to the laws of nations before an impartial tribunal the issue would have been far from certain.

Louis ordered his council and certain theologians to examine his claims, and they judged them indisputable; but the council and confessor of the widow of Philip IV. found them very poor. For herself, she had a very powerful reason—the express law of Charles V.; but the laws of Charles V. seemed to bear very little weight in the court of France.

One of the pretexts put forward by the king's council was that the five hundred thousand crowns of his wife's dowry had never been paid; but they forgot that the dowry of Henri IV.'s daughter had likewise remained unpaid. France and Spain at first fought with documents, quoting bankers' figures and lawyers' arguments; but the all-powerful reason was a state one, and it was sufficiently extraordinary. Louis XIV. was about to wage war on a child of whom he should naturally have been the protector since he was his brother-in-law. How could he imagine that the Emperor Leopold, regarded as the head of the House of Austria, would let him crush his house and seek aggrandisement in Flanders? Who would believe that the Emperor and the King of France had already in imagination shared the spoils of the young Charles of Austria, King of Spain?

Some traces of this sad truth are to be found in the Memoirs of the Marquis de Torci, but they are rather obscure. Time has at length unveiled this mystery and proved that among princes expediency and the right of the strongest take the place of justice, especially when that justice appears in doubt.

All the brothers of Charles II., King of Spain, were dead, and Charles himself had a weak and sickly constitution. During his infancy Louis XIV. and Leopold entered into a partition treaty almost identical with that which they concluded after his death. By this treaty, which is still in the archives of the Louvre, Leopold was to allow Louis XIV. to take possession of Flanders, on condition that on the death of Charles, Spain should immediately pass under the Emperor's rule. It is not stated if any money passed over this strange transaction. As a rule this important article of such treaties is kept secret.

Leopold had no sooner signed the document than he repented of it; at least he insisted that other courts should know of it, that no duplicate copy should be made as was the usual custom, and that the sole document to be preserved should be enclosed in a metal casket, of which the Emperor should have one key and the King of France the other. This casket was to be placed in the keeping of the Grand Duke of Florence. For this purpose the Emperor committed it into the hands of the French ambassador at Vienna, and the king sent sixteen men of his bodyguard to the gates of Vienna to escort the courier for fear that the Emperor should change his mind and forcibly recover the casket on the way. It was, however, brought to Versailles and not to Florence; this makes one suspect that Leopold had received money, since he dared not protest.

In this manner did the Emperor suffer the King of Spain to be robbed of his estates.

Louis, relying rather on his troops than on his legal arguments, marched to certain victory in Flanders. (1667) He himself was at the head of thirty-five thousand men, another corps of eight thousand was despatched towards Dunkirk, and one of four thousand towards Luxembourg. Turenne was commanding his army under him. Colbert had trebled the resources of the state in order to provide for these expenses, and Louvois, the new minister of war, had made immense preparations for the campaign. Stores of every kind were distributed along the frontier. Louvois was the first to introduce this excellent system of victualling the army by means of storing-places, which, owing to the weakness of the government, had been impracticable up till then; whatever siege the king wished to undertake, to whichever side he wished to turn his arms, supplies of every kind were at hand, the troops' billets were assigned and their routes arranged. Discipline, which was daily more strictly enforced by the resolute severity of the minister, kept all the officers firmly to their duty. The presence of a young king, the idol of his army, made the very hardship of this duty easy and dear to them. Military rank from that time took on an importance greater than that of birth. Services were taken account of, not ancestors, a thing practically unknown before; officers of the lowest birth were thus encouraged, while those of the highest had nothing of which to complain. The infantry, on whom fell the whole burden of war, now that the uselessness of lances was recognised, shared the rewards which the cavalry had formerly received. The new principles of the government inspired a new courage.

The king, having under him a general and a minister who, being equally capable and mutually jealous, served him but the better, at the head of the best troops in Europe, and once more allied with Portugal, attacked with all these advantages the badly defended province of a ruined and broken kingdom. His only opponent was his mother-in-law, a weak woman, ruled by a Jesuit, whose despised and unsuccessful government left the Spanish monarchy defenceless. The King of France possessed everything that Spain lacked.

The art of besieging towns was not yet perfected as it is to-day, since the arts of fortification and of defence were alike largely unknown. The frontiers of Spanish Flanders were practically unfortified and without garrisons.

Louis had only to make his appearance on the frontier.

In June 1667 he entered Charleroi as he might enter Paris; Ath and Tournai were taken in two days; Furnes, Armentières and Courtrai held out not much longer. He himself visited the trenches in front of Douai, which surrendered the next day (July 6). Lille, the most prosperous city of the country, the only one well fortified, and with a garrison of six thousand men, capitulated (27 August) after a nine days' siege. The Spanish had only eight thousand men to oppose the victorious army; even the rearguard of this petty army was cut to pieces (31 August) by the Marquis, afterwards Marshal de Créqui. The remainder shut themselves up in Brussels and Mons, leaving Louis to conquer without a blow.

This campaign, fought in the midst of affluence, and accompanied by such easy successes, seemed like the peaceful progress of a court. Good cheer, luxury and pleasures were then introduced into the army, at the very time when discipline was being made more strict. The officers carried out their military duties with much greater punctiliousness but under more refined conditions. The Marshal de Turenne had long had to eat from iron plates in the field: the Marquis d'Humières was the first at the siege of Arras in 1658 to have his meals served on silver dishes in the trenches, meals moreover which included delicacies of the table such as *hors d'œuvres* and savouries. But in the campaign of 1667, when a young king, delighting in pomp, was eager to exhibit the splendour of his court amidst the hardships of war, everybody prided himself on the lavishness and good taste of his table, of his clothes and of his carriage. Such luxury, a sure sign of wealth in a great state, and often the cause of decadence in a small one, was, however, little in comparison with what has since been seen. The king, his generals, and his ministers would attend meetings on horseback; to-day there is not a cavalry-captain, not an officer's secretary who would not ride in a post-chaise with glass windows and springs, more calmly and comfortably than one could then travel from one quarter of Paris to another.

The fastidiousness of officers did not prevent them from appearing in the trenches armed with casque and cuirass. The king himself set the example; he went thus armed into the trenches before Douai and Lille. This wise conduct was the making of more than one great man. It has since been too much neglected by less sturdy youngsters full of valour but indolent, who seem to fear fatigue more than danger.

The swiftness of these victories filled Brussels with alarm; the people were already conveying their goods and chattels to Antwerp. It seemed possible that the conquest of all Flanders might be the work of one campaign. The king only lacked sufficient numbers of troops to guard the towns, which were ready to surrender to his arms. Louvois advised him to draft large garrisons into the conquered towns and fortify them. Vauban, one of those great men of genius who appeared in this age for the service of Louis XIV., was placed in charge of these fortifications. He constructed them according to a new method of his, which is to-day accepted by all expert engineers. Astonishment was expressed at seeing the towns surrounded by outworks hardly higher than the surrounding country. High and towering fortifications were only the more exposed to the battering of artillery; the lower they were made the less liable were they to attack. He built the fortress of Lille on these principles (1668). The government of a town had never before been separated in France from the command of a fortress. A precedent was formed in the case of Vauban; he was the first governor of a fortress. It may be noted that the first plan in relief that one may still see in the gallery of the Louvre is the plan of the fortifications of Lille.

The king now hastened to receive the acclamations of his people, the homage of his courtiers and mistresses, and to join in the rejoicing of his court.

CHAPTER IX

THE CONQUEST OF FRANCHE-COMTÉ. PEACE OF AIX-LA-CHAPELLE

(1668) Diversion was the order of the day at Saint-Germain, when, in January, in the heart of winter, troops were seen with amazement in line of march on every side coming and going on the roads to Champagne in the Trois-Evêchés; trains of artillery, wagon-loads of ammunition halted under various pretences on the route leading from Champagne to Burgundy. Movements were taking place throughout the whole of this part of France for some reason unknown. Both foreigners and courtiers exhausted themselves in conjecture, the former from interest, the latter out of curiosity; Germany was alarmed; but the object of these preparations and irregular marches was kept a close secret from everybody. Never indeed has a secret plot been better concealed than was this enterprise of Louis XIV. At length, on 2 February, Louis himself leaves Saint-Germain, with the young Duke d'Enghien, son of the great Condé, and a few courtiers; the other officers join the troops at the appointed meeting-places. He travels on horseback and arrives at Dijon by forced marches. Twenty thousand men, who have arrived by twenty different roads, find themselves the same day in Franche-Comté, and but a few leagues from Besançon; the great Condé appears at their head, having as his chief lieutenant-general his friend Montmorenci-Boutteville, now Duke of Luxembourg, who had remained faithful to him alike in good and evil times. Luxembourg was Condé's pupil in the art of war; and on account of his merit Condé had forced the king to employ him, though Louis did not like him.

Intrigues played their part in this hastily considered expedition; the Prince de Condé was jealous of Turenne's glory, and Louvois of his favour with the king; Condé was jealous as a hero, Louvois as a minister. The prince in his capacity of Governor of Burgundy, which adjoins Franche-Comté, had formed the plan of making himself master of it in winter in less time than Turenne had taken the preceding summer to conquer French Flanders. He first revealed his plan to Louvois, who eagerly embraced it, thinking to belittle Turenne and at the same time serve his master.

The province of *Franche-Comté*, some hundred and twenty miles long by sixty wide, poor in money but fertile and well populated, was "free" not only in name but in fact.

The kings of Spain were rather its protectors than its masters, and although the country was under the government of Flanders it depended but little upon it. The whole administration was divided and disputed between the parliament and the governor of Franche-Comté. The people enjoyed great privileges, which were always respected by the court of Madrid, who treated with consideration a province that was jealous of its rights and a neighbour of France. Besançon was even self-governed like an imperial city. Never did a people live under a more indulgent administration, nor was ever a people more attached to its sovereigns. Their love for the House of Austria has lived on for two generations, but at bottom this love was the love of their own liberty. In a word, Franche-Comté was happy but poor, and being a kind of republic, there were factions.

Whatever Pellisson may say, France did not confine herself to employing force.

At first some of the citizens were won over by gifts and promises. The Abbé Jean de Watteville was prevailed upon, brother of him who had insulted the French ambassador in London, and by this outrage had been responsible for the humiliation of the Spanish branch of the House of Austria. This abbé, formerly an officer, later a Carthusian friar, then for a long time a Mussulman among the Turks, and finally a priest, was promised an archdeaconship and certain other livings. A few magistrates and officers were bought cheaply; and in the end even the Marquis d'Yenne, the governor-general, became so pliable that after the war he publicly accepted a large pension and the rank of Lieutenant-General of France. These secret intrigues had hardly been begun when they were backed by twenty thousand men. Besançon, the capital of the province, was surrounded by the Prince de Condé; Luxembourg hastened to besiege Salins, and on the morrow both towns surrendered. On capitulation Besançon only stipulated for the preservation of a holy shroud that was greatly venerated in the city; this was very readily agreed to. The king arrived at Dijon. Louvois, who had rushed to the frontier to direct these operations, came to tell him that these two towns had been besieged and taken. The king hastened immediately to show himself to Fortune, who thus smiled upon him.

He set out to besiege Dôle in person. The town was thought to be well fortified; its governor was Count de Montrevel, a man of great courage, loyal, as was his nature, to the Spaniards whom he hated, and the parliament which he despised. His garrison consisted of not more than four hundred soldiers and the citizens, and he dared to defend the place. The trench had not been fully fortified. Hardly was it taken than a crowd of young volunteers of the king's own company rushed to attack the counterscarp and succeeded in gaining a hold there; the Prince de Condé, to whom age and experience had imparted an unshaken courage, came to their support at an opportune moment, and shared the danger of their position in attempting to rescue them from it. The prince was everywhere in the field with his son and afterwards came to make a full report to the king, as though he were an officer

who had his fortune to make. The king in his quarters showed
rather the dignity of a monarch in his court than any display
of impetuous ardour, for which there was no necessity. All
the ceremonial of Saint-Germain was observed. He had his
petit coucher, his public and private receptions, an audience
chamber in his tent. He moderated the royal pomp only by
having his staff officers and their aides-de-camp to eat at
his table. Amidst the ardours of war there was never seen
in him the rash courage of Francis I. and Henri IV., who
sought every kind of danger. He rather contented himself
with showing no fear of dangers and with encouraging his
men to brave them fearlessly. On 14 February, 1667, he
entered Dôle after a four days' siege, and twelve days after
leaving Saint-Germain; finally, in less than three weeks, the
whole of Franche-Comté had submitted to him. The council
of Spain, amazed and indignant at this feeble resistance,
wrote to the governor "that the King of France might well
have sent his lackeys to take possession of the country
instead of going there in person."

Such great success allied to such great ambition roused
Europe from her slumber; the Empire began to bestir itself,
and the Emperor hastened to raise troops. The Swiss, neighbours of the Francs-Comtois, trembled for their liberty—
almost their only valuable possession. The rest of Flanders
might be invaded in the coming spring. The Dutch, who had
always been eager to have the French as friends, trembled
at the thought of having them as neighbours. Spain looked
for help to Holland, and was, in fact, protected by that
small nation, which she had formerly regarded as merely
contemptible and rebellious.

Holland was governed by John De Witt, who, at the age of
twenty-eight, had been elected chief magistrate, a man as
eager for his country's freedom as for personal distinction.
Accustomed to the frugality and simplicity of the Republic,
he had but a single lackey and domestic and walked on foot
in The Hague, while in the councils of Europe his name was
coupled with those of the greatest kings. He was a man
whom no task could fatigue, prudent, assiduous in affairs
of state, an excellent citizen, a great politician, but who in
later years was nevertheless very unfortunate.

He had contracted a friendship such as is rare among
ministers with Sir William Temple, English ambassador at
The Hague. Temple was a philosopher who combined liter-

ature with his official duties; a worthy man, despite the charges of atheism brought against him by Bishop Burnet; born with the spirit of a moderate republican, loving Holland as much as his own country, because she was free, and as jealous of that freedom as the chief magistrate himself. These two citizens united with Count Dhona, the Swedish ambassador, to check the advance of the French king.

Events moved rapidly at this period. Flanders, that is to say, French Flanders, had been conquered in three months, Franche-Comté in three weeks. The treaty between Holland, England and Sweden, to maintain the balance of power in Europe and restrict the ambition of Louis XIV., was proposed and concluded within five days. The Emperor Leopold's council did not dare to take part in this intrigue, for the Emperor was bound by the secret treaty he had made with the King of France to despoil the young King of Spain. He secretly encouraged the alliance of England, Sweden and Holland, but took no open measures.

Louis XIV. was indignant that such a petty state as Holland should presume to limit his conquests and make herself the arbiter of kings; his indignation was not lessened by the fact that she was capable of doing so. This action of the United Provinces was an insult which he felt but which he had to swallow, and for which from that moment he meditated vengeance.

Ambitious, proud and vengeful as he was, he nevertheless averted the storm which was gathering in every quarter of Europe. He himself held out the branch of peace. France and Spain chose Aix-la-Chapelle as the place for conference and the new Pope, Rospigliosi, Clement IX., as arbitrator.

The Court of Rome, to deck out her weakness by a show of apparent authority, sought by every means the honour of acting as arbiter between the crowns of Europe. She had been unable to obtain such an honour at the treaty of the Pyrenees; at the peace of Aix-la-Chapelle she at least appeared to have done so. A nuncio was despatched to the Congress as a phantom arbitrator among phantom plenipotentiaries. The Dutch, already jealous of their glory, had no wish to share that of concluding what they had commenced. All the terms, in fact, were discussed at Saint-Germain through the agency of their ambassador, Van Beuning. What had been secretly agreed to by him was then transmitted to Aix-la-Chapelle, to be signed with due solemnity by the ministers assembled at the congress. Who would have said thirty years before that a citizen of Holland would force France and Spain to accept his arbitration?

This Van Beuning, a sheriff of Amsterdam, had the quickness of a Frenchman and the pride of a Spaniard. He took pleasure in shocking on every occasion the imperious arrogance of the king, and opposed a republican firmness to the tone of superiority that the French ministers began to adopt. "Do you not trust the word of a king?" M. de Lyonne asked him at one of the conferences. "It is nothing to me what the king *wants* to do," said Van Beuning, "I am considering what he *can* do."

Finally, on 2 May, 1668, at the court of the proudest monarch in Europe, a burgomaster had power to conclude a peace by which the king was compelled to surrender Franche-Comté. The Dutch would infinitely rather he had restored Flanders, and thus have been relieved of so formidable a neighbour; but other nations thought Louis sufficiently moderate in giving up Franche-Comté. Nevertheless, in keeping the Flemish towns he gained more than he lost: he was opening the door to Holland, to whom he was making concessions, but at the same time planning to destroy.

CHAPTER X

THE WORKS AND MAGNIFICENCE OF LOUIS XIV. STRANGE
AFFAIR IN PORTUGAL. CASIMIR IN FRANCE. AID FOR
CANDIA. CONQUEST OF HOLLAND

LOUIS XIV., now at peace for some time, continued the work he had begun of putting his kingdom in order, of fortifying it, of beautifying it. He showed that an absolute monarch, anxious to do good, succeeds without difficulty in everything he may undertake. He had only to command, and success in administration was as rapid as it had been in military conquest. It was truly a marvellous sight to behold the seaports, formerly deserted and fallen into ruins, now surrounded by structures which were at once their ornament and their defence, teeming with ships and sailors, and already containing nearly sixty large vessels which could be armed for war. New colonists under the protection of the French flag were departing from every port for America, for the East Indies, and for the coasts of Africa. Meanwhile in France under his very eyes, great buildings were employing thousands of men, and all the arts that architecture brings in its train; and in the interior of his court and capital, still nobler and more ingenious arts were giving France pleasures and a glory which earlier centuries had not even dreamed of. Letters flourished; good taste and reason penetrated into the schools of barbarism. Every detail of the nation's glory and felicity will find its proper place in this history; here we shall only speak of general and military matters.

About this time a strange scene was enacted in Portugal. Dom Alfonso, the unworthy son of the excellent Dom John of Braganza, was ruling there; he was a maniacal imbecile. His wife, daughter of the Duke of Nemours, and enamoured of Dom Pedro, the brother of Alfonso, was bold enough to conceive the idea of dethroning her husband and marrying her lover. The brutish character of the husband justified the wickedness of the queen. He was abnormally virile; he had publicly acknowledged a child of his by a courtesan; and for a very long time he had cohabited with the queen. Despite all this she accused him of impotence; and having secured by her adroitness the authority which her husband had forfeited by his frenzy, she had him put away (November 1667), and soon obtained from Rome a bull permitting her to marry her brother-in-law. It is surprising, not that Rome should have granted the bull, but that persons so powerful should have had need of it. What Julius II. had granted without difficulty to Henry VIII., King of England, Clement IX. granted to the wife of a King of Portugal. The most trivial intrigue achieves at one time what the greatest efforts cannot bring about at another. There are always two sets of weights and measures for the rights of kings and peoples, and they have obtained at the Vatican since the Popes first influenced the affairs of Europe.

The force of custom can alone explain how it is that the European nations have allowed the Roman pontiff to assume so singular an authority.

This event, which was not a revolution in the Kingdom of Portugal, but merely in the royal family, since it effected no change in European affairs, deserves attention only on account of its peculiarity.

Soon afterwards France welcomed a king who left his throne for a very different reason. In 1668 John Casimir, King of Poland, imitated the example of Queen Christina.

Tired of the cares of government and wishing to live at peace, his choice of retreat fell upon the monastery of Saint-Germain in Paris, of which he was the abbé. Paris, which for some years past had become the home of all the arts, was a delightful place for a king who sought the pleasures of social life and who was a lover of learning. Before being a king he had been both a Jesuit and a cardinal, and now, disgusted alike with royalty and the church, he desired only to retire into a private and studious life, and would never permit anyone in Paris to address him as Your Majesty.

But a more important matter claimed the attention of all Christian princes.

The Turks, less formidable, it is true, than in the times of Mahomet, of Selim and Solyman, but still dangerous and powerful by our very disunion, having blockaded Candia for eight years, were now regularly besieging it with all the forces of their empire. It is difficult to say which was more astonishing, that the Venetians should have so long defended themselves or that the kings of Europe should have abandoned them.

Times have indeed changed. Formerly, when Christian Europe was in a state of barbarism, a Pope, or even a monk, rallied millions of Christians to fight against the Mohammedans in their empire; the European states exhausted men and money in order to conquer the miserable and barren province of Judæa; and now, when the island of Candia, reputed the bulwark of Christendom, was overrun by sixty thousand Turks, the Christian kings looked on at the disaster with indifference. A few galleys from Malta and the Pope were the sole assistance sent to defend this republic from the Ottoman Empire. The Venetian senate, as powerless as it was prudent, was unable to resist the grand vizier, Kiuperli, with mercenary troops and such feeble aid; Kiuperli himself was a fine minister, and a better general, master of the Turkish Empire, with formidable troops and even good engineers at his command.

Louis vainly set an example to other princes by sending help to Candia. His galleys and vessels, newly built in the port of Toulon, conveyed seven thousand men there under the command of the Duke of Beaufort; but in the face of such a danger the assistance was too slight, since the magnanimity of France found no imitation.

La Feuillade, a plain French gentleman, performed an

action whose like must be sought in the ancient days of chivalry. He took a company of nearly three hundred gentlemen to Candia at his own expense, though far from being a rich man. If another nation had sent help to the Venetians to the same extent as La Feuillade, Candia might well have been saved. As it was, the help that was given served but to delay its capture for a few days and caused needless loss of life. The Duke of Beaufort was killed in a sortie, and when on 16 September, 1669, the town capitulated, Kiuperli entered it to find it but a heap of ruins.

In this siege the Turks showed their superiority over the Christians even in their knowledge of the military arts. The largest cannon that had yet been seen in Europe were cast in their camp. They constructed for the first time parallel lines of trenches. We have since borrowed the method from them, and they themselves took it from an Italian engineer. It cannot be doubted that conquerors such as the Turks, with the experience, courage, wealth and tenacity for work that were then typical of them, would have conquered Italy and captured Rome in a very short space of time; but the cowardice of their later emperors, their poor generals, and the defects of their government have been the salvation of Christendom.

But little affected by these distant events, the king nourished his ambitious scheme of conquering the whole of the Netherlands, beginning with Holland. Every day the opportunity became more favourable. The small republic ruled the seas; but on land no country was in a weaker state. Allied with Spain and England and at peace with France, she relied too confidently on her treaties and the advantages of an immense trade. If her naval forces were well-trained and invincible, her armies on land were badly organised and indeed contemptible. The cavalry consisted merely of citizens who never left their homes and who paid the dregs of the populace to serve in their stead. The infantry was on very much the same footing. Officers, even commanders of fortresses, were the sons or relatives of burgomasters, fostered in ignorance and indolence, who regarded their appointments as certain priests regard their benefices. The chief magistrate, John De Witt, had wanted to reform these abuses, but had not insisted with sufficient force: it was one of the great errors of this great republican.

(1670) It was first necessary to detach England from

Holland. Once this support was removed from the United
Provinces their ruin seemed inevitable. Louis XIV. did not
find it difficult to induce Charles to fall in with his schemes.
The English monarch was indeed not very sensible of the
disgrace to himself as ruler and to his country of having his
ships burnt in the very mouth of the Thames by the Dutch
fleet. He thirsted neither for conquest nor revenge. He wished
to lead a life of pleasure and to rule as a more absolute
monarch. It was through this weakness that it was possible
to persuade him. Louis, who could have money for the asking,
promised it in plenty to Charles, who could not obtain it
without the sanction of parliament. In France this secret
liaison between the two kings was confided only to Madame
(the sister of Charles II. and the wife of the king's only
brother, Monsieur), to Turenne, and to Louvois.

(May 1670) A princess of twenty-six years was chosen
as the plenipotentiary to conclude the treaty with King
Charles. A journey which the king wished to make to his
newly conquered territories round Dunkirk and Lille was
the pretext given for the princess's crossing to England.
The pomp and splendour of the ancient kings of Asia were
eclipsed by the magnificence attending this journey. Thirty
thousand men attended the king's progress, some intended
to reinforce the garrisons of the conquered countries, others
to work on the fortifications, still others to make good roads.
The king was accompanied by his queen, all the princesses
and the most beautiful ladies of the court. Madame shone
amongst them and enjoyed to the full all the magnificent
show which accompanied her voyage. It was one continuous
fête from Saint-Germain to Lille.

The king, who wished to gain the hearts of his new subjects
and dazzle his neighbours, scattered his bounties everywhere
with a liberal hand; gold and jewels were lavished on anyone
who had the slightest pretext for speaking with him. Princess
Henrietta embarked at Calais to see her brother who had
come as far as Canterbury to meet her. Charles, won over
by his love for his sister and the gold of France, signed
everything that Louis wished and paved the way for Holland's
downfall in the midst of pleasure and entertainments.

The sudden and distressing death of the princess on her
return threw unjust suspicions on her husband, but in no
wise altered the plans of the two kings. The spoils of the
Republic, which was to be overthrown, were already appor-

tioned by the secret treaty between the courts of France and England, just as Flanders had been shared with the Dutch in 1635. Thus views, allies and enemies all are changed, and one's plans are often completely deceived. News of the coming venture began to be spread abroad; but Europe listened in silence. The Emperor, occupied with disturbances in Hungary, Sweden lulled by negotiations, Spain as usual weak, vacillating and slow, allowed free scope for the ambition of Louis XIV.

To complete her misfortune Holland was divided into two parties; the one of strict republicans, to whom the least breath of despotic authority seemed monstrous and contrary to the laws of humanity; the other of moderate republicans, who wished the young Prince of Orange, famous afterwards as William III., to assume the title of his ancestors. The chief magistrate, John De Witt, and his brother Cornelius, were the leaders of the strict partisans of liberty; but the party of the young prince was beginning to get the upper hand. Thus the Republic, more occupied with its internal troubles than its danger from abroad, contributed to its own downfall.

An astonishing custom known for more than seven hundred years among the Christians, permitted priests to be temporal lords and warriors. Louis paid the Archbishop of Cologne, Maximilian of Bavaria, and that same Van Galen, Bishop of Münster, abbé of Corbach in Westphalia, just as he paid Charles II., King of England. He had previously aided the Dutch against that bishop; now he paid him to crush them. Van Galen was a singular man, the details of whose life should be known to history. Son of a murderer and born in the prison where his father was confined for fourteen years, he had risen to be Bishop of Münster by intrigues favoured by fortune. Scarcely was he elected bishop than he had attempted to deprive the city of its privileges. It offered resistance and he besieged it; he swept with fire and sword the country which had chosen him to be its pastor. He treated his Abbey of Corbach in the same way. He was looked upon as a hired brigand, who at one time received money from the Dutch to make war on their neighbours, and at another from France to make war on the Republic. Sweden did not attack the United Provinces; but she abandoned them on seeing them threatened and renewed her old alliance with France in return for certain subsidies. Everything conspired for Holland's ruin.

It is singular and worthy of remark that of all the enemies that were about to fall upon this petty state not one could allege an excuse for making war. The agreement was very similar to that formed between Louis XII., the Emperor Maximilian and the King of Spain, when they planned the downfall of the Venetian Republic, because she was rich and proud.

In consternation the States - General wrote to Louis humbly asking if the great preparations he was making were in truth to be directed against them, his old and faithful allies. In what way had they offended him? What satisfaction did he require? He replied, "That he would employ his troops as his dignity demanded, for which he was not account-able to anyone." The whole reason assigned by his ministers was that the Dutch gazette had been too insolent and that Van Beuning was said to have struck a medallion that was offensive to Louis XIV. There was a rage for emblems in France at that time. Louis XIV. had received the device of a sun with this motto: *Nec pluribus impar.* It was alleged that Van Beuning had also represented himself with a sun accompanied by these words as motto: "IN CONSPECTU MEO STETIT SOL"—"Beholding me the sun stood still"! This me-dallion never existed. It is true that the Netherland States had struck a medallion on which they had inscribed the glories of the Republic: "*Assertis legibus; emendatis sacris; adjutis, defensis, conciliatis regibus; vindicata marium libertate; stabilita orbis Europae quiete*"—"Laws established; religion purified; kings assisted, defended and reconciled; liberty of the seas proclaimed; Europe pacified."

In truth they were not boasting of anything they had not accomplished; nevertheless they broke up the mould of this medallion in order to pacify Louis XIV.

The King of England, for his part, complained that they had not dipped their flag to an English ship, and furthermore alleged that a certain picture of Cornelius De Witt, the brother of the chief magistrate, depicted him with all the emblems of a conqueror. The fact was that captured and burning vessels might certainly be seen in the background of the picture. Cornelius De Witt, who had indeed taken a great part in the maritime exploits of his country against England, had permitted this feeble memorial to his glory to be painted, but the almost forgotten picture hung in a room where hardly anyone ever entered. The English ministers who put in writing the complaints of their king against Holland specified *abusive pictures*. The Dutch, who always translated the notes of ministers into French, translated the word *abusive* by the words *fautifs* (defective) and *trompeurs* (deceptive), and replied that they did not know what they meant by these "deceptive pictures." Indeed they never guessed that a portrait of one of their fellow-citizens was in question, and could not conceive of such an excuse for war.

All that the promptings of ambition and human foresight could suggest to prepare the way for the destruction of a nation, Louis XIV. had done. No small enterprise has ever had more formidable preparations. Conquerors who have invaded new continents did not begin their conquests with so many regular troops and so much treasure as Louis employed to subjugate the petty state of the United Provinces. Fifty millions, which to-day would represent ninety-seven, were spent in preparations. Thirty ships, each with fifty pieces of cannon, joined up with the English fleet, itself a hundred strong. The king proceeded with his brother to the frontiers of Spanish Flanders and Holland, near Maestricht and Charleroi, with more than a hundred and twelve thousand men. The Bishop of Münster and the Elector of Cologne had about twenty thousand. The generals of the king's army were Condé and Turenne. Luxembourg was in command under them, and Vauban was to direct the sieges. Louvois was everywhere with his customary watchfulness. Never had there been seen such a magnificent army and at the same time one better disciplined.

The newly-formed household troops of the king provided in themselves an extraordinarily imposing sight. There were four companies of bodyguards, each comprising three hundred gentlemen, among whom there were many young cadets, unpaid, but subject like everyone else to the strict rules of the service; there were also two hundred guardsmen, two hundred light horse, five hundred musketeers, all of gentle birth, young and of good appearance; twelve companies of men-at-arms, afterwards increased to sixteen; the hundred Swiss guards accompanied the king, and his regiments of French and Swiss guards mounted guard in front of his house and tent. These troops, whose uniforms were covered for the most part with gold and silver, were at once the terror and admiration of people to whom every kind of splendour was unknown. The added strictness of the discipline had resulted in a new rank in the army. Before this time there had been no inspectors of cavalry and infantry, as there have been since; but two men, each without a rival in his particular sphere, now assumed those duties. Martinet was responsible for the discipline of the infantry which prevails to-day: the Chevalier de Fourilles performed the same work in the cavalry. A year before, Martinet had introduced the use of the bayonet into certain regiments; before his day it had not been regularly used. This last invention, perhaps the most terrible of all the inventions of the military art, was known, but little practised on account of the prevalence of the pike. Martinet had also designed certain pontoons of copper which could be easily conveyed on carts. With so many advantages, certain of his fortune and his glory, the king took with him a historian whose duty it should be to record his victories; this was Pellisson, of whom we shall speak later in the chapter on the fine arts, a writer who found it easier to write well than to refrain from flattery.

What further contributed to the ruin of the Dutch was that the Marquis de Louvois had bought from them, through the agency of the Count de Bentheim, who was secretly won over, a large part of their munitions, which, while greatly depleting their stores, contributed at the same time to their destruction. It is not at all surprising that merchants, who daily sell such provisions to their enemies during the most desperate campaigns, should have done so before the outbreak of war. It is well known that a Dutch merchant once replied to Prince Maurice, who was rebuking him for such a transaction: "Sire, if it were possible to do some profitable business at sea with the powers of hell, I would risk burning my sails to go there." But what is surprising is that it has been stated that the Marquis de Louvois himself went in disguise to see to his purchases in Holland. Could any venture be more misplaced, dangerous and useless!

Against Turenne, Condé, Luxembourg, Vauban, a hundred and thirty thousand fighting men, a prodigious amount of artillery, and money which was constantly being used to seduce the governors of enemy towns, Holland could oppose but a young prince of feeble constitution, ignorant alike of a siege or battle, and about twenty-five thousand inferior troops who constituted the sole defence of the country. Prince William of Orange at twenty-two years of age had just been elected Captain-General of the land forces by the vote of the nation: the chief magistrate, John De Witt, had been forced to agree to it. Beneath an exterior typically Dutch in its impassiveness this prince cherished a fierce desire for glory, that later perpetually showed itself in his actions without ever being betrayed by his words. His manner was cold and severe, his mind active and acute; his unquenchable spirit enabled his feeble body to sustain hardships that were really above his strength. He was valiant without ostentation, ambitious, but an enemy of pomp, born with a stubborn calmness well adapted to struggle against adversity, fond of politics and warfare, acquainted neither with the pleasures of greatness nor with those of ordinary humanity—in a word, almost the exact opposite of Louis XIV.

At first he was unable to stem the torrent that burst upon his country. His forces were inadequate, his power limited by the States-General. The French armies suddenly hurled themselves upon Holland, and she had no one to whom to apply for help. The ill-advised Duke of Lorraine, desirous of raising troops to join his fortune with that of the Republic, saw the whole of Lorraine seized by the French armies with the same ease that Avignon is taken when the Pope is out of favour.

Meanwhile the king pushed his armies towards the Rhine, into those countries bordering on Holland, Cologne and Flanders. He distributed money in all the villages to pay for the damage his troops might cause. If any gentleman of the district came to complain he was sure to receive a present. An envoy from the governor of the Low Countries, coming to make a representation to the king about certain damage committed by his troops, received from the king's own hands his portrait set in diamonds, and worth some twelve thousand francs. Such conduct won the people's admiration and increased their fear of his power.

The king was at the head of his household brigades and his finest troops, numbering some thirty thousand men; Turenne was in command under him. The Prince de Condé had an army equally strong. The other divisions, sometimes led by Luxembourg, sometimes by Chamilli, were formed into separate armies or reunited as occasion demanded. They commenced operations by besieging simultaneously four towns, the names of which, Rheinberg, Orsoy, Wesel, Burg, would not be worth mentioning were it not for the singularity of this event. They were taken almost as soon as

they were invested. Rheinberg, which the king wished to
besiege in person, did not attempt to fire a shot; and in
order to make still surer of its capture, the precaution was
taken of bribing the lieutenant of the town, by name Dosseri,
an Irishman, who was base enough to sell the place and
foolish enough to fall back at once on Maestricht, where the
Prince of Orange had him punished by death.

All the towns bordering the Rhine and the Issel surrendered. Some governors delivered up their keys on seeing
a few French squadrons merely passing in the distance, several
officers fled from towns where they were garrisoned before
the enemy had so much as put foot in their territory; consternation reigned everywhere. The Prince of Orange had
not sufficient troops to appear in the field. All Holland
expected to pass under the yoke as soon as the king had
crossed the Rhine. The Prince of Orange had trenches dug
in haste beyond this river, but once completed he recognised
the impossibility of holding them. The only question was
that of knowing the spot at which the French would attempt
to build a bridge of boats and to oppose them if possible at
that point. The intention of Louis was indeed to cross the
river on a bridge of the little boats invented by Martinet.
Some country folk informed the Prince of Orange that the
dryness of the season had formed a ford of the Rhine close
to an old tower which was used as a toll-house and was
known as *Tollhuys* (the Toll-house), and in which there were
seventeen soldiers.

The king ordered the Count de Guiche to sound the ford.
There were but twenty paces to be swum in the middle of
this arm of the river, so writes Pellisson, who was an eye-
witness, in his letters, and this is corroborated by what
the inhabitants have told me. Such a distance was nothing,
for several of the horses of the van broke the current of the
stream which was far from swift. The landing was easy; on
the other side of the river there were only four or five hundred
cavalrymen and two feeble infantry regiments without any
cannon. The French artillery riddled their flank. While the
king's household troops and the flower of the cavalry to the
number of about fifteen thousand men crossed over without
danger (12 June, 1672), the Prince de Condé guarded their
flank in one of the copper boats. But few Dutch horsemen
entered the water to make any pretence of fighting, and a
moment afterwards they fled before the multitude that

advanced against them. Their infantry at once threw down their arms and asked for quarter. In this crossing the only casualties were the Count de Nogent and a few horsemen, who got out of their depth and were drowned; and had it not been for the foolhardiness of the young Duke de Longueville not a single man would have lost his life that day. It is said that being full of wine, he drew his pistol on the enemy, who were asking for their lives upon their knees, and shouting "*No quarter for this rabble*," he fired at and killed one of their officers. The Dutch infantry in despair immediately took up their arms and fired a volley, killing the Duke de Longueville. A captain of cavalry named Ossembrock, who had not fled with the others, rushed at the Prince de Condé, who was about to mount his horse after crossing the river, and held his pistol to his head. With a quick movement the prince turned aside the shot which shattered his wrist. This was the only wound that Condé ever received in all his campaigns. Exasperated, the French threw themselves on the infantry who fled in all directions. Louis XIV. crossed on a bridge of boats with the infantry, having himself directed the advance.

Such was the crossing of the Rhine, celebrated as a glorious and unique achievement, and considered worthy to be treasured in the minds of men. The air of greatness with which the king invested all his actions, the immediate success of his conquests, the splendour of his reign, the adoration of his courtiers, and finally, the tendency of his people (especially of the Parisians) towards exaggeration, combined with their ignorance of war, such as is common amid the comforts of large towns—all this made the crossing of the Rhine seem to the people of Paris a marvellous event, and they accordingly magnified it still further. The general opinion was that the whole army had swum across the river in the face of an entrenched army and notwithstanding the fire of an impregnable fortress known as the *Tholus*. It was quite true that this crossing was of immense importance to the enemy, and that if they had had a body of trustworthy troops on the other side, the attempt would have been highly dangerous.

No sooner was the Rhine crossed than Doesburg, Zutphen, Arnhem, Nosembourg, Nimeguen, Schenck, Bommel, Crève-cœur and other towns were taken. Hardly an hour passed during the day that the king did not receive news of some capture. An officer named Mazel sent word to Turenne:

"If you will send me fifty horse, I shall be able to take two or three towns."

On 20 June, 1672, Utrecht delivered up her keys and surrendered, with the whole province that bears that name. Louis made his triumphal entry into the city on 30 June, accompanied by his grand almoner, his confessor and the titular Archbishop of Utrecht. The great church was solemnly dedicated to the Catholics. The archbishop, who bore but the empty title, enjoyed for a brief time a real authority. The religion of Louis XIV. proved as all-conquering as his arms. In the opinion of Catholics he justly acquired such a right over the Dutch.

The provinces of Utrecht, Over-Yssel and Guelderland were subjected; Amsterdam awaited only the moment of her bondage or of her ruin. The Jewish residents hastened to offer to Gourville, the commissary and friend of the Prince de Condé, two million florins to preserve themselves from plunder.

Naarden, the neighbouring town to Amsterdam, was already taken. Four marauding horsemen advanced right up to the gates of Muiden, which is only a league from Amsterdam, and where the locks are situated that can flood the country. In their fright the magistrates of Muiden came out to deliver their keys to these four soldiers; but then seeing that the troops were not advancing they took back their keys and closed the gates. A moment's diligence and Amsterdam would have fallen into the king's hands. This capital once taken, not merely the republic would have perished but Holland as a nation would have been no more, and in a short time even the land itself would have disappeared. The wealthiest families and those most eager for liberty were preparing to flee to the ends of the world and to embark for Batavia. They counted up all the ships that were fit to undertake the voyage and the number of people that could embark. It was found that fifty thousand families would be able to sail for the new country. Holland would have existed, but in the extreme East; her European provinces, who only buy their wheat with the wealth they draw from Asia, who are dependent for their existence on their trade and one may dare to say on their liberty, would have been almost at one blow ruined and depopulated. Amsterdam, the market and storehouse of Europe, where two hundred thousand men carry on commerce and cultivate the arts, would have soon become a vast waste of marshes. The whole of the adjoining territory requires enormous expense and thousands of men to keep in repair the dykes; in all probability men as well as money would have been lacking and the country would at length have been submerged, leaving to Louis XIV. naught save the lamentable glory of having destroyed the finest and the most remarkable monument ever raised by human industry.

The desolation of the country was still further increased by divisions common to those in misfortune, who are too ready to impute to each other the responsibility for public calamities.

The chief magistrate, De Witt, believed that it was only by asking for peace from the victor that what remained of his country could be saved. Republican to the core and jealous of his own authority, he was still more fearful of the elevation of the Prince of Orange than of the conquests of the King of France; he had even insisted on this prince taking his oath to observe a permanent decree which excluded him from the office of stadtholder. Honour, power, party spirit, self-interest, all bound De Witt to insist on this oath. He would rather see the Republic enslaved by a victorious king than subject to a stadtholder.

The Prince of Orange, on the other hand, more ambitious than De Witt, yet as much attached to his country, more patient in public adversity, willing to entrust all to time and his own unwavering resolution, was aspiring to the stadtholderate with the same ardour that he combated the idea of peace. The States-General decided to sue for peace in spite of the prince; but the prince was made a stadtholder in spite of De Witt.

Four deputies repaired to the king's camp to beg for clemency in the name of a republic that six months previously had thought itself the arbiter of kings. They were far from being received by Louis XIV.'s ministers with that French politeness which mingles an easy civility with the harshness of authority. Louvois, stern and arrogant, born to serve his master well rather than make him loved, received the petitioners with haughtiness and even insulted them by raillery. They were obliged to return several times before the king at length made known his will to them. He required the States to cede all the land that they possessed beyond the Rhine, together with Nimeguen, and certain towns and fortresses in the heart of the country; to pay him twenty millions; the French to be in control of the great highways of Holland by sea and land, without paying any tolls or dues; the Catholic religion to be re-established everywhere; the Republic to send him every year an extraordinary embassy with a gold medallion, on which an inscription was to be engraved to the effect that they received their liberty from Louis XIV.: finally they should add to these reparations those which they owed to the King of England and to the princes of the Empire, such as those of Cologne and Münster, by whom Holland was still further despoiled.

Such conditions of peace which approximated so nearly to slavery seemed intolerable, and the arrogance of the conqueror inspired the vanquished with the courage of despair. They resolved to die fighting. All hearts and hopes were turned towards the Prince of Orange. The people cried out in fury against the chief magistrate who had asked for peace; and such sedition was but fomented by the policy of the prince and the rage of his party. An attempt was first made on the life of the chief magistrate, John De Witt; Cornelius, his brother, was then accused of having attempted that of the prince: he was put to the torture. On the rack he repeated the first lines of Horace's Ode, *Justum et tenacem,* etc., fit subject for his plight and for his courage:

> The man that's just and resolute of mood
> No craze of people's perverse vote can shake,
> Nor frown of threat'ning monarch make
> To suit a purposed good.

Finally, on 20 August, 1672, the infuriated populace butchered the two brothers De Witt in The Hague—of whom one had worthily ruled the state for nineteen years and the other had served his country with his sword.

All the fury of which a mob is capable was spent upon their battered bodies—horrors common to every nation and which the Marshal d'Ancre, Admiral Coligni and others had suffered at the hands of the French; for the populace is nearly everywhere the same. The friends of De Witt were also persecuted. Even Ruyter, the Chief Admiral of the Republic, who alone fought for them with success, was beset by assassins in the streets of Amsterdam.

In the midst of these disturbances and calamities the magistrates showed evidence of virtues rarely seen save in republics. Citizens who possessed bank-notes rushed in a crowd to the Bank of Amsterdam; they feared that the public treasure had been drawn upon. Everyone was eager to be paid from the little money which was thought to remain. The magistrates opened the vaults where the public treasure was kept, and it was found there intact as it had been deposited sixty years before: the very silver was still blackened from the fire which had burnt down the Town Hall a few years previously. Bank-notes had thus been duly cashed up to that moment and the public treasury had not been drawn upon. Such husbandry and good faith were all the more praiseworthy in comparison with the fact that Charles II., in order to be able to carry on the war against the Dutch and provide for his own pleasures, not content with the money he received from France, had made his own subjects bankrupt. It was as shameful for this king thus to violate public trust as it was glorious for the magistrates of Amsterdam to have kept such a trust at a time when they might permissibly have been found wanting.

To this republican virtue they united a courage which dares to take extreme measures in desperate straits. They broke down the dykes that shut out the sea. The country houses scattered in large numbers around Amsterdam, the villages, the neighbouring towns, Leyden and Delft, were flooded. The peasants did not complain when they saw their herds drowned in the fields. Amsterdam stood like a vast fortress in the midst of the waters, surrounded by ships of war who could sail close up to the city. Famine was widespread among the people, above all they lacked fresh water which was sold at six sous a pint, but such privations seemed more bearable than slavery. It is a thing worthy of note that while Holland was thus vanquished on land, no longer existing as a state, she yet remained formidable at sea; it was her natural element.

While Louis XIV. was crossing the Rhine and capturing three provinces, Admiral Ruyter, with about a hundred ships of war and more than fifty fire-ships, approached near to the coast of England. The united forces of England and France had not been able to put to sea a stronger fleet than that of the Republic. The English and the Dutch fought like nations accustomed to dispute the supremacy of the seas. This, the Battle of Southwold, lasted the whole of 7 June, 1672. Ruyter, who gave the signal of battle, attacked the English admiral's flagship, on board which was the king's

brother, the Duke of York. The glory of this particular
fight remains with Ruyter. The Duke of York, compelled
to change his ship, did not again oppose himself directly to
the Dutch admiral. The thirty French ships took little part
in the action, and the result of this battle was that the
coasts of Holland were secured.

Afterwards, Ruyter despite the fears and opposition of
his countrymen conducted the merchant fleet from the Indies
into the Texel; thus defending and enriching his country
on the one side while it perished on the other. Dutch
commerce was indeed maintained; theirs was the only flag
to be seen in the Pacific. One day when a French consul
was telling the King of Persia that Louis XIV. had conquered nearly the whole of Holland, that monarch replied,
"How can that be, since there are always twenty Dutch
ships to one French in the port of Ormuz?"

Meanwhile, the Prince of Orange was eager to show himself
a good citizen. He offered the revenues of his office to the
state, and all his property, to preserve his country's liberty.
He flooded the districts through which the French might
enter the rest of the country. His negotiations, as prompt as
they were secret, roused the Emperor, the imperial princes,
the Council of Spain, and the Governor of Flanders from
their lethargy. He even disposed England to peace. The king
entered Holland in May, and by July Europe had begun to
plot against him.

Monterey, Governor of Flanders, despatched in secret a few
regiments to the relief of the United Provinces. Emperor
Leopold's council sent Montecuculi at the head of nearly
twenty thousand men. The Elector of Brandenburg with
twenty-five thousand soldiers in his pay began to move.

In July 1672 the king took leave of his army.

No further conquests could be made in a flooded country.
The garrisoning of the captured provinces was becoming
difficult. Louis wished his glory to be secure, but unwilling
to acquire it at the cost of unremitting toil, he found it
slipping from his grasp. Satisfied at having taken so many
towns in two short months he returned to Saint-Germain
at the height of summer, leaving Turenne and Luxembourg
to finish the campaign while he enjoyed the triumph. Monuments were erected to perpetuate his conquest, while the
European powers were conspiring to rob him of it.

CHAPTER XI

EVACUATION OF HOLLAND. SECOND CONQUEST OF FRANCHE-COMTÉ

It is perhaps necessary to remind readers of this book that it is not a bare record of campaigns, but rather a history of the manners of men.

There are plenty of books filled with the most minute particulars of military operations and details of human passions and misery. The aim of this history is to depict the chief characteristics of such revolutions, clear away the innumerable small events that obscure the great ones, and finally, if possible, to depict the spirit that informed them.

France was then at the height of her glory. The names of her generals were held in veneration. Her ministers were regarded as men of genius superior to the advisers of other princes, and Louis was looked upon as the only king in Europe. Indeed, the Emperor Leopold was never seen with his armies; Charles II. of Spain, Philip IV.'s son, was little more than a child; the King of England was actively concerned only with his pleasures.

All these princes and their ministers committed great mistakes. England acted against all principles of reason in uniting with France to exalt a power which it was her interest to weaken. The Emperor, the Imperial princes and the Spanish council made a still greater error in not immediately opposing this torrent. Finally, Louis himself committed the gravest error of all in not pursuing such conquests with greater rapidity. Condé and Turenne wished to destroy the greater number of the Dutch strongholds: they insisted that states were conquered not by garrisons, but by armies, and that while holding one or two fortresses in case of retreat, they should rapidly advance and conquer the whole country. Louvois, on the other hand, was all for fortified towns and garrisons; his genius lay in that direction, and such a plan was pleasing to the king. Louvois consequently had more offices at his disposal, and extended the powers of his ministry; he took pleasure in contradicting the two greatest captains of the age. Louis trusted him, and was mistaken, as he afterwards confessed; he missed the opportunity of entering the capital of Holland; he weakened his army by dividing it among too many towns; he gave his enemy breathing-space. The history of the greatest princes is often a record of the faults of men.

After the king's departure affairs assumed a different aspect. Turenne was obliged to march towards Westphalia to bar the advance of the Imperial troops. Monterey, Governor of Flanders, though not commanded to do so by the timid Council of Spain, reinforced the small army of the Prince of Orange with about ten thousand men. The prince was thus enabled to hold his own against the French until the winter. It was much to be able to fight on level terms. At length winter arrived, and the flooded parts of Holland were covered with ice. Luxembourg, who was in command in Utrecht, invented a new method of war unknown to the French, and placed Holland in a fresh danger, which was as terrible as any that had preceded.

One night he mustered nearly twelve thousand foot-soldiers from the neighbouring garrisons. The soles of their shoes were rough-shod. Putting himself at their head, he marched over the ice towards Leyden and The Hague; but a thaw set in, The Hague was saved, and surrounded by water, his army, without either a road of retreat or supplies, was near to perishing. To return to Utrecht his men had to march along a narrow and miry dyke, on which they could scarcely walk four abreast. Moreover, they could only reach this dyke by attacking a fort that appeared impregnable without the help of artillery; and had this fort stopped their progress for but one day, the whole army would have died of hunger and fatigue. Luxembourg was at the end of his resources; but chance, which had saved The Hague, saved his army, through the cowardice of the governor of the fort, who deserted his post for no apparent reason. In war, as in civil life, there are a thousand incomprehensible events; this was one of them. The only outcome of this expedition was an exhibition of cruelty which made the name of France hateful throughout the whole country. Bodegraven and Zwammerdam, two important market towns, rich and well-populated, very similar to French country towns of moderate size, were given over to the soldiers for pillage, as a recompense for their hardships. They set fire to both; and in the light of the flames rioted in debauch and cruelty. It is astonishing that the French soldiery should be so barbarous, commanded as they are by so many officers who have justly gained the reputation of being as humane as they are brave. This pillaging made such a profound impression that more than forty years later I have seen Dutch children's reading-books which recount the deed and thus inspire hatred of the French in future generations.

(1673) Meanwhile the king was agitating the councils of all the European princes by his negotiations. He won over the Duke of Hanover. On the commencement of war the Elector of Brandenburg had concluded a treaty, but it was soon broken. There was not a court in Germany where Louis' agents were not to be found. They stirred up strife in Hungary, which had been harshly treated by the Treaty of Vienna. Money was lavished on the King of England to persuade him to continue the war against Holland, and this in spite of the protests of the whole English nation, who were indignant at assisting to build the greatness of Louis XIV., which they would have more gladly weakened. Europe was disturbed alike by the arms and the diplomacy of Louis. He could not at length prevent the Emperor, the Empire and Spain from allying themselves with Holland and solemnly declaring war against him. He had so changed the course of affairs that the Dutch, his natural allies, had become the friends of the House of Austria. The Emperor Leopold was slow in sending help, but he displayed great animosity. It is related that on going to Egres to review the troops there assembled, he took the sacrament on the way, and after communion he took the crucifix in his hand and called God to witness the justness of his cause. Such an action would have been fitting at the time of the Crusades; Leopold's prayers, however, were powerless to stay the progress of the King of France.

It was immediately apparent that the French navy had been greatly improved. Instead of the thirty ships that had been sent to join the English fleet the year before, forty were now sent, in addition to fire-ships. The officers had learnt the skilful manœuvres of the English, with which they had outwitted those of their enemies, the Dutch. The Duke of York, afterwards James II., had invented the method of giving orders at sea by means of flags. Before that time the French did not know how to arrange a fleet in line of battle. Their method was simply to fight one ship against another; they had no knowledge of concerted movements or of imitating at sea the evolutions of armies on land, by which separate regiments mutually support and assist one another. They did almost as the Romans of old, who in one year learnt from the Carthaginians the art of naval warfare, and became the equals of their masters.

Vice-Admiral d'Estrées and his lieutenant Martel brought honour to the military ardour of the French nation in three consecutive naval battles on the 7th, 14th and 21st of June, 1673, between the Dutch fleet and that of France and England. Admiral Ruyter achieved greater glory than ever in these three actions. D'Estrées wrote to Colbert: "I would have given my life for the glory that Ruyter has recently gained." D'Estrées deserved to have been spoken of in such terms by Ruyter. Valour and resolution were so equal on either side that the victory remained uncertain.

Louis, having made sailors of his Frenchmen by the efforts of Colbert, made further improvements in the art of war on land by the industry of Vauban. He came in person to besiege Maestricht at the time when these three naval battles were being fought. Maestricht was the key to the Low Countries and the United Provinces; it was a place very strongly defended by a dauntless governor, one Fariaux, a French-man who had crossed over to the service of Spain and later to that of Holland. The garrison was composed of five thousand men. Vauban, who conducted the siege, made use for the first time of parallel lines of trenches invented by Italian engineers for the Turks in front of Candia. He also added certain saps to the trenches, in which troops can be drawn up in battle order and the better rallied in case of sorties. In this siege Louis displayed greater exactness and perseverance than he had ever shown before. By his example he taught the value of patience in toil to a nation which up till then had been accused of possessing but an impetuous courage which was quickly exhausted by fatigue. Maestricht surrendered at the end of eight days (29 June, 1673).

To strengthen military discipline still further he used a severity which seemed to err on the side of excess. The Prince of Orange, who had but officers without ambition and soldiers without courage, to oppose to these rapid conquests, had drilled them into shape with great harshness, handing over to the executioner those who deserted their posts. The king also dealt out punishment the first time that he lost a town. A gallant officer named Du-Pas surrendered Naarden to the Prince of Orange on 14 September, 1673. It is true that he had only held it for four days; but he only surrendered after a fight lasting some five hours, with poor defences at his disposal, and in order to avoid a general assault, which a feeble and reduced garrison would not have been able to repulse. The king, angered at the first check that his arms had received, ordered him to be exposed in Utrecht, a broom in his hand, and his sword was publicly broken: this was a useless disgrace for French officers whose love of glory makes it unnecessary to control them by the fear of shame. It must be mentioned that the royal letters issued to the governors of fortresses certainly lay it down as their duty to resist three assaults, but they belong to that class of orders which are never carried out. A year later Du-Pas let himself be killed at the siege of the little town of Grave, where he was serving as a volunteer. His courage and his death must have inspired regret in the heart of the Marquis de Louvois, who had punished him so severely. The sovereign power may ill-treat a brave man; it cannot dishonour him.

The toils of the king, the genius of Vauban, the stern vigilance of Louvois, the experience and matchless skill of Turenne, the intrepid courage and activity of the Prince de Condé, all could not repair the error that had been made in garrisoning too many towns, in thus weakening the army, and in failing to take Amsterdam.

The Prince de Condé desired in vain to penetrate into the heart of flooded Holland. Turenne could neither hinder Montecuculi from joining forces with the Prince of Orange nor prevent the Prince of Orange from taking Bonn. The Bishop of Münster, who had sworn to destroy the States-General, was himself attacked by the Dutch. The English parliament forced its king to enter genuinely upon negotiations for peace, and to cease to be the mercenary tool of French aggrandisement. It had now become necessary to evacuate the three Dutch provinces as rapidly as they had been conquered. This was not done without exacting ransoms; the commissary, Robert, collected in one year from the Province of Utrecht alone 668,000 florins. They were in such haste to evacuate a country which had been so quickly conquered that 28,000 Dutch prisoners were liberated at a crown a head. The triumphal arch at the gateway of Saint-Denys and the other monuments of the conquest were scarcely finished when the conquest was already being abandoned. In the course of this invasion the Dutch could boast of having disputed the empire of the sea and of having skilfully transferred the theatre of war outside their own country. In Europe Louis XIV. was regarded as having rejoiced too soon and too loudly over a short-lived triumph. The expedition resulted in his being engaged in a desperate war against the united forces of Spain, the Empire and Holland, in being deserted by England, later by Münster and even Cologne, and in leaving more hatred than admiration for his name in the countries he had invaded and abandoned.

The king stood alone against all the enemies that he had made. The foresight of his government and the resources of the state appeared to but greater advantage when he had to defend himself against a number of allied powers and their famous generals, than when he had taken in his stride French Flanders, Franche-Comté and half Holland, from enemies who were off their guard.

Especially noteworthy was the advantage that an absolute king possesses over other monarchs, provided his finances are in good order. At one and the same time he furnished Turenne with an army of about 23,000 men to oppose the Imperial forces, and Condé with 40,000 to oppose the Prince of Orange; another regiment was on the frontier of Roussillon; a fleet laden with soldiers was sent as far as Messina to make war on Spain, and he himself marched on Franche-Comté to make himself master of that country for the second time. He defended himself and attacked in every part at the same time.

At first, in his new expedition upon Franche-Comté, the superiority of his government appeared to be unquestionable. It was important to gain to his side, or at any rate to allay the suspicions of, the Swiss, a nation valiant but poor, always in arms, jealous to excess of their liberty, and invincible on their frontiers, but already murmuring, and disturbed at seeing Louis XIV. a second time in their neighbourhood. The Emperor and Spain appealed to the thirteen cantons to allow at least a free passage to their troops, so as to send aid to Franche-Comté, which was left defenceless through the negligence of the Spanish Government. On his side the king urged the Swiss to refuse such a passage; the Emperor and Spain were prodigal of nothing but reasons and entreaties; the king persuaded the Swiss to do what he desired by means of hard cash, and the passage was refused.

Accompanied by his brother and the son of the great
Condé, Louis besieged Besançon. He took great delight in
siege warfare and might well consider that he understood
the art as well as Condé and Turenne; but jealous as he was
of his own glory, he confessed that those two great men knew
more about open warfare than himself. Moreover he never
besieged a town without being certain of taking it. Louvois
made such complete preparations, the troops were so well
provided for, Vauban, who conducted nearly all the sieges,
was such a past-master in the art of taking towns, that
the king's glory was assured. Vauban directed the attacks on
Besançon, which was taken in nine days (15 May, 1674), and
in six weeks the whole of Franche-Comté had surrendered
to the king. It still belongs to France and seems destined
to be a monument of the weakness of the Austrian-Spanish
government and of the strength of that of Louis XIV.

CHAPTER XII

GLORIOUS CAMPAIGN AND DEATH OF MARSHAL DE TURENNE. LAST BATTLE OF THE GREAT CONDÉ AT SENEFFE

WHILE the king was thus rapidly and easily subduing
Franche-Comté with that splendour already characteristic
of his destiny, Turenne, whose only task was to defend the
frontiers of the Rhine, was showing the greatest and most
gifted qualities that can be displayed in the art of war. The
esteem of men is accorded in proportion to the difficulties
they surmount, and to this is due the great reputation of
this campaign of Turenne's.

(June 1674) He first undertook a long and rapid march,
crossed the Rhine at Philippsburg, marched during the whole
night to Sinsheim, and took the town; at the same time he
attacked and put to flight Caprara, the Emperor's general,
and the old Duke of Lorraine, Charles IV.—a prince whose
whole life was spent in losing his states and raising troops
—and who had just joined his small army to one of the
Emperor's divisions. Turenne not only beat him, but pursued
him, and again defeated his cavalry at Ladenburg (July
1674); thence he advanced to attack another Imperial
general, the Prince de Bournonville, who was only awaiting

fresh forces to open the way to Alsace; he prevented the meeting of these troops, attacked him and forced him to flee from the field (October 1674).

The Empire gathered all its forces against him; there were 70,000 Germans in Alsace; and Brisach and Philippsburg were blockaded by them. Turenne had no more than 20,000 fit men at the most in December of that year.

The Prince de Condé sent a few cavalry from Flanders to his help; he proceeded to cross the mountains still covered with snow, passing through Tanne and Belfort, and suddenly appeared in Upper Alsace in the enemy's quarters. They imagined him to be still resting in Lorraine and the campaign over. At Mühlhausen he defeated the regiments who opposed him, and took two regiments prisoner. He marched to Colmar, where the Elector of Brandenburg, known as the Great Elector, and at that time the commander-in-chief of the Imperial armies, had made his headquarters. He arrived at the moment that this prince and the other generals were sitting down to table; they had barely time to escape, and the country was covered with fugitives.

Turenne, considering that he had done nothing since there still remained so much to do, continued to wait close to Türkheim, watching for a detachment of the enemy's infantry. The advantages of the position he had taken up made victory certain and the body of infantry were defeated (5 January, 1675). Thus an army of 70,000 men found itself beaten and dispersed almost without a single large battle. The king continued to hold Alsace and the Imperial troops were obliged to recross the Rhine. All these successive actions, directed with such skill, planned with such patience and carried out with such rapidity, were admired equally by the French and by their enemies. The glory of Turenne was but further increased when it was known that all that he had done in this campaign had been done in spite of the court and the repeated orders of Louvois given in the king's name. To resist the all-powerful Louvois and take upon himself the responsibility for the result despite the outcries of the court, the orders of Louis XIV. and the hatred of his minister, was not the least mark of Turenne's courage nor the least achievement of the campaign.

It must be confessed that those who have more humanity than reverence for warlike deeds will lament this glorious campaign. It was noteworthy for the misery of the common people as much as for the marches of Turenne. After the Battle of Sinsheim, the Palatinate, a peaceful and fertile country, covered with cities and wealthy market-towns, was devastated by fire and carnage. The Elector Palatine, from the heights of his castle of Mannheim, gazed on the flames of two towns and twenty-five villages: in his despair he challenged Turenne to single combat in a letter full of reproaches. Turenne having sent the letter to the king, who forbade him to accept the challenge, replied only with a vague and meaningless compliment to the Elector's reproaches and defiance. It was always Turenne's custom to express himself with moderation and ambiguity.

With the same calmness he burnt part of the countryside of Alsace to destroy the enemy's means of subsistence. Later he allowed his cavalry to lay waste Lorraine. His troops committed such depredations that the commissary, who, on his side, laid waste Lorraine with his pen, wrote to him and frequently asked him to put a stop to these excesses. He replied coldly, "I will see that it is announced in the orders of the day." He preferred to be called the father of the soldiers, who were under his care, than of the people, who, according to the rules of war, are always sacrificed. All the evil that he did seemed necessary; his glory covered all. Moreover, the 70,000 Germans whom he prevented from entering France would have done much more damage there than he did in Alsace, Lorraine and the Palatinate.

Such has been the position of France since the beginning of the sixteenth century, that every time that she has gone to war she has been obliged to fight Germany, Flanders, Spain and Italy at the same time. The Prince de Condé made headway against the young Prince of Orange in Flanders, while Turenne was driving the Germans from Alsace. Turenne's campaign was successful, Condé's desperately fought. The short engagements of Sinsheim and Türkheim were decisive; the great and famous Battle of Seneffe was a carnage. The great Condé, who fought this battle while Turenne was accomplishing his secret marches in Alsace, achieved no advantage from it, whether because the situation was less favourable to him, or because he had taken less skilful precautions, or more probably because he had cleverer generals and better troops against him. The Marquis de Feuquières insists that Seneffe should be called not a pitched battle, but merely an engagement, since the action was not fought between two armies in line and all the regiments were not engaged, but general agreement gives the name of *battle* to this fierce and bloody day. The clash of 3000 men in line, with every company engaged, would only be an engagement. The importance of an event always decides its name.

The Prince de Condé had to carry on the campaign with about 45,000 men, against the Prince of Orange, who, it was said, had 60,000. He waited until the enemy army was passing through a narrow pass at Seneffe near Mons, and on 11 August, 1674, attacked part of the rear-guard, composed of Spanish troops, and gained a decided advantage. The Prince of Orange was blamed for not having taken sufficient precautions in the passage of the defile, but was praised for the way in which he restored order, and Condé was reproved for immediately recommencing the fight against an enemy who was too well entrenched. The fight was renewed three times. In this medley of mistakes and great deeds both generals displayed equal courage and presence of mind. Of all the battles of the great Condé it was in this one that he most exposed his own life and the lives of his soldiers. Three horses were killed under him. After three desperate charges he wished to attempt a fourth. An officer who was present said that there seemed to be nobody but the Prince de Condé who was still eager to fight. The most remarkable part of this action was, however, that in the evening, after a series of the most bloody and desperate encounters, the troops on both sides took to flight in panic. On the morrow both armies had retired, neither of them in possession of the field, neither victorious, but both equally weakened and defeated. On the French side there were nearly 7000 dead and 5000 prisoners; the enemy suffered equal losses. The useless expenditure of so many lives precluded either army from undertaking any further considerable action.

So important is it to uphold the reputation of one's army that the Prince of Orange immediately besieged Oudenarde in order to make believe that he had won the battle, but the Prince de Condé proved that he had not lost it by immediately raising the siege and pursuing the Prince of Orange.

France and the Allies alike performed the futile ceremony of giving thanks to God for a victory which they had never obtained, a custom instituted to encourage the people, whom it is important always to deceive.

In Germany, Turenne with a small army continued a progress which was only made possible by his genius. The Council of Vienna no longer venturing to entrust the fortunes of the Empire to princes who had so badly defended it, again placed Montecuculi at the head of its armies; he it was who defeated the Turks in the battle of Saint Gothard, and who, in spite of Turenne and Condé, had joined the Prince of Orange and checked the progress of Louis XIV. after the conquest of three Dutch provinces.

It has been remarked that the greatest generals of the Empire often came from Italy. In spite of her decadence and bondage, that country still produces men who remind one of what she was. Montecuculi was the only one worthy to be an opponent of Turenne. Both had reduced war to a fine art. They spent four months in following and mutually watching each other during marches and in encampments, months which earned them greater esteem in the eyes of French and German officers than any number of victories would have done. Each judged what his opponent was going to do by the step he himself would have taken in his place, and they were never mistaken. They vied with each other in patience, in cunning, in ceaseless activity; at length they were ready to come to blows and risk their reputation on a battle near the village of Salzbach, when Turenne, reconnoitring in search of a spot to place a battery, was killed by a cannon-ball on 27 July, 1675. There is no one who does not know the circumstances of his death; but one cannot abstain from relating the chief of them, for the very reason that they are still commonly spoken of.

Indeed, it can hardly be too often described how the same shot that killed him took off the arm of Saint-Hilaire, lieutenant-general of artillery, whose son bursting into tears threw himself upon him. "Do not weep for me," said Saint-Hilaire, "weep for that great man"—heroic words, comparable with the most heroic that history records and the worthiest panegyric of Turenne. It is rare indeed that under a monarchy, where men are only concerned with their own interests, those who have served their country are mourned by the public when they die. Yet Turenne was wept for by the soldiers and by the common people. Louvois alone did not regret him; public opinion charged both him and his brother, the Archbishop of Rheims, with having indecently rejoiced over the loss of that great man. It is well known what honours the king paid to his memory, that he was buried at Saint-Denys as had been the high constable, Du Guesclin, and that popular opinion deems him as superior to that knight as the age of Turenne surpasses the age of the high constable. Turenne had not always known success in war; he had been defeated at Marienthal, at Rethel and at Cambrai; he said himself that he had committed errors, and was great enough to acknowledge them. He made no brilliant conquests and never fought one of those pitched battles the result of which sometimes makes one nation the mistress of another; but as he was always repairing his defeats and doing great deeds with slender forces he was regarded as the cleverest captain in Europe, at a time when the art of war was more deeply studied than ever before. And so, though he might be reproached for disloyalty in the wars of the Fronde, though at the age of nearly sixty years love tempted him to reveal a state secret, though he may have been guilty of cruelties in the Palatinate for which there was no apparent reason, nevertheless he preserved the reputation of an honourable, prudent and moderate man, because the virtues and great talents which belonged to him alone made one forget the weaknesses and faults which he had in common with so many other men. If he is to be compared with any one of the generals of earlier ages it should be with Gonsalvo di Cordova, surnamed *the great captain*, to whom he bears most resemblance.

Born a Calvinist, he became a Catholic in the year 1668. No Protestant, no philosopher even, thought that persuasion alone had brought about this change in a soldier and politician now past fifty years of age, who still indulged in mistresses. It is known that, when Louis XIV. appointed him Chief Marshal of his armies, he had spoken these very words to him, as they are recorded in the letters of Pellisson and elsewhere: "I wish that you would oblige me to do something more for you." These words, in their opinion, might in time have brought about such a conversion. The post of high constable might tempt an ambitious spirit. It is also possible that his conversion was sincere. The human heart often contains within itself politics, ambition, the weaknesses of passion and deep religious feelings. Finally, while it was very probable that Turenne only left the religion of his fathers for reasons of policy, the Catholics who exulted at the conversion refused to believe that the soul of Turenne was capable of deceit.

The events in Alsace which immediately followed the death of Turenne made his loss still more felt. Montecuculi, held back for three whole months on the farther side of the Rhine by the strategy of the French general, crossed the river directly he learnt that he had no longer Turenne to fear, and fell upon a part of the army which was under the bewildered command of Lorges and Vaubrun, two lieutenants-general who were both disunited and vacillating. The army defended itself courage-ously but could not prevent the Imperial troops from pene-trating into Alsace, which Turenne had hindered them from doing. It had need of a commander, not only to lead them, but to redeem the recent defeat of Marshal de Créqui, a man of rash courage, capable of the finest and most daring actions, but as dangerous to his country as he was to his enemies.

Créqui had recently been defeated on 11 August, 1675, at Saarbrück. His small army was cut to pieces and put to flight by a force of 20,000 Germans who were besieging Trèves. It was with difficulty that he saved a quarter of his men. In the face of fresh dangers he hastened to throw himself into Trèves, which he should have relieved with caution and which he defended with courage. He wished to bury himself under the ruins of the town; a breach had been made, but he persisted in holding out. The garrison murmured. Captain Bois-Jourdain at the head of the mutineers went to surrender at the breach. Never was a cowardly act committed with such effrontery. He threatened to kill the marshal if he did not sign. Créqui retired with a few faithful officers into a church, preferring capture rather than surrender.

To replace the men that France had lost in so many sieges and battles, Louis XIV. was advised not to call up the militia recruits as was usual but to enlist the nobles and their re-tainers. According to an ancient custom now obsolete, owners of fiefs were compelled to go to war at their own expense in the service of their sovereign lord and remain under arms for a certain number of days.

Such service made up the greater part of the laws of bar-barian nations. To-day all is changed in Europe; there is no state which does not recruit soldiers who are continuously kept in reserve under the colours, and who form disciplined regiments.

On one occasion Louis XIII. had recruited the nobles of his kingdom. Louis XIV. now imitated his example. The corps of nobles marched under the command of the Marquis, then

Marshal, de Rochefort to the frontiers of Flanders, and afterwards to those of Germany, but the regiment was neither numerous nor useful, and indeed could not well be either. The officers in command of the troops were noblemen fond of fighting and capable of doing good service; some through age or disloyalty remained at home, and did not attempt to join; others, who were engaged in cultivating their estates, reluctantly enlisted to the number of about 4000. Nothing could be less like a warlike troop. All differently mounted and armed, inexperienced and unfit, neither able nor willing to undergo regular service, they were only a source of trouble, and caused a general disgust which has ever since remained. This was the last trace in the regular army of that ancient chivalry of which armies were formerly composed, and which while possessing all the courage inherent in the nation has never carried on warfare efficiently.

(August and September 1675) With Turenne dead, Créqui defeated and a prisoner, Trèves captured and Montecuculi laying Alsace under contribution, Louis turned to the Prince de Condé as the only one who could restore confidence to the troops, discouraged as they were by the death of Turenne. Condé left Marshal de Luxembourg to uphold the fortunes of France in Flanders and pushed on to check Montecuculi's advance. He had recently shown impetuosity at Seneffe; he now gave proof of patience. His genius, pliant and accommodating itself to everything, betrayed the same artistry as that of Turenne. Two encampments alone checked the advance of the German army and forced Montecuculi to raise the sieges of Haguenau and Saverne. After this campaign, which was less striking but more esteemed than that o Seneffe, the prince ceased to appear in the field. He wished his son to assume command, and offered to assist him with his advice, but the king wanted neither young men nor princes as generals; it was with some reluctance that he had employed even the Prince de Condé. Louvois' jealousy of Turenne, as much as the name of Condé, had contributed to his being put at the head of armies.

The prince retired to Chantilly and came but seldom to Versailles to see his glory eclipsed in a place where the courtiers' only respect is paid to favour. He passed the rest of his life tormented by gout, but consoling himself in his retreat with the conversation of men of genius in every sphere of life. France was then full of such men. He was worthy of such conversation, being a stranger to none of the arts or sciences in which they shone.

He was still revered in retirement, but at length the consuming fire, which had made of him in his youth a hero at once impetuous and impassioned, wore out the forces of his body; born rather agile than robust, he fell into a decline before his time, and his mind growing weaker with his body, nothing remained of the great Condé during the last two years of his life; he died in 1686. Montecuculi retired from the Emperor's service at the same time that the Prince de Condé relinquished the command of the French armies.

The contemptible tale is widely spread that Montecuculi resigned his command on the death of Turenne, because, said he, there was no longer a rival worthy of him. Even had there been no Condé it would have been a foolish remark. But far from making the foolish remark which has thus been credited to him, he continued to fight against the French and forced them to recross the Rhine in the same year. Moreover, what general of an army would ever have said to his master, "I do not wish to serve you any longer, since your enemies are too weak, and my merit is too superior"?

CHAPTER XIII

FROM THE DEATH OF TURENNE TO THE PEACE OF NIMEGUEN IN 1678

AFTER the death of Turenne and the retirement of the Prince de Condé, the king continued the war against the Empire, Spain and Holland, with no less success. He was served by officers trained by those two great men. He had Louvois, more valuable to him than any general, since his foresight enabled generals to undertake everything they wished to do. Victorious for so long, the troops were emboldened by the same spirit which was excited by the presence of a king who was ignorant of defeat.

In the course of the war he took in person Condé (26 April, 1676), Bouchain (11 May, 1676), Valenciennes (17 March, 1677) and Cambrai (5 April, 1677). At the siege of Bouchain he was reproached with having been afraid to engage battle with the Prince of Orange, who appeared with 50,000 men to attempt to relieve the town. The Prince of Orange was likewise reproached for having been in a position to give battle to Louis XIV. and for not having done so. Such is the lot of kings and generals that they are always blamed, alike for what they do and what they leave undone; but neither the king nor the Prince of Orange was to blame. On his side, the prince did not give battle, although he wished to do so, because Monterey, the governor of the Netherlands, who was with his army, did not wish to expose his government to the risk of a decisive battle; yet the glory of the field remained with the king, since he achieved what he wished to do and took a town in the face of the enemy.

Valenciennes, on the contrary, was taken by assault, by one of those remarkable actions typical of the impetuous courage of the nation. The king conducted this siege, having with him his brother and five Marshals of France, d'Humières, Schomberg, La Feuillade, Luxembourg and de Lorge. Each marshal commanded in turn for one day. Vauban directed the whole of the operations.

None of the outworks of the place had yet been taken, and the besiegers were first obliged to attack two half-moon fortifications. Behind these was a great earthwork palisaded and fraised, surrounded by a ditch cut by several traverses. Within this earthwork there was yet another fortification surrounded by another ditch. After taking all these entrenchments, an arm of the Escaut would have to be crossed, after which there was still another obstacle known as the *pâté*. Behind this flowed the main stream of the Escaut, deep and swift, serving as a moat round the wall. Finally the wall itself was supported by broad ramparts. All these fortifications bristled with cannon, and a garrison of 3000 men was preparing a lengthy resistance.

The king held a council of war to decide on the method of attacking the outermost fortifications. The custom was always to make these attacks during the night, so as to advance upon the enemy without being seen and to spare the lives of the soldiers. Vauban proposed to make the attack in full daylight. All the French marshals protested against this; Louvois condemned it. Vauban, however, remained firm with the confidence of a man who is certain of what he proposes. "You wish," he said, "to spare the soldiers' lives; you will do so more surely if you attack by daylight, thus obviating confusion and tumult, and the fear that some of our men will fire on the others, as only too often happens. Our aim is to surprise the enemy, who is always on the look-out for night attacks; we shall certainly surprise him when, exhausted with the weariness of watching, he is obliged to sustain the attacks of our fresh troops. Add to this that if in this army there are men who are faint-hearted, night favours their timidity, but in the daytime the eye of their general inspires valour and raises men above themselves."

The king was convinced by Vauban's reasons, in spite of Louvois and five Marshals of France.

On 17 March, 1677, at nine o'clock in the morning, two companies of musketeers, about a hundred grenadiers, a battalion of the guards and one from a Picardy regiment, scaled the crowned fortification on every side. Their orders were simply to take up a position on it, and it was no slight achievement; but some of the black musketeers penetrated by a narrow pathway into the interior entrenchment of this fortification, and made themselves masters of it. At the same time the grey musketeers assaulted it in another quarter. The guards' battalions followed them; the defenders were pursued and killed, the musketeers lowered the drawbridge connecting this fort with the others, and pursued the enemy from one entrenchment to the other, over the small arm of Escaut and over the main stream. The guards advanced in a body. The musketeers were already in the town before the king knew that the first fort had been carried.

This was not the most extraordinary part of this action. It was natural that young musketeers carried away by their success should throw themselves blindly on the troops and citizens who advanced to oppose them in the streets; and that there they would perish or the town be pillaged; but these young men, led by a cornet named Moissac, drew themselves up in fighting order behind carts, and, while the troops as they arrived formed up without haste, other musketeers seized the neighbouring houses to protect those who were in the street by their fire; hostages were given on all sides; the town council met, and a deputation was sent to the king; all this occurred without there being any pillage, confusion or mistakes of any kind. The king made the garrison prisoners of war and entered Valenciennes astonished at having mastered it. The singular nature of this action accounts for our entering into so much detail.

(9 March, 1678) He had also the glory of taking Ghent in

four days and Ypres in seven (25 March). These were his personal achievements. The successes of his generals were still greater.

(September 1676) On the German front, the Marshal Duke of Luxembourg, it is true, allowed Philippsburg to be taken before his eyes, and attempted in vain to relieve it with an army of 50,000 men. The general who took Philippsburg was Charles V., the new Duke of Lorraine, the heir of his uncle Charles IV., and like him deprived of his estates. He had all the good qualities of his unfortunate uncle without his defects. He commanded the Imperial armies for a long period, during which he covered himself with glory; but in spite of the capture of Philippsburg and the fact that he was at the head of 60,000 men, he was never able to regain his estates. It was in vain that he inscribed on his standards, *Aut nunc aut nunquam*—" Now or never."

Marshal de Créqui, ransomed from prison and become more careful after his defeat at Saarbrück, prevented him from entering Lorraine. On 7 October, 1677, he defeated him in the little Battle of Kochersberg in Alsace. He harassed and exhausted him, giving him no respite. On 14 November, 1677, he took Freiburg under his eyes and some time afterwards again beat a detachment of his army at Rheinfeld. In July 1678 he crossed the River Kinzig in the face of his troops, pursued him towards Offenburg, and charged his retreating army; immediately afterwards having taken the fort of Kehl, he advanced sword in hand to set fire to the bridge of Strasburg, over which that town, which was still free, had so many times allowed the Imperial arms to pass. Thus did Marshal de Créqui make amends for one day's recklessness with a series of successes gained by cautiousness, and had he lived he would have perhaps acquired a reputation equal to that of Turenne.

The Prince of Orange was no more successful in Flanders than the Duke of Lorraine in Germany; he was not only obliged to raise the sieges of Maestricht and Charleroi, but, after allowing Condé, Bouchain and Valenciennes to fall into the hands of Louis XIV., he was defeated on 11 April, 1677, in the Battle of Mont-Cassel by Monseigneur, while endeavouring to relieve Saint-Omer. The Marshals de Luxembourg and d'Humières were in command of the army under Monsieur. It is claimed that a mistake on the part of the Prince of Orange, and a skilful movement on that of Luxembourg, decided the victory. Monsieur charged with a bravery and presence of mind unexpected in an effeminate prince. Never was there a better example that courage is far from being incompatible with effeminacy. This prince, who frequently dressed like a woman, and indeed had the disposition of one, now acted as a captain and a soldier. His brother, the king, seemed to be jealous of his glory. He said but little to him about his victory. He did not even go to see the field of battle, although he was in the vicinity. Some of the servants of Monsieur, more discerning than the rest, predicted then that he would not again be placed in command of an army, and they were not mistaken.

The successes of Louis XIV. in this war were not confined to the capture of many towns and the winning of numerous battles in Flanders and Germany. The Count of Schomberg and Marshal de Navailles also beat the Spaniards at Lampourdan, at the foot of the Pyrenees: and the Spaniards were attacked even in Sicily.

Sicily, since the time of the tyrants of Syracuse, under whom at any rate she had counted for something in the world, has always been subject to foreign nations, the slaves in turn of the Romans, Vandals, Arabs and Normans, and the vassals of the Pope, the French, the Germans and the Spaniards—nearly always hating their masters and rebelling against them, but not making any real efforts worthy of freedom, and continually stirring up sedition with the only result of changing their masters.

The magistrates of Messina had recently begun a civil war against their rulers and called upon France for help, but a Spanish fleet blockaded the port, and they were reduced to extremes of famine.

The Chevalier de Valbelle first arrived on the scene with a few frigates, and broke through the Spanish fleet, bringing food, arms and troops to Messina. After him came the Duke de Vivonne with seven warships of sixty cannon, two of eighty and several fire-ships; he defeated the enemy's fleet on 9 February, 1676, and made a victorious entry into Messina.

In order to defend Sicily, Spain was obliged to implore the help of her former enemies, the Dutch, still looked upon as the masters of the seas. Ruyter came to her aid from the Zuyder Zee, passed the straits and added twenty-three large warships to the twenty Spanish ships.

Upon this the French, who allied with the English had

been unable to beat the fleets of Holland, were now victorious over the united fleets of Holland and Spain (8 January, 1676). The Duke de Vivonne, obliged to remain in Messina to hold in check the people who were already discontented with their defenders, surrendered the command of this battle to Duquesne, a lieutenant-general of the fleet, and a man as remarkable as Ruyter; one like him, moreover, who had risen to command by merit alone, but had never before commanded a fleet, and was indeed better known as a privateer than as a general. But indeed a man who has genius for his calling and a power of command finds no difficulty in passing rapidly from little things to great.

Duquesne showed himself to be a great admiral, even when opposed to Ruyter. To secure a slight advantage over the Dutch admiral was in itself sufficient proof. He engaged in a second naval battle with the two enemy fleets off Agosta on 12 March, 1676. Wounded in this action Ruyter there ended his glorious career. He is one of the men whose memory is still greatly revered in Holland. He had begun his career as a valet and a cabin-boy, and was respected but the more for it. The name of the Princes of Nassau is not above his own. The Council of Spain gave him the title and letters-patent of Duke, a strange and impertinent honour for a republican. The letters came only after his death, and his children, worthy of their father, refused a title which is so coveted in our monarchies, but which must ever give place to the name of a good citizen.

Louis XIV. had sufficient greatness of soul to be grieved at his death. It was pointed out to him that he was rid of a dangerous enemy. He replied, " That one could not help being moved at the death of a great man."

For a third time, Duquesne, the Ruyter of France, attacked the two fleets after the death of the Dutch admiral. He sent some to the bottom, burnt others and captured a few of their ships. Marshal the Duke de Vivonne was the commander-in-chief in this battle; but Duquesne was, nevertheless, responsible for the victory. Europe was amazed to see France become in so short a time as formidable on sea as she was on land; although it is true that such arms and victories served but to spread alarm among the other nations.

The King of England, who had entered the war in the interests of France, was now bent on leaguing himself with the Prince of Orange, who had just married his niece. Moreover, the triumphs of Sicily had been bought at too dear a price. The French accordingly evacuated Messina on 8 April, 1678, at the very moment when it was thought that they were about to conquer the whole island. Louis XIV. was freely reproached for having entered upon undertakings in this war which were not carried through, and for having abandoned Messina as he did Holland, after gaining useless victories.

Nevertheless, he was assuredly formidable in the extreme, if his only misfortune were to be unable to retain all his conquests. He pressed his enemies from one end of Europe to the other. The Sicilian war had cost him much less than it had Spain, who was now exhausted and defeated in every part. He stirred up fresh enemies against the House of Austria. He fomented troubles in Hungary, and his ambassadors at the Ottoman Court urged her to make war on Germany, although for appearance' sake he might still find it necessary to send the Empire help against the Turks. Singlehanded he overwhelmed all his enemies. For at that time, Sweden, his only ally, was engaged in an unsuccessful war with the Elector of Brandenburg. The Elector was father of the first King of Prussia, and was beginning to acquire for his country a respect which has since steadily increased; about this time he captured Pomerania from the Swedish.

It is curious that during this war overt negotiations for peace were almost continuously being made; first at Cologne through the fruitless mediation of Sweden, later at Nimeguen at the instance of England. The mediation of England was indeed a ceremony almost as idle as had been the arbitration of the Pope at the treaty of Aix-la-Chapelle. Louis XIV. was in fact the only arbiter. On 9 April, 1678, he proposed certain conditions in the midst of his conquests, and gave his enemies until 10 May to accept them. He afterwards allowed an extension of six weeks to the United Provinces, who humbly asked for the time to be extended.

His ambition no longer turned towards Holland. The Republic had been fortunate or skilful enough to appear nothing more than an auxiliary in a war designed to bring about his ruin. The Empire and Spain, once minor antagonists, had ended by being the principal parties concerned.

Louis in his terms of peace encouraged Dutch trade; he restored Maestricht, and gave back to the Spanish several towns, which would serve as a barrier against the Netherlands; these included Charleroi, Courtrai, Oudenarde, Ath, Ghent, Limburg; but he retained Bouchain, Condé, Ypres, Valenciennes, Cambrai, Maubeuge, Aire, Saint-Omer, Cassel, Charlemont, Poperinghe, Bailleul, etc.; which constituted a good part of Flanders. He also kept Franche-Comté, which he had twice conquered, and these two provinces represented a fairly substantial gain from the war.

He wanted only Freiburg or Philippsburg in Germany, and left the choice to the Emperor. He restored the two brothers Fürstenberg to the see of Strasburg and their estates; they had been deprived of the latter by the Emperor, and one of them had been cast into prison.

He stoutly defended his unfortunate ally, Sweden, against the King of Denmark and the Elector of Brandenburg. He required Denmark to restore all that she had taken from Sweden, reduce passage tolls in the Baltic, and restore his estates to the Duke of Holstein; Brandenburg was to surrender Pomerania which she had conquered, and the treaties of Westphalia were to be rigorously observed. His will was law from one end of Europe to the other. It was in vain that the Elector of Brandenburg wrote him a most humble letter, addressing him according to custom as *Monseigneur*, imploring him to allow him to retain his conquests, and assuring him of his devotion and loyalty; his submissions were as futile as his resistance, and the conqueror of Sweden was obliged to surrender all his conquests.

Upon this, French ambassadors refused to treat with the electors. The Elector of Brandenburg offered every inducement to persuade the Count, afterwards Marshal, d'Estrades, ambassador to the United Provinces, to treat with him at Clèves. The king would not permit a man who represented him to give place to an elector, and the Count d'Estrades was not able to come to terms.

Charles V. had placed the grandees of Spain and the electors on an equal footing: a footing which the peers of France have accordingly claimed. It may be seen to what extent things have altered at the present day, since at the Imperial diets ambassadors of the electors are treated in the same way as those of kings.

As regards Lorraine he offered to restore the new duke, Charles V.; but he was determined to remain master of Nancy and of all the great highways.

These terms were laid down with the arrogance of a conqueror; nevertheless they were not so outrageous as to render his enemies desperate and force them to reunite against him in a final effort: he spoke to Europe as a master, but at the same time acted as a statesman.

He succeeded in sowing jealousy among the allies at the conference of Nimeguen. The Dutch hastened to sign peace, in spite of the Prince of Orange, who wanted to continue the war at whatever cost: they said that Spain was not strong enough to help them should they refuse to sign.

Seeing that Holland had accepted terms of peace, Spain also signed, declaring that the Empire had not made sufficient efforts in the common cause.

Finally, Germany, abandoned by Holland and Spain, was the last to sign, giving up Freiburg, and confirming the treaties of Westphalia.

None of the conditions laid down by Louis XIV. was altered. His enemies would have bluffed in vain had they submitted better terms to cloak their weakness: Europe received not only laws but peace from Louis. The Duke of Lorraine alone dared to refuse a treaty which seemed to him too odious; preferring to be a wandering prince within the Empire than a sovereign with neither power nor dignity in his own estates, he trusted to time and courage to restore his fortunes.

(10 August, 1678) While the conferences proceeded at Nimeguen and four days after the plenipotentiaries of France and Holland had signed the peace, the Prince of Orange showed himself to be a most dangerous enemy. Marshal de Luxembourg, who was blockading Mons, had just received news of peace. He remained quietly at the village of Saint-Denys and was dining with the commissary of the army, when suddenly, on 14 August, the Prince of Orange fell upon his flank, broke through with all his forces and engaged him in a long, bloody and stubborn fight, from which with good reason he expected a signal victory; for not only was he on the attack, which is an advantage, but he was attacking troops who relying on the treaty were taking their rest. Marshal de Luxembourg resisted with great difficulty, and if there were any advantage in this battle, it was on the side of the Prince of Orange, since his infantry remained masters of the ground where they had fought.

If ambitious men regarded the lives of other men as of any consequence, the Prince of Orange would never have engaged

in this battle. There can be no doubt that he knew that peace
was signed, and that the peace was advantageous to his
country; yet he risked his life and the lives of several thousands of men as the first fruits of a general peace which he
could not have prevented even by beating the French. The
battle, noteworthy for its inhumanity as for its greatness, and
at that time more admired than censured, produced no new
article of peace, and fruitless as it was, it cost the lives of
two thousand French and as many of the enemy. This peace
is a good example of how contradictory are the designs of
men and their subsequent results. Holland, against whom
alone the war had been waged and who should have been
ruined, lost nothing ; indeed she gained a barrier ; all the
other powers who had guaranteed her from annihilation
lost something.

The king was at this time at the height of his greatness.
Victorious since he had begun to reign, having besieged no
place which he had not taken, superior in every way to his
united enemies, for six years the terror of Europe and at
last her arbitrator and peacemaker, he now added Franche-
Comté, Dunkirk and half Flanders to his possessions; moreover, and he might well count this the greatest of his
advantages, he was the king of a nation happy in itself
and the model of all others.

Some time afterwards, in 1680, the Council of Paris conferred the title of *Great* upon him with due solemnity and
decreed that henceforth the title alone should be used
in all public records. Since 1673 a few medals had been struck
bearing his cognomen. Europe, though jealous, made no protest against such honours. Nevertheless the name of *Louis-
Quatorze* has prevailed in the public mind over that of *the
Great*. Custom is all-powerful: Henri, justly surnamed *the
Great* after his death, is commonly known as *Henri-Quatre*,
and the name speaks loudly enough. The Prince de Condé is
always called *the great Condé*, not merely on account of his
heroic deeds, but because it is easier to distinguish him by
that surname from the other princes of the same name. Had
he been called *Condé the Great*, the title would not have clung
to him. We speak of *the great Corneille* to distinguish him from
his brother. We do not say *the great* Virgil, nor *the great* Homer,
nor *the great* Tasso. *Alexander the Great* has come to be known
as Alexander, and Cæsar is never called *the Great*. Charles V.,
whose career was more brilliant than that of Louis XIV., has

never had the title of *great*, and the title survives in Charlemagne only as a proper name. Posterity has no use for titles; the name of a man who has done great deeds inspires more reverence than any epithet.

CHAPTER XIV

CAPTURE OF STRASBOURG. BOMBARDMENT OF ALGIERS. SURRENDER OF GENOA. EMBASSY FROM SIAM. THE POPE DEFIED AT ROME. ELECTORATE OF COLOGNE DISPUTED

THE ambitions of Louis XIV. were not restrained by the general peace. While the Empire, Spain and Holland all demobilised their special forces, Louis retained his; he made of peace a nursery of conquests (1680); he was so sure of his power that he set up at Metz and Brisach tribunals for the purpose of uniting under his crown all lands, which might once have been under the dependency of Alsace or the Trois-Évêchés, but which from time immemorial had passed into other hands. Many of the sovereigns of the Empire, the Elector Palatine, even the King of Spain, who owned some small estates in these countries, and the King of Sweden, as Duké des Deux-Ponts, were summoned before these tribunals to do homage to the King of France or to suffer the confiscation of their estates. Since the time of Charlemagne no prince had thus been seen to act as the lord and judge of sovereigns, and to conquer countries by decrees of law.

The Elector Palatine and the Elector of Trèves were deprived of the seigniories of Falkenburg, Germersheim, Velden and others. In vain they complained to the Imperial Assembly at Ratisbon, which confined itself to making protests.

The king was not satisfied with possessing the prefecture of the ten free towns of Alsace with the same privileges as the Emperors had possessed; already in these towns they no longer dared to speak of liberty. Strasbourg remained a great and wealthy city, mistress of the Rhine, by reason of her bridge which spanned that river; she formed in herself a powerful republic, famed for her arsenal, which contained nine hundred pieces of cannon.

Louvois had long planned to obtain possession of it for

his master. Bribery, intrigue, terrorism, which had opened the gates of so many towns to him, were used to bring about an entry into Strasbourg on 30 September, 1681. The magistrates were won over. The people were dismayed to see suddenly twenty thousand French around the ramparts; the forts which protected them on the side of the Rhine were assaulted and taken in a moment; Louvois was at the gates, and the burgomasters were speaking of surrendering; the lamentations and despair of the citizens, eager of freedom, were powerless to prevent the magistrates from proposing a treaty of surrender or Louvois from taking possession of the city within the short space of twenty-four hours. Vauban later made of it, by the fortifications which still surround it, the strongest fortress in France.

The king no longer treated Spain with any consideration; in the Netherlands he demanded the town of Alost, together with the land surrounding it, which, he said, his ministers had forgotten to include in the terms of peace, and owing to the delays of Spain he blockaded the town of Luxembourg (1682).

At the same time he bought, in 1681, the strong town of Casal from a petty Prince Duke of Mantua, who would have sold the whole of his estates to provide for his pleasures.

The fears of Europe were reawakened on seeing Louis XIV. extending his power on all sides and acquiring in time of peace more than his ten predecessors on the throne had gained by their wars. The Empire, Holland, and even Sweden, offended with the king, contracted a treaty of alliance. England was threatening, Spain eager for war, and the Prince of Orange busy pulling every string, but no power was bold enough to strike the first blow.

Feared everywhere as he was, the king's sole aim was to heighten those fears. By 1680 he had increased his navy beyond the hopes of the French and the fears of Europe; he now had sixty thousand sailors.

A discipline which was as severe as that of the army kept these rough men to their duty. England and Holland, maritime powers though they were, had neither so many sailors nor such good discipline. Companies of cadets in frontier towns and marine-guards in the ports were established; they were formed of young men who were taught the whole art of their profession by instructors paid out of public funds.

On the Mediterranean the port of Toulon was constructed

at immense cost to hold a hundred ships of war, together with a splendid arsenal and powder-magazine. On the Atlantic the port of Brest was formed on the same grand scale. Dunkirk and Hâvre-de-Grace were filled with ships, and at Rochefort nature herself was brought under subjection.

At last the king had more than a hundred ships of the line, several of which carried a hundred cannon and some more. They did not remain idle in port. His squadrons, under the command of Duquesne, swept the seas, which were infested by the corsairs of Tripoli and Algiers. He took vengeance on Algiers by the aid of a new invention, which owed its discovery to the pains he had himself taken to inspire every genius of the time. This deadly but wonderful invention was known as the bomb-ship, and by it maritime towns could be reduced to ashes. A young man named Bernard Renaud—and known as *little Renaud*—who, without ever having served on board ship was nevertheless an excellent sailor by sheer force of genius, had attracted the attention of Colbert, who had an eye for hidden merit: he had often summoned him to the naval council, even in the presence of the king, and it was owing to Renaud's industry and knowledge that for some short time a more exact and easy method of building ships had been practised. He ventured to propose in council that Algiers should be bombarded by a fleet, but the idea of mortar-pieces being placed anywhere but on solid land seemed inconceivable, and the proposal was rejected. Renaud endured the opposition and jeers which every inventor must expect; but his persistence, and an eloquence which men keenly impressed with their invention usually possess, determined the king to permit the innovation to be tried.

Renaud built five ships of smaller size than usual, but of thicker wood, and having only one false deck in the bottom of the hold, in which hollows were formed and in which the mortars were placed. He set out with this vessel under the orders of the aged Duquesne, who was in command of the undertaking, and did not expect that it would be successful. Duquesne and the Algerians alike were amazed at the effect of the bombs (28 October, 1681), part of the town being actually demolished and burnt: but this invention, soon copied by other nations, served but to increase the sum of human calamities and was more than once disastrous to France—the country in which it had been invented.

This improvement of the navy within a few short years must be attributed to the industry of Colbert. Louvois meanwhile fortified over a hundred citadels in the most perfect manner. In addition, Hüningen was built, Saarlouis, the fortresses of Strasbourg, Mont-Royal, etc., and while the kingdom was being thus strengthened without, at home the arts were honoured, food was plenteous, and pleasure was rife. Foreigners flocked in crowds to see the wonders of Louis XIV.'s court. His name penetrated to every nation of the world.

His prosperity and glory were but the more enhanced by the weakness of most other kings and the unhappiness of their peoples. The Emperor Leopold lived in fear of the revolted Hungarians, and in still greater fear of the Turks, who, at the invitation of the Hungarians, were preparing to overrun Germany. The policy of Louis XIV. was to persecute Protestants in France, since he thought it well to put them in a position where they could not injure him: but he secretly protected the Protestant Hungarian rebels who could be of service to him. Prior to the peace of Nimeguen his ambassador at the Ottoman Court had urged the arming of the Turks. The Sultan singularly enough nearly always waited until the Emperor was at peace before declaring war against him. He did not make war on Hungary until 1682, and in the following year the Ottoman army (said now to be more than two hundred thousand strong and strengthened more-over by Hungarian troops), finding neither fortified towns in their line of march such as France possessed, nor any army corps capable of checking their progress, advanced right up to the gates of Vienna, having laid waste the whole of the country behind them.

The Emperor Leopold hurriedly left the city on the approach of the Turks and withdrew first to Linz, but on hearing that they had invested Vienna, his only action was to retreat still farther to Passau, leaving the Duke of Lor-raine at the head of a small army, which had already been somewhat harried by the Turks in their advance, to uphold as he could the fortunes of the Empire.

No one doubted but that the Grand Vizier, Kara Mustapha, in command of the Ottoman army, would soon take pos-session of Vienna, a poorly fortified town, which had been abandoned by her ruler, though defended, it is true, by a garrison which could not have been less than sixteen thousand men, though its effective strength did not exceed eight thousand. It seemed the eve of a terrible revolution.

Louis XIV. hoped that Germany, with her lands laid waste by the Turks, and with a ruler whose flight but increased the general terror, would be obliged to seek the protection of France, as seemed very probable. He had consequently an army on the frontiers of the Empire ready to defend it against the very Turks whom his previous negotiations had brought there: by this means he could become the defender of the Empire, and make his own son King of the Romans.

He had first combined such generous overtures with his political schemes from the moment that the Turks had menaced Austria; not that he had again sent help to the Emperor, but he had declared that he would not attack the Netherlands, and had thus left the Spanish branch of the House of Austria free to assist the German branch, which was on the point of succumbing. As the price of such inaction he asked for satisfaction on several doubtful points in the Treaty of Nimeguen, and especially with regard to the lands surrounding Alost which had through negligence not been included in the treaty. He raised the blockade of Luxembourg in 1682 without waiting for satisfaction and abstained from hostilities for a whole year. This magnanimity at length belied itself during the siege of Vienna. The Council of Spain, so far from appeasing him, provoked him; and Louis again took up arms in the Netherlands at the very moment that Vienna was about to fall; this was at the beginning of September; but, contrary to all expectations, Vienna was saved. The presumption of the Grand Vizier, his indolence, his brutal contempt for the Christians, his ignorance and his dilatoriness were his downfall, and there was need of all these faults in their most extreme form for Vienna to avoid being taken. John Sobieski, King of Poland, had time to come up, and aided by the Duke of Lorraine, he had but to appear before the Ottoman hosts to rout them (12 September, 1683). The Emperor returned to his capital with the regret of having quitted it. He re-entered the city at the moment that his deliverer was leaving the church where the *Te Deum* had been sung and the preacher had taken as his text: "There was a man sent from God, called John"—words which Pope Pius V. had already applied to Don John of Austria, after the victory of Lepanto. That which appears new is often but a repetition. The Emperor was at once triumphant and humiliated. The King of France, having no longer to move carefully, bombarded Luxembourg. In November 1683 he captured Courtrai and Dixmude in Flanders. He took Trèves and destroyed its fortifications; all this was done, so it was said, to carry out the spirit of the treaties of Nimeguen. The Empire and Spain were actually negotiating with him at Ratisbon while he was taking their towns; the peace of Nimeguen thus infringed was changed in August 1684 to a truce of twenty years, by which the king kept the town of Luxembourg and its principality which he had just taken.

(April 1684) He was still more feared on the coasts of Africa, where, before his time, the French had been known only as slaves on the occasion of their capture by the barbarian inhabitants.

After being twice bombarded, Algiers sent delegates to sue for pardon and make peace; they set free all Christian slaves, and, in addition, paid over large sums of money—the greatest punishment that pirates can know.

Tunis and Tripoli made similar submissions. It is interesting to note that when Damfreville, the captain of the ship, arrived at Algiers to set free all Christian slaves in the name of the King of France, he found among them a number of English, who, on being taken on board, persisted in maintaining that it was out of regard for the King of England that they were set at liberty. Upon this the French captain summoned the Algerian slave-masters, and had the English put on shore again. "These men," he said, "claim that they have been set free in the name of *their* king, so that my sovereign cannot take the liberty of offering them his protection; I return them to you; it is for you to know what you owe to the King of England." The English were immediately clapped into irons. English pride, the weakness of Charles II.'s government, and the respect of other nations for Louis XIV.—all are clearly shown by this incident.

So great was this universal respect that fresh honours were bestowed on his ambassador at the Ottoman Court—that of the sofa in particular: this, at the very time that he was humiliating the African nations who are under the protection of the Sultan.

Genoa humbled itself before him still more than Algiers: that republic had sold powder and bombs to the Algerians, and was building four galleys for the service of Spain. The

king sent orders by his envoy, Saint-Olon, one of his gentlemen-in-waiting, forbidding them to launch the galleys, and
threatened them with swift punishment if they did not
carry out his wishes. The Genoese, exasperated by this
attack on their liberty and counting too much on the assistance of Spain, gave him no satisfaction. Immediately forty
large ships, twenty galleys, ten bombing ships and several
frigates set sail from the port of Toulon. Seignelai, the new
naval secretary, who, on the advice of his father, the famous
Colbert, had already seen service in this department before
his father's death, was himself on board. This young man,
full of ambition, courage, spirit and activity, wished to be
at the same time warrior and minister; eager for every kind
of glory, zealous in everything he undertook, he united
pleasure and duty without impairing the latter. The aged
Duquesne was in command of the ships, the Duke de Mortemar of the galleys; but both were followers of the secretary
of state. They arrived before Genoa; the ten bombing ships
hurled fourteen thousand bombs into the city (17 March,
1684), and reduced to ashes many of those marble buildings
which had earned for the city the name of *Genoa the superb*.
Fourteen thousand soldiers landed, advanced to the gates,
and burnt the suburb of San Pietro d'Arena. Finally, on
22 February, 1685, submission had become the only means
of preventing the total destruction of the city.

The king ordered the doge of Genoa and four of the chief
senators to come and implore his forgiveness at his palace
of Versailles; and, fearing that the Genoese would evade
giving him this satisfaction and deprive him in some measure
of his glory, he ordered that the doge who came to ask for
pardon should continue in his office, in spite of the immutable
law of Genoa by which a doge who is absent for one moment
from the city loses his dignity.

Imperiale Lescaro, doge of Genoa, with senators Lomellino,
Garibaldi, Durazzo and Salvago, came to Versailles to do all
that the king demanded of them. The doge, in ceremonial
dress, wearing a cap of red velvet, which he frequently doffed,
was the spokesman; his speech and tokens of submission
were dictated by Seignelai. The king heard him, seated and
with head covered; but uniting as always courtesy with
dignity, he treated Lescaro and the senators with as much
kindness as pomp. The ministers Louvois, Croissi and Seignelai, however, made them feel the pride of France. Thus the

doge remarked: "The king banishes liberty from our hearts by the manner in which he receives us; but his ministers restore it to us." This doge was a man of great wit. His reply to the Marquis de Seignelai when asked what he found most remarkable at Versailles is well known. "*To find myself there*," he said.

(1684) Louis' extreme fondness for glitter and pomp was still further indulged by the embassy that he received from Siam, a country that till then had been unaware of France's existence. By one of those singular occurrences which prove the superiority of European over other nations, it had happened that a Greek, son of a tavern-keeper in Cephalonia, Constantine Phaulkon by name, had become *Barcalon*, that is to say, prime minister or grand vizier of the Kingdom of Siam. This man, eager to consolidate his position and rise still higher and needing the assistance of foreigners, had yet not ventured to confide in either the English or the Dutch, since they are too dangerous neighbours in the Indies. The French had, however, recently established settlements on the coasts of Coromandel and the reputation of their king had thus penetrated to the ends of Asia. Constantine thought Louis XIV. likely to be flattered by homage which came from such a distance and so unexpectedly. Religion, the resort of politics from Siam to Paris, was also made to serve his designs. In the name of his master, the King of Siam, he despatched a solemn embassy with sumptuous gifts to Louis XIV., giving him to understand that the Indian monarch, captivated by his renown, was desirous of making a treaty of commerce with none other nation than the French, and that he was not far from becoming a Christian. The king was induced by such flattery of his greatness and the deference paid to his religion, to send two ambassadors and six Jesuits to the King of Siam, adding later eight hundred soldiers and their officers; but the pomp and show occasioned by this Siamese embassy was the only tangible result. Constantine perished four years afterwards, the victim of his own ambition; the few French who remained with him were massacred, others were compelled to fly, and his widow, from being on the point of becoming queen, was condemned by the King of Siam's successor to serve in the royal kitchens, an occupation for which she was eminently fitted.

The thirst for glory which led Louis XIV. to outrival other kings in every detail was also displayed in the haughti-

ness which he affected towards the Court of Rome. Odescalchi, Innocent XI., the son of a Milanese banker, occupied
the papal throne. A virtuous man, a wise pontiff, a poor
theologian, but a courageous, resolute and magnificent
prince, he aided the Empire and Poland against the Turks
with his own money and the Venetians with his galleys. He
condemned the conduct of Louis XIV. in uniting with the
Turks against the Christians. It was thought surprising that
a Pope should so eagerly take the part of Emperors who
style themselves Kings of the Romans, and who, if they
could, would rule in Rome; but Odescalchi was born under
the Austrian rule, and had waged two campaigns with the
Milanese troops. Men are ruled by habit and temperament.
His pride was irritated by that of Louis, who, for his part,
took every opportunity of mortifying him that a King of
France can take while still remaining in communion with
him. There had long existed at Rome an abuse which was
difficult to eradicate, since it rested on a point of honour
upon which all the Catholic monarchs prided themselves.
Their ambassadors at Rome extended the rights of franchise
and sanctuary belonging to their houses to a very great
distance, the district being known as a *quarter*: and such
claims, continuously upheld, converted the half of Rome into
a safe asylum for every manner of crime. There was another
abuse by which all who entered Rome under the name of
an ambassador escaped paying the entrance toll. Trade
suffered by it, and the public treasury was impoverished.

At length Innocent XI. obtained promises from the
Emperor, the King of Spain, the King of Poland and the
new King of England, James II., a Catholic monarch, that
they would forgo these odious rights. The nuncio Ranucci
proposed to Louis XIV. that like other monarchs he should
take his part in ensuring the peace and good order of Rome.
Louis, much offended with the Pope, replied, "That he had
never ruled his conduct on the example of others, and it
was for him to set the example." He despatched the Marquis
de Lavardin with an embassy to Rome to defy the Pope.
On 16 November, 1687, in spite of the pontiff's interdiction,
Lavardin entered Rome, escorted by four hundred marine
guards, four hundred volunteer officers and two hundred
liveried men, all in arms. He took possession of his palace,
his quarters and the church of Saint-Louis, posted sentinels
and patrolled the place as though it had been a fortress.

The Pope is the only sovereign to whom such an embassy could be sent, for the superiority that he affects over the crowned heads of Europe makes them eager to humiliate him, and the weakness of his position allows him to be insulted with impunity. All that Innocent XI. could do in opposition to the Marquis de Lavardin was to make use of the worn-out weapon of excommunication, which is no longer considered formidable at Rome any more than anywhere else, but is still employed as an ancient formula, just as the soldiers of the Pope are armed only as a matter of form. Cardinal d'Estrées, a man of spirit, but frequently an unfortunate negotiator, was at that time France's *chargé d'affaires* at Rome. Having often had occasion to see the Marquis de Lavardin, he could not afterwards be admitted to an audience of the Pope without receiving absolution; it was in vain that he excused himself. Innocent XI. insisted upon granting it him so as to preserve that imaginary authority which is founded upon such customs.

With the same arrogance and as always with an underlying political motive, Louis wished to endow Cologne with an Elector. Eager to divide the Empire as to defeat it, he proposed appointing to this electorate Cardinal de Fürstenberg, Bishop of Strasbourg, his tool and the dupe of his policy, a deadly enemy of the Emperor, who had imprisoned him in the last war as a German who had sold himself to France.

The Chapter of Cologne, like all other chapters in Germany, has the right to nominate its own bishop who thereby becomes Elector. The holder of this see, Ferdinand of Bavaria, once the ally and now, like so many other princes, the enemy of the king, was ill and on the point of death. The king's bribes, which were suitably distributed among the canons, and intrigues and promises, succeeded in obtaining the election of Cardinal de Fürstenberg as coadjutor, and on the death of the prince he was again elected by a majority of votes. The Pope, by the terms of the Germanic concordat, has the right of conferring the bishopric on the elected party, and the Emperor that of sanctioning the electorate. The Emperor and Pope Innocent XI., convinced that to allow Fürstenberg to remain on the electoral throne would be to place Louis XIV. upon it, united to give this principality to the young Prince of Bavaria, brother of the dead Ferdinand. (October 1688) The king revenged himself on the Pope by seizing Avignon, and prepared to make war on the Emperor.

At the same time he disquieted the Elector Palatine with regard to the rights of *Madame*, the Palatine Princess, the second wife of Monsieur, rights which she had renounced by her marriage contract. The war against Spain in 1667 for the rights of Maria Theresa in spite of a similar renunciation, plainly shows that contracts are binding upon individuals, but not upon nations. In this manner the king while at the height of his greatness estranged, despoiled or humiliated practically every prince in Europe; it was not surprising that nearly all united against him.

CHAPTER XV

KING JAMES DETHRONED BY HIS SON-IN-LAW, WILLIAM III, AND SHELTERED BY LOUIS XIV

More ambitious than Louis XIV., the Prince of Orange had planned vast schemes which might seem fantastic in a Dutch stadtholder, but which were justified by his ability and courage. He aimed at humbling the King of France and dethroning the King of England. He had no difficulty in leaguing Europe little by little against France. The Emperor and a part of the Empire, Holland and the Duke of Lorraine had entered into a secret alliance at Augsburg in 1687: later Spain and Savoy joined these powers. The Pope, without definitely allying himself with them, encouraged them all by his intrigues, and Venice supported them without openly declaring herself. All the Italian princes were for them. In the North, Sweden was at that time on the side of the Imperialists and Denmark was a futile ally of France. More than five hundred thousand Protestants, flying from the persecution of Louis, took with them out of France at once their industry and the hatred they bore the king, and thus constituted new enemies, who travelled all over Europe stirring up nations who were already anxious for war. (An account of this flight will be found in the chapter on religion.) The king was surrounded by enemies on all sides and had no other friend but King James of England.

James, the successor of his brother, Charles II., was like him a Catholic, but Charles had only consented to die a Catholic in order to please his mistress and his brother; in reality his religion was nothing more than mere deism; his extreme indifference to all disputes which commonly divide men, had contributed not a little to his reigning peacefully in England. James, on the other hand, attached from his youth to the Roman community, united the spirit of party and religious ardour to his faith. Had he been a Mahommedan or a follower of Confucius the English would never have disturbed his reign; but he was determined to re-establish Catholicism within his kingdom, a religion regarded with abhorrence by these republican royalists as the religion of slavery.

It is sometimes an easy matter to establish a religion in a country: Constantine, Clovis, Gustavus Vasa, and Queen Elizabeth, each without danger and by different means introduced a new religion; but to effect such changes two things are entirely necessary, a profound knowledge of policy and favourable conditions; James was lacking in both. It hurt his pride to see so many kings in Europe absolute: that the monarchs of Sweden and Denmark were becoming so, and that, in short, out of the whole world Poland and England alone remained where the liberty of the people existed side by side with royalty. Louis XIV. encouraged him to become an absolute monarch, and the Jesuits urged him to restore their religion together with their good name. He undertook the task so disastrously that he succeeded in shocking all his subjects. He acted at the start as though he had already achieved what he had set out to do; he publicly received a nuncio of the Pope at his court, together with Jesuits and Capuchins; imprisoned seven Anglican bishops whom he might have won over; deprived the city of London of her privileges, when he should rather have increased those she already possessed; arrogantly rescinded laws which he should have secretly undermined: in a word, behaved so indiscreetly, that the cardinals at Rome declared in jest "that he ought to be excommunicated, as he bade fair to lose the remnant of Catholicism which still remained in England." Innocent XI. anticipated that nothing would come of James's activities and steadily refused his demand of a cardinal's hat for his confessor, the Jesuit Peters. This Jesuit was an over-jealous schemer, consumed with the ambition of becoming cardinal and primate of England, who urged his master to the precipice. The chief men of the state assembled secretly to thwart the king's designs and sent a deputation to the Prince of Orange. Their plot was hatched with such caution and secrecy that the suspicions of the court were never aroused.

The Prince of Orange fitted out a fleet large enough to carry fourteen or fifteen thousand men. This prince was nothing more than a famous individual with an income hardly exceeding five hundred thousand florins, but his policy was so well-judged that money, the fleet and the hearts of the Netherlanders were all at his disposal. By his skilful policy he was actually king in Holland, while James had ceased to be so in England by his rashness. It was announced that this armed fleet was to be employed against France, and the secret was kept by more than two hundred persons. Barillon, the French ambassador in London, a man of pleasure, better acquainted with the intrigues of James's mistresses than with those of Europe, was duped at once. Louis was not deceived; he offered help to his ally who at first confidently refused it, but afterwards demanded it, when it was too late and the fleet of his son-in-law, the Prince of Orange, had already set sail. All resources failed, and not least the resources of his own spirit.

In October 1688 he wrote vainly to the Emperor Leopold, who replied: "What has happened to you is only what we had already foretold." He relied on his fleet, but it allowed the enemy's ships to pass through. He could at least defend himself on land; he had an army of twenty thousand men, and had he led them into battle without giving them time for reflection they would probably have been victorious; but he allowed them time to consider on which side they should fight. Several general officers deserted him; among them was the famous Churchill, as fateful afterwards to Louis as he was to James, and renowned as the Duke of Marlborough. He was the favourite and the tool of James, the brother of his mistress, and a lieutenant-general in his army; nevertheless, he deserted him and went over to the camp of the Prince of Orange. The Prince of Denmark, James's son-in-law, and lastly, his own daughter, the Princess Anne, abandoned him.

At length, finding himself attacked and pursued by one of his sons-in-law and abandoned by the other, opposed by his two daughters and his own friends, hated even by those subjects who still remained loyal to the throne, he gave up all hope of victory: flight, the last resource of a beaten monarch, was the course he took without striking a blow. Finally, having been stopped in his flight by the populace and roughly handled by them, led back to London and forced to receive with calmness the orders of the Prince of Orange in his own palace, to see his guard replaced by that of the prince without a shot being fired, driven from his home, and kept a prisoner at Rochester, he at last made use of the liberty which was given to him to forsake his kingdom and seek a refuge in France.

It was an era of veritable liberty in England. The nation represented by its parliament fixed the limits, so long disputed, of the rights of king and people, and having prescribed the terms on which the Prince of Orange would have to reign, they chose him for their king, jointly with his wife, Mary, daughter of King James. Henceforth he was known in the greater part of Europe under no other name than that of William III., lawful King of England and liberator of the nation. But in France he was regarded only as the Prince of Orange, usurper of the kingdom of his father-in-law.

In January 1689 the fugitive king, accompanied by his wife, a daughter of a Duke of Modena, and the Prince of Wales as yet an infant, came to crave protection of Louis XIV. The Queen of England, who arrived before her husband, was astonished at the splendour that surrounded the King of France, at the magnificent prodigality of Versailles, and above all at the manner in which she was received. The king went before her as far as Chatou. "I am rendering you but a sad service, Madame," he said, "but I hope very soon to render you greater ones of happier augury." These were his very words. He conducted her to the Castle of Saint-Germain, where she was waited on as though she had been the Queen of France; she was supplied with everything requisite to comfort and luxury, with presents of all kinds of silver, gold, plate, jewellery and stuffs.

Among all these gifts there was a purse of ten thousand golden louis on her dressing-table. The same attentions were paid her husband who arrived the day after. Six hundred thousand francs were settled on him annually for the maintenance of his household, besides the innumerable presents which were made him. He was attended by royal officers and guards. This reception was but a small affair compared with the preparations made for restoring him to his throne. Never had Louis appeared to greater advantage, nor James to less. The inhabitants of courts and cities who decide men's reputations had little esteem for him. He saw few people

but Jesuits. He went to visit them in Paris in the Rue Saint-
Antoine. He told them that he was himself a Jesuit; and the
most remarkable thing is that it was true. While still Duke of
York he had been admitted to this Order with certain ceremonies by four English Jesuits. Such baseness in a prince,
together with the way in which he had lost his crown, rendered
him so contemptible that the courtiers' daily amusement
was to compose songs about him. Driven from England he
was mocked in France. He gained no favour for being a
Catholic. The Archbishop of Rheims, brother of Louvois,
loudly exclaimed in his antechamber at Saint - Germain:
"There goes a simpleton who has lost three kingdoms for a
Mass." From Rome he received only indulgence and pleasantries. In short, during the whole revolution his religion did
him so little service that when the Prince of Orange, the
leader of Calvinism, had set sail to dethrone his father-in-
law, the minister of the Catholic king at The Hague had caused
masses to be said for the successful issue of his voyage.

Amid the humiliations of this fugitive king and the generosity of Louis XIV., it was a noteworthy sight to see James
touching the sick at the little English convent; perhaps the
English kings claim this singular prerogative as pretenders
to the throne of France, or else this ceremony has been
established since the time of the first Edward.

It was not long before Louis sent him to Ireland, where
the Catholics still seemed to have a considerable party. A
squadron of thirty ships of the first rate lay in the roads at
Brest to escort him. All officers, courtiers, and even priests,
who had come to join James at Saint-Germain, were carried
thence to Brest, at the expense of the King of France. The
Jesuit Innes, rector of the Scottish college at Paris, was his
Secretary of State. An ambassador (by name M. d'Avaux)
was appointed to the service of the dethroned king and
followed in his train with pomp. Arms and munitions of
every kind were embarked on this fleet, even furniture of
the cheapest and also of the most expensive kind was provided. The king came to say farewell to him at Saint-Germain.
As a parting gift he gave him his cuirass, and said, as he
embraced him: "The best that I can wish you is that we
shall never see each other again." Scarcely had James dis-
embarked in Ireland on 12 May, 1689, with these forces than
he was followed by twenty-three more warships under the
command of Château-Renaud and a tremendous number of

transports. This fleet successfully put into port after having put to flight and scattered the English fleet which disputed its passage; and capturing seven Dutch merchant vessels on its return, it put back to Brest victorious over England and laden with the spoils of Holland.

Shortly afterwards, in March 1690, a third relief fleet set out from Brest, Toulon and Rochefort. The Irish ports and the English Channel were overrun with French ships.

At length Tourville, Vice-Admiral of France, with seventy-two large ships, fell in with a combined English and Dutch fleet of about sixty sail. They fought for ten hours (July 1690); Tourville, Château-Renaud, d'Estrées and Nemond distinguished themselves by their courage and skill which gave France a renown to which she had hitherto been a stranger. The English and the Dutch, till then masters of the sea, and from whom the French had learnt in so short a time the art of fighting pitched battles, were totally defeated. Seventeen of their ships broken and dismasted ran aground, and were burnt on their shores. The remainder sailed for the Thames for shelter or among the shoals of Holland. The French did not lose a single dinghy. What Louis XIV. had hoped for during the last twenty years, but which had seemed so unlikely, was now actually come to pass; he possessed the empire of the sea, though indeed it was of short duration. The enemy's ships of war hid themselves from his fleets. Seignelai, bold for anything, launched his galleys from Marseilles, and they were seen off the English coast for the first time. By their means a raid upon Teignmouth was easily made.

More than thirty merchant vessels were burnt in the bay; and the privateers of Saint Malo and the new port of Dunkirk enriched both themselves and the State by continual prizes. For nearly two years only French ships were to be seen on the high seas.

In Ireland James did not take full advantage of the assistance of Louis XIV. He had with him nearly six thousand French and fifteen thousand Irish. Three-quarters of the kingdom declared in his favour. His rival, William, was absent; nevertheless, he did not profit from such opportunities. His fortunes fell at the very beginning before the little town of Londonderry; for four months he enforced a stubborn but badly-directed siege. The town was defended by a Presbyterian minister named Walker, who had placed himself at the head of the city militia. He led them in preaching and in fighting, encouraged them to brave hunger and death, and finally compelled the king to raise the siege. This initial reverse in Ireland was soon followed by a greater calamity; William landed and advanced against him, the River Boyne being between them. On 11 July, 1690, William essayed to cross it in sight of the enemy. There were three places where it was just fordable.

The cavalry swam across and the infantry were up to their shoulders in water; on the opposite shore there was still a marsh to be crossed, and after this, a steep bank forming a natural rampart. William succeeded in crossing at the three fords and opened the attack. The Irish, who, as we have seen, make good soldiers in France and Spain, have always fought badly in their own country. There are some nations that seem fated to be subject to others. The English have always been superior to the Irish in genius, in wealth and in arms. Ireland has never been able to shake off the English yoke since she was first mastered by a plain English lord. The French fought at the Battle of the Boyne, the Irish fled; James, who appeared neither at the head of the French nor of the Irish during the fight, was the first to retreat. He had indeed always shown great valour, but there are occasions when despondency prevails over courage. William had his shoulders grazed by a cannon-shot before the battle, and rumour had it in France that he was dead. The false news was received in Paris with indecent and shameful joy. Some of the lesser magistrates encouraged the people to illuminate the city, and the bells were rung. In several quarters wicker figures, representing the Prince of Orange, were burnt just as they burn the Pope in London. The cannon of the Bastille was fired, not by order of the king, but by the ill-considered zeal of its governor. One would imagine from these expressions of relief and the testimony of so many writers that this unbridled joy at the supposed death of an enemy was due to the excessive fear that he had inspired. All writers, both French and foreign, have declared that these rejoicings were in themselves the greatest eulogy of King William. But if the circumstances and the ruling spirit of the time be taken into account, it will be clearly seen that fear was not the cause of such transports of joy. The common people only fear an enemy when he menaces their town, and so far from being frightened at the name of William, the common people of France at that time were sufficiently ill-judged to despise him. He had nearly always been beaten by French generals, and the vulgar herd was unaware that he had achieved veritable glory even in defeat. William, the conqueror of James in Ireland, did not yet appear in the eyes of the French to be an enemy worthy of Louis XIV. Paris idolised her king and thought him in very truth invincible. The rejoicings were, therefore, not the result of fear, but of hate. Most Parisians of that time, born under the reign of Louis, and with necks used to the despotic yoke, looked upon the throne as divine and usurpation as the height of sacrilege. The populace, who had seen James daily going to mass, hated William as a heretic. The thought of a son-in-law and a daughter driving out their father, of a Protestant reigning in place of a Catholic, above all, of an enemy of Louis XIV., roused the Parisians to a kind of frenzy; nevertheless, the wiser spirits formed a more moderate judgment.

James returned to France, leaving his rival to gain fresh victories in Ireland and strengthen his position on the throne. The French fleets were busy in bringing back the French troops who had fought in vain, and Irish Catholic families, who, poverty-stricken in their own country, wished to come to France and subsist on the bounty of the king.

In all probability chance played little part in the whole of this revolution from beginning to end. The respective characters of William and James were enough. Those who choose to see the causes of events in the conduct of men will observe that William granted a general pardon after his victory, while the defeated James in passing through the little town of Galway had several citizens hanged for having wished to close the gates against him. Of two men who behaved in such ways it was not difficult to see which of them was bound to succeed.

A few towns in Ireland still remained faithful to James— among others, Limerick, where there were twelve thousand of his troops. The King of France, continuing to uphold James's cause, despatched three thousand regular troops to that town. With excess of generosity he sent all that could be necessary for the requirements of a large population and the troops. Forty transport vessels, escorted by a dozen war-ships, brought all possible assistance in the way of men, utensils and equipment, engineers, gunners, bombers and two hundred masons; saddles, bridles, horse-cloths, sufficient

for more than twenty thousand horses, cannons with their
carriages, muskets, pistols, swords, for the arming of twenty-
six thousand men, provisions, clothes and even twenty-six
thousand pairs of shoes. Limerick, besieged but provided with
such help, expected to see her king fighting in her defence.
But James would not come. Limerick surrendered, and the
French vessels again returned to the coasts of Ireland,
bringing back to France about twenty thousand Irish, half
soldiers and half fugitive citizens.

That Louis XIV. did not lose heart was perhaps the most
surprising thing. He was engaged in a desperate war against
practically the whole of Europe. Yet he made one last
attempt to turn the fortune of James by a decisive move,
and prepared a descent on England with twenty thousand
men. He was counting on James's adherents in England.
Troops were mustered between Cherbourg and La Hogue.
More than three hundred transport ships were in readiness
at Brest. Tourville, with forty-four large warships, was
awaiting them off the coast of Normandy; and d'Estrées
arrived from Toulon with thirty more. While there are misfortunes due to bad conduct of affairs, there are also some
which can only be attributed to chance. The wind, which was
at first favourable to d'Estrées' squadron, changed, and he
was unable to join Tourville whose forty ships were attacked
by the combined fleets of England and Holland, nearly a
hundred strong. Superiority of numbers carried the day, and
the French gave way after a fight lasting ten hours (29 July,
1692). Russell, the English admiral, pursued them for two
days. Fourteen large ships, two of which carried a hundred
and four pieces of cannon, ran aground and were set fire to
by their captains to avoid their being burnt by the enemy.
James, who witnessed this disaster from the shore, gave
up all hope.

This was the first check to Louis XIV.'s power on the
seas. Seignelai, who, in succession to his father, Colbert, had
improved the navy, had died at the end of 1690. Pontchartrain, who had risen from the first presidency of Brittany to
be secretary of state for the fleet, maintained its efficiency.
The same spirit still prevailed in the government. In the
year following the disaster of La Hogue, France possessed
a fleet as numerous as ever; Tourville had sixty ships of
the line under his command, and d'Estrées thirty, without
counting those in the ports (1696); moreover, four years

later the king had a still larger fleet for the purpose of conveying James to England at the head of twenty thousand French; but this fleet merely showed itself, since the plans of James's party had been as badly devised in London as those of his protector had been thoroughly carried out in France.

The one resource left to the dethroned king's party lay in conspiring against his rival's life. Those who conspired perished almost without exception on the scaffold, and it is probable that even had they succeeded he would never have regained possession of his kingdom. He passed the remainder of his days at Saint-Germain, where he lived on the bounty of Louis and a pension of seventy thousand francs, which he was weak enough to receive from his daughter Mary, by whom he had been dethroned. He died in 1701 at Saint-Germain, and a few Irish Jesuits declared that miracles were performed at his tomb. After his death they even spoke at Rome of canonising him, though that court had consistently neglected him during his lifetime.

Few monarchs have been more unhappy than he, and history provides no other instance of a royal house so long unfortunate. The first of the kings of Scotland, his ancestors, by name also James, after being kept a prisoner for eighteen years in England, was assassinated with his wife at the hands of his subjects. His son, James II., was killed at the age of twenty-nine while fighting against the English. James III., imprisoned by his own people, was later killed in battle by the rebels. James IV. perished in a fight in which he was defeated. His granddaughter, Mary Stuart, driven from her throne, a fugitive in England, languished in prison for eighteen years, and was condemned to death and executed by English judges. Charles I., grandson of Mary, King of Scotland and England, sold by the Scots and condemned to death by the English, died on a public scaffold. James, his son, seventh of the name and the second in England, with whom we are here concerned, was driven from three kingdoms, and, as a last misfortune, even the legitimacy of his son was disputed. His son's attempts to re-ascend the throne of his fathers served only to bring his friends to the scaffold, and in our own times Charles Edward has in vain displayed the virtues of his forefathers and the courage of his maternal grandfather, John Sobieski, King of Poland, performing deeds and suffering misfortunes alike beyond belief. There are those who believe in a fatality which nothing can avert, and such a belief is strengthened by this continuous series of misfortunes which has dogged the House of Stuart for more than three hundred years.

CHAPTER XVI

EVENTS ON THE CONTINENT WHILE WILLIAM III. WAS INVADING
ENGLAND, SCOTLAND AND IRELAND UP TO 1697. FRESH
OUTBREAK OF THE PALATINATE. VICTORIES OF MARSHALS
CATINAT AND LUXEMBOURG, AND OTHER EVENTS

NOT wishing to break the sequence of affairs in England, I now return to what was happening on the Continent.

The king, in thus creating a maritime power, such as no other state has ever surpassed, had to defend himself against the Emperor and the Empire, Spain, the two maritime powers, England and Holland (each become more formidable under a single ruler), Savoy, and nearly the whole of Italy. One of these enemies alone, such as England or Spain, had formerly been powerful enough to bring France to her knees; now all together could not compass such a result. During this war Louis XIV. nearly always had five army corps in the field, sometimes six, and never less than four. The combined strength of his armies in Germany and Flanders amounted more than once to a hundred thousand combatants. Frontier towns were, however, not left unprotected. The king had four hundred and fifty thousand men in arms, including the marines. The Turkish Empire, powerful as it is in Europe, Asia and Africa, has never had so many; the Roman Empire never had more, and at no period had she to carry on so many wars at the same time. Those who blamed Louis XIV. for having made so many enemies, admired him for the steps he took to defend himself against them and even to anticipate them.

They had not yet all declared themselves, nor were they completely united; the Prince of Orange had not yet left Texel to drive out his father-in-law, and already the armies of France were stationed on the frontiers of Holland and the Rhine. The king had sent his son, the Dauphin (known as *Monseigneur*), into Germany in command of a hundred thousand men; he was a prince of gentle manners, modest in bearing, seeming to take entirely after his mother, and twenty-seven years of age. It was the first time that he was entrusted with a command, but he had already given proof by his character that he would not abuse it. On his departure on 22 September, 1688, the king publicly said to him: "My son, in sending you to command my armies, I give you opportunities of making your merit known; show it to all Europe, so that when I come to die, no one will perceive that the king is dead."

The prince received a special commission for his command, as though he were simply one of the generals selected by the king. His father addressed it: "To my son, the Dauphin, my lieutenant-general, commanding my armies in Germany."

Every precaution had been taken and all arranged that the son of Louis XIV., who contributed to this expedition with his name and presence, should suffer no set-back. Marshal Duras was the real commander of the army. Boufflers had a body of troops this side of the Rhine, and Marshal d'Humières another towards Cologne to keep watch on the enemy. Heidelberg and Mayence were taken, and the siege of Philippsburg (always a necessary preliminary when France makes war on Germany) was begun. Vauban conducted the siege. All details outside his province devolved on Catinat, then lieutenant-general, a man capable of anything and competent to fill any post. *Monseigneur* arrived after the army had been six days entrenched. He imitated the conduct of his father, exposing himself as was necessary, but never recklessly, affable with everybody, and generous to the soldiers. The king was genuinely delighted to have a son who imitated him without effacing him, and who made himself loved by all without making himself feared by his father.

Philippsburg was taken in nineteen days; Mannheim on 11 November, 1688, in three; Frankenthal in two: and Speyer, Trèves, Worms and Oppenheim surrendered as soon as the French appeared before their gates on 15 November, 1688.

The king had decided to lay waste the Palatinate as soon as these towns were taken. His object was rather to cut off the enemy's means of subsistence than to avenge himself on the Elector Palatine, who had committed no crime but that of doing his duty, and combining with the rest of

Germany against France. In February 1689, an order was issued to the army by Louis, signed by Louvois, to reduce the country to ashes. It was in the heart of winter; the French generals could not but obey, and accordingly announced to the citizens of all those flourishing and well-ordered towns, to the inhabitants of the villages, and to the masters of more than fifty castles, that they would have to leave their homes, which were to be destroyed by fire and sword. Men, women, old people and children departed in haste. Some went wandering about the countryside; others sought refuge in neighbouring countries, while the soldiery, who always carry out to the letter orders of exceptional severity and fail to observe more merciful ones, burnt and sacked their country. They began with Mannheim and Heidelberg, the seats of the Electors; their palaces as well as the houses of common citizens were destroyed; their tombs were opened by the rapacious soldiery, who thought to find treasures there; and their ashes were scattered. For the second time this beautiful country was ravaged by Louis XIV., but the flames of the two towns and twenty villages which Turenne had burnt in the Palatinate were but sparks compared with this conflagration. Europe was horror-struck. The officers who executed the orders were ashamed to be the instruments of such severity. They placed the responsibility on the Marquis de Louvois, who had become less humane through that hardening of sensibilities which a lengthy ministry produces. He had indeed advised this course, but Louis had been master enough not to agree to it. Had the king been a witness of the sight he would himself have extinguished the flames. Within the precincts of his palace at Versailles and in the midst of pleasures, he signed the destruction of an entire country; and he saw in this order nothing but his own power and the unfortunate prerogative of war; but as an eye-witness he could have seen nothing but its horror. Nations who until then had only blamed his ambition while they admired it, now cried out against his severity and even blamed his policy; for should his enemies invade his country as he had invaded his enemies', they would likewise burn his cities to the ground.

The danger was a real one; by posting his frontiers with a hundred thousand men Louis had prompted Germany to similar efforts. With a larger population than France that country can raise larger armies. They are raised, mobilised, and paid with greater difficulty, they appear late in the field, but their discipline and endurance of fatigue make them as formidable at the end of a campaign as are the French at the beginning. Charles V., Duke of Lorraine, commanded them: unable to regain his estates of which he had been deprived by Louis XIV., he had saved the Empire for Emperor Leopold and had brought him victory over the Turks and Hungarians. With the Elector of Brandenburg, he proceeded to counterbalance the successes of the King of France. He recaptured Bonn and Mayence, towns badly fortified, but protected by defences which were regarded as models of their kind. Bonn only surrendered on 12 October, 1689, after three and a half months of siege and after its governor, Baron d'Asfeld, had been wounded in a general assault.

The Marquis d'Uxelles, afterwards a Marshal of France, one of the wisest and most far-seeing of men, made such excellently thought-out plans for the defence of Mayence, that the garrison were but little fatigued by long hours of guard. Besides his toils within the walls he made twenty-one sorties against the enemy and killed more than five thousand of them. He even made two sorties in full daylight; at last, having run out of powder, he had to surrender after seven weeks of siege. This defence deserves a place in history, not only for itself, but for the way in which the public received it. Paris, that immense city, full of idle people always ready to judge, with ears and tongues for everything, but with little discernment, regarded d'Uxelles as both faint-hearted and ill-advised. He was justly praised by every sober-minded officer, yet at the theatre on his return from the campaign he was received by the public with boos and shouts of *Mayence*. He was obliged to retire, despising like a wise man a people so blind to merit, whose praises nevertheless are so eagerly sought after.

(June 1689) About the same time Marshal d'Humières was defeated in the Netherlands, at Valcour on the Sambre, by the Prince of Waldeck; but this repulse, while injuring his reputation, did but little harm to the French arms. Louvois, whose follower and friend he was, felt obliged to deprive him of the command of his army, and he had to be replaced.

The king's choice fell on Marshal Luxembourg, against the wishes of his minister who hated him, as he had hated

Turenne. "I promise you," the king said to him, "I shall take care that Louvois plays fair. I shall oblige him to sacrifice his hatred for you to the good of my service; you will write to no one but myself and your letters will not pass through his hands." Luxembourg consequently commanded in Flanders and Catinat in Italy. In Germany the troops fought well under Marshal Lorges. The Duke of Noailles had some success in Catalonia, while in Flanders under Luxembourg and in Italy under Catinat, it was one continuous series of victories. These two generals were at that time the most famous in Europe.

The character of the Duke of Luxembourg resembled in some respects that of the great Condé, whose pupil he had been; his was a fiery spirit, having great promptitude in action, and quick discernment, a mind eager for knowledge, but full of various and ill-sorted facts, continually involved in feminine intrigues; always in love and often loved, though deformed and far from handsome, possessing rather the qualities of a hero than those of a philosopher.

Catinat had qualities of industry and quickness which made him capable of anything, without his ever applying himself diligently to it. He would have made as good a minister or chancellor as he was a great general. He had begun his career as a barrister, but quitted that profession at the age of twenty-three on losing a suit which he thought just. He took up the profession of arms and enrolled as an ensign in the French guards. In 1667, at an attack on the fortress of Lille, in the presence of the king, he performed an action which required both ability and courage. The king remarked it; and it proved the starting-point of his fortunes. From that time he rose steadily without help or favour, remained a philosopher in the midst of luxury and war, the two greatest obstacles to moderation, and continued free from all prejudices, without the affectation of appearing unduly to despise them. Flattery and the art of the courtier were alike unknown to him. Instead he cherished friendships and was made but the more worthy by them. Throughout his life he was as much the enemy of self-interest as of pomp: he died as he had lived, a philosopher in all things.

Catinat was then commanding in Italy. His adversary was the Duke of Savoy, Victor Amadeus, a prince distinguished for his prudence and diplomacy, yet still more for his misfortunes; a courageous soldier, leading his armies in person, exposing himself as a common soldier, and understanding as well as anyone the war of cunning that had to be waged in a country that was mountainous and intersected with rivers, such as his own; active, vigilant, and a lover of order, but making mistakes both as a prince and as a general. According to reports he was at fault in the drawing up of his army against Catinat.

(18 August, 1690) The French general took advantage of this and gained a complete victory, in sight of Saluces near the abbey of Staffarde, which gives its name to the battle. When there are many killed on one side and hardly any on the other, it is undoubted proof that the defeated army was so situated that it must of necessity have been overwhelmed.

Only three hundred French were killed, while 4000 of the allies commanded by the Duke of Savoy lost their lives. After the battle the whole of Savoy—with the exception of Mont-mélian—surrendered to the king. (1691) Catinat marched into Piedmont, forced the lines of the enemy near Susa, took Susa, Villafranca, Montalban, Nice, considered impregnable, Veillane, Carmagnole and finally returned to Montmélian, which he captured after a stubborn siege.

After such great successes the ministry reduced the army under his command while the Duke of Savoy increased his own. Catinat, now weaker than the enemy he had conquered, remained for some time on the defensive; but at last having received reinforcements he descended the Alps towards Marsiglia, where on 4 October, 1693, he won a second pitched battle, more glorious in that Prince Eugene of Savoy was one of the enemy generals.

(30 June, 1690) At the other end of France towards the Netherlands, Marshal Luxembourg won the Battle of Fleurus, and, in the opinion of all the officers, this victory was due to the superior genius of the French general over the Prince of Waldeck, then in command of the allied armies. Eight thousand prisoners, six thousand dead, two hundred flags and banners, cannon, baggage, the possession of the field—all were obtained by this victory. Victorious over his father-in-law, King William had just returned from England. This man of genius, fertile in resources, gained more advantage from defeats than France often gained from her victories. In order to procure troops and money he was obliged to resort to intrigue and negotiations, as compared with a king who

had only to say, *I will.* (19 September, 1691) Nevertheless, after the defeat of Fleurus, he was able to confront Marshal Luxembourg with an army as powerful as that of the French.

Each army numbered about eighty thousand men, but on 9 April of that year Mons had already been invested by Marshal Luxembourg, and William thought that the French troops had not come out of their winter quarters. Louis XIV. advanced to the siege, and at the end of nine days' open trench warfare entered the town in full view of the enemy. He then immediately returned along the road to Versailles, leaving Luxembourg to dispute the ground inch by inch for the rest of the campaign, which ended with the Battle of Loos, on 19 September, 1691; this was a remarkable action in which twenty-eight squadrons of the king's household cavalry and infantry kept at bay seventy-five squadrons of the enemy.

The king also appeared at the siege of Namur, which, owing to its situation at the juncture of the Sambre and the Meuse and its rock-built fortress, was the strongest town in the Netherlands. He took the town in eight days in June 1692, and its forts in twenty-two, while the Duke of Luxembourg prevented William from crossing the Méhaigne with eighty thousand men and thus raising the siege.

Louis returned to Versailles again after this victory, leaving Luxembourg once more to face the enemy's forces. It was then that the Battle of Steenkerque was fought; noteworthy alike for its display of strategy and of valour. A spy in the pay of the French general was discovered among the retainers of King William: and before his death was forced to write a false message to Marshal Luxembourg. Acting on this false advice, Luxembourg took certain measures by which he was certain to be undone. His army was attacked when asleep at early dawn, and one brigade had been already put to flight before the general was so much as even aware of the attack. It was only by great diligence and bravery that all was not lost.

It was not enough to be a great general; seasoned troops were necessary, capable of being rallied, together with staff-officers with sufficient ability and courage to restored order; for had a single superior officer wished to take advantage of the confusion to allow his general to be defeated, he could easily have done so without committing himself.

Luxembourg was ill, a disastrous occurrence at a moment which demanded fresh activity. It was 3 August, 1692, and danger restored his strength; prodigies were necessary to avoid defeat; and he performed them. To shift his ground, draw up his army on a new field of battle, restore the right wing which was in total disorder, thrice to rally his troops, and thrice to charge at the head of the household cavalry, was the work of less than two hours. In his army there was Philip, Duke of Orleans, then Duke of Chartres and afterwards Regent, grandson of the King of France, and at that time not yet fifteen years old. He could do nothing to strike a decisive blow; but it greatly emboldened the soldiers to see a grandson of France, still a child, charging with the household troops, wounded in the fight and returning again to the charge in spite of his wound.

A grandson and a grand-nephew of the great Condé were both serving as lieutenants-general; one was Louis de Bourbon, known as *Monsieur le Duc*, the other François-Louis, Prince de Conti; they were rivals alike in courage, spirit, ambition and reputation; *Monsieur le Duc*, of a sterner character, possessed perhaps more solid qualities and the Prince de Conti more brilliant ones. Both called to the command of armies by the public voice, they passionately desired that honour; an honour that they never obtained, since Louis, aware of their ambitions as of their merit, never forgot that the Prince de Condé had made war upon him.

The Prince de Conti was the first to restore order, rallying some of the brigades, and moving others forward: *Monsieur le Duc* carried out the same manœuvre though not needing the spur of rivalry. The Duke of Vendôme, grandson of Henri IV., was also a lieutenant-general in the army. He had served since twelve years of age, and although now forty, had not attained to the chief command. His brother, the Grand Prior, was with him.

It was essential that the princes should unite and place themselves at the head of the household cavalry with the Duke of Choiseul, to dislodge a body of English who were guarding a strategic position, on which the success of the battle depended. The household cavalry and the English were the finest troops in the world: the slaughter was terrible. Finally, the French, encouraged by such an assemblage of princes and young lords fighting around their general, carried the position. The Champagne regiment engaged King

William's English guards, and when the English were beaten the rest were forced to surrender.

At that very moment, Boufflers, afterwards a Marshal of France, who was several miles away from the field of battle, rushed up with his dragoons and completed the victory.

William, having lost about seven thousand men, retired in the same orderly manner that had characterised his attack; though defeated he was still to be feared, and he did not abandon the campaign. The victory, due to the valour of these young princes and the flower of the nobility, produced an impression on the court, on Paris and on the provinces such as no other success had previously made.

On their return, *Monsieur le Duc*, the Prince de Conti, the Duke of Vendôme and their friends found the roads lined with people, almost frenzied in their expressions of triumph and joy. Every woman attempted to attract the heroes' eyes. The men at that time used to wear lace cravats which were arranged with a great expenditure of time and trouble. The princes, dressing hurriedly for the fight, had tied them carelessly round their necks; women now wore flounces of the same pattern, they were called *Steenkerques*. All novelties in jewellery were *à la Steinkerque*. A young man who had fought in this battle was regarded with respect. The people flocked in crowds around the princes, and they were liked the more, in that their favour at court was not equal to their glory.

It was in this battle that the young Prince de Turenne lost his life, nephew of the hero who was killed in Germany; he had already given hopes of rivalling his uncle. His manners and courage had already endeared him to Paris, to the court, and to the army.

The general, in giving the king an account of this memorable battle, did not even deign to tell him that he was ill at the time when he was attacked.

The same general, with the same princes and troops taken by surprise and yet victorious at Steenkerque, surprised William in the following campaign by a march of seven miles, and overtook him at Neerwinden, a village close to La Gheete and some miles from Brussels. William had time to entrench during the night and place his troops in order of battle.

The attack was launched at daybreak on 29 July, 1693. William was at the head of the Ruvigni regiment, composed entirely of French noblemen, who had been forced to leave and hate their country by the fatal revocation of the Edict of Nantes and the subsequent persecutions. They revenged on their country the intrigues of the Jesuit, La Chaise, and the cruelties of Louvois. Followed by such spirited troops, William at first routed the squadrons opposed to him, but was then driven back, his horse being killed under him. He mounted again and continued the combat with the most desperate perseverance.

Sword in hand, Luxembourg twice fought his way into the village of Neerwinden: the Duke de Villeroi was the first to leap into the enemy's trench, and the village was twice taken and retaken.

It was also at Neerwinden that Philip, Duke of Chartres, showed himself a worthy grandson of Henri IV. He charged thrice at the head of his squadron, and on the troop being repulsed he found himself cut off in a hollow, surrounded on all sides by men and horses either dead or wounded. An enemy squadron bore down upon him, and called upon him to surrender; he was seized but defended himself single-handed, wounded the officer who held him prisoner, and freed himself. His men immediately rallied to him, and extricated him from the position. The Prince de Condé, known as *Monsieur le Duc*, and the Prince de Conti, his rival, who had so distinguished themselves at Steenkerque, fought with equal distinction at Neerwinden for their lives, as for their glory, and were called upon to kill their enemies in hand-to-hand fighting, a rare experience for present-day staff-officers, now that firearms have become the dominant factor in warfare.

Marshal Luxembourg distinguished himself and exposed himself more than ever; his son, the Duke de Montmorenci, threw himself in front of him and received the shot intended for his father. Finally, the general and the princes recaptured the village for the third time and the battle was won.

Few battles have been more sanguinary. The killed amounted to nearly twenty thousand, twelve thousand on the Allies' side and eight on that of the French. It was on this occasion that it was said that the *De Profundis* should be sung rather than the *Te Deum*.

Could anything allay the horrors of this war it would be the word of the Count de Salm, wounded and a prisoner in Tirlemont. Marshal Luxembourg was assiduous in his attentions to him: "What a nation you are!" the prince said to him. "There are no enemies more to be feared in battle and no more generous friends after victory."

These battles resulted in great glory, but few material advantages. The Allies, though beaten at Fleurus, Steenkerque and Neerwinden, had not once been completely defeated. William always retreated in excellent order, and fifteen days after one battle, another had become necessary if the victor was to remain master of the field. The Cathedral of Paris was filled with enemy standards. Prince de Conti called Marshal Luxembourg the *Upholsterer of Notre-Dame*. Victory was on everyone's lips. Yet while formerly Louis XIV. had conquered half Holland and Flanders and the whole of Franche-Comté without fighting a single battle, now, after tremendous efforts and most desperate victories, he was unable to break through the United Provinces; he was unable even to besiege Brussels.

On the 1st and 2nd of September, 1692, Marshal Lorges had also gained a great victory near Speyerbach; he had actually taken prisoner the aged Duke of Würtemburg, and had penetrated into his country; but though invading it as a victor he was soon compelled to evacuate it. Heidelberg, which had been retaken by the enemy, was now recaptured and sacked a second time by *Monseigneur*, who was then obliged to act on the defensive against the Imperial troops.

Marshal Catinat, after his victory at Staffarde and the conquest of Savoy, was unable to save Dauphiny from being invaded by the Duke of Savoy, nor to save the important town of Casal after his victory at Marsiglia.

In Spain Marshal Noailles also gained a victory (27 May, 1694) on the banks of the Ter. He took Gerona and several small towns, but his forces were inadequate, and after his victory he was obliged to fall back on Barcelona. Everywhere victorious and yet weakened by their successes, the French found that in the Allies they were fighting a hydra that was continually springing up again. It was beginning to be difficult to raise recruits in France and still more difficult to find money. The severity of the season, which at this time destroyed the produce of the land, brought famine in its train. People were dying of starvation with the sound of *Te Deums* and rejoicings ringing in their ears. That spirit of confidence and superiority which was the very soul

of the French army was already subsiding a little. Louis XIV.
no longer appeared at the head of his troops, Louvois had
died on 16 July, 1691, and his son, Barbesieux, provoked
general dissatisfaction. Finally, the death of Marshal Luxembourg in January 1695, under whose leadership the soldiers
believed themselves invincible, seemed to put an end to the
rapid succession of French victories.

The art of bombarding coastal towns from ships was now
used against the inventors. It is true that the infernal machine
with which the English attempted to burn Saint-Malo, and
which failed in its object, did not owe its origin to French
workmanship. Similar machines had been attempted long
before in Europe. It was the art of projecting bombs from a
moving vessel as effectively as from solid ground that the
French had invented, and it was by this art that Dieppe,
Hâvre-de-Grâce, Saint-Malo, Dunkirk and Calais were
bombarded by the English fleets in July of 1694 and 1695.
Dieppe, the most easily approachable, was the only port to
suffer real damage. The town with its pleasant rows of
orderly houses owes its present beauties to its past misfortunes, for it was almost totally reduced to ashes. At Hâvre-
de-Grâce not more than twenty houses were destroyed and
burnt by bombs; but the fortifications of the port were
demolished. In this sense the medallion struck in Holland
is correct, although so many French authors have exclaimed
against its falsity. It bears inscribed in Latin: *The port of
Hâvre burnt and destroyed*, etc. The inscription does not say
that the town was destroyed, which would have been false,
but that the port was burnt, which was true.

Some time afterwards Namur was recaptured by the
Allies. In France praises had been showered on Louis XIV.
for having taken it, and jeers and obscene lampoons thrown
at the head of William for not having been able to relieve
it with an army of eighty thousand men. William regained
possession of it in the same manner that he had seen it
captured. He attacked it in the face of an army still stronger
than his had been when Louis XIV. besieged it. Vauban
had built fresh fortifications, and the French garrison
defending it was an army in itself, for at the commencement
of the siege Marshal Boufflers had thrown himself into the
town with seven regiments of dragoons. Namur was thus
defended by sixteen thousand men, and a hundred thousand
were ready to relieve it at any moment.

Marshal Boufflers was a man of great attainments, an active and competent general, and a good citizen, thinking only of the good of the service, and as prodigal of toil as of life itself. The Marquis de Feuquières in his *Memoirs* censures him for several mistakes in the defence of this town and citadel; he also blames him for the defence of Lille, which has reflected great honour on him. Those who have written the history of Louis XIV. have slavishly followed the Marquis de Feuquières in all details of warfare as they have the Abbé de Choisi in anecdotes of private life. They were evidently not aware that Feuquières, in other respects an excellent officer, with both practical and theoretical knowledge of warfare, was a man not less disappointed than he was enlightened—the Aristarchus and sometimes the Zoilus among generals; he alters facts in order to have the pleasure of censuring faults. He complained of everybody and everybody complained of him. He was said to be the bravest man in Europe, since he slept in the midst of a hundred thousand enemies. His abilities not having been rewarded with a marshal's baton, he was over‑zealous in employing his qualities of mind against those who were serving the state— qualities which would have been in the highest degree useful had he possessed a mind as conciliating as it was keen, diligent and fearless.

He reproached Marshal Villeroi for more numerous and vital errors than Boufflers. Villeroi, at the head of about eighty thousand men, had to relieve Namur, but even in the rare event of the Marshals Villeroi and Boufflers doing all that could be done, it was impossible that Namur could be relieved, owing to the nature of the ground, and she would have had to surrender sooner or later. The banks of the Méhaigne, occupied by an observation army which had inter‑ cepted the relief troops of William, now necessarily formed a check to those of Marshal Villeroi.

Marshal Boufflers, the Count de Guiscard, governor of the town, and the Count du Châtelet de Lomont, com‑ manding the infantry, together with all ranks from officer to private, defended the town with marvellous obstinacy and courage, but they were unable to postpone its capture by more than two days. When a town is besieged by superior numbers, and, the weather being favourable, operations are well directed, it is almost certain how soon it will be taken, no matter how stout the defence may be. William captured the town and citadel in September of 1695 after a longer siege than that of Louis XIV.

While losing Namur the king ordered Brussels to be bombarded—a fruitless revenge on the King of Spain for towns which had been bombarded by the English. Such conduct made the war ruinous and disastrous to both sides.

After two centuries one of the results of the ingenuity and frenzy of men is that the ravages of our wars are not confined to Europe. We exhaust ourselves of men and money in going to the ends of Asia and America in order to bring about our mutual destruction. The Indians whom we have either forced or persuaded to receive our settlements, and the Americans, whose blood we have spilt and whose continent we have ravaged, look upon us as the enemies of mankind, who rush from the ends of the earth to swallow them up only to proceed by destroying ourselves.

The French had no colonies in the Indies other than Pondicherry, planted at enormous expense by the efforts of Colbert, and whose fruits would not be reaped until the end of several years. The Dutch easily seized it and ruined French trade in the Indies before it had scarcely begun.

In 1695 the English destroyed the French plantations at San Domingo, and in the next year a privateer of Brest ravaged their African possessions in Gambia. The privateers of Saint-Malo took their revenge on the eastern coast of Newfoundland, which the English possessed. French squadrons harassed the English island of Jamaica, ships were captured and burnt, and their coasts were ravaged.

Pointis, a squadron commander, with several of the king's ships and a few American privateers succeeded in May 1697 in surprising the town of Cartagena, almost on the Equator, the storehouse and depository of the treasures that Spain had extracted from Mexico. The damage that he inflicted was estimated at twenty millions of our livres and the spoils at ten million. It is always necessary to deduct something from these calculations, but nothing from the extreme calamities of which such glorious expeditions are the cause.

Dutch and English merchant ships were daily captured by French privateers, especially by Du Guay-Trouin, a man unique of his kind, who only lacked large fleets to acquire the fame of a Dragut or a Barbarossa.

Jean Bart also achieved great fame among the corsairs

From an ordinary sailor he at length became a squadron leader like Du Guay-Trouin. Their names are still famous.

The enemy captured fewer French merchant ships because there were fewer to be captured, Colbert's death and the war having greatly reduced trade.

The result of expeditions by sea and land was thus universal misery. Those more sensitive to humanitarian considerations than to politics will note that Louis XIV. was in arms against his brother-in-law, the King of Spain; against the Elector of Bavaria, whose sister he had married to his son, the Dauphin; against the Elector Palatine, whose country he burnt after having married his eldest brother to the Palatine princess. James, King of England, was driven from his throne by his daughter and his son-in-law. Still later the Duke of Savoy was seen leagued against France, where one of his daughters was the Dauphiness, and against Spain, where his other daughter was queen. The majority of wars between Christian princes are in the nature of civil wars.

The most criminal enterprise of the whole war was the only one really successful. William was uniformly successful in England and Ireland. Elsewhere success was evenly balanced. In describing this enterprise as criminal, I am not enquiring whether the nation, after shedding the father's blood, was right or wrong in proscribing the son and forbidding alike his religion and his rights; I am simply stating that if there is any justice on the earth, it was not the part of the daughter and son-in-law of King James to drive him from his kingdom. Such an action would be horrible among private individuals; the interest of nations seems, however to establish a different moral code for princes.

CHAPTER XVII

TREATY WITH SAVOY. MARRIAGE OF THE DUKE OF BURGUNDY. PEACE OF RYSWICK. STATE OF FRANCE AND EUROPE. DEATH AND TESTAMENT OF CHARLES II., KING OF SPAIN

FRANCE still maintained her supremacy over all her enemies. She had crushed some of them, such as Savoy and the Palatinate; she had made war on the frontiers of others. She resembled now a powerful and vigorous body, fatigued by lengthy resistance and exhausted by her victories. A well-chosen blow would have made her stagger. A country fighting several enemies at the same time can in the long run only find safety in their division or in peace. Louis XIV. soon procured both.

Victor Amadeus, Duke of Savoy, was the first of all the princes to come over to his side, when it became a question of breaking his pledges to serve his interests. It was to him that the Court of France made overtures. The Count de Tessé, afterwards Marshal of France, a clever and likeable man, naturally of a pleasing disposition, which is the primary requisite of a diplomatist, at first negotiated secretly at Turin. Marshal Catinat, as ready in peace as in war, brought the affair to a successful issue. It did not need two clever men to persuade the Duke of Savoy to benefit himself.

His country was to be restored, money was to be given to him; the marriage of his daughter was proposed with the young Duke of Burgundy, son of *Monseigneur* and heir to the throne of France. They were soon agreed (July 1696); the duke and Catinat concluded the treaty at Notre-Dame de Lorette, where they went on the pretence of making a devotional pilgrimage which did not deceive anyone. Innocent XII., who was then Pope, entered eagerly into the negotiations. His aim was to free Italy both from the invasions of the French and the continual taxes exacted by the Emperor to pay his troops. It was desired that the Imperialists should allow Italy to remain neutral. The Duke of Savoy undertook in the treaty to procure this neutrality. At first the Emperor refused, for the Court of Vienna hardly ever made a decision until in extremity. Upon this the Duke of Savoy united his forces with the French army. In less than a month this prince changed from being generalissimo of the Emperor to being generalissimo of Louis XIV. In 1697 his eleven-year-old sister was brought to France to marry the Duke of Burgundy, who was but thirteen. As at the Peace of Nimeguen, following the defection of the Duke of Savoy, each of the allies came forward to negotiate. First the Emperor agreed to the neutrality of Italy; then the Dutch proposed that conferences for a general peace should be held at the Castle of Ryswick, close to The Hague. Four armies which the king had in the field helped to expedite matters. There were eighty thousand men under Villeroi in Flanders. Marshal Choiseul had forty thousand on the banks of the Rhine. Catinat had a like number in Piedmont. The Duke of Vendôme, having at length attained the rank of general, after passing successively every rank from that of guardsman like any soldier of fortune, was in command in Catalonia, where he won a battle, and in August 1697 took Barcelona. Fresh efforts and fresh successes such as these proved the strongest argument for mediation.

The Court of Rome again offered to arbitrate, but was refused, as at Nimeguen. Charles XI., King of Sweden, was chosen as mediator. At length, in September and October 1697, peace was concluded, no longer accompanied by that arrogance and those advantageous conditions which had signalised the greatness of Louis XIV., but with an ease and surrender of his rights which equally astonished the French and the Allies. It has long been thought that this peace was prepared with the most profound statecraft.

It was claimed that the great aim of the King of France was necessarily that of preventing the succession of the huge Spanish monarchy from falling to the other branch of the House of Austria. It was said that he hoped to wrest at least some portion of it for the House of Bourbon, and that perhaps one day she would obtain entire possession of it. The express renunciations of the wife and mother of Louis XIV. were apparently merely valueless signatures, which fresh plans would obliterate. In this scheme, which exalted either France or the House of Bourbon, it was necessary to display some moderation to the rest of Europe in order not to arouse the ever-watchful suspicions of such numerous powers. Peace would give him time to make new allies, restore his finances, win over those whose help was necessary, and raise fresh troops within the state. It was necessary to give up something in the hope of obtaining much more.

Such were thought to be the secret motives of the Peace of Ryswick, which in the event procured the throne of Spain for the grandson of Louis XIV. The supposition, apparently so true, is nevertheless false; neither Louis XIV. nor his council held the views which it seems should obviously have occurred to them. It is a good example of the power of revolutions in this world, which catch up and carry along the very men by whom they seem to be brought about. The obvious importance of obtaining a part or the whole of Spain at an early date did not influence the Peace of Ryswick in the slightest. The Marquis de Torci acknowledges as much in his as yet unpublished Memoirs. Peace was made out of weariness of war, and the war had been largely objectless, at any rate on the part of the Allies, who had merely the vague design of humbling the greatness of Louis XIV.; and the latter, as a result of his very greatness, had no intentions of yielding. William had won over to his cause the Emperor and the Empire, Spain, the United Provinces and Savoy. Louis XIV. had found himself too much involved to retreat, and the most beautiful part of Europe had been laid waste because the King of France had used his new-won power with an excess of arrogance after the Peace of Nimeguen. It was against him personally that the Allies were leagued rather than against France. The king believed the glory obtained by his arms to be now secure; he desired now to gain renown for moderation, and the exhausted state of his finances made such moderation easy.

The political situation was discussed in the council and resolutions taken. The Marquis de Torci, still a young man, was only entrusted with carrying them out. The whole of the council voted for peace. The Duke de Beauvilliers, especially, urged with some passion the poverty of the common people; Mme. de Maintenon was touched and the king was not insensible. Such poverty was all the more striking in comparison with the flourishing state to which Colbert had brought the kingdom. Huge buildings of every kind had wasted immense sums which economy was now powerless to replace. People were startled by this bad state of affairs at home, for such a thing had not been known since Louis XIV. took up the reins of government himself. These were actually the causes that led to the Peace of Ryswick, though of course generous sentiments had their share of influence, for those who imagine that kings and their ministers are for ever sacrificing unconditionally to ambition are no less mistaken than those who think that they constantly make sacrifices for the happiness of the world.

Louis accordingly restored to the Spanish branch of the House of Austria all that he had taken in the Pyrenees, together with his conquests in Flanders during the recent war, that is to say, Luxembourg, Mons, Ath and Courtrai. He recognised William as the rightful King of England, whom he had hitherto treated as the Prince of Orange, usurper and tyrant. He promised to give no assistance to his enemies. James, whose name was omitted from the treaty, remained at Saint-Germain with the worthless title of king, and in receipt of a pension from Louis XIV. Sacrificed by his protector to necessity, his actions were now confined to issuing manifestoes; and he was already forgotten by the rest of Europe.

The judgments delivered in the chambers of Brisach and Metz against so many European sovereigns and the additions made to Alsace, monuments of a power and pride alike dangerous, were abolished, and the lands thus juridically seized were restored to their rightful owners.

In addition Freiburg, Brisach, Kehl and Philippsburg were ceded to the Empire, and Louis agreed to raze the fortresses of Strasburg on the Rhine, Fort-Louis, Trarbach and Mont-Royal, works upon which Vauban had exhausted his art and the king his money. Europe was astonished and France ill-pleased to see Louis XIV. making peace as though he had been vanquished. Harlai, Créci and Callières, who signed it, did not dare to show themselves at court or in the city; they were overwhelmed with reproaches and ridicule as though they had taken a step not ordered by the government. The Court of Louis XIV. reproached them with having betrayed the honour of France, and later praised them for having prepared the way by this treaty for the Spanish succession; in reality they were equally undeserving of both the censure and the praise.

It was by this peace that France restored Lorraine to the house which had possessed it for seven hundred years. Duke Charles V., the prop of the Empire and the conqueror of the Turks, was dead. By the Treaty of Ryswick his son Leopold gained possession of his sovereignty, deprived, it is true, of his full rights, for he was not permitted to raise ramparts to his capital; but he could not be denied a more glorious right, that of doing good to his subjects, a right which no prince has ever better used.

May it ever be remembered in the minds of men that the ruler who has done the most good for his people was one of the least sovereigns in Europe. He found Lorraine desolate and deserted; he re-peopled and enriched it. While the rest of Europe was ravaged by war he succeeded in maintaining peace unbroken in his own country. He was wise enough to remain on good terms with France and yet keep the favour of the Empire, successfully preserving that middle way between two great powers which a weak monarch has rarely ever maintained. He brought his people an affluence which they had never known. The nobility reduced to utter poverty was restored to opulence solely by his benefactions. If he saw the house of a nobleman in ruins he had it rebuilt at his own expense; he paid their debts; arranged the marriages of their daughters; was lavish in his presents, but possessed that art of giving which is worth more than the gift itself; he gave with the magnificence of a prince and the delicacy of a friend. The arts, held in honour in his small province, produced a new circulation of wealth, such as adds to the riches of states. His court was modelled on that of France. At Versailles and Lunéville one might almost imagine oneself at the same place. Following the example of Louis XIV. he encouraged letters and established a kind of university at Lunéville, where without pedantry the young German nobles came to finish their education. Even the sciences were taught there in the schools, where visible demonstrations in physics were made with the aid of admirable apparatus. The duke sought out talent even in the shops and forests in order to bring it to light and encourage it. In short, during the whole of his reign his only care was to procure peace, wealth, learning and pleasures for his country. "I would leave my kingdom to-morrow," he said, "if I could not do good." And he thus tasted the happiness of knowing himself beloved; long after his death I have seen his subjects break into tears at the sound of his name. Dying, he left an example for the greatest kings to follow, and contributed not a little towards preparing the way for his son's accession to the Imperial throne.

At the time when Louis XIV. was occupied with the Peace of Ryswick, which was destined to yield him the Spanish succession, the crown of Poland became vacant. It was the only royal crown in the world that was then elective; citizens and foreigners might compete for it; but to secure it one of two things was necessary; either merit so outstanding and so supported by intrigues as to gain votes, as in the case of the last king, John Sobieski; or the possession of sufficient wealth to buy the kingdom, which is nearly always accessible to bidders.

The Abbé, afterward Cardinal, de Polignac, succeeded at the beginning in securing votes for the Prince de Conti, well known for his valorous deeds at Steenkerque and Neerwinden. He had never been commander-in-chief, and was not a member of the king's council; *Monsieur le Duc* had as great a reputation in war as he, and Monsieur de Vendôme still greater; yet his fame eclipsed that of all others, possessing as he did the great art of pleasing and of making himself esteemed— an art which no one knew better than himself. Polignac, an adept in the sister-art, persuasion, first influenced the people in his favour, and counterbalanced by his eloquence and promises the money so lavishly poured out by Augustus, Elector of Saxony.

On 27 June, 1697, Louis François, Prince de Conti, was elected king by the larger party and thus proclaimed by the primate of the realm. Two hours later Augustus was elected by a smaller party; but he was a sovereign and a powerful prince, and had troops posted ready on the Polish frontiers. The Prince de Conti was absent and without money, troops or power; with only his name and Cardinal de Polignac to help him. Louis XIV. had either to forbid him to receive the offer of the crown or allow him the means of ousting his rival. The French ministry was considered to have done too much in sending the Prince de Conti, and too little in allowing him but a weak squadron and a few bills of exchange, with which he arrived in the roads of Danzig. The affair seemed to be conducted with that half-hearted policy which begins a task only to abandon it. The Prince de Conti was not even received at Danzig. His bills of exchange were questioned. The intrigues of the Pope and the Emperor, the money and troops of Saxony, already assured his rival of the crown. He returned with the glory of having been elected, and France had the mortification of displaying to Europe that she was not powerful enough to make a King of Poland.

This set-back of the Prince de Conti did not disturb peace among the Christian nations of the North, and the south of Europe was soon calmed after the Peace of Ryswick. The only war remaining was that of the Turks against Germany, Poland, Venice and Russia, and in this war the Christians, though badly governed and divided amongst themselves, had the upper hand. On 1 September, 1697, the Battle of Zenta was fought in which Prince Eugene defeated the Sultan in person; a grand vizier fell together with seventeen pashas and more than twenty thousand Turks; the Ottoman pride was humbled and the Peace of Carlowitz secured in 1699, at which terms were dictated to the Turks. Venice received Morea; Russia, Azov; Poland, Kaminietz, and the Emperor, Transylvania.

Christendom was at last tranquil and happy. The whole world was at peace.

Public woes, however, soon began afresh. From the year 1700 onwards, Northern Europe was disturbed by two of the most remarkable men then living. One was Czar Peter Alexivitch, Emperor of Russia, and the other the young King of Sweden, Charles XII. Peter the Great, in advance of his time as he was of his nation, may justly be considered by his works the reformer, or rather the founder of his empire. Charles XII., more valorous but of less service to his subjects, born to command soldiers but not a nation, was the greatest hero of his time; yet he died with the reputation of a reckless monarch. The devastation of Northern Europe by a war which lasted eighteen years was due to the ambition of the Czar, the King of Denmark and the King of Poland, who resolved to take advantage of Charles XII.'s youth by robbing him of a portion of his kingdom. (1700) At the age of sixteen years Charles defeated all three of them. He became the terror of the North and was already regarded as a great man at an age when other men have not yet finished their education. For nine years he was the most formidable king in Europe and for another nine the most unhappy.

The disturbance of Southern Europe had a different origin. It was a question of apportioning the inheritance of the King of Spain, whose death was near. The powers who in imagination were already dividing this vast inheritance were acting just like the relatives of a childless but rich old man during his last illness. Wife, relations, priests and officers deputed to receive the last wishes of the dying, surround him on all sides in order to drag from him some favourable promise: some of the heirs agree to divide the spoils; others hasten to dispute them.

Louis XIV. and the Emperor Leopold had equal claims; both were descended from Philip III. in the female line,— but Louis was the son of the elder. The Dauphin had a still greater advantage over the Emperor's children in that he was the grandson of Philip IV., whereas the children of Leopold were not related. All natural rights of succession were therefore with France, as a glance at the following table will plainly show:

FRENCH BRANCH   KINGS OF SPAIN   GERMAN BRANCH

PHILIP III.

Anna Maria the elder, married *Louis XIII.* in 1615.	PHILIP IV.	*Maria Anna*, the younger, married *Ferdinand III.*, Emperor, in 1613.
Maria Theresa, elder daughter of *Philip IV.*, married *Louis XIV.* in 1660.	CHARLES II.	*Margarita Theresa*, younger daughter of *Philip IV.*, married in 1666 *Leopold*, son of *Ferdinand III.* and *Maria Anna.*
Monseigneur.		*Marie - Antoinette Josèphe*, married the *Elector of Bavaria, Maximilian Emmanuel.*
Duke of Burgundy. *Duke of Aniou,* KING OF SPAIN. *Duke of Berri.*		*Joseph Ferdinand Leopold of Bavaria*, heir to the entire Spanish monarchy at the age of four.

The Emperor, however, relied on, first, the authentic and approved renunciations of Louis XIII. and Louis XIV. to the Spanish crown, and in addition the name of Austrian; the blood of Maximilian from whom both Leopold and Charles II. were descended; the almost unbroken unity which had prevailed between the two Austrian branches; the still more persistent hatred of the two branches for the Bourbons; the ill-will at that time existing between the Spanish nation and the French; and finally the fact that the Emperor had the power of controlling the decisions of the Council of Spain.

Nothing seemed more natural at that time than that the throne of Spain should be perpetuated in the House of Austria. The whole of Europe expected it before the Peace of Ryswick; but since the year 1696 the weakness of Charles had disturbed this order of succession, and the Austrian title had already been sacrificed in secret. The King of Spain had a grand-nephew, son of the Elector of Bavaria, Maximilian Emmanuel. The king's mother, who was still living, was the great-grandmother of this young Bavarian prince, at that time four years old, and although this queen-mother was of the House of Austria, being the daughter of Emperor Ferdinand III., nevertheless she persuaded her son to disinherit the Imperial line. She was offended with the Court of Vienna;

and cast her eyes on this Bavarian prince, hardly out of his cradle, as the future monarch of Spain and the New World. Charles II., completely under her influence, made a secret will in 1696 in favour of the Elective Prince of Bavaria: but later, having lost his mother, he came under the dominion of his wife, Maria Anne of Bavaria-Neuburg. This Bavarian princess, sister-in-law of the Emperor Leopold, was as much attached to the House of Austria as the Austrian queen-mother had been devoted to the Bavarian line. The natural course of things was thus for ever being reversed in this affair which concerned the largest monarchy in the world. Maria Anne of Bavaria tore up the will which appointed the young Bavarian to the succession, and the king promised his wife that he would have no other heir than a son of Emperor Leopold, and that he would not ruin the House of Austria. The matter stood thus at the Peace of Ryswick. The Houses of France and Austria mutually feared and observed each other; and both had Europe to fear. England and Holland, still a powerful state, whose interest it was to maintain a balance of power between the sovereigns, were not inclined for a moment to allow the same head to wear both the crown of Spain and that of the Empire of France.

The most extraordinary thing, however, was that the King of Portugal, Peter II., entered the lists as a claimant. This was absurd; he could derive his claim but from a certain John I., natural son of Peter the Just in the fifteenth century: but this fantastic claim was upheld by Count Oropesa of the House of Braganza, who was a member of the Council. He was bold enough to speak of it and was immediately disgraced and dismissed.

Louis XIV. could neither permit a son of the Emperor to inherit the succession nor ask for it himself. It is not definitely known who was the first man to think of making a premature and unprecedented partition of the Spanish monarchy during the lifetime of Charles II. Very probably it was the minister, Torci; for it was he who first made overtures of such a partition to Bentinck, Earl of Portland, William III.'s ambassador at the Court of Louis XIV.

(October 1698) William entered eagerly into this new scheme. With Count de Tallard at The Hague he disposed of the Spanish succession. The young Prince of Bavaria was to receive Spain and the West Indies, for they were unaware that Charles had previously already left him all his states.

The Dauphin was to receive Naples, Sicily and the province of Guipuzcoa, with several towns. Archduke Charles, second son of the Emperor Leopold, was left but the Duchy of Milan, while Archduke Joseph, elder son of Leopold, and the heir to the Empire, received nothing whatever.

The fate of a part of Europe and half America being thus decided, Louis promised by this partition treaty to renounce in its entirety the Spanish succession. The Dauphin also promised and subscribed to the same provision. France thought to gain fresh territory; England and Holland believed that they were securing peace for a part of Europe; but all this diplomacy was so much vanity. The dying king was indignant on learning that his kingdom was being thus parcelled up while he was still alive. On this it was thought that he would appoint as his successor either the Emperor Leopold or one of the Emperor's sons as his successor, as a reward for having refused to participate in the partition, and that the greatness and influence of the House of Austria would dictate the terms of his will. He did indeed make one, but for the second time nominated that same Prince of Bavaria as the sole heir to all his estates (November 1698). The Spanish nation, fearing nothing so much as the disruption of the Empire, approved of this arrangement. Peace, it seemed, would inevitably follow; but again this hope was as vain as the treaty itself. The Prince of Bavaria, the king designate, died at Brussels on 6 February, 1699.

The House of Austria was unjustly accused of his sudden death on the unsupported evidence that crimes are committed by those who benefit by them. Once more intrigues were set on foot at the courts of Madrid, Vienna, Versailles, London, The Hague and Rome.

Once more Louis XIV., William, and the States-General planned in imagination a distribution of the Spanish monarchy. (March 1700) They assigned to Archduke Charles, younger son of the Emperor, the part previously allotted to the boy prince, who had just died. The Dauphin was to have Naples, Sicily and all that had been allotted to him by the former treaty.

Milan was given to the Duke of Lorraine, and Lorraine itself, so often invaded and then surrendered by France, was to be annexed to the latter country in perpetuity. This treaty, which aroused the diplomatic activities of every European prince, either in opposition or support, was as fruitless as the first. Europe was again deceived in her expectations, as so often happens.

The Emperor, on its being proposed that he should sign the partition treaty, would have none of it, since he hoped to obtain the whole succession. The King of France, who had urged his signature, was awaiting events with some incertitude. On this fresh affront becoming known at the Court of Madrid, the king was near dying with grief, and his wife at the height of her rage smashed the furniture of her apartment, especially the mirrors and other ornaments which had come from France; passion, be it noted, knows no difference of class. These visionary partitions, intrigues, and quarrels affected but individual interests. The Spanish nation was regarded as a cipher. It was never consulted, never asked what king it really desired. It was proposed to call the *cortes*, the parliament; but Charles trembled at the very name.

In this pass the unhappy prince, seeing himself near death in the prime of life, decided to give all his possessions to Archduke Charles, his wife's nephew and the second son of the Emperor Leopold. He dared not leave them to the eldest son, so strong was the influence of a putative balance of power, and so certain was he that the fear of seeing Spain, Mexico, Peru, large settlements in the Indies, the Empire, Hungary, Bohemia and Lombardy in same hands, would suffice to set the rest of Europe in arms. He demanded that the Emperor Leopold should send his second son Charles to Madrid at the head of ten thousand men; but neither France, England, Holland nor Italy would have permitted this: all were in favour of a partition. The Emperor was not at all inclined to send his son alone to be at the mercy of the Council of Spain, and could not spare ten thousand men for the purpose. His one care was to despatch troops to Italy in order to secure that part of the Austro-Spanish possessions. Then occurred in a matter of the highest importance between two kings what occurs daily between ordinary individuals over trifling affairs; they disputed, and the dispute grew bitter; German boisterousness came into collision with Castilian pride. The Countess of Perleps, who ruled the wife of the dying king, alienated people at Madrid, whom she should rather have won over, and the Council of Vienna but further estranged them by its arrogance.

The young archduke, afterwards Emperor Charles VI., always spoke of the Spanish in offensive terms. He gave

an example of how much princes should weigh their words.
A bishop of Lerida, the Spanish ambassador at Vienna,
disliking the Germans, noted these words of abuse, heightened
them in his despatches and in his turn wrote insults about
the Council of Austria greater than the archduke had ever
uttered against the Spanish. "The minds of Leopold's
ministers," he wrote, "are like the horns of the goats in my
country — small, hard and crooked." This letter became
public. The Bishop of Lerida was recalled, and on his return
to Madrid but increased the hatred of the Spaniards for
the Germans.

While the Austrian party was disgusting the Court of
Madrid, the Marquis, afterwards Duke, d'Harcourt, the
French ambassador, was winning all hearts by his lavishness
and magnificence as by his tact and great capacity for
pleasing. He was at first ill received at the Court of Madrid,
but he accepted every rebuff without complaining; three
whole months elapsed before he could obtain an audience
of the king. He employed this time in making friends. He
was the first to substitute a feeling of goodwill for that
antipathy which the Spanish nation had felt towards the
French since the time of Ferdinand the Catholic, and his
discretion paved the way for the renewal of those ancient
bonds between France and Spain which had united them
before the time of Ferdinand, *crown to crown, people to people,
man to man*. He accustomed the Spanish Court to be friendly
towards the ruling house of France, his ministers to be no
longer alarmed by the renunciations of Maria Theresa and
Anne of Austria, and Charles II. himself to waver between
his own house and that of Bourbon. He was thus the prime
mover of the greatest revolution in government and the
minds of men. The change was, however, still distant.

The Emperor entreated, threatened. The King of France
maintained his rights, but without ever venturing to demand
the whole succession for one of his grandsons. His business
was to flatter the invalid. The Moors besieged Ceuta. Immediately the Marquis d'Harcourt offered ships and troops to
Charles, who was deeply moved by this action; but the
queen was alarmed by it, fearing that her husband would
display only too much gratitude, and she curtly refused
the assistance.

The Council of Madrid did not yet know which side to
take, and as Charles II. felt death approaching he became

more uncertain than ever. The Emperor Leopold in irritation recalled his ambassador, the Count von Harrach, but sent him back to Madrid shortly afterwards, and the hopes of the House of Austria revived. The King of Spain wrote to the Emperor that he would nominate the archduke as his successor. On this, the King of France, threatening in his turn, mustered an army on the Spanish frontiers and the Marquis d'Harcourt himself was recalled from his embassy in order to command the army. At Madrid there only remained an infantry officer who had been secretary to the embassy and thus became *chargé d'affaires*, as the Marquis of Torci put it. In such plight the dying king, threatened in turn by those who claimed the succession, and seeing that the day of his death would herald the declaration of war, with the consequent parcelling-up of his estates, approached his end lacking both consolation and resolution, and in the midst of alarms.

In this desperate crisis, Cardinal Portocarrero, Archbishop of Toledo, Count Monterey and other grandees of Spain resolved to save their country. They joined themselves together for the purpose of preventing the disruption of the Empire. Their hatred of the German government gave added strength to reasons of state and all unconsciously played into the hands of the Court of France. They persuaded Charles II. to choose a grandson of Louis XIV. in preference to a prince living farther from them and thus incapable of defending them. This in no way reversed the solemn renunciations by the mother and wife of Louis XIV. of the crown of Spain, since such renunciations had been made only to prevent the direct line from uniting the two kingdoms under its rule, and no prince in the direct line was being chosen. Justice would be done to the claims of blood and at the same time the Spanish monarchy would be preserved from partition. The conscientious king consulted certain theologians, who confirmed the opinion of his council; then, ill as he was, he wrote with his own hand to Pope Innocent XII. asking also for his advice. The Pope, believing that the freedom of Italy depended upon the weakening of the House of Austria, wrote to the king "that the laws of Spain and the good of Christendom required him to give the preference to the House of France." The Pope's letter was dated 16 July, 1700. He treated this matter which concerned the conscience of a king as though it were an affair of state.

whilst the King of Spain made of this important matter a question of conscience.

Louis XIV. learnt the news from Cardinal de Janson, who was at that time living in Rome; the Versailles cabinet took no further part in the affair. Six months had passed since the French ambassador had left Madrid. It was perhaps a mistake, and yet a mistake which possibly secured the Spanish monarchy to the House of France.

On 2 October, 1700, the King of Spain made his third will, long thought to be his only one, in which he bequeathed all his states to the Duke of Anjou. A moment was seized when his wife was absent to obtain his signature. In such a manner the whole business was settled.

Europe believed that this will of Charles II. had been dictated from Versailles, but in reality the dying king had only considered the interests of his kingdom, the wishes and even the fears of his subjects; for the King of France was advancing his troops on the frontier in order to make certain of a portion of the inheritance, at the very moment that the dying king was deciding to give him all. Nothing is more true than that the reputation of Louis XIV. and the consciousness of his power were the sole instigators of this great revolution.

Charles, after signing the ruin of his house and the greatness of that of France, lingered for another month before ending on 1 November, 1700, at the age of twenty-nine, the undistinguished life he had led on the throne. It is not perhaps wholly unprofitable with a view to throwing light on the workings of the human spirit to mention that some months before his death Charles had caused the tombs of his father, his mother and his first wife, Marie Louise of Orleans, to be opened at the Escurial. It was said that he had consented to the death by poison of his first wife. He now kissed the remains of these corpses, perhaps in imitation of the old kings of Spain, perhaps wishing to accustom himself to the horrors of death, or simply from a secret superstition that the opening of these tombs would delay the hour when he should be carried to his own.

Charles had been born weak in mind as in body, and the weakness infected all his estates. It is the fate of monarchies that their prosperity depends on the character of a single man. Such was the profound ignorance in which Charles had been brought up that when the French were besieging

Mons he thought the place belonged to the King of England. He did not know where Flanders was, nor what his possessions were in that country. He thus left all his possessions to the Duke of Anjou, grandson of Louis XIV., without knowing what he was actually leaving to him.

The will was kept so secret that the Count von Harrach, the Emperor's ambassador, still flattered himself that the archduke was the recognised successor. He stood for a long time awaiting the result of a meeting of the great council which was held immediately after the king's death. The Duke of Abrantes came out to him with open arms; at that moment the ambassador no longer doubted that the archduke was king; but his hopes were dashed as the Duke of Abrantes embraced him with the words, *"Vengo á despedirme de la casa de Austria"*—"I come to take my leave of the House of Austria."

Thus, after two hundred years of wars and negotiations over certain frontiers of the Spanish states, the House of France, by one stroke of the pen, obtained the whole empire, without either treaty or intrigue, without even having entertained any hopes of the succession. It has been thought necessary to make known the simple truth of an affair which has so far been obscured by innumerable ministers and historians, deceived by prejudices and appearances such as are nearly always deceptive. All that has been related in one volume and another, of money poured out by Marshal d'Harcourt and of Spanish ministers thus won over to secure the signing of the will, belongs to the category of political falsehoods and popular misconceptions. The King of Spain, in choosing as his heir the grandson of a king for many years his enemy, had always in mind the results which the idea of a general balance of power made inevitable. The Duke of Anjou, grandson of Louis XIV., was only called to the Spanish succession because he could not hope for the crown of France, and the same will which in default of younger members of Louis XIV.'s family nominated the Archduke Charles, afterwards Emperor Charles VI., expressly stated that the Empire and Spain should never be united under the same sovereign.

Louis XIV. could still hold to the partition treaty which benefited France. He could also accept the will which was advantageous to his house. It is certain that the matter was discussed at an extraordinary meeting of the council.

The chancellor, Pontchartrain, and the Duke of Beauvilliers were in favour of holding to the treaty: they foresaw the dangers of having to support a new war. Louis was no less aware of them, but had accustomed himself not to fear them. On 11 November, 1700, he accepted the will, and on meeting the Princesses de Conti with *Madame la Duchesse* as he left the council, he said to them smilingly: "Well, which side will you take?" Then without waiting for their reply, he added: "Whichever side I take, I am well aware that I shall be blamed for it."

The actions of kings, flattered though they be, are also so keenly criticised that the King of England himself was subjected to reproofs from his own parliament, and his ministers were reproached for having framed the partition treaty. The English, who reason better than any other nation, but whose reasoning powers are sometimes obscured by the fury of party spirit, exclaimed both against William, who had made the treaty, and against Louis XIV., who broke it.

Europe seemed for a moment to stand paralysed, amazed and impotent, on seeing the Spanish monarchy come under the domination of France, whose rival she had been for three centuries. Louis XIV. appeared the most prosperous and powerful monarch in the world. At the age of sixty-two he found himself surrounded by a numerous progeny, and one of his two grandsons was about to rule under his orders, Spain, America, half Italy and the Netherlands. The Emperor dared only voice his complaints.

William III., become weak and feeble at the age of fifty-two, no longer appeared a dangerous enemy. Before making war he had to obtain the consent of his parliament, and Louis had sent money over into England with which he hoped to influence not a few parliamentary votes. William and Holland, not being strong enough to declare themselves, addressed Philip V. in February 1701 as the legitimate King of Spain. Louis had no fears of the Elector of Bavaria, father of the young prince who had died after being nominated King of Spain. This Elector, governor of the Netherlands in the name of the late King Charles II., at once assured the possession of Flanders to Philip V., and opened the highway to Vienna to the French armies which passed through his territory, in case the Emperor should dare to make war. The Elector of Cologne was as intimately associated with France as his brother, the Elector of Bavaria, and both princes seemed to have chosen the right side since the House of Bourbon was incomparably the stronger. The Duke of Savoy, already father-in-law to the Duke of Burgundy, was now to be father-in-law of the King of Spain; he was given the command of the French armies in Italy. No one had ever foreseen that the father of the Duchess of Burgundy and the Queen of Spain would ever be called upon to make war on his two sons-in-law.

The Duke of Mantua, sold to France by his minister, sold himself again and received a French garrison in Mantua. The Milanese acknowledged the grandson of Louis XIV. without hesitation. Even Portugal, the natural enemy of Spain, at first united with her. In short, from Gibraltar to Antwerp, and from the Danube to Naples, everything seemed to be in the hands of the Bourbons. The king was so vain of his success that in conversation with the Duke de La Rochefoucauld on the subject of the propositions which the Emperor was then making to him, he made use of this expression: "You will find them still more insolent than they have been represented to you."

In September 1701, William, the undying enemy of Louis' greatness, promised the Emperor that he would arm England and Holland in his cause; he also engaged Denmark in his interests; finally, at The Hague he signed the league already concerted against the House of France. Louis, however, remained unmoved, relying upon the divisions that his money would cause in the English parliament and still more on the combined forces of France and Spain; he seemed to despise his enemies.

On 16 September, 1701, James II. died at Saint-Germain. Louis could acquiesce in what seemed both appropriate and politic in not hastening to recognise the Prince of Wales as King of England, Scotland and Ireland, after having recognised William III. by the Treaty of Ryswick. A feeling of pure generosity at first led him to give the young Pretender the consolation of an honour and a title which his unhappy father had retained until his death, and of which the Treaty of Ryswick was powerless to deprive him. All the leaders of the council were of a contrary opinion. The Duke of Beauvilliers especially drew a vivid picture with convincing eloquence of all the horrors of war that would result from such dangerous magnanimity. He was governor of the Duke of Burgundy, and in everything followed the views of that prince's tutor, the celebrated Archbishop of Cambrai, distinguished for his humane precepts of government and for the precedence he gave to the people's interests over the greatness of kings. The Marquis de Torci adduced principles of policy to give added weight to what the Duke of Beauvilliers had spoken as a citizen. He urged that it was not expedient to provoke the English nation by any sudden step. Louis yielded to the unanimous advice of his council and firmly decided in his own mind not to acknowledge the son of James II. as king.

On the same day Mary of Modena, James's widow, came to speak with Louis XIV. in Mme. de Maintenon's private apartment. She besought him in tears not to affront her son, herself and the memory of a king whom he had protected, by refusing a mere title, the only remnant of such greatness; her son had always been accorded the honours of a Prince of Wales; surely he should be treated as a king after his father's death. William could not complain of this, provided that he was allowed to enjoy his usurpation. She strengthened these reasons by appealing to Louis XIV.'s personal glory. Whether or not he recognised the son of James II., the English would not be less antagonistic to France and he would be left with the regret of having sacrificed the nobility of his feelings to vain considerations of policy. These remonstrances and tears were supported by Mme. de Maintenon. The king reverted to his former opinion and to the glory of supporting the cause of persecuted kings to the best of his power. In a word, James III. was recognised as such on the very day that it had been decided in council that such recognition should not be granted.

The Marquis de Torci has often admitted the truth of this singular story. It was not inserted in the manuscript of his Memoirs, because, he said, he did not think it creditable to his master that two women should have made him alter a decision arrived at in his council. Several Englishmen have told me that had it not been for this step it is possible that their parliament would never have taken sides between the Houses of Bourbon and Austria; but that to recognise as their king a prince whom they had banished seemed an insult to the nation and a sign that Louis was eager to exercise a despotism over Europe. The instructions given by the City of London to its members were violent in the extreme:

"The King of France makes himself a viceroy in bestowing

the title of our sovereign upon a pretender who claims to be Prince of Wales. We should indeed be in sorry plight if we were to be ruled by the pleasure of a prince who has used fire, sword, and the galleys to exterminate Protestants from his dominions; would he display more humanity towards us than towards his own subjects?"

William expressed himself in parliament with the same vigour. James III. was declared guilty of high treason, and a bill of attainder was brought against him; that is to say, that like his grandfather he was condemned to death and it was by virtue of this bill that a price was afterwards put upon his head. Such was the fate of this unfortunate house whose misfortunes were not yet even at an end. It must be admitted that it was a barbarous reply to the generosity of the King of France.

It seems very probable that England would still have declared against Louis XIV. even had he refused the empty title of king to James III. The fact that the Spanish monarchy was in the hands of his grandson seemed bound to rouse the maritime powers against him. The bribing of a few members of parliament would not have stopped the impetuous torrent of the whole nation. It was a pretty problem as to whether Mme. de Maintenon's judgment was better than that of the whole council and whether Louis XIV. was right in allowing himself to be ruled by the nobility and delicacy of his feelings.

Emperor Leopold was the first to begin operations in Italy in the spring of 1701. Italy has always been the country most coveted by the Empire. The Emperor's arms could most easily penetrate into the interior by way of Tyrol and the state of Venice; for Venice, though apparently neutral, leant nevertheless more to the side of Austria than to that of France. Moreover, she was obliged by treaties to give free passage to German troops, and the treaties were fulfilled without difficulty.

Before attacking Louis XIV. from the side of Germany the Emperor waited until the German corps should revolt in his favour. He had spies and friends in Spain from whom he could receive information, but such information was useless unless one of Leopold's sons could gather it in person; and the Emperor's son could only reach Spain with the help of the Dutch and English fleets. William hastened his preparations. His mind, more active than ever though contained in an enfeebled and almost lifeless body, stirred up everything, eager rather to humble Louis XIV. than to assist the House of Austria.

At the beginning of 1702 he was to put himself at the head of his armies, but death forestalled his plans. A fall from his horse seriously injured his already weakened body, and a slight attack of fever carried him off. He died on 16 March, 1702, paying no attention to the spiritual attentions of priests around his bed, and showing no other anxiety than for the troubled state of Europe.

He left behind him the reputation of a great statesman, though he had never been popular; and that of a general to be feared, though he had lost many battles. Always deliberate in his conduct and never animated except in the hour of battle, he reigned peacefully in England simply because he did not attempt to be absolute. He was called, as is well known, the King of the English and the Stadtholder of the Dutch. He knew all the languages of Europe, but none with facility, his mind being more prone to reflection than imagination. His character was exactly opposed to that of Louis XIV.; where Louis was affable, he was melancholy, reserved, serious, cold and taciturn. He hated women as much as Louis was attracted by them. Louis made war as a king, William as a soldier. He had fought against the great Condé and against Luxembourg; both he and Condé had claimed the victory at Seneffe, and it had taken him but a short time to redeem his defeats at Fleurus, Steenkerque and Neerwinden. He was proud as Louis XIV. but with that gloomy and melancholy pride which repels rather than imposes. While the fine arts flourished in France owing to the efforts of her king, they were neglected in England, where they were replaced by a harsh and uneasy policy agreeing with the temper of its ruler.

Those who value higher the merit of defending his country, and the expediency of acquiring a kingdom without natural right, of maintaining his position there without being loved, of ruling Holland with regal power and yet not tyrannising over her, of being the mind and leader of half Europe, possessing at once the resources of a general and the courage of a soldier, of persecuting no one for his religion, of despising all the superstitions of mankind, of being simple and unassuming in his manners—doubtless, such persons will give the name of "great" rather to William than to Louis. But those who are more impressed by the pleasures and glitter of a brilliant court, by magnificence, patronage of the arts, zeal for public welfare, a passion for glory, and a gift for ruling; who are more struck by the arrogance with which ministers and generals annexed whole provinces to France on a simple order from their king; who are more astonished at seeing a single state resist so many powers; who esteem a King of France who succeeds in bestowing Spain upon his grandson, rather than a Dutch stadtholder who dethrones his father-in-law; in a word, those who admire the protector rather than the persecutor of James will give the preference to Louis XIV.

CHAPTER XVIII

MEMORABLE WAR OF THE SPANISH SUCCESSION. DEEDS OF MINISTERS AND GENERALS UP TO 1703

PRINCESS ANNE succeeded William III. She was the daughter of James and a granddaughter of Hyde, a lawyer who became chancellor, and one of the great men of England. She was married to the Prince of Denmark, who was but her highest subject. From the moment she ascended the throne she adopted all William's schemes although she had openly disagreed with him, and these schemes were in accordance with the will of the people. Elsewhere the people have blindly to acquiesce in the designs of their kings; but at London the king must acquiesce in those of his people.

The measures taken by England and Holland to place if possible the Archduke Charles on the throne of Spain, or at least to resist the Bourbons, deserve perhaps the attention of every age. Holland on her side had to maintain 102,000 troops either in garrisons or in the field. The huge Spanish empire fell far short of being able to furnish as many at this juncture. Thus a nation of merchants who thirty years before had been almost completely vanquished in the short space of two months was now more powerful than the rulers of Spain, Naples, Flanders, Peru and Mexico. England promised forty thousand men in addition to her fleets.

It always happens in alliances of this kind that in the long run considerably fewer troops are furnished than were originally promised. England, on the contrary, however, supplied fifty thousand men in the second year in the place of forty; and towards the end of the war she was maintaining as many troops as the rest of the Allies together, posted on the frontiers of France, in Spain, Italy, Ireland and America, and manning her fleets, in all nearly two hundred thousand soldiers and sailors under arms. The expenditure is almost unbelievable, when one considers that England by herself is but a third of the size of France, and that the total amount of money in circulation in England at that time was but half of that in France; but the expenditure presents nothing extraordinary to the eyes of those who know the power of trade and credit. England throughout bore the greatest burden in this alliance. That of the Dutch was gradually lessened; for, after all, the republic of the States-General is but a great commercial company, whereas England is a fertile country, as rich in tradesmen as in warriors.

The Emperor was to furnish ninety thousand men, apart from the help of the Empire and those allies whom he hoped to separate from the House of Bourbon; meanwhile the grandson of Louis XIV. was already reigning peaceably in Madrid; and Louis himself at the beginning of this century was at the height of his glory and his power; but those who had an intimate knowledge of the courts of Europe, and especially that of France, began to fear a change for the worse. Weakened under the last kings of the blood of Charles V., Spain was still further enfeebled during the first days of the reign of a Bourbon. The House of Austria had partisans in more than one province of that monarchy. Catalonia seemed ready to shake off the new yoke and go over to the Archduke Charles. Portugal sooner or later could not but range herself with the House of Austria. Her obvious course was to encourage a civil war among her natural enemies, the Spaniards, from which Lisbon would inevitably profit. The Duke of Savoy, but lately become the father-in-law of the new King of Spain, and bound to the Bourbons, both by ties of blood and by treaties, seemed already dissatisfied with his sons-in-law. Fifty thousand crowns a month, afterwards increased to two hundred thousand francs, did not seem to him a sufficient inducement to maintain his allegiance. He must have at least Montferrat, Mantua and a part of Milan. The insolence he endured from the French generals and the ministry of Versailles gave him good cause to fear that he would soon count for nothing with his two sons-in-

*G 780

law, whose territory surrounded his estates on every side. He had already abruptly abandoned the Emperor's party for France. It seemed probable that, being so little esteemed by France, he would desert her at the first opportunity.

As for the Court of Louis XIV. and his kingdom, shrewd minds already observed a change there, which the more vulgar only discern when decadence has already arrived. The king, now more than sixty years of age and grown more retiring, had lost as a consequence his power of judging men; he saw things from too far off, with eyes less diligent, eyes, above all, which had been dazzled by long years of prosperity. Mme. de Maintenon, with all her excellent qualities, had not the strength, the courage, nor the greatness of mind necessary to uphold the glory of a state. She contrived to obtain the appointment of her tool, Chamillart, as Minister of Finance in 1699, and as Minister of War in 1701—an honest fellow rather than a minister, who had pleased the king by his modest behaviour when in charge of Saint-Cyr. In spite of his unassuming manner, he was foolish enough to think himself capable of bearing the burden of these two offices, a burden which Colbert and Louvois had with difficulty shouldered. The king, relying on his own experience, believed that he could successfully direct his ministers. After the death of Louvois he had said to James: "I have lost a good minister; but your business and mine will fare none the worse." On choosing Barbesieux to succeed Louvois at the ministry of war, he said to him: "I trained your father; I will do the same for you." He said almost as much to Chamillart. A king who had striven so long and so successfully seemed to have the right to speak thus; but his confidence in his own perspicacity deceived him.

The generals he employed were often embarrassed by precise orders, like ambassadors who are not allowed to deviate from their instructions. In the private apartments of Mme. de Maintenon he directed the plan of campaign with Chamillart. If a general wished to undertake some great enterprise he often had to despatch a courier to the king asking for permission; on his return the courier would find either the opportunity passed or the general defeated.

Military honours and rewards were lavishly distributed under Chamillart's ministry. Too many young men hardly more than boys were allowed to buy the command of regiments; while on the enemy's side a regiment was the reward of twenty years' service. The difference was afterwards only too apparent on more than one occasion when an experienced colonel could have avoided a total defeat. The Cross of the Knights of Saint Louis, an award originated by the king in 1693, and at first the source of eager rivalry among officers, was freely sold from the beginning of Chamillart's ministry. They could be bought for fifty crowns apiece at the war office. Military discipline, the very backbone of the service, which had been enforced by Louvois, was now ruinously slackened; the numbers of soldiers in the companies were deficient, as were those of the officers in the regiments. The ease with which commissaries could be bribed and the negligence of the ministry were responsible for this confusion. This caused an inferiority which, other things being equal, would inevitably lose battles. For, in order to oppose an equal front to the enemy, the French were forced to place weak battalions opposite to those at full strength. Stores were no longer so abundant nor so readily at hand: arms were no longer of first-rate quality. Consequently those who perceived the faults of the government and who knew what generals there were to draw upon, feared for France even in the midst of initial advantages which promised her greater glories than ever.

The first general to counterbalance the superiority of France was a Frenchman; for so Prince Eugene may well be called, although he was the grandson of Charles Emmanuel, Duke of Savoy. His father, the Count of Soissons, had settled in France, was made Lieutenant-General of the armies and Governor of Champagne, and had married on 18 October, 1663, Olympia Mancini, one of the nieces of Cardinal Mazarin. The fruit of this marriage, unhappy in other ways, was the prince afterwards so dangerous to Louis XIV., who was born in Paris, but remained unknown to the great monarch in early youth. He was first known in France as the *Chevalier de Carignan*. He then entered the church and was known as the *Abbé of Savoy*. It is said that he asked the king for a regiment, and had the mortification of being scolded in addition to having his request refused. Unable to distinguish himself under Louis XIV., he entered the Emperor's service against the Turks in 1683, and the two Princes of Conti joined him there in 1685; but the king ordered these princes and all who had accompanied them to return: the Abbé of Savoy alone disobeyed. He had already declared that he renounced his country. The king, on hearing this, said to his courtiers, "Don't you agree that I have lost a great man there?" but the courtiers assured him that the Abbé of Savoy would always be a madcap, a man incapable of anything great. They were judging him by a few indiscretions of his youth, such as men should never be judged by. This prince, too lightly despised by the French Court, was born with the qualities of a hero in war and of a great man in peace; a mind imbued with as high a sense of justice as of pride, and a courage alike unshaken in the command of armies and in his own study. Like all generals he made mistakes, but they were eclipsed by the number of his great achievements. He shook the greatness of Louis XIV. and the Ottoman power; he ruled the Empire, and during all his victories and his ministry he scorned alike the temptations of pomp and wealth. He even practised the art of letters and encouraged it to the best of his powers at the Court of Vienna. Now, at thirty-seven years of age, his experience was the richer for his victories over the Turks and for the mistakes made by the Imperial troops during the recent wars, in which he had fought against France.

He descended into Italy by way of the Trentino to the plains of Venice with thirty thousand men and entire freedom as to how he should employ them. The King of France at first forbade Marshal Catinat to check the advance of Prince Eugene, either because he did not wish to commence hostilities—a bad policy when one is already under arms—or in order to maintain friendly relations with the Venetians, who were in reality less dangerous than the German army.

This first mistake on the part of the court had the result of making Catinat commit others.

Success comes rarely to him who carries out a plan not his own. Moreover it is obvious how difficult it is, in a country intersected by rivers and streams, to prevent a skilful enemy from crossing them. Prince Eugene combined great subtlety of plan with remarkable swiftness in execution. In addition, the nature of the country round about the banks of the Adige caused the French army to be more spread out, while the enemy's troops were more concentrated. Catinat wished to advance upon the enemy; but several lieutenants-general put difficulties in his way and plotted against him. He was weak enough not to insist upon obedience: and this moderation led him to commit a grave error. Eugene first forced the position at Carpi, on the Canale Bianco, defended by Saint-Fremont, who did not fully carry out his general's order and allowed himself to be defeated. By this success, the German army was master of the country lying between the Adige and the Adda; it penetrated into Bressan, and Catinat fell back behind the Oglio. Many experienced officers approved of this retreat, which appeared to them sound, and, it must be added, inevitable by the lack of munitions promised by the ministry. Courtiers, and especially those who were hoping to succeed Catinat in the command, expressed the opinion that he had disgraced the name of France by his conduct. Marshal Villeroi urged that he should redeem the nation's honour. The confidence with which he spoke and the king's liking for him procured him the command in Italy, and Marshal Catinat, in spite of his victories at Staffarde and at Marsiglia, was obliged to serve under him.

The Marshal Duke de Villeroi, son of the king's tutor, and brought up with him, had always enjoyed his favour; he had shared alike in his campaigns and in his pleasures; he was a man of pleasing and imposing appearance, as brave as he was honourable, a good friend, sincere in all social relationships, and in everything magnificent. But his enemies said that, as general of an army, he was more occupied with the glory and pleasure of commanding than with the plans proper to a great captain. He was blamed for holding to his own opinions and refusing to defer to those of anyone else.

He came to Italy to give orders to Marshal Catinat and offence to the Duke of Savoy. Indeed he gave him to understand that as a favourite of Louis XIV. in command of a mighty army he really considered himself above a prince; he addressed him merely as *Mons. de Savoie*; and treated him as a general in the pay of France rather than as a sovereign, master of the barriers which nature has set between France and Italy. The friendship of this sovereign, though essential to France, was not sought with the care that it demanded. The court imagined that fear was the only bond which would restrain him, and that a French army by which the six or seven thousand Piedmontese were continuously surrounded would guarantee his loyalty. Marshal Villeroi treated him as an equal in everyday affairs and as an inferior in matters of command. The Duke of Savoy bore the empty title of generalissimo, an office which Marshal Villeroi fulfilled in fact. His first orders were to attack Prince Eugene in his position at Chiari, close to the Oglio, on 11 September, 1701. The staff officers considered that it was against all the canons of warfare to attack this position, and for decisive reasons: the place itself was of no importance, and the trenches were untakable: nothing would be gained by taking it, and failure would mean loss of reputation in the whole campaign. Villeroi told the Duke of Savoy that he must advance and sent an *aide-de-camp* to order Marshal Catinat on his side to attack. Catinat had the order repeated three times, then turning to the officers of his staff he said: "Well, gentlemen, we must obey." They advanced on the trenches. The Duke of Savoy at the head of his troops fought like a man who was well content to ally himself with France. Catinat did his best to seek death. He was wounded; but wounded as he was, on seeing the king's troops repulsed and Marshal Villeroi issuing no orders, he conducted the retreat; after this he left the army and went to Versailles to give the king an account of his conduct, without lodging complaints against anyone.

Prince Eugene continued to keep the upper hand over Marshal Villeroi. At length, on 2 February, 1702, in the middle of winter when the marshal was securely sleeping in Cremona, a strongly fortified town furnished with a large garrison, he was awakened by the sound of musketry. He rose hastily and mounted his horse; the first thing he encountered was an enemy squadron. The marshal was immediately made prisoner and led out of the town, without knowing what had happened and unable to conceive the cause of so extraordinary an occurrence. Prince Eugene was already in Cremona. A priest, named Bozzoli, provost of Santa Maria la Nuova, had let in the German troops by an underground passage. Four hundred soldiers, who had entered the priest's house by means of this passage, had at once butchered the guards at the two gates; the two gates being opened, Prince Eugene entered with four thousand men. All this was done before the governor, a Spaniard, suspected anything, and before Marshal Villeroi was even awake.

Secrecy, order, diligence, all possible precautions had contributed to the success of the enterprise. As soon as the Spanish governor appeared in the streets with a few soldiers, he was killed by a musket shot; and all the staff officers were either killed or taken prisoners with the exception of the Count de Revel, lieutenant-general, and the Marquis du Praslin.

Chance, however, confounded the discretion of Prince Eugene.

On that very day the Chevalier d'Entragues was to hold in the town a review of the ships' regiments of which he was the colonel, and the soldiers were already assembling at four o'clock in the morning at one end of the town at the very moment when Prince Eugene was entering at the other. D'Entragues hastened through the streets with his soldiers, offered resistance to the Germans that he met, and thus gave the rest of the garrison time to muster. The streets and public places were filled with officers and soldiers, hurrying pell-mell, some armed, others rushing about scarcely dressed, without discipline or order. They fought in the midst of confusion, made trenches from street to street, and from square to square. Two Irish regiments, which formed part of the garrison, checked the advance of the Imperial troops. Never was town surprised with greater dexterity or defended with greater courage. The garrison comprised about five thousand men, and not more than four thousand of Prince Eugene's men had yet entered the town. A large detachment of his army was to arrive by the bridge over the Po: his measures had been well taken, but again an unfortunate chance upset everything. The bridge over the Po, insufficiently guarded by about a hundred French soldiers, was to have been seized first of all by the German cuirassiers who were ordered to go and take possession of it as soon as Prince Eugene entered the town. In order to do this, since they had entered by the south gate close to the underground passage, it was necessary for them immediately to hasten out of Cremona on the north side by the Po and rush to the bridge. They did this; the guide who was leading them, however, was killed by a musket shot from a window, and the cuirassiers mistook their road and went a long way round. In this short interval the Irish fell upon the Po gate, and attacked and repulsed the cuirassiers; the Marquis du Praslin took advantage of the opportunity, and ordered the bridge to be destroyed: the assistance which the enemy were awaiting was thus unable to reach them, and the town was saved.

Having fought all day without ever losing possession of the gate by which he had entered, Prince Eugene retired, taking with him as prisoners Marshal Villeroi and several staff officers, but having failed to take Cremona, which his enterprise and circumspection, aided by the governor's negligence, had given into his hands, but of which he was robbed by a stroke of bad fortune and the valour of the French and Irish troops.

Marshal Villeroi was extremely unfortunate on this occasion; he was condemned by the courtiers at Versailles with all the severity and bitterness that could be inspired by the favouritism of which he had been the object and by his personal pride, which they thought approached too near to vanity. The king, who pitied him in place of blaming him, incensed that the man of his choice should be so severely blamed, so far forgot himself as to say, "They inveigh against him simply because he is my favourite"; it was the only occasion in his life on which he used the expression. The Duke of Vendôme was thereupon nominated to the command in Italy.

The Duke of Vendôme, grandson of Henri-Quatre, was, like him, dauntless, pleasant, generous, not standing upon ceremony, and a stranger alike to envy and revenge. He was haughty only with princes; with everyone else he bore himself as an equal. He was the only general under whom soldiers were not driven into battle by the exigence of military service, and that instinct of purely animal, even mechanical fury, which blindly obeys the orders of officers; his soldiers fought for their leader, the Duke of Vendôme himself, and they would give their lives to retrieve him from a false step in which the recklessness of his genius sometimes engaged him. He was not thought to ponder upon his plans so deeply as Prince Eugene, or to understand so well the art of maintaining an army. He paid too little attention to details, and allowed military discipline to fall into neglect, too much of his time being taken up with eating and sleeping; in this he resembled his brother. This laxity put him more than once in danger of being dismissed; but in the day of action he redeemed all by a presence of mind and a power of judgment which danger only served to make keener, and such days of action he was continually seeking; from all accounts he was adjudged less fitted to carry on a defensive war than Prince Eugene, but quite as capable of taking the offensive.

The disorder and negligence which he introduced into the army was seen carried to a singular excess in his own household, and even his own person; detesting luxury, he fled to the other extreme of observing a contemptuous slovenliness, of which there is no other example; and his disinterestedness, in itself the noblest of virtues, became in him a failing which, by its very excess, made him lose more than he ever gained by benefits bestowed. He was known to have been often in want of the necessities of life. His brother, the grand prior, who commanded under him in Italy, had all his faults, which he even carried still farther, and only redeemed by a like valour. It was, indeed, an amazing thing to see two generals who often did not leave their beds until four o'clock in the afternoon, two princes even, grandsons of Henri-Quatre, so negligent of their own persons that the basest of men would have been ashamed to be seen thus.

What is still more surprising is the mingling of activity and indolence with which Vendôme carried on the war against Eugene, a war conspicuous for cunning, surprises, marches, the crossing of rivers, skirmishes often as useless as private murders, and sanguinary battles in which both sides claimed the victory; such a battle was that of Luzzara, fought on 15 August, 1702, for which *Te Deums* were sung both at Vienna and Paris. Vendôme was victorious on every occasion that he was not directly engaged with Prince Eugene in person; but as soon as the latter was at the head of his troops France ceased to hold the advantage.

(January 1703) In the midst of these battles and the sieges of numerous castles and petty towns, secret intelligence was received at Versailles that the Duke of Savoy, grandson of a sister of Louis XIII., and father-in-law of the Duke of Burgundy and Philip V. of Spain, was about to desert the Bourbons and thus buy the Emperor's support. Everyone was surprised to see him desert not only his two sons-in-law, but also, as they thought, his real interests. But the Emperor promised him all that his sons-in-law had refused him: Montferrat, Mantua, Alexandria, Valencia, the country between the Po and the Tanaro, and more money than even France was giving him. The money would have to be found by England, for the Emperor had scarcely enough with which to pay his own armies. England, the wealthiest of the Allies, was contributing more than all of them to the common cause. The Duke of Savoy might have little regard for the laws of nations and of nature, but, after all, that is a question of ethics with which the conduct of sovereigns is little concerned. The result of itself eventually showed that he did not lack, at least in his treaty, a knowledge of the laws of policy; he was, however, guilty of neglecting another and essential point—in leaving his troops to the mercy of the French while he was negotiating with the Emperor.

On 19 August, 1703, the Duke of Vendôme disarmed them. There were, it is true, but five thousand men, but it was no slight set-back to the Duke of Savoy.

Scarcely had the House of Bourbon lost this ally than she learnt that Portugal had declared against her. Peter, King of Portugal, acknowledged the Archduke Charles as King of Spain. Accordingly the Imperial Council divided in favour of Peter II., and in the name of the archduke, a monarchy of which as yet it did not possess a single town; by one of those treaties which are never fulfilled the council granted him Vigo, Bayonne, Alcantara, Badajoz, part of Estremadura, and the whole country situated to the west of the Plate River in South America; in a word, it apportioned out what it did not possess in order to acquire all that it could in Spain.

The King of Portugal, the Prince of Darmstadt, minister of the archduke, and his adherent, the Admiral of Castile, even solicited the help of the King of Morocco. They not only made treaties with this barbarian in order to obtain horses and wheat, but they asked for troops. Muley Ismail, Emperor of Morocco, and at that time the most warlike and subtle of the Mahommedan despots, would only consent to send troops on conditions perilous to Christendom and shameful to the King of Portugal; he demanded one of the king's sons as hostage, and several towns. The treaty consequently was not concluded. The Christians proceeded to fight among themselves without bringing in the aid of barbarian troops. The help from Africa was in any case not so valuable as that of England and Holland to the House of Austria.

Churchill, afterwards Earl and Duke of Marlborough, appointed general of the combined English and Dutch troops from 1702 onwards, was the most fatal antagonist to France's greatness that had appeared for several centuries. He was not one of those generals to whom a minister gives a written plan of campaign, and who, after carrying out the orders of the cabinet at the head of an army, returns to request the honour of serving again. On the contrary, he dominated the Queen of England herself, both by the need she had of him and the powerful influence exerted by his wife. He ruled parliament by the authority of his position and that of the Lord Chancellor, Godolphin, whose son had married his daughter. In such a fashion, master of the court, of parliament, of the war department, and of finance, more of a king than William had ever been, as good a statesman and much greater a leader, he accomplished more than the Allies dared to hope. He possessed above all the generals of his time that calmness of courage in the midst of tumult, that serenity of mind in time of danger, which the English call *cool-headedness.*

It is perhaps owing to that quality, the most essential gift of nature for him who wishes to command, that the English have gained on other occasions such victories over the French as were seen on the plains of Poitiers, of Crécy and of Agincourt.

An indefatigable soldier during campaigns, Marlborough proved himself an equally active diplomatist during the winter. He visited The Hague and all the courts of Germany: he persuaded the Dutch to do everything in their power to humble France: he stirred up the resentment of the Elector Palatine: he flattered the dignity of the Elector of Brandenburg at a time when that prince wished to become king, humbling himself indeed so far as to present a napkin to him at table, and thus securing help from him to the number of seven to eight thousand soldiers.

No sooner had Prince Eugene for his part finished one campaign than he repaired in person to Vienna to direct the preparations of another.

It is well known that armies are better provided for when the general is his own minister. These two men, sometimes commanding together, sometimes separately, were always in agreement with each other; they frequently conferred together at The Hague with the grand pensionary, Heinsius, and the registrar Fagel, who ruled the United Provinces as wisely as the Barneveldts and the De Witts and with yet more fortune. Always acting in concert, they drew up the forces of half Europe against the House of Bourbon; and the French ministry was powerless to withstand for long these united forces. The secret of their plans of campaign was always rigorously kept between them: they formulated their own plans and only confided them to those who would have to carry them out at the moment of execution.

Chamillart, on the contrary, being no statesman, soldier, nor even financial expert, yet entrusted with the rôle of prime minister, was entirely incapable of making plans on his own initiative, and had consequently to receive them from the hands of his subordinates. Secret plans were thus on occasion made public even before he knew precisely what was to be done. The Marquis de Feuquières rightly blamed him for this, and Mme. de Maintenon admits in her letters that the man she had chosen turned out an incompetent minister. In that incompetence lay one of the principal causes of France's misfortunes.

Once in command of the allied armies in Flanders, Marlborough was not slow in showing that he had learnt the art of war under Turenne. In former days he had fought his first campaigns under that general as a volunteer, and had been known in the army as the *bel Anglais*; but the Viscount de Turenne had prophesied that the handsome Englishman would one day be a great man. His first actions were to promote subaltern officers till then unknown whose merit he discerned, refusing to be bound by the usual system of military service, known in France as the *ordre du tableau*. He was well aware that healthy rivalry is at an end when promotion is made only by seniority, and that an officer is not always better than another for having been longer in the service. (1702) His first care was to fashion men. He succeeded in gaining territory from the French without striking a blow.

The first month, the Earl of Athlone, the Dutch general, disputed the command with him, but in the second he was obliged to defer entirely to him. The King of France had sent against him his grandson, the Duke of Burgundy, a wise and just prince, born to make men happy, whose army was commanded by Marshal Boufflers, a man of untiring courage.

The Duke of Burgundy, however, returned to Versailles in the middle of the campaign. During September and October of 1702, Boufflers remained the sole witness of Marlborough's triumphs: the English general took Venloo, Ruremonde, Liège, in quick succession, advancing continuously and never for a moment losing the advantage.

On his return to London after this campaign Marlborough was accorded all the honours it is possible to enjoy, both in a monarchy and a republic; he was made a duke by the queen, and what was still more flattering, was thanked by the two houses of parliament whose members came to his private house to congratulate him.

Meanwhile, however, in France a man was coming to the

front who, it seemed, would restore her fortunes; this was the Marshal Duke de Villars, then lieutenant-general, and later at the age of eighty-two generalissimo of the armies of France, Spain and Sardinia, an officer full of daring and self-confidence. By his resolute determination to do more than his duty he had been the artificer of his own fortune. On several occasions he offended Louis, and what was more dangerous, Louvois, by addressing them with the same fearlessness with which he served them. He was reproached for not displaying a modesty appropriate to his valour; but at length it was perceived that he had a genius for warfare and was eminently fitted to lead the French. In a few years he was promoted to the highest post after having long remained in obscurity.

Few men have excited more jealousy by their success and with less cause. He became a Marshal of France, duke and peer, and the governor of a province; but he saved the state; and others by whom the state was lost or who were no more than courtiers have reaped very much the same rewards. He has even been reproached for his wealth, moderate as it was, and obtained by taxes levied on enemy country—a legitimate recompense for his valour and his leadership; yet others, who have amassed fortunes ten times as great by shameful means, have enjoyed them with universal approbation. He was eighty almost before he began to enjoy his fame. He had need to outlive the whole court to taste the fullness of his glory.

It is not unprofitable to enquire why men are thus unjust: the reason is to be found in the fact that Marshal Villars possessed no tact. He had neither the art of making friends with straightforwardness and spirit, nor the power of winning esteem, although he habitually spoke of himself as he deserved that others should speak of him.

On one occasion, when leaving to take command of the army, he said to the king in the presence of the whole court: "Sire, I go to fight the enemies of your majesty and I leave you in the midst of mine." He said to the courtiers of the Duke of Orleans, Regent of the kingdom, who had become wealthy by subversions of the state known as the *System*: "For myself I have never won anything except from the enemy." Such words, which displayed the same courage as his actions, humbled the pride of lesser men already sufficiently exasperated by his triumphs.

At the beginning of this war he was one of the lieutenants-general who commanded detachments in Alsace. The Prince of Baden at the head of the Imperial army had just taken Landau, which had been defended for four months by Mélac. The prince was making progress. He had the advantage of numbers, of the ground and the prestige of a campaign well begun. His army lay among the mountains of Breisgau, which border the Black Forest, and this immense forest separated the Bavarian troops from the French. Catinat was in command at Strasburg. His cautiousness forbade him to advance and attack the Prince of Baden with so many disadvantages; for the French army would be irretrievably lost and the way to Alsace opened in the event of failure. Villars, who had determined to become a Marshal of France or perish, ventured to do what Catinat dared not attempt. He obtained the consent of the court, advanced upon the Imperial troops towards Friedlingen with an inferior force, and fought on 14 October, 1702, the battle which bears that name.

The cavalry was engaged on the plain while the French infantry climbed the heights and attacked the German infantry entrenched in the woods. I have heard it said more than once, that when the battle was won and as Marshal de Villars was marching at the head of the infantry, a voice cried, "We are cut off." At these words his regiments took to flight as one man. He ran after them, shouting, "Come, my friends, the victory is ours! Long live the king!" The soldiers tremblingly replied, "Long live the king!" but continued their flight. The general's greatest difficulty was thus in rallying the victors. Had two enemy regiments appeared at that moment of blind panic the French would have been defeated; thus does Fortune play her part in the winning of battles.

The Prince of Baden, after losing three thousand men, his cannon and the field of battle, after being pursued two leagues through woods and defiles, and with the fortress of Friedlingen taken as proof of his defeat, nevertheless reported to Vienna that he had gained a victory and had the *Te Deum* sung, a more shameful action than that of losing the battle.

The French soldiers, having recovered from their terror, proclaimed Villars Marshal of France on the field of battle, and a fortnight later the king confirmed what the voices of his soldiers had bestowed.

In April 1703 Marshal Villars at length joined his victorious forces with those of the Elector of Bavaria, whom he found also victorious, gaining territory and in possession of the Imperial town of Ratisbon, where the assembled council of the Empire had but recently planned his ruin.

Villars was better fitted to serve the state by following his own genius than by collaborating with a prince. He conducted or rather hurried the Elector across the Danube, and the river once crossed, the Elector regretted his action, perceiving that the slightest check would leave his country at the Emperor's mercy. The Count of Styrum at the head of a body of nearly twenty thousand men was advancing to join up with the main army of the Prince of Baden near Donau-wörth. "We must prevent them," the marshal said to the prince, "we must fall on Styrum and march without delay." The Elector procrastinated, replying that he must consult his generals and ministers. "I am both your minister and your general," Villars retorted. "Do you need any other advice than mine when it is a question of giving battle?" Thinking only of the danger of his country and annoyed with his general, the prince still held back. "Very well," Villars told him, "if your Electoral Highness is unwilling to seize this opportunity with your Bavarians, I intend to fight them with my French," and he at once gave the order to attack. The indignant prince, seeing only recklessness in the Frenchman's action, was obliged to fight in spite of himself; and the battle took place on 20 September, 1705, on the plains of Höchstädt, near Donauwörth.

After the first charge the power of chance over the results of battles was again demonstrated. Both armies, French and German, seized with panic, took flight at the same time, and for several minutes Marshal Villars found himself left practically alone upon the field; he rallied his troops, renewed the fight and won the battle. Three thousand of the Imperial troops were killed, four thousand were made prisoners, and they lost their cannon and baggage. The Elector was master of Augsburg, the road to Vienna was opened, and the question of evacuating the capital was openly discussed in the Emperor's council.

The Emperor's panic was pardonable; he had been defeated everywhere. On 6 September, but a fortnight before, the Duke of Burgundy with the Marshals Tallard and Vauban under his command had taken the aged Brisach prisoner. On

14 November, 1703, Tallard not only recaptured Landau, but also near Spires defeated the Prince of Hesse, afterwards King of Sweden, who attempted to relieve the town. If one is to believe the Marquis de Feuquières, so experienced an officer and judge of the military art, but always very severe in his judgments, Marshal Tallard only won this battle through the enemy's mistakes and over-confidence. However, he wrote to the king from the field of battle, "Sire, your army has taken more than one enemy standard for every life laid down by a private soldier."

The bayonet inflicted greater slaughter in this action than in any other of the war. It is an arm which the French with the impetuosity of their race employ to great advantage; but it has since become more threatening than deadly. Sustained and well-directed fire has prevailed over it. The Germans and the English were trained to fire in divisions with greater order and promptitude than the French. The Prussians were the first to load their guns with iron ramrods. The second King of Prussia trained them so that they could easily fire six shots a minute. Three ranks firing simultaneously and then immediately and swiftly advancing—that is the dominating factor in battles of to-day. Field cannon are no less formidable in their effect. Battalions shaken by this fire will not face a bayonet charge, and cavalry will succeed in breaking them up. The bayonet thus terrifies rather than kills, and the sword has become absolutely useless to the infantry. The bodily strength, dexterity and courage of an individual combatant are no longer of any use to him. Battalions have become vast machines, the better equipped of which necessarily breaks down the opposing battalion. It is precisely for this reason that Prince Eugene gained his celebrated victories of Temesvar and Belgrade against the Turks, where the superior numbers of the Turks would probably have given them the advantage had there occurred what is known as a *mêlée*. The art of destruction is thus completely different not merely from what it was before the invention of gunpowder, but from what it was a hundred years ago.

Meanwhile, the fortunes of France having been at first so successfully upheld on the German side, it was thought that Marshal Villars would extend them still further, with that impetuosity of his, which was so disconcerting to German tardiness; but his very character, which made him so redoubtable a leader, brought him into disagreement with the

Elector of Bavaria. The king liked his generals to be arrogant only towards the enemy, and the Elector of Bavaria was ill-judged enough to ask France for another marshal.

Villars himself, disgusted with the petty intrigues of a restless and self-seeking court, with the vacillations of the Elector, and still more so with Chamillart, the Minister of State, whose letters to him were as full of prejudice as they were of ignorance, asked the king's permission to retire. This was the sole reward for military operations of the highest genius and the winning of a pitched battle. To France's misfortune Chamillart sent him to the heart of the Cevennes to quell fanatical peasants, and thus deprived the French armies of the only general besides the Duke of Vendôme who could inspire them with an invincible courage. We shall speak of these fanatics in the chapter on religion. At that time Louis XIV. had enemies at once more terrible, more successful and more inexorable than the inhabitants of the Cevennes.

CHAPTER XIX

DEFEAT OF BLENHEIM, OR HÖCHSTÄDT, AND ITS CONSEQUENCES

AT the beginning of 1703 the Duke of Marlborough had recommenced his campaign in the neighbourhood of the Netherlands with the same skill and the same success. He had taken Bonn, the seat of the Elector of Cologne. Thence he had retaken Huy and Limburg and made himself master of the whole of the Lower Rhine. Marshal Villeroi, on being released from prison, was in command in Flanders and enjoyed no more success against Marlborough than previously against Prince Eugene. It was to no purpose that Marshal Boufflers with a detachment of the army had gained a small advantage against Obdam, the Dutch general, at the Battle of Eckeren. A success which has no results is worth nothing.

Nevertheless, if the English general did not march to the Emperor's help, the House of Austria, it seemed, was lost. The Elector of Bavaria was master of Passau. Thirty thousand French, under the orders of Marshal Marsin, who had succeeded Villars, were pouring into the country beyond the Danube. Advance parties were overrunning Austria. Vienna was threatened on the one side by the French and Bavarians and on the other by Prince Rakoczy, at the head of Hungarians fighting for their liberty and assisted by French and Turkish money. Prince Eugene thereupon hurriedly left Italy and came to take over the command of the German armies; at Heilbronn he saw the Duke of Marlborough. The English general, who was entirely unhampered in his schemes, the Queen of England and the Dutch having given him full powers to carry them out, hastened to the assistance of the central part of the Empire. He took with him ten thousand English infantry and twenty-three squadrons, and advanced by forced marches in the direction of the Danube; he arrived close to Donauwörth opposite the lines of the Elector of Bavaria, where some eight thousand French and as many Bavarians lay entrenched, guarding the territories they had conquered. After a two hours' fight on 2 July, 1704, Marlborough broke through their ranks at the head of three English battalions and routed the Bavarians and the French. It is said that he killed six thousand of the enemy and lost nearly as many: but the number of dead is of small consequence to a general when he attains his object. He took Donauwörth, crossed the Danube, and laid Bavaria under contribution.

Marshal Villeroi, who had intended to pursue him during his initial marches, had suddenly lost sight of him, and only learnt of his whereabouts when he heard of this victory of Donauwörth.

Marshal Tallard, with a corps of about thirty thousand men, came up by another route to bar Marlborough's advance and joined up with the Elector; at the same time Prince Eugene arrived and united his forces with those of Marlborough.

At length the two armies met quite close to Donauwörth itself and on the same plains where Marshal Villars had been victorious the year before. The latter was then in the Cevennes. It is within my knowledge that on receiving a letter from Tallard's army written on the eve of battle by a soldier who explained the position of the two armies and the tactics which Marshal Tallard intended to adopt, Villars wrote to his brother-in-law, the President de Maisons, saying that if Marshal Tallard gave battle defending that position, he would be inevitably defeated. The letter was shown to Louis XIV., and was afterwards made public.

(13 August, 1704) Including the Bavarians, the French army consisted of eighty-two battalions and one hundred

and sixty squadrons, amounting to some sixty thousand
fighting men, since the corps were not up to complement.
The enemy's army contained sixty-four battalions and one
hundred and fifty-two squadrons, though not more than
about fifty-two thousand men strong, for armies are always
made out to be stronger than they are. So bloody and decisive
a battle deserves especial attention. The French generals have
been blamed for many mistakes, the principal one being
that of placing themselves in a position where a battle was
inevitable, instead of letting the enemy's army perish for
want of food, and thus giving Marshal Villeroi time to fall
on the unprotected Netherlands or to advance on Germany.
But as an answer to this reproach it must be remembered
that the French army, being slightly stronger than that of
the Allies, might well hope to defeat them, and that such a
victory would have dethroned the Emperor. The Marquis
de Feuquières enumerates twelve cardinal faults made by
the Elector, Marsin and Tallard, both before and after the
battle. One of the most serious was that of omitting to have
a large body of infantry in the centre and in having separated
their two army corps. I have often heard it said by Marshal
Villars that such a disposition was inexcusable.

Marshal Tallard was on the right wing, the Elector with
Marsin on the left. Marshal Tallard had all the impetuous
courage and ardour of a Frenchman, and was in addition
active, acute, fertile in every kind of expedient and resource.
It was he who had concluded the partition treaties. He had
acquired fame and fortune by every means open to a man of
spirit and courage. He had gained great credit at the Battle
of Spires in spite of the criticisms of Feuquières; for a victorious general has no faults in the eyes of the public, just
as a defeated one is always in the wrong however judicious
his conduct may have been.

Marshal Tallard, however, suffered from a misfortune
which was dangerous in the extreme to a general; his sight
was so weak that he could not distinguish objects at a
distance of twenty feet. Those who knew him well have also
told me that his fiery courage, the opposite of that of Marlborough, which burnt still brighter in the heat of action, did
not permit him a requisite freedom of judgment. The failing
arose from his dry, hot-blooded nature. It is well known that
all the qualities of our minds depend upon our *temperaments*.

Marshal Marsin had never before held the chief command,

and while a man of sense and honour, it was said that he had the experience rather of a good officer than of a general.

As for the Elector of Bavaria, he was considered less as a great captain than as a brave and amiable prince, beloved by his subjects, of a temper more magnanimous than persevering.

At last, between the hours of twelve and one, the battle began. Crossing a stream, Marlborough and the English were already charging the cavalry under Tallard, who but a short time before had visited the left wing to see how it was disposed. This constituted a preliminary disadvantage in that Tallard's army had to fight without its general to lead them. The army of the Elector and Marsin had not been engaged by Prince Eugene. Marlborough thus attacked the French right wing nearly an hour before Eugene came up with the Elector on the left.

As soon as Marshal Tallard learnt that Marlborough was attacking his wing, he hastened back to find a furious fight raging, and the French cavalry three times rallied and three times repulsed. He proceeded to the village of Blenheim, where he had stationed twenty-seven battalions and twelve squadrons, as a small separate army, which kept up a continuous fire upon Marlborough's troops. From this village, whence he issued his orders, he flew back to the spot where Marlborough, with the cavalry and battalions and squadrons mixed, was driving back the French cavalry.

M. de Feuquières is certainly in error when he says that Marshal Tallard was not there, but was taken prisoner on returning from Marsin's wing to his own. All reports agree; and it is only too true that he was present on the spot. He himself was wounded and his son received a mortal blow at his side. The whole of his cavalry was routed before his eyes. Marlborough, victorious, broke through on one side between the two French armies, and on the other his general officers broke through between the village of Blenheim and Tallard's army, still cut off from the little army stationed in Blenheim itself.

In this grievous predicament Marshal Tallard hastened to rally a few squadrons, but, owing to his weak sight, he took one of the enemy's squadrons for a French one, and was taken prisoner by the troops of the Duke of Hesse who were in the pay of England. At the moment when the general was captured, Prince Eugene, after being repulsed three times, at last gained the upper hand. The rout was already complete, and the army corps under Marshal Tallard took to headlong flight. The dismay and confusion of the whole of the right wing was indeed so great that officers and soldiers threw themselves into the Danube without knowing where they were going. Not a single general officer gave the order to retreat; not a single one thought either of saving the twenty-five battalions and twelve squadrons of the best troops in France still so unfortunately cooped up in Blenheim, or of bringing them into action.

Marshal Marsin then beat a retreat. The Count du Bourg, afterwards a Marshal of France, saved a small section of the infantry by retreating through the marshes of Höchstädt; but not he, nor Marsin, nor anyone gave a thought to the army that still remained in Blenheim awaiting orders which it never received. Eleven thousand men were stationed there, and they were the most experienced troops. There are several examples of smaller armies who have defeated fifty thousand men, or at any rate made glorious retreats, but the situation in which they are placed decides everything. They could not sally forth from the narrow streets of a village and place themselves in battle order in the face of a victorious army, which might at any moment have overwhelmed them with a larger front and with their artillery, which had already been increased by the very guns of the defeated army. The general officer who should have commanded them, the Marquis de Clérembault, son of Marshal Clérembault, hastened to ask for orders from Marshal Tallard, learnt that he had been taken prisoner and, seeing nothing but fugitives, fled with them and was drowned in the Danube.

Sivières, a brigadier who was stationed in the village, attempted a bold stroke; he called out to officers from Artois and Provence to accompany him, and together with several officers from other regiments, they fell upon the enemy, as if making a sortie from a besieged town; but after the sortie they were obliged to return to the village. One of the officers, named Denonville, returned to the village a moment later on horseback with Hamilton, Earl of Orkney. "Are you bringing us an English prisoner?" exclaimed the officers surrounding him. "No, gentlemen," was the reply, "I am a prisoner myself and come to tell you that there is nothing for it but to deliver yourselves up as prisoners of war. Here is the Earl of Orkney who proposes that you

surrender." The old soldiers trembled; the Navarre regiment
tore up their colours and buried them, but were obliged in
the end to bow to necessity, and the army surrendered without fighting. Lord Orkney has since told me that the body
of troops in question could not do otherwise in such difficult
circumstances. Europe was amazed that the finest French
troops should have suffered such ignominy in a body.
Their misfortune was attributed to cowardice; but several
years afterwards the instance of fourteen thousand Swedish
surrendering at discretion to the Russians in open country
vindicated the French.

Such was the famous battle which in France bears the name
of Höchstädt, in Germany of Blindheim, and of Blenheim
in England. Of the victors there were nearly five thousand killed and nearly eight thousand wounded, the largest
number belonging to Prince Eugene. The French army was
almost entirely destroyed. Of sixty thousand men victorious
for so long, not more than twenty thousand effective troops
could be mustered.

About twelve thousand dead, fourteen thousand prisoners,
all the guns, an immense number of standards and flags,
tents, equipment, the general of the army and twelve hundred
distinguished officers in the power of the victor—these were
the fruits of the battle for France. The fugitives were scattered
and nearly a hundred leagues of territory were lost in less
than one month. The whole of Bavaria passed under the
Emperor's yoke, and experienced to the full the severity of
an exasperated Austrian government and the extremes of
greed and barbarity of which a victorious soldier is capable.
The Elector, fleeing to Brussels, met his brother, the Elector
of Cologne, on the road; he also had been driven from his
estates, and they embraced with tears. Amazement and consternation filled the Court of Versailles, so long accustomed
to success. The news of the defeat arrived in the midst of
rejoicings on the birth of a great-grandson to Louis XIV.
No one dared to inform the king of so cruel a fact. Finally,
Mme. de Maintenon was compelled to take upon herself the
duty of telling him that he was no longer invincible.

It has been said and written and all histories have repeated
that the Emperor erected a monument of this defeat upon
the plains of Blenheim which bore an inscription ignominious
to the King of France; but such a monument never existed.
It was only in England that a monument was erected, and

that in honour of the Duke of Marlborough. The queen and parliament had a vast palace built for him on his principal estate, to which the name of Blenheim was given; and the battle is commemorated in pictures and in tapestry. The thanks of both houses of parliament, of the towns and villages, in a word, the applause of England, these were the first rewards he reaped from his victory. The poem composed by the celebrated Addison, a more lasting memorial than Blenheim Palace, is accounted by that warlike and ingenious nation among the most honourable of the rewards accorded to the Duke of Marlborough. The Emperor made him a prince of the Empire, giving him the principality of Mindelheim, which was afterwards exchanged for another; but he has never been known under this title, the name of Marlborough having become the most glorious that he could bear.

On dispersal of the French army, the road from the Danube to the Rhine lay open to the Allies. They accordingly crossed the Rhine and invaded Alsace. Prince Louis of Baden, a general famous for his encampments and marches, besieged Landau which the French had recaptured. Joseph, King of the Romans, eldest son of the Emperor Leopold, was present at this siege. Landau was taken on the 19th, and Trarbach on the 23rd November, 1704.

The loss of one hundred leagues of territory did not prevent the frontiers of France from being drawn back still farther. Louis XIV. was supporting his grandson in Spain and was victorious in Italy. Great efforts were necessary in Germany to check Marlborough, and they were made. The remains of the army were assembled, garrisons were depleted, and the militia was called up. Money was borrowed by the ministry from all sides. An army was finally formed, and Marshal Villars was recalled from the Cevennes to take up the command. He arrived to find himself close to Trèves, facing the English general with inferior forces. Both were eager to engage in fresh battle. But as the Prince of Baden had not arrived in time to unite his forces with the English, Villars had at least the glory of obliging Marlborough to decamp (May 1705). It was no small feat at this juncture. The Duke of Marlborough had sufficient esteem for Marshal Villars to wish to be esteemed by him in turn, and wrote to him as he was decamping: "Do me the justice to believe that my retreat is the fault of the Prince of Baden, and that my esteem for you is greater than my vexation with him."

The French had therefore still a defensive barrier in Germany. Flanders, where Marshal Villeroi, released from prison, was in command, had not been invaded. In Spain, Philip V. and the Archduke Charles both nourished expectations of the crown; the former by reason of his grandfather's power and the goodwill of the majority of the Spanish; the latter by English help and his partisans in Catalonia and Aragon. The archduke, afterwards Emperor, but then merely the second son of the Emperor Leopold, possessing nothing but his title, had gone towards the end of 1703 to London practically without a retinue in order to entreat the help of Queen Anne.

Then the whole might of the English was displayed. This nation, a stranger as it was to the dispute, supplied the Austrian prince with two hundred transport ships, thirty warships, together with ten Dutch ships, nine thousand fighting men, and enough money to conquer a kingdom. But the superiority which power and the consciousness of benefits bestowed can give, did not prevent the Emperor in his letter to Queen Anne, which the archduke presented, from refusing that sovereign, his benefactress, the title of *Majesty*; he addressed her but as *Serenity*, according to the style of the Court of Vienna, a style which custom alone could justify and which reason afterwards altered when pride was forced to yield to necessity.

CHAPTER XX

LOSSES IN SPAIN. DEFEATS AT THE BATTLES OF RAMILLIES AND TURIN, AND THEIR CONSEQUENCES

ONE of the first exploits of the English forces was the taking of Gibraltar, which men had good reason to believe impregnable. A long ridge of precipitous rocks forbids all approach on the land side, and there is no harbour. A wide bay, unsafe and stormy in the extreme, exposes ships to tempests and gun-fire from the fortress and the mole; the citizens of this town could alone defend it against a thousand ships and a hundred thousand men; but the very strength of the place was the cause of its capture. The garrison consisted of only a hundred men; the number was sufficient, but they neglected a duty which they thought unnecessary. The Prince of Hesse had landed with eighteen hundred soldiers on the isthmus which lies to the north and at the back of the town; but from this side a precipitous cliff makes the town impregnable. In vain the fleet fired fifteen thousand cannon-shots. At last a few sailors, who were out merry-making, approached in their rowing-boats under the lee of the mole, in which position they should have been blown up by the guns, but they were not even fired at. They climbed on to the mole and took possession of it; the troops came up, and in such a way the impregnable town was compelled to surrender on 4 August, 1704. It still belongs to the English at the time I am writing. Spain, once more a first-class power under the government of the Princess of Parma, second wife of Philip V., and later victorious in Africa and Italy, still sees with impotent bitterness Gibraltar in the hands of a Northern nation, whose ships two centuries ago were scarcely ever seen in the Mediterranean.

Immediately after the capture of Gibraltar, the English fleet, mistress of the seas, attacked the Count of Toulouse, Admiral of France, in sight of Malaga; the battle, it is true, was indecisive, but it marked the last phase of Louis XIV.'s power. His natural son, the Count of Toulouse, was in command of fifty vessels of the line and twenty-four galleys. He withdrew without loss and not entirely without glory. But later, in March 1705, the king, having sent thirteen ships to attack Gibraltar, while Marshal Tessé besieged it by land, both army and fleet were lost by such twofold temerity. Part of the fleet was broken up by storms; another part was boarded and taken by the English after a noble resistance, and yet another burnt on the coasts of Spain. After that day no large French fleets were to be seen either on the Atlantic or in the Mediterranean. The navy sank again to the same state from which Louis XIV. had rescued it, like so many other brilliant undertakings which, during his rule, were seen to rise and wane.

The English, who had captured Gibraltar for themselves, now conquered Valencia and Catalonia in six short weeks for Archduke Charles. They took Barcelona by an accident which arose from the temerity of the besiegers.

The English were under the orders of one of the most remarkable men ever produced by that country so prolific in proud, valiant, and singular men. This was the Earl of

Peterborough, a man made in the image of those heroes which Spanish imagination has depicted in so many books. At fifteen he had set out from London to take part in the war against the Moors in Africa; at twenty he was one of the leaders of the revolution in England, and was the first to join the Prince of Orange in Holland; but fearing that the object of his voyage would be suspected, he embarked for America, and from there sailed on a Dutch vessel to The Hague. More than once he lost or gave away all his worldly wealth, and then again restored his fortunes. He was carrying on the war in Spain practically at his own expense, and at the same time was supporting the archduke and all his household. It was he who besieged Barcelona with the Prince of Darmstadt. He suggested to him a sudden attack on the entrenchments guarding Fort Mont-Joui and the town. These trenches, where the Prince of Darmstadt himself lost his life, were carried at the point of the sword. A bomb burst within the fort in the powder magazine and blew it up; the fort was immediately taken and the town surrendered. The viceroy was parleying with Peterborough at the gate of the town, and the terms were not yet signed, when suddenly a hubbub of cries and yells arose. "You have betrayed us," exclaimed the viceroy; "we surrendered in good faith, and here, your English have entered the town by the ramparts. They are pillaging and destroying everything." "You are mistaken," replied the Earl of Peterborough; "they must be the Prince of Darmstadt's troops. There is now only one way of saving your town, and that is to allow my men to enter at once; I will quell all disturbance and return to the gate to conclude the terms of surrender."

He spoke with a tone of sincerity and authority which at a time of such immediate danger convinced the governor, and he was allowed to enter. He advanced quickly with his officers to find the Germans and Catalonians, together with the dregs of the town, occupied in sacking the houses of the chief citizens; he pursued them, and forced them to abandon the booty that they were carrying away; in doing so he came upon the Duchess of Popoli in the hands of common soldiers who were about to violate her, and restored her to her husband. Finally, having quelled all disturbance, he returned to the gate and signed the capitulation. The Spaniards were amazed at such chivalry in the English, whom the mob had always taken for pitiless barbarians, since they were heretics.

The loss of Barcelona was followed, moreover, by the mortification of a vain attempt to recapture it. Philip V., with nearly all Spain on his side, had yet no generals, no engineers and hardly any soldiers. France provided everything. The Count of Toulouse returned to blockade the port with twenty-five ships that still remained to France. Marshal Tessé organised the siege with thirty-one squadrons and thirty-seven battalions; but the English fleet came on the scene, the French retreated, and Marshal Tessé hurriedly raised the siege. He left behind in his camp an immense store of provisions and abandoned in his flight fifteen hundred wounded to the mercy of the Earl of Peterborough. These losses were considerable; it was debated whether it once cost France more to conquer Spain than it now did to aid her. Louis XIV.'s grandson, however, still retained the affection of the Castilian nation, a nation which prides itself upon its fidelity, and now remained faithful to its choice.

In Italy all went well. Louis XIV. was revenged on the Duke of Savoy. At the commencement of the campaign the Duke of Vendôme had gloriously repulsed Prince Eugene at the Battle of Cassano, near by the Adda, on 16 August, 1705; it was a bloody encounter, one of those indecisive battles for which each side sings the *Te Deum*, but whose only result is the slaughter of men, with neither side gaining an advantage. Following Cassano, he won decisively at Calcinato on 19 April, 1706, Prince Eugene being absent; on the morrow of the battle Eugene arrived and witnessed another detachment of his troops totally defeated. The Allies were finally obliged to surrender the whole plain to the Duke of Vendôme. There remained practically only Turin to take. The siege was begun, and it seemed impossible to relieve it. Marshal Villars was pushing the Prince of Baden back towards Germany. In Flanders Villeroi was commanding an army of eighty thousand men and was confident of repairing against Marlborough the defeats he had sustained when fighting Prince Eugene. His excessive confidence in his own ability proved on this occasion more fatal than ever to France.

Marshal Villeroi had encamped his army near the Méhaigne and towards the source of the little river Gheet. His centre was at Ramillies, a village which has since become as famous as Blenheim. He could have avoided giving battle, and this was what his general officers advised; but he was carried away by a blind craving for glory (23 May, 1706). He disposed his forces, or so it is maintained, in such a way that no experienced officer could have predicted anything but failure. Freshly recruited troops, undisciplined and short of their full complement, were stationed at the centre; the baggage was allowed to remain between the army's lines, and his left wing was placed behind a marsh, as though he wished to prevent it from engaging the enemy.

Marlborough, who observed all these blunders, arranged his army so as to take advantage of them: seeing that the left wing of the French army could not advance to attack his right, he immediately depleted this right wing, so as to fall upon Ramillies with superior numbers. M. de Gassion, a lieutenant-general who observed these movements of the enemy, exclaimed to the marshal: "If you do not alter your order of battle you are lost. Reduce your left wing, so as to encounter the enemy with equal numbers, and close up your lines. If you hesitate a moment, the opportunity will be lost." Several officers seconded this sound advice, but the marshal did not heed them. Marlborough attacked. He was engaging enemies drawn up in just such a position as he would have wished to place them himself in order to defeat them. All France has declared it, and history is in part the record of men's opinions; but should it not also be said that the allied troops were better trained and that their confidence in their leaders and former successes prompted them to greater deeds of daring? Were there no French regiments who ill-performed their duty? and do not the battalions, that are most steadfast under fire, mould the destiny of nations? The French troops did not hold their ground for half an hour. They had fought for nearly eight hours at Blenheim, and killed nearly eight thousand of the victors; but at Ramillies they killed no more than two thousand five hundred; it was a complete rout; the French lost twenty thousand men, the nation's honour, and the hope of regaining the upper hand. Blenheim had lost them Bavaria and Cologne; Ramillies lost them the whole of Spanish Flanders. Marlborough entered victorious into Antwerp, and then into Brussels; he took Ostend, and Menin surrendered to him.

In despair, Marshal Villeroi dared not send news of this defeat to the king. For five days he forbore to despatch couriers. At length he wrote confirming the news which had already struck the Court of France with dismay: and when he re-appeared before the king, Louis, instead of heaping reproaches on him, simply said, "Sir Marshal, at your age there is no success."

The king at once recalled the Duke of Vendôme from Italy, where he thought him no longer needed, in order to send him to Flanders to retrieve this disaster if it were possible. He hoped at least, and apparently on good grounds, that the taking of Turin would console him for so many losses. Prince Eugene was not near enough to be able to relieve the city. He was stationed beyond the Adige, a river which, guarded on the nearer side by a long line of trenches, seemed to render his crossing impossible. The great city itself was being besieged by forty-six squadrons and a hundred battalions.

The Duke de La Feuillade, who was in command, was the most distinguished and amiable man in the kingdom, and, although the minister's son-in-law, was extremely popular. He was a son of that Marshal de La Feuillade who erected the statue of Louis XIV. in the *Place des Victoires*. One could see in him his father's courage, the same ambition and the same brilliancy, but with higher qualities of intellect. He was expecting as reward for the conquest of Turin the baton of a Marshal of France. Chamillart, his father-in-law, who loved him dearly, had been prodigal in every sort of supplies to assure his success. Imagination is appalled at the particulars of the preparations for this siege. Readers who have not the opportunity of obtaining information on these matters will perhaps be interested to learn the details of all that immense and useless apparatus.

140 cannons had been brought up, and, be it noted, that each large mounted cannon costs about 2000 crowns. There were 110,000 bullets, 106,000 cartridges of one kind and 300,000 of another, 21,000 bombs, 27,700 grenades, 15,000 sacks of earth, 30,000 tools for digging, and 1,200,000 pounds of powder. To these munitions must be added lead, iron, tin, ropes, everything for the use of miners, sulphur, saltpetre, and tools of every kind. There can be no doubt that the expense of all these preparations for destruction would be sufficient to found and support in a flourishing condition the largest colony. All sieges of large towns demand some tremendous outlay; but when a ruined village at home requires rebuilding it is neglected.

The Duke de La Feuillade, full of zeal and energy, better qualified than any for enterprises demanding courage alone, but little qualified for those requiring skill, thought and time, hurried on this siege against all canons of military art. Marshal Vauban, perhaps the only general who loved his country better than himself, proposed to the Duke de La Feuillade to come and direct the siege as an engineer, serving meanwhile in his army as a volunteer; but La Feuillade in his pride imagined that Vauban's offers were prompted by arrogance under a veil of modesty. He was annoyed that the finest engineer in Europe should attempt to give him advice. He wrote in a letter which I have seen: "I am hoping to take Turin *à la Cohorn*." Cohorn was the Vauban of the Allies, a fine engineer and a good general, who had more than once captured towns fortified by Vauban. After such a letter there was nothing for it but to take Turin; his having attacked the fort, however, which was the strongest part, and not even having completely surrounded the town, enabled both help and provisions to enter, and the Duke of Savoy to sally out; the more vehemently the Duke de La Feuillade made his repeated and fruitless attacks, the longer the siege dragged on.

The Duke of Savoy then rode out of the town with a few cavalry troops in order to divert the attention of the Duke de La Feuillade, who desisted from the siege to pursue the prince: but the latter, better acquainted with the ground, escaped his pursuers, and thus La Feuillade not only failed to capture the Duke of Savoy, but hindered the progress of the siege.

Nearly all historians have maintained that the Duke de La Feuillade had no intention of taking Turin; they declare that he had sworn to the Duchess of Burgundy to spare her father's capital; they point out that that princess induced Mme. de Maintenon to take all possible measures for the safety of the town. It is true that nearly all the officers of La Feuillade's army have long believed this, but, in fact, it was one of those popular rumours which discredit the judgments of newsmongers and dishonour those of historians. It would have been indeed inconsistent for the same general to wish to capture the Duke of Savoy and yet fail to take Turin.

From 13 May to 30 June the Duke of Vendôme assisted the besiegers from the banks of the Adige; and with seventy battalions and sixty squadrons under his command he counted upon barring all routes to Prince Eugene.

The general in command of the Imperial troops lacked both men and money. The London mercers lent him about six millions of our livres, and at length he sent for troops from various parts of the Empire. The delay in sending this help might have lost Italy, had not the delay over the siege of Turin been still greater.

Vendôme had already been appointed to retrieve the losses in Flanders, but, before leaving Italy, he allowed Prince Eugene to cross the Adige, even the Canale Bianco, and finally the Po itself, a river larger and in some places more difficult of passage than the Rhône. The French general only withdrew from the banks of the Po when he saw that Prince Eugene was in a position to advance close on Turin. He thus left matters at a momentous crisis in Italy, and they appeared no less desperate in Flanders, Germany and Spain.

The Duke of Vendôme accordingly proceeded to muster the remnants of Villeroi's army near Mons, and the Duke of Orleans, Louis XIV.'s nephew, proceeded to take command of the Duke of Vendôme's troops near the Po. The troops were in disorder, as though they had just been defeated. Eugene had crossed the Po in sight of Vendôme; he now crossed the Tanaro before the eyes of the Duke of Orleans, took Carpi, Correggio and Reggio, stole a march on the French, and finally joined forces with the Duke of Savoy near Asti. All that the Duke of Orleans could do was to join the Duke de La Feuillade in his camp before Turin. Prince Eugene followed him in a field-coach. Two courses were now open to the French; one, to await Prince Eugene in their lines surrounding the city; and two, to advance against him while he was still close to Veillane. The Duke of Orleans summoned a council of war, composed of Marshal Marsin, who had lost the Battle of Blenheim, Duke de La Feuillade, Albergotti, Saint-Fremont and other lieutenants-general. "Gentlemen," said the Duke of Orleans, "if we remain in our lines we shall lose the battle. Our trenches extend round the city for miles in length; we cannot line them all. Here, you can see the marines are only two men deep; in other places the lines are completely empty. The Dora, which flows through our camp, will prevent our troops from mutually assisting one another. If the French wait to receive an attack they lose what is their greatest advantage, that impetuosity and those first moments of enthusiasm which have so often turned the tide of battle in their favour." The lieutenants-

general were unanimous in their reply: "We must advance."
At this juncture Marshal Marsin drew an order of the king
from his pocket, which ordered them to defer to his opinion
in case of action; his advice was to remain within their lines.

The Duke of Orleans was indignant to see that he had
been put in command of the army, not as a general, but
merely as a prince of the blood; obliged, however, to follow
Marshal Marsin's instructions, he made preparations for
battle under such disadvantageous conditions.

The enemy apparently intended to make several attacks
at the same time, and their movements kept the French
camp in suspense. The Duke of Orleans wanted one thing,
Marsin and La Feuillade another, and in spite of argument
they came to no decision. Finally, they allowed the enemy
to cross the Dora, and eight columns, twenty-five men deep,
advanced against them. It was essential that battalions
of equal strength and depth should be immediately opposed
to the advancing enemy.

Albergotti, stationed at some distance from the main army,
on the Mount of the Capuchins, had twenty thousand men
under him and only militia troops in front of him, who dared
not attack him. The general sent asking for twelve thousand
men. He replied that he could not spare them; gave certain
plausible reasons, which were listened to, and thus time was
wasted. On 7 September, 1706, Prince Eugene attacked the
entrenchments, and carried them after two hours' fighting.
The Duke of Orleans was wounded and had retired from the
field to have his wounds dressed. Hardly had the surgeons
begun to attend to him when he learnt that all was lost,
the enemy was in possession of the camp, and the rout was
complete. Immediate flight was his only course; lines and
trenches were abandoned and the army scattered. The
whole of the baggage, provisions, ammunition and money
for the troops fell into the hands of the victor.

Wounded in the thigh, Marshal Marsin was taken prisoner.
One of the Duke of Savoy's surgeons amputated the limb,
and the marshal died a few minutes after the operation.
Sir Paul Methuen, English ambassador to the Duke of Savoy,
the most generous, open-hearted, and courageous Englishman ever employed by his country on an embassy, had
continued to fight by the side of this prince. He saw Marshal
Marsin taken prisoner and witnessed his last moments. He
told me that Marsin's own words to him were: "Believe, sir,

at least, that it was against my advice that we waited in our lines to receive your attack." These words seem expressly to contradict what had taken place in the council of war, but they were nevertheless true; the fact was that Marshal Marsin, on taking his leave from Versailles, had pointed out to the king how necessary it would be to attack the enemy, supposing he appeared to relieve Turin; but Chamillart, intimidated by former defeats, had persuaded the king to decide that it should be left to the enemy to open the battle; so that an order given at Versailles caused the rout of sixty thousand men. Not more than two thousand French were killed in the battle, but it is well known that actual slaughter does less damage than panic.

The necessity of food, which sometimes causes even a victorious army to retire, now brought the troops back into the Dauphiny after their defeat. All was in such confusion that the victory of Count Medavi-Grancei, who was then with a body of troops in Mantua, over an Imperial army commanded by the Landgrave of Hesse (afterwards King of Sweden), at Castiglione on 9 September, 1706, was useless although complete. In a short time, Milan, Mantua, Piedmont, and finally the Kingdom of Naples, were all lost.

CHAPTER XXI

FURTHER REVERSES OF FRANCE AND SPAIN. LOUIS XIV. SENDS HIS CHIEF MINISTER TO SUE FOR PEACE, BUT IN VAIN. BATTLE OF MALPLAQUET LOST, AND OTHER MATTERS

THE Battle of Blenheim had cost Louis XIV. an extremely well-equipped army and the whole of the country between the Danube and the Rhine; it had cost the House of Bavaria all its estates. Ramillies had resulted in all Flanders being lost up to the gates of Lille. As a consequence of the defeat at Turin the French were driven out of Italy, as they have always been in every war since the days of Charlemagne. A few troops remained in the Milanese and the small victorious army under the command of Count Medavi. A few towns were still occupied. It was proposed to surrender everything to the Emperor, provided that he allowed these troops, who numbered nearly fifteen thousand men, to depart. The

Emperor accepted the terms of this surrender, and the Duke of Savoy also agreed. Thus by a stroke of the pen the Emperor became the undisturbed master of Italy. He was assured of the conquest of the kingdoms of Naples and Sicily, and all territories regarded as feudatory in Italy were treated by him as subject states. He taxed Tuscany to the extent of one hundred and fifty thousand pistoles and Mantua to the extent of forty thousand; Modena, Lucca and Genoa, in spite of their being free towns, were included in these taxations.

The Emperor who enjoyed all these advantages was not that Leopold, the former rival of Louis XIV., who under a pretended moderation had quietly cherished far-reaching ambitions: but his eldest son, Joseph, quick-tempered, haughty and passionate, but nevertheless no greater soldier than his father. If ever Emperor seemed born to subdue Germany and Italy, it was Joseph I. He made his mastery felt from beyond the mountains; he levied contributions on the Pope; in 1706, on his sole authority, he placed the Electors of Bavaria and Cologne under the ban of the Empire; he deprived them of their electorate; and imprisoned the children of the Bavarian Elector, depriving them even of their name. Their father had no other recourse but to publish his misfortune throughout France and the Netherlands. Later, in 1712, Philip V. surrendered to him the whole of Spanish Flanders. Had he retained that province, which was a more valuable possession than Bavaria, he could have freed himself from the thraldom of the House of Austria; but he was only able to keep the towns of Luxembourg, Namur and Charleroi; the rest went to the conquerors.

All seemed now to threaten Louis, who but a little time before had threatened all Europe. The Duke of Savoy was in a position to invade France: England and Scotland were united together to form a single kingdom; or rather Scotland had become a province of England, and thus increased the power of her former rival. Towards the end of 1706 and the beginning of 1707 all France's enemies seemed to be putting on new strength while France was moving to her downfall. She was pressed on all sides, on land and on sea. Of those great fleets which Louis XIV. had gathered together hardly thirty-five ships remained. Strasburg was still a frontier town, but the loss of Landau exposed Alsace to continual danger. Provence was threatened with invasion, both by land and sea: what France had lost in Flanders made her fear for the rest. Nevertheless, in spite of so many disasters, France herself was still untouched: and in a war so disastrous to her, she had as yet but lost her former conquests.

Louis XIV. confronted his enemies on all sides. Though weakened everywhere, he resisted, defended and even attacked right and left. But he was as unsuccessful in Spain as he had been in Italy, in Germany and in Flanders. It was alleged that the siege of Barcelona was conducted with still greater incompetence than that of Turin.

The Count of Toulouse had appeared only to convey his fleet back to Toulon. With Barcelona relieved and the siege abandoned, the French army, reduced by half and short of ammunition, retreated into Navarre, a small kingdom belonging to the Spanish, yet whose title our kings still add to that of France, by a usage which seems unworthy of their greatness.

To these disasters was added another, which seemed decisive. The Portuguese, with a few English, took all the towns in their path, and advanced from the Portuguese into the Spanish Estremadura. They were commanded by a Frenchman who had become an English peer, the Earl of Galway, formerly Count de Ruvigny; while at the same time the Duke of Berwick, an Englishman and a nephew of Marlborough, was at the head of the French and Spanish troops, who were no longer able to check the progress of the victorious army.

Uncertain of his fate, Philip V. remained in Pampeluna. His rival, Charles, meanwhile, was strengthening his party and his forces in Catalonia; he was master of Aragon, of the province of Valencia, of Cartagena and of part of the province of Granada. The English had possessed themselves of Gibraltar, and had handed over to him Minorca, Iviza and Alicante. To top all, the road to Madrid was open to him. On 26 June, 1706, Galway entered the city unopposed, and proclaimed Archduke Charles as king. A single detachment also proclaimed him king at Toledo.

Philip V.'s position now appeared so hopeless that Marshal Vauban, foremost among engineers, and the most loyal of citizens, a man always occupied with some scheme or other, sometimes useful, sometimes impracticable, but always highly ingenious, suggested to the Court of France that Philip V. should be sent to reign in America; the prince agreed to this course. He was to have embarked with the

Spaniards still attached to his party. Spain would have been delivered up to civil strife. The trade of Peru and Mexico would have passed into the hands of the French, and in the family reverse of Louis XIV., France would have once more regained her greatness. The plan was deliberated upon at Versailles, but the loyalty of the Castilians and the mistakes of his enemies resulted in Philip's retaining the crown. The populace loved Philip as being the king they had chosen, and his wife, the daughter of the Duke of Savoy, earned their affection by her desire to please, displaying fearlessness superior to her sex, and a constancy which no misfortune could shake. She went herself from town to town, cheering all hearts, stirring up their zeal and accepting the gifts the people brought her. In this way she provided her husband with more than two hundred thousand crowns in three weeks. Not one of the nobles who had sworn fealty broke his word. When Galway proclaimed the archduke in Madrid, the shout of *Long live Philip !* was heard; and at Toledo, the incited populace drove those who had proclaimed the arch- duke from the town. Up till then the Spanish had made small efforts to uphold their king; but they did prodigies when they saw him beaten, and on that occasion displayed a kind of courage different from that of other nations, who begin by great efforts and then become disheartened. It is difficult to give a nation a king against its will. The Portu- guese, English and Austrians, who were in Spain, were harried everywhere; they lacked food and committed such errors as are mostly unavoidable in a foreign country: little by little they were beaten back. At length, on 22 September, 1706, three months after he had turned his back on Madrid as a fugitive, Philip V. re-entered the city in triumph and was received with acclamations as heartfelt as the indifference and hostility lately shown towards his rival.

Louis XIV. redoubled his efforts when he saw that the Spanish were willing to do their part, and, while keeping a watchful eye on the safety of the French coast-line and the Mediterranean and posting them with militia, while main- taining an army in Flanders, one in the vicinity of Strasburg, an army corps in Navarre, and another in Roussillon, he continued to send fresh troops to Marshal Berwick in Castile.

It was with these troops, aided by the Spanish, on 25 April, 1707, that Berwick won the important battle of Almanza over Galway. Built by the Moors, Almanza is a town on the

frontiers of Valencia; and this lovely province was the reward
of victory. Neither Philip V. nor the archduke was present
at the battle, and it was upon this occasion that the famous
Earl of Peterborough, remarkable for everything he did,
exclaimed "that it was very good of the English to fight for
them at all." That is what he wrote to Marshal Tessé and
what I have heard from his own lips. He added that it was
only slaves who would fight for a single man, and they were
fighting for a nation. The Duke of Orleans, who wished to
be present at the engagement, and was to take over the
command in Spain, only arrived on the next day; but he
took advantage of the victory, and captured several towns,
including Lerida, the stumbling-block of the great Condé.

On 22 May, 1707, on another front, Marshal Villars, entrusted once more with the command of the French armies,
solely because they needed him, redeemed in Germany the
disaster of the Battle of Blenheim. He broke through the
lines of Stolhofen beyond the Rhine, dispersed all the
enemy's troops, levied taxes within a circuit of fifty leagues,
and advanced as far as the Danube. The momentary success
afforded a breathing-space on the German frontier, but in
Italy all was lost. The Kingdom of Naples, defenceless and
accustomed to a change of ruler, bowed to the yoke of the
victors; and the Pope, who had been unable to prevent the
German troops from passing through his territories, saw,
without daring to complain, that the Emperor was become
his vassal in spite of him. It is a good example of the power
of accepted opinions and the force of habit, that Naples can
always be seized without consulting the Pope, but that no
one ever dares to refuse him homage for it.

While his grandson was losing Naples, Louis himself was
on the point of losing Provence and the Dauphiny. The Duke
of Savoy and Prince Eugene had already crossed the Col
di Tenda and entered Provence. These frontiers were not
guarded like those of Flanders and Alsace, the eternal
theatre of war, bristling with fortresses built from fear of
aggression. There were no similar precautions near the Var,
none of those fortified towns that check the enemy and allow
time for armies to be mustered. This frontier has been neglected up to the present day, and no other reason perhaps
can be given than that men are rarely attentive to all their
obligations. Grievously exasperated, the King of France
perceived that the very Duke of Savoy who, the previous

year, had possessed little else than his capital and Prince Eugene who had been brought up in the French Court, were about to wrest Toulon and Marseilles from him.

In August 1707 Toulon was besieged and hard pressed; an English fleet, mistress of the sea, was bombarding it. A little more perseverance, a little greater care and unanimity, and Toulon would have fallen. Marseilles also, being without defences, would have been lost; and it seemed probable that France was going to lose two provinces. But the probable does not always happen. There was time to despatch help. Directly these provinces had been threatened, troops had been detailed from Marshal Villars' army; and what had been gained in Germany was sacrificed to save a part of France. The country through which the enemy was advancing was dry, barren and mountainous; food was scarce, and retreat beset with difficulties. Disease, moreover, afflicted the enemy's army, and thus further aided Louis XIV. On 22 August, 1707, the siege of Toulon was raised, and soon after Provence was liberated and the Dauphiny free from danger; an invasion is indeed rarely successful unless the invaders have a good knowledge of the country. Charles V. failed in his attempt, and in our day the Queen of Hungary's troops were also unsuccessful.

Nevertheless, the invasion, while costly to the allies, was not less so to the French; a large expanse of her country had been laid waste and her forces divided.

Europe was far from expecting at a time of exhaustion, when France was counting it a great success to have escaped an invasion, that Louis XIV. would have sufficient greatness and resources to attempt himself an invasion of Great Britain, notwithstanding the altered state of his naval forces, and in spite of the English fleets which covered the seas. The scheme was broached by certain Scotch adherents of the son of James II. Success was doubtful; but Louis XIV. foresaw certain glory in the mere undertaking of it. He confessed himself that he was impelled by this motive, as much as by political interests.

To carry war into Great Britain, while supporting with difficulty the burden of so many other fronts, and to attempt to restore at least to the throne of Scotland the son of James II. while scarcely able to maintain Philip V. on his Spanish throne, was indeed an ambitious scheme, and one after all not wholly devoid of probability.

Among the Scots, all those who had not been seduced by the Court of London groaned under the English yoke. Their unspoken cry was unanimously in favour of the descendant of their ancient kings, banished in his cradle from the throne of England, Scotland and Ireland, and whose birth had even been called in question. They assured Louis that he would find thirty thousand men in arms ready to fight for him, if he could only land near Edinburgh with some support from France.

Louis XIV., who in times of past prosperity had made such efforts for the cause of James, now did as much for the son at a time of misfortune. Eight ships of war, and seventy transport ships, were fitted up at Dunkirk. In March 1708, six thousand men embarked. Count Gacé, afterwards Marshal Matignon, was in command of the troops, and the Chevalier de Forbin Janson, one of the greatest seamen, commanded the fleet. The opportunity appeared favourable; there were not more than three thousand regular troops in Scotland, and England's resources were drained. Her soldiers were employed in Flanders under the Duke of Marlborough. But it was necessary to arrive, and the English had a fleet of nearly fifty ships of war afloat. The venture was exactly similar to that which we have seen in our own days undertaken in 1744, on behalf of James II.'s grandson. It was anticipated by the English, and untoward circumstances upset the scheme. The ministry in London had time to recall a dozen battalions from Flanders. and in Edinburgh the suspected ringleaders were arrested. Finally, when the Pretender appeared off the coast of Scotland he perceived none of the signals agreed upon, and all that the Chevalier de Forbin could do was to return to Dunkirk. The fleet was saved, but the whole result of the venture was lost. Matignon alone gained anything. While at sea he opened the orders received from the court and there discovered his promotion to Marshal of France, a reward for something that he was willing but unable to do.

Some historians have assumed that Anne was in league with her brother. It would be altogether too ridiculous to believe that she would invite her rival to come and dethrone her. They have mistaken the particular period; they believed that she was then befriending him because she afterwards secretly looked upon him as her heir. But who could ever wish to be driven from a throne by his successor?

While France's fortunes sank daily lower, it was suggested

to the king that if his grandson, the Duke of Burgundy, appeared at the head of the armies in Flanders, the presence of the heir-presumptive would revive that desire for glory which was now for the first time lacking. The prince was of a resolute and fearless nature, pious, just and a philosopher. He was born to command men. A pupil of Fénelon, Archbishop of Cambrai, he loved duty; he also loved mankind, and wished to make men happy. Trained in the art of war, he looked upon that art rather as the scourge of the human race and an unfortunate necessity, than as a source of true glory. This prince-philosopher was pitted against the Duke of Marlborough; and the Duke of Vendôme was appointed to assist him. Then happened what occurs only too often: the great captain's advice was not sufficiently heeded; and too often the prince's opinion was set against the general's reasons. Two parties were thus formed, whereas in the Allies' army there existed but one, that of the common cause. Prince Eugene was then on the Rhine, but on every occasion that he was with Marlborough they were always unanimous in their views.

The Duke of Burgundy had the superiority of numbers; France, whom Europe thought exhausted, had supplied him with an army of nearly one hundred thousand men, and the Allies at that time had but eighty thousand. Moreover, he had more favourable opportunities for negotiations in a country so long under Spanish rule, weary of Dutch garrisons, and where many of the citizens leant to the side of Philip V. A friendly understanding opened the gates of Ghent and Ypres to him; but his actual movements in the field dissipated the results of such political moves. Differences of opinion, and hence uncertainty in the council of war, led to an advance in the direction of the Dender, and two hours afterwards to a retreat towards the Scheldt at Oudenarde; time was thus lost. On 11 July, 1708, the French came upon Prince Eugene and Marlborough, who had made good use of their opportunities and had joined forces. They were routed near Oudenarde; it was not a great battle, but it was a fatal retreat. Blunders were multiplied. Regiments marched where they could in default of any orders. More than four thousand men were taken prisoners on the road by the enemy some miles from the field of battle.

Disheartened, the army retreated in disorder on Ghent, Tournai and Ypres, and quietly allowed Prince Eugene in possession of the field to besiege Lille with an army of inferior numbers.

To lay siege to a town as large and well-fortified as Lille, without having first taken Ghent, only able to draw his convoys from Ostend, and only able to convey them along a narrow highway, with the risk of their being intercepted at any moment, was regarded by Europe as a rash undertaking, but one which was rendered excusable by the misunderstanding and uncertainty that prevailed in the French army; and which was finally justified by success. The large convoys, which might have been captured, were left unmolested. The troops who escorted them, and who should have been vanquished by superior numbers, were victorious. The Duke of Burgundy's army, which could have attacked the as yet unfinished entrenchments of the enemy, neglected to do so. On 23 October, 1708, Lille was captured, to the great astonishment of all Europe, who had thought the Duke of Burgundy in a better position to attack Eugene and Marlborough than these generals to besiege Lille. Marshal Boufflers defended the town for nearly four months.

The inhabitants had become so used to the noise of cannon and to all the horrors that attend a siege, that plays were performed in the town as frequently as in times of peace and a bomb falling near the theatre in no way interrupted the play.

Marshal Boufflers had established such perfect order everywhere that the inhabitants of that large town remained calm, trusting in his labours. His defence earned for him the esteem of his enemies, the affection of the citizens, and the reward of the king. Historians, or rather Dutch writers, who have affected to blame him should remember that to contradict public opinion it is necessary to have been a witness, and an irreproachable one, or to be in a position to prove what is advanced.

Meanwhile, the army which had looked on at the siege of Lille gradually decreased in numbers; it allowed the enemy to take Ghent, then Bruges and all its positions, one after the other. There have been few campaigns so disastrous. The officers attached to the Duke of Vendôme threw all the blame for these blunders on the Duke of Burgundy's council, and that council in turn assigned it all to the Duke of Vendôme. Everyone became embittered by these misfortunes. One of the Duke of Burgundy's courtiers said one day to the Duke of Vendôme: "This is what happens from never going to mass; so you see to what our misfortunes are due." "Do you imagine," replied the Duke of Vendôme, "that Marlborough attends mass more often than I do?" The rapid successes of the Allies elated the mind of the Emperor Joseph. A despot within the Empire, master of Landau, he now saw the road to Paris practically open after the capture of Lille. A Dutch detachment had already had the audacity to advance from Courtrai to within close distance of Versailles and had carried off the king's chief equerry, thinking they had captured the Dauphin himself, father of the Duke of Burgundy. Terror reigned in Paris.

The Emperor's expectations of establishing his brother Charles in Spain were quite as great as Louis XIV.'s hopes of maintaining his grandson on the throne. The succession which the Spanish wished to preserve indivisible, was already divided between three individuals. The Emperor had taken Lombardy and the Kingdom of Naples as his share, while his brother Charles still held Catalonia and part of Aragon. The Emperor then forced Pope Clement XI. to acknowledge the archduke as King of Spain. This pope, who was said to resemble Saint Peter, because he affirmed, denied, repented and wept, had always acknowledged Philip V., imitating the example of his predecessor, and he was attached to the House of Bourbon. The Emperor punished him for this by declaring that many of the fiefs, which up till that time had belonged to the popes, were dependencies of the Empire, especially Parma and Piacenza, and proceeded to lay waste certain ecclesiastical estates and take possession of the town of Comacchio.

In former times a pope would have excommunicated any emperor who should have contested the most trivial of his rights, and such an excommunication would have lost the emperor his throne; but the powers of the holy keys having been reduced to just such a point, or almost so, as is becoming, Clement XI., encouraged by France, had dared on this occasion to employ the power of the sword. He took up arms, and soon repented of having done so; for he perceived that, under a wholly sacerdotal rule, the Romans were not fitted to wield the sword. He accordingly laid down his arms, surrendered Comacchio in trust to the Emperor, and consented to write to the archduke: *To our very dear son, Catholic King in Spain.* An English fleet in the Mediterranean and German troops within his territories soon forced him to write.

To our very dear son, King of the Spains. This support of the
Pope, which was worth nothing in the German Empire, was
of some importance to the Spanish people, who had been
made to believe that the archduke was unworthy to reign,
since he was protected by the heretics who had taken
possession of Gibraltar.

(August 1708) In addition to the mainland there remained
to the Spanish monarchy the islands of Sardinia and Sicily.
An English fleet gave Sardinia to the Emperor Joseph, for
the English were resolved that his brother, the archduke,
should have Spain alone. It was their arms which made
partition treaties. They reserved the conquest of Sicily for
another time, preferring to use their ships to search for
galleons from America on the high seas (some of which were
captured), than to give the Emperor fresh territories.

France's pride, like Rome's, was humbled, but she was
in greater danger; her resources were exhausted, and her
credit destroyed; her people, who had idolised their king
in times of prosperity, murmured against Louis XIV. now
that he had fallen on evil days.

Partisans, to whom the ministry had sold the nation for
ready money in its pressing needs, thrived on the public
calamities and outraged the people's misfortunes by their
extravagance. All their loans had been spent. Had it not
been for the undaunted efforts of a few merchants, especially
those of Saint-Malo, who sailed for Peru and brought back
thirty millions, half of which they loaned to the state,
Louis XIV. would have been unable to pay his troops. The
war had ruined France and a few merchants saved her. The
same state of affairs existed in Spain. The galleons which
were not taken by the English helped to defend Philip. But
such resources, sufficient as they were for a few months, did
not make the recruiting of soldiers any easier. Chamillart,
appointed to the ministry of finance and war, resigned as
Minister of Finance in 1708, and left the department so
disorganised that no means were found to restore order in it
throughout the reign, and in 1709 he resigned from the
ministry of war, which had become as arduous as the former
office. He was blamed for many mistakes. The public, yet
more harsh on account of its sufferings, did not consider that
there are times of misfortune when mistakes are inevitable.
Voisin, who succeeded him in the war department, and
Desmarets, who became Minister of Finance, could neither

draw up more successful plans of war nor restore a credit which did not exist.

The bitter winter of 1709 reduced the nation to despair. The olive trees, which are a great source of revenue in the south of France, perished, and nearly all the fruit trees were killed by the frost. All hopes of harvest were blighted. Stocks were extremely low. Grain, which could be obtained at great expense from the seaports of the Levant and from Africa, was liable to be seized by the enemy's fleets, to oppose which there were scarcely any ships left. The distress occasioned by this winter was felt all over Europe; but the enemy had greater resources. The Dutch especially, who had been for long the factors of other nations, had sufficient stores to be able to keep the flourishing armies of the Allies in plenty, whilst the French troops, reduced in numbers and disheartened, seemed doomed to perish from want.

The king sold his gold plate for four hundred thousand francs. The highest lords sent their silver plate to the mint. For some months nothing but black bread was eaten in Paris. Several families even at Versailles lived on oaten bread, Mme. de Maintenon giving the example.

Louis XIV., who had already taken steps to sue for peace, did not hesitate, under these distressing circumstances, to ask it from the Dutch themselves, whom he had formerly treated so harshly.

Since the death of King William, the United Provinces had had no stadtholder and the Dutch magistrates, who had already given their families the cognomen of *patrician families*, were so many kings. The four Dutch commissioners appointed to the army behaved most arrogantly to the thirty German princes who were in their pay. *Tell Holstein to come here*, they said; *tell Hesse to come and speak with us.* Thus did merchants express themselves, who, by the simplicity of their dress and the frugality of their meals, delighted to humble at once the conceit of Germans who were in their pay and the pride of a great king who in former times had been their conqueror.

They were known to have sold their attachment to Louis XIV. for a low price in 1665, to have endured their adversities in 1672, and to have retrieved them with undaunted courage; and now they wished to take advantage of their fortune. They were far from being satisfied with letting men see, from the mere demonstration of their superiority, that there is no true greatness without power: they wished to acquire supreme authority over ten towns in Flanders, among others Lille, which was already in their possession, and also Tournai, which was not yet so. The Dutch thus claimed to reap the fruits of victory, not only at the expense of France, but also at the expense of Austria, for whom they were fighting, just as Venice had formerly enlarged her possessions by the territories of all her neighbours. At bottom the republican spirit is as ambitious as that of a monarchy.

Such was plainly apparent a few months afterwards; for when these illusive negotiations had come to naught, and the Allies' arms had obtained still further successes, the Duke of Marlborough, more powerful at that time than his sovereign in England, and won over by Holland, concluded with the United Provinces in 1709 the famous Barrier Treaty by which they were to remain in possession of all the frontier towns they might take from France, were to have the right to maintain garrisons in twenty Flemish towns at the country's expense, in Huy, Liège and Bonn, and were to have sovereign powers in Upper Guelders. In fine, they would become rulers of seventeen provinces in the Netherlands, and would have supreme power in Liège and in Cologne. They wished thus to exalt themselves even on the ruins of their allies, and were already contemplating such ambitious schemes, when the king secretly despatched President Rouillé to endeavour to enter into negotiations with them.

The diplomatist went first to Antwerp, where he saw two magistrates from Amsterdam, Bruys and Vanderdussen, who spoke in the lofty tones of conquerors, and treated the delegate of the most imperious of kings with the same arrogance to which they had been subjected in 1672. They then pretended to enter into negotiations with him in one of the villages which Louis XIV. had formerly put to fire and sword. When they had trifled with him sufficiently, they declared that the King of France must compel his grandson, the King of Spain, to abdicate from the throne without any compensation; that the Elector of Bavaria, François Marie, and his brother, the Elector of Cologne, must sue for pardon, or treaties would be decided by the fate of arms alone.

One after another the council received the despairing despatches of President Rouillé at a time when the kingdom was reduced to the most calamitous and distressing misery. The winter of 1709 had wrought fearful havoc; the people were dying of hunger. The troops had no pay; everywhere was desolation. The groans and consternation of the public still further increased the evil.

The council was composed of the Dauphin, his son the Duke of Burgundy, the Chancellor of France, Pontchartrain, Duke of Beauvilliers, the Marquis de Torci, Chamillart, the Secretary of State for War, and the Comptroller-General, Desmarets. The Duke of Beauvilliers drew such a pathetic picture of the state to which France was reduced that the Duke of Burgundy burst into tears and the whole council joined with him. The chancellor judged it wise to make peace at whatever price. The ministers of war and finance admitted that they were without resources. "It would be difficult," said the Marquis de Torci, "to describe so melancholy a scene, even if it were permissible to disclose the secret which formed the most pathetic part of it." The tears which were shed constituted the only secret.

In this crisis the Marquis de Torci proposed that he himself should go and take upon himself the insults offered to the king in the person of President Rouillé; but how could he hope to obtain what the victors had already refused? He could only expect more exacting terms.

The Allies were already opening their campaign. Torci travelled under an assumed name to The Hague itself. (22 May, 1709) The Grand Pensionary, Heinsius, was, indeed, astonished when he was informed that he who was regarded by foreigners as the chief minister of France, was at that moment in his anteroom. On a former occasion Heinsius had been sent to France by King William for the purpose of upholding his rights respecting the principality of Orange. He had addressed himself to Louvois, Secretary of State for the Department of the Dauphiny, on whose frontier Orange is situated. William's minister spoke with spirit, not only for his master's cause, but for the claims of Orange. Is it credible that Louvois answered him by saying *that he would have him put into the Bastille*?

It was a detestable remark to have made, even to one of Louis' own subjects, but to make it to a foreign minister was a gross outrage on the rights of nations. It may be imagined what deep-felt impressions he engraved on the mind of the representative of a free people.

There are few examples of such arrogance followed by such humiliation. The Marquis de Torci, a suppliant at The

Hague in the name of Louis XIV., addressed himself to Prince Eugene and the Duke of Marlborough after having effected nothing with Heinsius. All three were in favour of continuing the war. The prince envisaged greatness and revenge by so doing; the duke personal glory and an immense fortune, for both of which he was equally ambitious; Heinsius, ruled by the other two, looked upon himself as a Spartan who was humbling the pride of a King of Persia. They proposed not peace, but a truce, during which complete satisfaction was to be accorded to all the Allies, but none to the allies of Louis, the conditions being that Louis should unite with his enemies in expelling his own grandson from Spain within the space of two months, and that as a guarantee he should surrender immediately ten towns in Flanders to the Dutch in perpetuity, cede Strasburg and Brisach, and renounce the sovereignty of Alsace. Louis XIV. had never thought, when on a former occasion he had refused a regiment to Prince Eugene, when Churchill was not yet a colonel in England, and when the name of Heinsius was almost unknown to him, that one day these three men would force upon him such conditions. Torci vainly endeavoured to tempt Marlborough with an offer of four millions; the duke, who loved glory as much as wealth, and whose victories had brought him immense sums of money, was unaffected by an offer of four millions, and the French minister had the bitterness of making a proposal which was both shameful and fruitless. Torci reported the orders of his enemies to the king, and Louis XIV. then did what he had never done before towards his subjects. He justified himself towards them; he addressed a circular letter to the governors of provinces, and the corporations of the towns, giving an account to his people of the burdens he had still to place upon them, by which he aroused at once their indignation, their respect and even their pity.

Politicians said that Torci only humbled himself at The Hague in order to put the enemy in the wrong, to justify Louis XIV. in the eyes of Europe, and to rouse the French to a sense of the insult offered to the nation through his person; but in reality his sole object was to sue for peace. President Rouillé even received orders to remain several days at The Hague to try and obtain more favourable terms; but the only answer of the United Provinces was to order Rouillé to leave within twenty-four hours.

On receiving such harsh replies Louis XIV. exclaimed before his assembled council: "Since I must make war, I will rather do so against my enemies than against my children." He accordingly made preparations to try once more his fortunes in Flanders. Famine, which was ravaging the country, was an aid to war. Those who lacked bread became soldiers. A great part of the land lay waste; but an army was formed. Marshal Villars, who, in the preceding year had been sent to command some troops in Savoy, whose courage he had revived, and who had gained some small successes, was recalled to Flanders, as being the one on whom the nation placed their hopes.

Marlborough had already taken Tournai on 20 July, 1709, to which Eugene had laid siege. These two generals were already advancing to invest Mons. Marshal Villars pushed forward to intercept them. He had with him Marshal Boufflers, his senior, who had asked to serve under him. Boufflers was, indeed, a man who loved his king and country above all things. On this occasion he proved (in spite of the maxim of a wit) that virtues do exist in a monarchical state, and especially under a good ruler. In such a state there are, without doubt, quite as many virtues as in a republic, accompanied perhaps by less enthusiasm, but more distinguished by what we know as honour.

As soon as the French advanced to prevent the investment of Mons, the Allies moved to attack them near to the woods of Blangies and the village of Malplaquet.

The Allies' army numbered about eighty thousand combatants, and that of Marshal Villars about seventy thousand. The French carried with them eighty pieces of cannon, the Allies one hundred and forty. The Duke of Marlborough commanded the right wing, composed of the English and German troops in the pay of England. Prince Eugene commanded in the centre; Tilly and a certain Count Nassau were on the left, together with the Dutch.

(11 September, 1709) Marshal Villars took over the command of the left wing himself and relinquished the right to Marshal Boufflers. He had hurriedly entrenched his army, a manœuvre probably well adapted to his troops, who were in inferior numbers, had long been unsuccessful, and were half of them fresh recruits, and adapted still more to the fortunes of France, in that a total defeat would have driven her to her last extremities. Some historians have blamed the general

for his disposition of the army. "He should have crossed a wide cleft," they said, "instead of leaving it in front of him." Those who pass such armchair judgments on what takes place on the field of battle must be held guilty of excessive cleverness.

All that I know is from the marshal's own words, that when the soldiers, who had been without bread for a whole day, at length received some, they threw part of it away, so that they could rush more swiftly into the fight. Not for several centuries has there been a battle so obstinately fought and so long prolonged, and none more sanguinary. I shall say nothing more about this battle than what is admitted by all the world. The enemy's left wing, where the Dutch fought, was almost completely routed, and pursued at the point of the bayonet. On the right Marlborough maintained a tremendous struggle. In order to withstand Marlborough's attack, Marshal Villars drew a few troops from his centre, and then this centre was also attacked. The entrenchments which guarded it were carried. The regiments of guards who were defending them were unable to resist. The marshal himself, hastening from the left wing to the centre, was wounded, and the battle was lost. The field was strewn with nearly thirty thousand dead and dying.

One could hardly walk, save on piled-up corpses, which were thickest where the Dutch had fought. France lost hardly more than eight thousand men in the battle. Her enemies left about twenty-one thousand dead and wounded, but as the centre had been broken through and the two wings cut off, it was the defeated side which had inflicted the heaviest slaughter.

Marshal Boufflers retreated in good order, with the assistance of Prince Tingri - Montmorenci, afterwards Marshal Luxembourg, who inherited the courage of his ancestors. The army retreated to a position between Quesnoi and Valenciennes, carrying away with them several flags and standards taken from the enemy. These spoils consoled Louis XIV., and the glory of having contested the fight for so long and having lost naught save the field of battle was counted as a victory. On his return to the court Marshal Villars assured the king that, had he not been wounded, he would have gained the victory. I know from experience that this general was convinced of what he said, but I have met with few persons who believed him.

One may be astonished that an army which had killed two-thirds more of their enemy than they themselves had lost, did not attempt to prevent those, who had gained no other advantage than that of lying down to rest with their dead, from laying siege to Mons. The Dutch feared to undertake it, and hesitated. But the very name of the place where they had lost a battle played upon the minds of the defeated and disheartened them. Men never do all that they are capable of, and the soldier who is reminded that he has been beaten goes in fear of being beaten again. So it came about that Mons was besieged and taken on 20 October, 1709, and again, as in the case of Tournai and Lille, it was handed over to the Dutch.

CHAPTER XXII

LOUIS XIV. CONTINUES TO SUE FOR PEACE AND TO DEFEND HIMSELF. THE DUKE OF VENDÔME ESTABLISHES THE KING OF SPAIN ON THE THRONE

IN this manner not only did the enemies advance step by step and capture all the French outposts on this front, but, with the help of the Duke of Savoy, they intended to surprise Franche-Comté and advance from both sides into the heart of the kingdom. General Merci, who was deputed to facilitate this undertaking by entering Upper Alsace by way of Basle, was fortunately checked on 26 August, 1709, near the isle of Neuburg on the Rhine by Count, afterwards Marshal, Du Bourg. I do not know by what fatality it is that those who have borne the name of Merci have always been as unfortunate as they were esteemed. This general of that name suffered the most complete defeat. The attack from the Savoy side came to nothing, but there was no less danger from the direction of Flanders, and affairs in the interior of the kingdom were in so desperate a condition that the king once more sued and begged for peace. He offered to acknowledge the archduke as King of Spain, to give no assistance to his grandson and to abandon him to his fate; to give up four towns as a guarantee of good faith; to surrender Strasburg and Brisach; to relinquish the sovereignty of Alsace, keeping only the prefecture; to fill up the port of Dunkirk,

for so long a formidable menace, and to raze its fortifications;
to surrender Lille, Tournai, Ypres, Menin, Furnes, Condé
and Maubeuge to the United Provinces. Such were the
principal conditions which were to serve as a basis for the
peace he sought.

The Allies wished once more to enjoy their triumph, by
discussing Louis XIV.'s offers of surrender. At the beginning
of 1710 they allowed his plenipotentiaries to come to the
small town of Gertruidenberg and present the petitions of
their monarch. Louis chose Marshal Uxelles, a frigid, taciturn
man, of a judicious cast of mind rather than exalted and
fearless, and the Abbé, afterwards Cardinal, de Polignac, one
of the wittiest and most eloquent men of his age, who commanded respect by his appearance and charm of manner.
But wit, prudence and eloquence in ministers are nothing
if their prince be unsuccessful. It is victories that make
treaties. Louis XIV.'s ambassadors were imprisoned in
Gertruidenberg rather than admitted to it. The deputies
listened to their proposals and reported them to The Hague,
to Prince Eugene, the Duke of Marlborough, and Count
Zinzendorf, the Emperor's ambassador, and their offers were
everywhere received with contempt. They were insulted by
outrageous libels, all of them composed by French refugees,
who had become greater enemies of Louis XIV.'s glory than
even Marlborough and Eugene. The French plenipotentiaries
humbled themselves so far as to promise that the king would
furnish money for the purpose of dethroning Philip V.; but
even then they were not listened to. As a preliminary condition, Louis XIV. was required to promise to drive his
grandson from Spain within two months, unaided by any
forces but his own. This preposterous piece of inhumanity,
much more outrageous than a refusal, was prompted by
fresh successes.

While the Allies were thus dictating terms, as superiors
nettled by the greatness and arrogance of Louis XIV., now
brought so low, they took the town of Douai (June 1710).
Soon afterwards they took possession of Bethune, Aire and
Saint-Venant, and Lord Stair proposed to despatch troops
as far as Paris.

Almost at the same time the archduke's army, commanded
in Spain by Guido von Staremberg, the German general whose
reputation was second only to that of Prince Eugene, gained
near Saragossa, on 20 August, 1710, a complete victory over

the army on which the adherents of Philip V. had placed
their hopes, and which was commanded by the unfortunate
Marquis de Bay. It was noted that the two princes, who
were contending for the throne of Spain, and who were both
within marching distance of their armies, were alike absent
from the battle. Of all the princes who were at that time
fighting in Europe, the Duke of Savoy was the only one who
conducted campaigns on his own initiative; and it was
regrettable that he only achieved this glory in fighting
against his two daughters, one of whom he wished to dethrone
in order to obtain a small piece of territory in Lombardy;
moreover, the Emperor Joseph was already putting obstacles
in the way of this and would deprive him of it at the first
opportunity.

The Emperor was successful everywhere, and nowhere
displayed moderation in his good fortune. On his authority
alone Bavaria was divided up, and he presented the various
fiefs to his relations and followers. He despoiled the young
Duke della Mirandola in Italy, and the Imperial princes
maintained an army for him near the Rhine, unaware that
they were exerting themselves to consolidate a power which
would become a menace to them; so dominant still was the
old hatred of the name of Louis XIV. in the minds of men,
a feeling which seemed to take precedence of all other
interests. Joseph's good fortune led him, moreover, to
triumph over the malcontents in Hungary. France had
incited against him Prince Rakoczy who took up arms
in support of her claims and those of his own country.
Rakoczy was defeated, his towns captured and his cause
ruined. Louis XIV. was thus equally unsuccessful abroad,
at home, on sea and land, in public affairs and in secret
intrigues.

All Europe expected that the Archduke Charles, brother
of the successful Joseph, would reign undisturbed in Spain.
Europe was threatened by a more formidable power than
that of Charles V.: and it was England, for so long the
enemy of the Spanish branch of Austria, and Holland, her
rebel vassal, who exhausted themselves in order to establish
her power. Philip V., a refugee in Madrid, again left the
city and withdrew to Valladolid, while the Archduke Charles
made his victorious entry into the capital. The King of
France could no longer assist his grandson: he had been
forced to do in part what his enemies had demanded at

Gertruidenberg—to forsake Philip's cause, and recall some
of the troops quartered in Spain, for his own defence. He
himself had scarcely sufficient forces to resist the enemy's
attacks from Savoy, the Rhine, and above all from Flanders,
where the hardest blows were struck.

The state of Spain was even more pitiable than that of
France. Nearly all her provinces had been laid waste by her
enemies and her defenders. She was attacked by Portugal.
Her trade was dying and great scarcity prevailed: but this
dearth was more fatal to the victors than to the vanquished,
because over a great part of the country the people loyally
refused everything to the Austrians and gave all to Philip.
The latter monarch had no longer either troops or a French
general to lead them. The Duke of Orleans, who had to a
slight extent retrieved his shaking fortunes, so far from
remaining in command of his armies, was looked upon as
his enemy. It cannot be doubted that in spite of the affection
of the people of Madrid for Philip, and notwithstanding the
loyalty of many grandees and of the whole of Castile, a large
part of Spain was definitely against him.

All the Catalonians, a warlike and stubborn people, clung
obstinately to his rival's cause. Half Aragon had also been
won over. One half of the nation awaited the turn of events;
the other hated the archduke still more than they loved
Philip. The Duke of Orleans, who also bore the name of
Philip, dissatisfied with the Spanish ministers and still more
so with the Princess de Ursinos who ruled them, thought he
could see his way to gain for himself the country which he
had come to defend; and when Louis XIV. himself proposed
to desert his grandson and there was already talk of an abdication in Spain, the Duke of Orleans thought himself entitled
to occupy the position which Philip V. was apparently bound
to relinquish. He was in possession of claims to the crown
which had been ignored in the will of the late King of Spain,
and which his father had publicly affirmed.

Through his agents he entered into a pact with certain of
the Spanish nobles by which they undertook to place him
on the throne in the event of Philip V.'s abdication. He would
in those circumstances have found many of the Spanish
eager to range themselves under the banner of a prince who
knew how to fight; and had the venture succeeded, it would
probably not have displeased the maritime powers, who
would then have less cause to fear the union of Spain and

France under one ruler; it would undoubtedly have removed obstacles in the way of peace.

The plot was discovered at Madrid, towards the beginning of 1709, while the Duke of Orleans was at Versailles. His agents were imprisoned in Spain, and Philip could not forgive his relation for having believed that he would abdicate, and for having entertained the idea of succeeding him. France cried out against the Duke of Orleans. *Monseigneur*, Philip V.'s father, suggested in council that proceedings should be instituted against the guilty party; but the king preferred to bury in oblivion an unformed and pardonable scheme rather than punish his nephew at a time when he saw his grandson moving to his ruin.

At length, shortly before the Battle of Saragossa, the King of Spain's council and most of the grandees, seeing that they had no leader to oppose to Staremberg, whom they considered a second Eugene, wrote a concerted letter to Louis XIV. asking for the Duke of Vendôme. That prince, who was in retirement at Anet, proceeded at once to Spain, and his presence was worth an army. The great reputation he had gained in Italy and of which the unfortunate campaign of Lille could not deprive him, impressed the Spanish: his popularity, his generosity which was lavish in the extreme, his frankness, his love for the soldiers, won their hearts. From the moment that he set foot in Spain, his name attracted a host of volunteers just as on a former occasion that of Bertrand de Guesclin had done. He had no money; but the municipal and village corporations and the religious orders provided him with it. A wave of enthusiasm swept over the nation. (August, 1710) The survivors of the battle of Saragossa gathered together under his flag at Valladolid. Everywhere they were eager to supply him with recruits. The Duke of Vendôme did not allow this fresh ardour to cool, but going in pursuit of the victors, brought the king back to Madrid and forced the enemy to retreat towards Portugal: he pursued them, swam the Tagus, and on 9 December took Stanhope prisoner with five thousand English in Brihuega: finally he overtook General Staremberg, and the next day engaged him in battle at Villa Viciosa. Philip V., who had never yet fought by the side of his former generals, emboldened by the Duke of Vendôme's energy, took the command of the right wing. The general commanded the left, and achieved a complete victory, so that in less than four months that prince, who had come on the scene when all hope was dead, had retrieved everything and established Philip on the throne of Spain for life.

While this startling change of events was striking the Allies with amazement, another change, more secret but not less decisive, was taking place in England. A German princess, by her maladroitness, lost to the House of Austria the entire succession of Charles V. and had thus been the prime mover of the war; now an English duchess by her indiscretion brought about peace. Sarah Jennings, Duchess of Marlborough, ruled Queen Anne, and the duke ruled the state. He controlled finance, through the Chancellor of the Exchequer, Godolphin, the father-in-law of one of his daughters. His son-in-law, Sunderland, Secretary of State, suborned the Cabinet. The whole of the queen's household, ruled by his wife, was at his commands. He was master of the army, and all military posts were bestowed by his orders. England was divided into two parties, Whigs and Tories; and the Whigs, with Marlborough at their head, did everything to increase his authority, while the Tories were obliged to respect him and hold their peace.

History must also add that the duke and duchess were the most handsome persons of their time, and this quality but further captivates the multitude when it is accompanied by honours and glory.

He had more power at The Hague than the Grand Pensionary and had great influence in Germany. Uniformly successful as a diplomatist and a general, no one man ever enjoyed such extensive power and glory. Moreover, he was able to consolidate his power with immense wealth, which he had acquired during his commands. I have heard his widow say that after the four children had received their shares, there remained to her, over and above any favours from the court, an income of seventy thousand pounds, which is worth more than 1,550,000 livres of present-day money.

Had not his parsimony equalled his greatness, he had formed a party which Queen Anne would have been powerless to break up; and had his wife been more complacent the queen would never have broken her bonds. But the duke could not overcome his fondness of money, nor the duchess her temper. The queen had an affection for her which bordered on submission and deprived her almost of any will of her own.

In such friendships it is usually the sovereign who evinces dislike, temper, arrogance, and takes advantage of his superior position; it is they who make the yoke felt, but on this occasion it was the Duchess of Marlborough who held the curb. It was necessary for Queen Anne to seek a favourite; she discovered such a one in Lady Masham, one of her ladies-in-waiting. The duchess's jealousy was aroused. Some pairs of gloves of curious workmanship refused by her to the queen, a bowl of water contemptuously let fall on Lady Masham's dress in the queen's presence—such trifles changed the face of Europe.

People began to get angry; the brother of the new favourite asked the duke for a regiment; the duke refused it and the queen bestowed. The Tories seized this opportunity to extricate the queen from such domestic bondage, diminish the Duke of Marlborough's power, change the ministry, make peace, and, if possible, restore the House of Stuart to the throne of England. Had the character of the duchess been capable of any pliancy she could still have retained her power. She and the queen were in the habit of writing to each other every day under assumed names. This secrecy and familiarity always left the way open for a reconciliation; but the duchess only employed this resource to wreck all.

She wrote in a domineering tone. In one letter she said: "Do me justice and make no reply." She was not slow to repent such words, and came to ask forgiveness: all that the queen said was: "You ordered me not to reply to you, and I shall make no reply." Henceforth the breach was irreparable. The duchess was seen no more at court, and some time afterwards a start was made by removing Sunderland, Marlborough's son-in-law, from the ministry, to pave the way for afterwards turning out Godolphin and the duke himself. In other countries this would have spelt disgrace; in England it means a change of government, and the change was still very difficult to bring about.

The Tories, though now masters of the queen, were not masters of the nation. They were obliged to bring in religion to their aid.

In Great Britain to-day there is hardly any religion save the little that is necessary to distinguish the political parties. The Whigs leant towards Presbyterianism. This was the party that had dethroned James II., persecuted Charles II., and executed Charles I. The Tories were for the Episcopacy;

they favoured the House of Stuart and desired passive obedience to their kings, by which the bishops hoped to receive greater obedience for themselves. They incited a preacher to proclaim this doctrine in St. Paul's Cathedral, and to portray Marlborough's administration and the party who had given the crown to William in the most offensive colours. But the queen, who befriended this priest, had not sufficient power to prevent him from being banned for three years by the two houses assembled in the Hall of Westminster, nor his sermon from being burnt. She was still more conscious of her weakness, when, in spite of her secret attachment to her own kith and kin, she found that she dared not open the way to the throne to her own brother, which had been closed to him by the Whig party. Writers who say that Marlborough and his adherents fell from power when they were no longer supported by the queen's favour, know nothing of England. The queen, though from that time desiring peace, did not dare to deprive Marlborough of the command of the army; and in the spring of 1711 Marlborough was again pressing upon France, though disgraced at court.

Towards the end of January of the same year, 1711, a stranger arrived at Versailles, a priest of the name of Abbé Gautier, who had formerly been assistant almoner to Marshal Tallard in his embassy to King William. Since then he had continued to live in London, his only duty being saying mass in the private chapel of Count Gallas, the Emperor's ambassador in England. Chance had admitted him to the confidence of a lord, who was the friend of the new ministry in opposition to the Duke of Marlborough. The unknown betook himself to the Marquis de Torci, and enquired without any preamble: "Do you wish to make peace, monsieur? I come to bring you the means of realising it." "It was like asking a dying man," said M. de Torci, "whether he wished to be cured."

Secret negotiations were soon entered into with the Earl of Oxford, Chancellor of the Exchequer, and St. John, Secretary of State, afterwards Lord Bolingbroke. These two men had no other interest in making peace with France, but that of depriving the Duke of Marlborough of the command of the army and of building their own power on his ruin. The step was dangerous; it was to betray the common cause of the Allies; it was to violate all their pledges, and expose themselves without any excuse to the hatred of the greater part of the nation, and an enquiry by parliament which might bring them to the block. It is extremely doubtful whether they could have succeeded, had not an unforeseen event facilitated the work. On 17 April, 1711, the Emperor Joseph I. died, and left the estates of the House of Austria, the German Empire and his claims in Spain and America to his brother Charles, who was elected Emperor a few months afterwards.

At the first news of this death the fears which had armed so many nations began to be dissipated in England through the efforts of the new ministry. Europe had wished to prevent Louis XIV. from ruling Spain, America, Lombardy, the Kingdom of Naples and Sicily in the name of his grandson. Why now should she be willing to unite so many estates under the hand of the Emperor, Charles VI.? For what had the English nation exhausted all her resources? She was paying out more than Germany and Holland combined. The expenditure of the present year amounted to seven millions sterling. Was she to ruin herself for a foreign cause and give a portion of Flanders to the United Provinces, her commercial rivals? All these arguments, which emboldened the queen, opened the eyes of a large section of the nation, and when a new parliament was convoked, the queen was at liberty to pave the way for peace in Europe.

But while preparing for it in secret she could not as yet publicly secede from her allies; and while the cabinet was negotiating, Marlborough was in the field. He continued to advance in Flanders; in August 1711 he broke through the lines which Marshal Villars had extended from Montreuil to Valenciennes; in September he took Bouchain, and marched on Quesnoi; there was hardly a rampart left between him and Paris.

It was at such a time of misfortune that the renowned Du Guay-Trouin, assisted by his valour and money given to him by a few merchants, having not yet attained to any rank in the navy, and owing all to himself, equipped a little fleet, and captured San Sebastian on the Rio de Janeiro, one of the principal towns of Brazil. (September and October, 1711) His fleet returned laden with riches, the Portuguese losing much more than he gained. But the mischief he did to Brazil could not alleviate the woes of France.

CHAPTER XXIII

VICTORY OF MARSHAL VILLARS AT DENAIN. GENERAL PEACE.
AFFAIRS PUT IN ORDER

NEGOTIATIONS at length publicly opened at London were more effective. The queen sent the Earl of Strafford as an ambassador to Holland, to communicate the proposals of Louis XIV. It was no longer Marlborough from whom mercy was asked. The Earl of Strafford forced the Dutch to nominate plenipotentiaries and to receive those of France.

There were three persons who were still opposed to peace. Marlborough, Prince Eugene and Heinsius persisted in their determination to crush Louis XIV. But on the English general's return to London at the end of 1711 he was deprived of all his offices. He discovered a new House of Commons, and had not a dominant party in the House of Lords. By creating new peers, the queen had weakened the duke's party and strengthened that of the crown. Like Scipio, he was accused of peculation; but by his glory and by his return, he extricated himself from the predicament in almost the same way as Scipio himself. In his fall he was still powerful. Prince Eugene did not hesitate to come to London in order to support his party. He was accorded a reception merited by his name and reputation and a refusal such as was merited by his proposals. The court gained the upper hand, and Prince Eugene returned to carry on the war alone; it was indeed but a fresh incentive to him to secure fresh victories, now that he was unencumbered by a partner to share the glory.

While the plenipotentiaries were assembling at Utrecht, and the French ministers, so hardly treated at Gertruidenberg, were now negotiating on more equal terms, Marshal Villars, who had retired behind the lines, again overran Arras and Cambrai. On 6 July, 1712, Prince Eugene took the town of Quesnoi and spread over the country an army of about a hundred thousand men. The Dutch had made great efforts; and as they had never yet provided the whole outlay that they had agreed to make for the war, their contingents were in advance of the number stipulated for that year. Queen Anne could not yet openly dissociate herself; she had despatched the Duke of Ormond with twelve thousand English troops to join Prince Eugene's army and was still paying many of the German troops. After burning the suburbs of Arras, Prince Eugene advanced on the French army and proposed to the Duke of Ormond to engage the enemy in battle. The English general's instructions, however, were not to fight. Private negotiations between England and France were in progress. A suspension of hostilities was publicly proclaimed by the two sovereigns. On 19 July, 1712, Louis XIV. handed over the town of Dunkirk to the English as a guarantee of good faith, and the Duke of Ormond withdrew in the direction of Ghent. He wished to draw off with his own English troops those who were in the queen's pay; but he was only able to persuade four of the Holstein squadrons and a Liège regiment to follow him. The troops of Brandenburg, the Palatinate, Saxony, Hesse and Denmark remained with Prince Eugene's colours, and were paid by the Dutch. Even the Elector of Hanover, who was to inherit the throne of Queen Anne, allowed his troops to remain with the Allies despite the queen, and made it clear that though his family might look forward to the crown of England, it was not on Queen Anne's patronage that it was relying.

Deprived of the support of the English, Prince Eugene still possessed a superiority of twenty thousand men over the French army; his position was superior, his stocks more plentiful, and he had the advantage of nine years of victories.

Marshal Villars was unable to prevent his laying siege to Landrecies. France, drained of men and money, was filled with dismay. Thoughtful people were not at all reassured by the conferences at Utrecht which might be rendered fruitless by Prince Eugene's successes. Already large detachments of his troops had laid waste part of Champagne and had advanced as far as the gates of Rheims.

Consternation already reigned at Versailles and in all other parts of the kingdom. The death of the king's only son, which had taken place within the year; the deaths of the Duke and Duchess of Burgundy in February 1712, and of their eldest son in March, all borne to the same tomb within a few months; the last of their children lying near to death; all these domestic misfortunes, together with troubles abroad and the misery of the people at home, led them to regard the end of Louis XIV.'s reign as a time set apart for calamities; and people began to expect disasters greater than the magnificence and glory of former days.

At this very time the Duke of Vendôme died in Spain on 11 June, 1712. The spirit of despondency, which pervaded the whole of France, and which I myself can remember, led people to fear again that Spain, though temporarily fortified by the Duke of Vendôme, would once more fall as a result of her loss.

Landrecies could not hold out for long. The question of the king withdrawing to Chambord on the Loire was raised at Versailles. Louis told Marshal Harcourt that in the event of a fresh disaster he would summon the whole of the nobility of the kingdom, would lead them in spite of his sixty-four years against the enemy, and would die at their head.

One error committed by Prince Eugene freed the king and France from much of their anxiety. It is alleged that his lines were too much extended; that the depôt for his stores in Marchiennes was too far away; that General Albemarle, who was stationed at Denain, between Marchiennes and the prince's camp, was not in a position to be reinforced with sufficient rapidity, should he be attacked. I have been told that there was in Marchiennes a very beautiful Italian, whom I saw some time afterwards at The Hague, and who at that time was a mistress of Prince Eugene, and that she was the cause of the spot having been chosen for the depôt of stores. It is to do scant justice to Prince Eugene to believe that a woman could have had a share in his preparations for war.

Those who are aware that a curé and a councillor of Douai, of the name of Le Fèvre d'Orval, strolling together in the neighbourhood of those quarters, were the first to perceive that Denain and Marchiennes could easily be attacked, will show by what secret and petty actions the great affairs of this world are often ruled. Le Fèvre communicated his views to the commissary of the province, and the latter to Marshal Montesquiou, who was second in command to Marshal Villars: the general approved of the idea and carried it out. This action, indeed, proved to be the salvation of France, even more so than the peace with England. Marshal Villars paid back Prince Eugene in his own coin. On 24 July, 1712, a corps of dragoons advanced within sight of the enemy's camp, as if about to attack it; and while these dragoons afterwards withdrew in the direction of Guise, the marshal marched on Denain with his army drawn up in five columns. He broke through General Albemarle's[1] entrenchments, which

[1] Joost van Keppel (1669–1718).

were defended by seventeen battalions, all of whom were killed or taken prisoners. The general surrendered together with two princes of Nassau, a prince of Holstein, a prince of Anhalt and all the officers. Prince Eugene arrived hurriedly with all the available troops he could master, but it was at the end of the action; he attempted to attack a bridge that led to Denain and which was in possession of the French; but losing men in the attempt he returned to his camp after having been a witness of the defeat.

All the positions towards Marchiennes, along the banks of the Scarpe, were one after another rapidly carried. On 30 July, 1712, the French pushed on to Marchiennes, which was defended by four thousand men; the siege was pressed so hard and with such vehemence, that at the end of three days the garrison was taken prisoner and all the munitions and food supplies accumulated by the enemy for the campaign were captured. After this all the advantage lay with Marshal Villars. During September and October of 1712 the disconcerted enemy raised the siege of Landrecies and witnessed the recapture of Douai, Quesnoi and Bouchain. The frontiers were safe. Prince Eugene's army retreated, reduced by nearly fifty battalions, forty of which had been captured from the Battle of Denain up to the end of the campaign. The most definite victory would not have yielded greater advantage.

Had Marshal Villars enjoyed the popular favour accorded to other generals, he would have been vociferously greeted as *the saviour of France*; but the debt of gratitude owing to him was grudgingly acknowledged, and in the public joy at such an unexpected success the feeling of envy still predominated.

Each advance of Marshal Villars hastened the Peace of Utrecht. Answerable alike to its country and to Europe, Queen Anne's ministry neglected no more the interests of England than those of the Allies, and the public safety. First, Philip V., now established on the throne of Spain, was required to renounce his claims to the throne of France which he had hitherto maintained, and his brother, the Duke of Berri, heir-presumptive to the throne of France after the only surviving great-grandson of Louis XIV., had likewise to renounce his claims to the Spanish crown, in the event of his becoming King of France. The Duke of Orleans was required to make a similar renunciation. Yet it had just been proved by twelve years of war how little men are bound by such treaties. There is as yet no recognised law which compels descendants to forgo their rights to a crown which their fathers have renounced.

Such renunciations are only effective when they continue to agree with common interests. But nevertheless they calmed for the moment a tempest of twelve years' duration, and it seemed probable that one day more than one nation would affirm these renunciations, which have become the basis of the equilibrium and peace of Europe.

By this treaty the Duke of Savoy acquired the island of Sicily with the title of King, and, on the continent, Fenestrelle, Exilles and the Valley o Pragelata. Thus lands were taken from the House of Bourbon to increase his power. A large strip of territory was given to the Dutch as a barrier such as they had always coveted; and while the House of France was robbed of some provinces to be given to the Duke of Savoy, land was also taken from the House of Austria to indemnify the Dutch, who were to become, at her expense, the guardians and the rulers of the strongest towns in Flanders. The commercial interests of Holland were considered, those of Portugal curtailed.

The Emperor was to retain the sovereignty of the eight and a half provinces of Spanish Flanders and the useful territory appertaining to the barrier towns. The kingdom of Naples and Sardinia was assured to him, with all his possessions in Lombardy and the four ports on the coasts of Tuscany. But the Council of Vienna thought itself too meanly dealt with and could not agree to such terms.

With regard to England, her glory and her interests were in safe keeping. She had the port of Dunkirk, the object of so much envy, demolished and filled up. Spain left her in possession of Gibraltar and the island of Minorca. France surrendered Hudson Bay, Newfoundland and Acadia. For her trade in America she obtained rights which were not granted to the French, though it was they who had placed Philip V. on the throne. Among the triumphant conditions laid down by the English ministry must be noted that of having made Louis set at liberty those subjects who were confined for their religious beliefs.

This was to dictate laws—but very worthy ones.

Finally Queen Anne, sacrificing to her country the rights of her kindred and the secret inclinations of her heart, promised and guaranteed her succession to the House of Hanover.

With regard to the Electors of Bavaria and Cologne, the Duke of Bavaria was to retain the duchy of Luxembourg and the countship of Namur, until he and his brother were re-established in their own electorates; for Spain had ceded these two sovereignties to the Bavarians as an indemnity for their losses, though the Allies had taken neither Namur nor Luxembourg.

As for France, who was to raze Dunkirk and surrender so many towns in Flanders formerly conquered by her arms and guaranteed to her by the treaties of Nimeguen and Ryswick, she recovered Lille, Aire, Bethune and Saint-Venant.

It would thus appear that the English ministry rendered justice to every one of the powers. But the Whigs would not render it to their own ministry; and soon half the nation was slandering the memory of Queen Anne, because she had accomplished the greatest good that any sovereign can do— that of bringing peace to many nations. She was upbraided for having been in a position to dismember France and not having done so.

All these treaties were signed one after another during the course of the year 1713. Either because of the obstinacy of Prince Eugene, or because of the misguided policy of the Emperor's council, that monarch did not participate in any of the negotiations. Had he shared at first the views of Queen Anne, he would certainly have obtained Landau and perhaps Strasburg. As it was, he persisted in carrying on the war and obtained nothing. Marshal Villars, having ensured the safety of the remaining part of French Flanders, turned towards the Rhine, and after taking possession of Spires, Worms and the surrounding country, took on 22 August, 1713, that very Landau which the Emperor could have kept by peace; he broke through the lines made by Prince Eugene; and on 20 October besieged and took Freiburg, the former capital of Austria.

The Council of Vienna solicited from all sides the help promised by the Imperial provinces, but such help was not forthcoming. Then it perceived that without England and Holland, the Emperor would be unable to stand against France, and too late it resolved to make peace.

Having thus brought the war to an end, Marshal Villars had also the glory of concluding peace at Rastadt with

Prince Eugene. This was perhaps the first time that two opposing generals were seen negotiating in the name of their masters at the end of a campaign. Both of them displayed at this meeting a characteristic frankness. I have heard that one of the earliest remarks of Marshal Villars to Prince Eugene was this: "Sir, we are no longer enemies; your enemies are at Vienna, mine at Versailles." Indeed, both generals were continually contending against plots at their respective courts.

In this treaty there was no question of the rights to the Spanish monarchy which the Emperor still claimed, nor of the empty title of Catholic King, which Charles VI. still assumed, though the kingdom was in Philip V.'s possession. Louis XIV. kept Strasburg and Landau, towns which he had previously offered to surrender; Hüningen and New Brisach, which he had himself offered to raze to the ground, and the sovereignty of Alsace, which he had offered to relinquish. But his noblest act was to reinstate the Electors of Bavaria and Cologne in their positions and estates.

It is indeed remarkable that in all her treaties with the Emperors, France has always protected the rights of the Imperial princes and the provinces. She laid the foundations of German liberty at Münster and there instituted an eighth electorate for this very House of Bavaria. The Treaty of Nimguen confirmed that of Westphalia. By the Treaty of Ryswick, she insisted on the restoration of all the possessions of Cardinal Fürstenberg. Finally, by the Peace of Utrecht, she reinstated the two electors. It must be admitted that during the whole of the negotiations that put an end to this long struggle, France submitted to the authority of England and made the Empire submit to hers.

The historical memoirs of the period, upon which so many compilations of the history of Louis XIV. have been based, relate that at the conclusion of the conferences, Prince Eugene bade the Duke de Villars embrace the knees of Louis XIV. for him, and present that monarch the assurances of his deepest respect as *from a subject to a sovereign*. First, it is not true that a prince, the grandson of a sovereign, remains the subject of another prince because he was born within his territory. Second, it is even less true that Prince Eugene, the Vicar-General of the Empire, could call himself a subject of the King of France.

Meanwhile, each country proceeded to take possession of

its new rights. The Duke of Savoy obtained recognition in Sicily without consulting the Emperor who complained in vain. Louis XIV. gained entry for his troops into Lille. The Dutch took possession of their barrier towns, and Flanders continued to pay them 1,250,000 florins every year, in order to enjoy their rights and liberty. Louis XIV. filled up the port of Dunkirk, razed the citadel to the ground, and pulled down all the coastal fortifications, under the eyes of an English commissary. The inhabitants of Dunkirk, seeing their commerce thus destroyed, sent a deputation to London to solicit the clemency of Queen Anne. It was a deplorable thing that Louis XIV.'s subjects should ask a favour from a Queen of England, but it was still more deplorable for them that Queen Anne was obliged to refuse them.

Some time afterwards Louis enlarged the Mardick Canal and, by means of locks, a port was constructed which was said to equal that of Dunkirk. The Earl of Stair, the English ambassador, indignantly protested to that monarch. In one of the best chronicles of the time it is related that Louis XIV. replied to the Earl of Stair in these words: "Sir ambassador, I have always been master of my own affairs, sometimes of other people's; do not remind me of it." I know for a positive fact that Louis XIV. made no such unseemly reply. He never had been master of the English, and he was far from being so. He was master in his own country, but it is to be questioned whether he was master enough to evade a treaty to which he owed his security and perhaps a large part of his kingdom.

The clause in the treaty which prescribed the destruction of the port of Dunkirk and its locks, did not bind him not to construct a port at Mardick. Books have been printed in which it has audaciously been stated that Lord Bolingbroke, who drew up the treaty, omitted this proviso because he had been bribed with a present of a million. This shameful calumny is to be found in *The History of Louis XIV.*, by a certain La Martinière, nor is this the only calumny which disgraces the book. Louis XIV. appeared to be within his rights in taking advantage of the carelessness of the English ministers and holding to the letter of the treaty; but he preferred to fulfil its spirit solely for the sake of peace: and so far from saying to Lord Stair *that he should not remind him that he had formerly been master of other people's affairs*, he was willing to yield to his remonstrances, which he might have resisted. In April 1715 he suspended the work at Mardick, and soon afterwards under the regency the works were demolished, and all the terms of the treaty thus fulfilled.

Philip V. was not yet in possession of the whole of Spain after the Peace of Utrecht and Rastadt: he had still to subdue Catalonia and the islands of Majorca and Iviza.

It should be mentioned that the Emperor Charles VI., having left his wife at Barcelona, and neither being able to carry on the war with Spain, nor inclined to surrender his rights and accept the Peace of Utrecht, nevertheless came to an agreement with Queen Anne, by which the Empress and his troops, now useless in Catalonia, were to be taken away in English ships. Catalonia indeed had been evacuated, and Staremberg on his departure had resigned his title of viceroy. But he left behind him the seeds of a civil war and the expectation of speedy assistance on the part of the Emperor and even of England. Those who enjoyed the greatest reputation in the province flattered themselves that they could form a republic under foreign protection, and that the King of Spain would not be strong enough to crush them. In this they displayed those characteristics so long ago attributed to them by Tacitus: "A fearless nation," he said, "who count their lives as of no value, when they are not risking them in fighting."

Catalonia is one of the most fertile and favourably situated countries in the world. Watered by beautiful rivers, streams and fountains, in favourable contrast to the arid regions of Old and New Castile, it produces everything necessary to the wants of man, and everything to satisfy his desires in the way of trees, wheat, fruit and vegetables of every kind. Barcelona is one of the finest ports in Europe and the country supplies everything necessary for the building of ships. Its mountains abound in marble quarries, jasper and rock-crystal, and are also rich in many kinds of precious stones. Mines yield plentiful supplies of iron, tin, lead, alum and vitriol; coral is found on the east coast. In short, Catalonia can dispense with the whole world, but her neighbours cannot dispense with her.

Far from being enervated by affluence and pleasures, the inhabitants have always been warriors and the mountain dwellers particularly fierce. But despite their valour and their love of liberty they have always been a subject people:

the Romans, the Goths, the Vandals and the Saracens have conquered them in turn.

They shook off the yoke of the Saracens only to place themselves under the protection of Charlemagne. They were annexed to the House of Aragon and afterwards to that of Austria.

We have seen that in the reign of Philip IV., provoked beyond endurance by the Count-Duke Olivares, the first minister, they attached themselves to Louis XIII. in 1640. All their privileges were preserved to them, and they were treated more as favourites than as subjects. In 1652 they came again under Austrian rule, and in the war of succession they took sides with the Archduke Charles against Philip V. Their stubborn resistance showed Philip that, even when he was rid of his rival, he could not subdue them unaided. Louis XIV., who, in the latter period of the war, could supply his grandson neither with soldiers nor ships in his struggle against his rival, Charles, now sent him some to fight against his rebellious subjects. A French squadron blockaded the port of Barcelona and Marshal Berwick besieged it by land.

The Queen of England, more loyal to her treaties than to the interests of her country, sent no relief to the city. The English were indignant at this treatment, and reproached themselves like the ancient Romans for having allowed Saguntum to be destroyed. The Emperor of Germany promised help which never came. The besieged defended themselves with a courage that savoured of fanaticism. Priests and monks rushed armed into the breaches, as though they were engaged in a war of religion. A vision of liberty made them deaf to all offers with which their rightful master tempted them. More than five hundred priests were killed with arms in hand during this siege. One can imagine how their words and their example had emboldened the people.

They hoisted a black flag over the breach, and repulsed more than one assault. Finally, when the besiegers broke through, they still fought from street to street, and, having retreated into the new town when the old one was taken, they demanded, on 12 September, 1714, that they should be allowed to preserve all their rights if they surrendered. They obtained but their lives and property. The greater part of their privileges were taken away from them, though of all the monks who had incited the people and fought against their king but sixty were punished; and even these were leniently treated, being only condemned to the galleys. Philip V. had treated the small town of Xativa more severely during the war; as an example to others not a stone of it was left standing; but while a small town of little importance may be razed to the ground, a large town is spared, especially when it possesses a port on the seaboard, the preservation of which is profitable to the state.

This outburst of fury on the part of the Catalonians, such as had not animated them when Charles VI. was in their midst, and which carried them away only when they were beyond assistance, was the last flame of the conflagration which had ravaged for so long the fairest part of Europe, and which had been lit by the last will and testament of Charles II., King of Spain.

CHAPTER XXIV

BIRD'S-EYE VIEW OF EUROPE FROM THE PEACE OF UTRECHT TO THE DEATH OF LOUIS XIV

I VENTURE to call this long war a civil war. The Duke of Savoy was fighting against his two daughters. The Prince of Vaudemont, who had sided with the Archduke Charles, very nearly took his own father prisoner in Lombardy, who was fighting for Philip V. Spain had been actually split up into factions, and whole regiments of French Calvinists had fought against their country.

To sum all, the whole cause of the war was a disputed succession between two branches of the same family, and it may be added that the Queen of England excluded her own brother, whom Louis XIV. had sheltered and whom she was compelled to banish, from the throne.

Human foresight and expectations were, as usual, thwarted in this war. Though twice installed in Madrid, Charles VI. was finally driven from Spain; Louis XIV., on the point of ruin, was saved by unforeseen discontents in England.

The Council of Spain, which had only invited the Duke of Anjou to the throne in order to prevent the monarchy from ever being split up, witnessed the loss of many provinces from it. Lombardy and Flanders remained in possession of the House of Austria; the House of Prussia obtained a small part also of Flanders, and the Dutch ruled over another part; yet a fourth part went to France. Thus the inheritance of the House of Burgundy became divided between four powers; and the one that apparently had most right to it did not obtain so much as a single farm. The Emperor retained Sardinia for some time, useless as it was to him. He also remained for some years in possession of Naples, that great fief of Rome, which has been so often and so easily captured. The Duke of Savoy occupied Sicily for four years, occupying it only to uphold against the Pope the strange but ancient prerogative of being Pope himself in that island, that is to say, of being, except in matters of doctrine, absolute ruler in ecclesiastical affairs.

The futility of diplomacy was still more evident after the Peace of Utrecht than during the war. It is unquestionable that Queen Anne's new ministry was desirous of making secret preparations for placing James II.'s son upon the throne. Queen Anne herself was inclined to listen to the voice of nature through the medium of her ministers, and was disposed to leave her crown to the brother on whose head she had set a price against her will.

Moved by the appeals of her favourite, Lady Masham, and intimidated by the remonstrances of the Tory prelates by whom she was surrounded, she reproached herself for such an unnatural proscription. The Duchess of Marlborough, I know, was convinced that the queen had had a secret meeting with her brother, that she had embraced him, and that had he been willing to abjure the Roman faith, regarded in England and by all Protestants as the mother of tyranny, she would have appointed him as her successor. Her antipathy to the House of Hanover increased her attachment to the House of Stuart. It is related that on the eve of her death, she cried out several times, "Oh! my brother! My dear brother!" She died of apoplexy at the age of forty-nine on 12 August, 1714. Both her adherents and her enemies agreed that she was a woman of very ordinary character. Nevertheless, her reign was the most glorious since those of Edward III. and Henry V.; never had there been greater captains on sea or land, never more ministers of genius, never more enlightened parliaments, never orators more eloquent.

Death forestalled all her plans. The House of Hanover which she disliked, regarding it as a foreign house, succeeded her; and her ministers were persecuted.

Viscount Bolingbroke, who had come over to grant peace to Louis XIV. with a grandeur rivalling that monarch's own, was compelled to seek shelter in France and make his reappearance as a suppliant. The Duke of Ormond, the life and soul of the Pretender's party, chose the same refuge, but Harley, Earl of Oxford, showed more courage. It was against him that envy was directed; but he remained boldly in his own country, and braved alike the prison into which he was cast and the death by which he was threatened. His was a serene soul, incapable of envy, above the lure of riches and the fear of hardship. His very fearlessness saved him, and his enemies in Parliament respected him too much to have him arrested.

Louis XIV.'s life was drawing to a close. It is difficult to believe that, at the age of seventy-seven years and in the midst of his country's misfortune, he should venture to expose himself to a fresh war in England, in favour of the Pretender, acknowledged by him as King, and who then bore the title of Chevalier of St. George; nevertheless, it is certain that he did so. It must be admitted that Louis ever possessed a greatness of soul which urged him to the accomplishment of great things in every sphere. The Earl of Stair, the English ambassador, had defied him. He had been forced to expel James III. from France, just as in his younger days Charles II. and his brother had been driven out. James III. was now in hiding at Commerci in Lorraine. The Duke of Ormond and the Earl of Bolingbroke flattered the King of France's glory and deluded him with hopes of a rising in England and especially in Scotland against George I. The Pretender had only to appear; all they required was a ship, a few officers and a little money. The ship and the officers were at once forthcoming, though the treaties did not allow of a warship being sent. The famous ship-owner, L'Épine d'Anicane, provided the transport ship, cannon and arms. As for money, the king had none. Only four hundred thousand crowns were asked and they could not be found. Louis XIV. wrote himself to his grandson, Philip V., King of Spain, who lent the money. It was with this help that the Pretender secretly crossed over to Scotland and did indeed find there a considerable party, but he was soon defeated by King George's English troops.

In the meantime Louis died; and the Pretender returned to Commerci, to submit to the cruel destiny that had dogged him all his life, while in England his partisans shed their blood upon the scaffold.

In the chapters devoted to private affairs and anecdotes, we shall see how Louis XIV. died in the midst of the abominable intrigues of his confessor and the most despicable theological disputes that have ever perplexed ignorant and restless minds. But I shall consider here the state in which he left Europe.

In the North, Russia's power was increasing day by day, and as yet France, Italy and Spain were too heedless of the advent of this new people and this new empire.

Sweden, France's old ally, and formerly the terror of the House of Austria, was unable to defend herself against the Russians, and Charles XII. was stripped of everything except his glory.

A single German electorate was beginning to transform itself into a dominating power. The second King of Prussia, the Elector of Brandenburg, by means of economy and a well-trained army, was laying the foundations of a power up to that time unknown.

Holland still enjoyed the reputation which she had acquired during the last war with Louis XIV.; but the influence that she had in the councils of nations was becoming daily less. England, though worried by disturbances during the first years of the reign of an Elector of Hanover, maintained all her power and influence. The states of the House of Austria languished under Charles VI.; but most of the Imperial princes brought their estates into a flourishing condition. Spain breathed again under Philip V., who owed his throne to Louis XIV. Italy remained quiet until the year 1717. There was no ecclesiastical dispute in Europe which could give the Pope a pretext to extend his claims or which could deprive him of the prerogatives he had preserved. Jansenism alone disturbed France, but without causing any schism and without stirring up a civil war.

CHAPTER XXV

INCIDENTS AND ANECDOTES OF THE REIGN OF LOUIS XIV

ANECDOTES are the gleanings left over from the vast harvest-field of history; they are details that have been long hidden, and hence their name of *anecdotes*: the public is interested in them when they concern illustrious personages.

Plutarch's *Lives of Great Men* is a collection of anecdotes more entertaining than accurate; how could he have had definite knowledge of the private lives of Theseus and Lycurgus? The majority of the maxims which he puts into the mouths of his characters are noteworthy for their moral content rather than their historical truth.

Procopius's *Secret History of Justinian* is a satire prompted by motives of revenge; and although revenge may sometimes speak the truth, this satire, which contradicts his own official history of the reign, seems to be false in several instances. One is not allowed nowadays to imitate Plutarch, still less Procopius. Historical truths must first be proved before they can be admitted. When contemporaries who were mutual enemies such as Cardinal de Retz and Duke de La Roche-foucauld confirm the same fact in their Memoirs, the matter is placed beyond a doubt; when they contradict, one must doubt: the principle is that what is probable should not be accepted, unless several trustworthy contemporaries unanimously testify to its truth.

The most useful and valuable anecdotes are those left in the secret writings of great princes, their natural candour thus revealing itself in permanent records; such are those which I am about to relate of Louis XIV.

Domestic details gratify merely the inquisitive: weaknesses brought to light give pleasure but to the spiteful, except when these very weaknesses are instructive, either on account of the misfortunes which they have caused or the virtues which have redeemed them.

The secret memoirs of contemporaries must always be suspected of partiality: those who write one or two genera-tions later must use the greatest care to omit the merely frivolous, to reduce exaggeration, and combat what has been dictated by motives of satire.

Louis XIV. invested his court, as he did all his reign, with

such brilliancy and magnificence, that the slightest details
of his private life appear to interest posterity, just as they
were the objects of curiosity to every court in Europe and
indeed to all his contemporaries. The splendour of his rule
was reflected in his most trivial actions. People are more eager,
especially in France, to know the smallest incidents of his
court, than the revolutions of some other countries. Such
is the effect of a great reputation. Men would rather know
what happened in the private council and court of Augustus
than details of the conquests of Attila or of Tamerlane.

Consequently there are few historians who have failed to
give an account of Louis XIV.'s early affection for the
Baroness de Beauvais, for Mlle. d'Argencourt, for Cardinal
Mazarin's niece, later married to the Count of Soissons, father
of Prince Eugene; and especially for her sister, Marie Mancini,
who afterwards married the High Constable Colonne.

He had not yet taken over the reins of government when
such diversions occupied the idleness in which he was encouraged by Cardinal Mazarin, then ruling as absolute
master. His attachment to Marie Mancini was in itself a serious
matter, for he was sufficiently in love to be tempted to marry
her, and yet sufficiently master of himself to abandon her.
This victory gained over his passion was the earliest sign
that he was born with a great soul. He gained a yet greater
and more difficult victory in allowing Cardinal Mazarin to
remain absolute master.

Gratitude prevented him from shaking off a yoke which
was beginning to irk him. The anecdote was often quoted at
court to the effect that after the cardinal's death he said:
"I do not know what I should have done, if he had lived
much longer."

He occupied his leisure in reading entertaining books,
especially in the company of Marie Mancini, wife of the
High Constable Colonne, a witty woman, like all her sisters.
He delighted in poetry and novels, which in describing gallant
and noble deeds secretly flattered his own character. He
read Corneille's tragedies and thus formed his taste, which is
nothing other than the result of good sense and the prompt-
ing of a rightly trained mind. The conversations of his
mother and the ladies of the court contributed not a little
to make him appreciate this supreme faculty of the intellect,
and to bring to perfection in him that remarkable refinement of manners which from that time began to characterise

the court. Anne of Austria had brought with her a certain dignified and haughty gallantry typical of the Spanish nation at that time, and had added a charm, a mildness and decorous freedom only to be found in France. The king made greater progress in this school of accomplishments from his eighteenth to twentieth year than he had ever made in the sciences under his tutor, the Abbé de Beaumont, afterwards Archbishop of Paris. He had been taught practically nothing. It was at least desirable that he should have been taught some history, and especially modern history; but the available histories were too badly written.

It was to be deplored that authors had as yet only succeeded in writing useless novels, and that important books were still remarkably unattractive. *A Translation of the Commentaries of Cæsar* was printed under Louis' name and one of *Florus* under that of his brother; but these princes had no other part in these books than that of having idly taken some passages from these authors for their exercises.

The tutor who had charge of the king's education under the first Marshal Villeroi was just such as he needed—learned and yet good-humoured: the civil wars, however, disturbed his education, and Cardinal Mazarin was very willing that the king should receive but little instruction. When he became attached to Marie Mancini he quickly learnt Italian for her sake, and later, at the time of his marriage, he studied Spanish with less success. The fact that his tutors had allowed him too much to neglect his studies in early youth, a shyness which arose from a fear of placing himself in a false position, and the ignorance in which he was kept by Cardinal Mazarin, gave the whole court to believe that he would always be ruled like his father, Louis XIII.

There was only one occasion on which those who can judge future events predicted what he would become; this was in 1665, following upon the suppression of the civil wars, and after his first campaign and coronation, when parliament again wished to assemble and discuss certain decrees; the king set out from Vincennes in hunting dress followed by all his court, entered parliament in top-boots, whip in hand, and uttered these words: "The misfortunes that your assemblies have brought about are well known; I order you to break up this assembly which has met to discuss my decrees. *M. le premier Président*, I forbid you to allow these meetings and a single one of you to demand them."

His figure, even now imposing, the nobility of his features, the masterful tone and air with which he spoke, impressed them more than did his rank, which up till then they had but little respected. These first signs of his greatness, however, seemed to wither almost immediately, and the fruits only became apparent after the cardinal's death.

Since the triumphant return of Mazarin the court was taken up with gaming, ballets and comedy, which, but lately born in France, had not yet the attained dignity of an art, and with tragedy, already become a sublime art in the hands of Pierre Corneille. A curé of Saint-Germain l'Auxerrois who inclined to the rigorous notions of the Jansenists had often written to the queen during the first few years of the regency, complaining of these performances. He maintained that anyone who attended them was doomed to perdition, and had even had this anathema signed by seven doctors of the Sorbonne; but the Abbé de Beaumont, the king's tutor, fortified himself by obtaining so many approvals from doctors that they outnumbered the condemnations of the stern curé. He thus calmed the scruples of the queen and, on becoming Archbishop of Paris, sanctioned the views he had upheld as an abbé. This fact is mentioned in the *Memoirs* of Mme. de Motteville, and as such may be taken as genuine.

It should be noted that since Cardinal Richelieu introduced regular performances of plays at court, which have now made Paris the rival of Athens, not only was there a special bench for the Academy, which included several ecclesiastics among its members, but also one for the bishops.

In 1646 and 1654 Cardinal Mazarin had Italian operas performed by singers specially come from Italy on the boards of the Palais-Royal theatre and the Petit-Bourbon, not far from the Louvre. This new entertainment had been recently invented in Florence, a state then favoured by fortune as well as by nature, and to which we owe the revival of several arts that had lain unknown for centuries, and even the creation of a few. There still remained in France a remnant of ancient barbarism which was opposed to the introduction of these arts.

The Jansenists, whom Richelieu and Mazarin endeavoured to suppress, revenged themselves on the pleasures which those two ministers introduced into the country. Lutherans and Calvinists had behaved in the same way in the time of

Pope Leo X. Indeed one had only to be an innovator to be austere. Men who overturn a whole nation to establish, often, an absurd doctrine, are the very ones to denounce innocent pleasures essential to a great city and arts which contribute to the glory of a nation. The suppression of the theatre is an idea more worthy of the age of Attila than of that of Louis XIV.

The dance, which may still be reckoned one of the arts since it is subject to rules and gives grace to the body, was one of the favourite amusements of the court. Louis XIII. had only once danced in a ballet, in 1625; and that ballet was of an undignified character which gave no promise of what the arts would become in France thirty years later. Louis XIV. excelled in stately measures, which suited the majesty of his figure without injuring that of his position. The ring jousts in which he sometimes engaged, and which were attended with great magnificence, strikingly displayed his dexterity in all kinds of military exercises. Everything breathed an air of luxury and magnificence so far as they were then known. It was little in comparison with what was seen when the king took the reins of government into his own hands; but it was something at which to marvel after the horrors of a civil war and the gloom of the melancholy and secluded life of Louis XIII. That sickly and disappointed prince had not been housed, furnished, or waited upon as befits a king. He did not possess more than a hundred thousand crowns' worth of crown jewels. Mazarin left but twelve hundred thousand; and to-day the crown jewels are worth about twenty million livres.

In 1660, the marriage of Louis XIV. was attended by a display of magnificence and exquisite taste which was ever afterwards on the increase. He made his entry accompanied by his bride, and Paris beheld with respectful yet loving admiration the beautiful young queen as she advanced, drawn in a superb carriage of novel design; the king, on horseback at her side, was adorned with everything that art could add to enhance his manly and heroic beauty which attracted every eye.

At the meeting of the roads at Vincennes a triumphal arch was erected on a base of stone; time did not permit the whole to be built of lasting material, and it was consequently made only of plaster which has since been entirely demolished. Claude Perrault designed it. The gate of Saint-

Antoine was rebuilt for the same occasion, a monument in poorer taste, but decorated with statues of considerable merit. All those who, after the Battle of Saint-Antoine, witnessed the dead or dying bodies of innumerable citizens brought back to Paris through that gate, at that time defended by a portcullis, and who now saw an entry so different, blessed God and gave thanks for so fortunate a change.

To celebrate the marriage the Italian opera *Ercole Amante* was performed at the Louvre by the orders of Cardinal Mazarin, but it failed to please the French. They were delighted only to see the king and queen dancing in it. The cardinal resolved to bring himself into prominence by providing a show more to the nation's taste. The Secretary of State Lyonne undertook to have a kind of allegorical tragedy written in the style of *Europe*, on which Cardinal Richelieu had worked. It was fortunate for the great Corneille that he was not chosen to complete this wretched sketch. The subject was that of *Lysis and Hesperia—Lysis* representing France and *Hesperia* Spain; and Quinault was entrusted with carrying it out. He had lately made a great reputation with a piece entitled *The False Tiberius*, which, poor though it was, had had a tremendous success. Matters fared differently with *Lysis*. It was performed at the Louvre, and its only merit was the stage-machinery employed. The Marquis de Sourdeac, to whom was due at a later date the establishment of opera in France, had at this very time at his own expense arranged a performance of Pierre Corneille's *Golden Fleece* in his castle at Neubourg with suitable stage-machinery. Quinault, young and of pleasing appearance, had the court on his side, Corneille had his name and France. The result is that we owe opera and comedy in France to two cardinals.

The king's marriage was followed by one long series of fêtes, entertainments and gallantries. They were redoubled on the marriage of *Monsieur*, the king's eldest brother, to Henrietta of England, sister of Charles II., and they were not interrupted until the death of Cardinal Mazarin in 1661.

Several months after the death of that minister an event occurred which is without parallel, and, what is stranger, all historians omit to mention it. An unknown prisoner, of height above the ordinary, young, and of an extremely handsome and noble figure, was conveyed under the greatest secrecy to the castle of the Island of Sainte-Marguerite, lying in the

Mediterranean off Provence. On the journey the prisoner wore a mask, the chin-piece of which had steel springs to enable him to eat while still wearing it, and his guards had orders to kill him if he uncovered his face. He remained on the island until an officer of the secret service by name Saint-Mars, governor of Pignerol, who was made governor of the Bastille in 1690, went in that year to Sainte-Marguerite, and brought him to the Bastille still wearing his mask. The Marquis de Louvois visited him on the island before his removal, and remained standing while speaking to him, evidently regarding him with respect. The unknown prisoner was conducted to the Bastille, where he was accommodated as well as was possible in that citadel, being refused nothing that he asked for. His greatest desire was for linen and lace of extraordinary fineness. He used to play on the guitar. He was given the greatest delicacies and the governor rarely seated himself in his presence. An old physician in the Bastille who often attended this remarkable man in illness declared that he never saw his face, although he had often examined his tongue and the rest of his body. He was a wonderfully well-made man, said his physician; his skin was rather dark; he charmed by the mere tone of his voice, never complaining of his lot nor giving a hint of his identity.

The unknown man died in 1703 and was buried by night in the parish church of Saint Paul. What is doubly astonishing is that when he was sent to the Island of Sainte-Marguerite no man of any consequence in Europe disappeared. Yet such the prisoner was without a doubt, for during the first few days that he was on the island, the governor himself put the dishes on the table and then withdrew, locking the door after him. One day the prisoner wrote something with his knife on a silver plate and threw it out of the window in the direction of a boat lying by the bank almost at the foot of the tower. A fisherman, to whom the boat belonged, picked up the plate and carried it to the governor. In amazement the latter asked him, "Have you read what is written on this plate, and has anyone seen it in your hands?" "I cannot read," replied the fisherman, "I have just found it, and no one else has seen it." The peasant was detained until the governor was convinced that he had not read it and that the plate had not been seen. "Go now," he said to him; "you are a very lucky man not to be able to read." Among those who have had first-hand knowledge of this affair a very trustworthy one is still alive. M. de Chamillart was, however, the last minister to be acquainted with the strange secret. His son-in-law, the second Marshal La Feuillade, told me that when his father-in-law lay dying, he implored him on his knees to tell him the name of this man who had been known simply as *the man in the iron mask.* Chamillart replied that it was a state secret and that he had sworn never to reveal it. Lastly, there are still many of my contemporaries who can confirm the truth of the affair that I have described, than which I know none more extraordinary, and at the same time better authenticated.

Meanwhile Louis XIV. was dividing his time between the pleasures befitting his age and the duties involved by his position. He used to hold a council every day, and would then work in secret with Colbert. This secret work brought about the downfall of the celebrated Fouquet, in which the Secretary of State, Guénégaud, Pellisson, Gourville, and so many others were involved. The fall of this minister, who was certainly less reproached than Cardinal Mazarin, shows that it is not everyone who can commit the same mistakes. His doom was already sealed when the king accepted an invitation to the magnificent fête which the minister held in his honour at his mansion at Vaux. This palace and the gardens had cost him eighteen millions, which would be worth about thirty-five to-day. He had twice built the palace and had bought three hamlets which were now contained in the enormous gardens, which had been planted in part by Le Nôtre, and were then regarded as the finest in Europe. The fountains of Vaux, afterwards less than mediocre in comparison with those of Versailles, Marli, and Saint-Cloud, were then considered marvellous. Nevertheless, however fine the mansion, an expenditure of eighteen millions—the accounts are still in existence—proves that his underlings had served him with as little regard for economy as he himself was serving the king. It could not be denied that Saint-Germain and Fontainebleau, the only country seats inhabited by the king, fell far short of the beauties of Vaux. Louis XIV. felt this and it annoyed him. The arms and motto of Fouquet were to be seen on every side, consisting of a squirrel with the words: *Quo non ascendam?* The ambition of the motto did not tend to pacify him.

The courtiers noticed that the squirrel was depicted everywhere, and was followed by an adder, which was the emblem of Colbert. The entertainment surpassed those given by Cardinal Mazarin, not only in magnificence, but in refinement. Molière's *Fâcheux* was there performed for the first time. Pellisson had composed the prologue, which was much admired. So true is it that at court public entertainments often conceal or prepare the way for the downfall of individuals, that had it not been for the queen-mother Pellisson and Fouquet would have been arrested at Vaux on the very day of the fête. What still further increased the anger of the king was that Mlle. de La Vallière, for whom he was beginning to feel a genuine passion, had been the object of Fouquet's passing fancy, and the latter had spared no efforts to satisfy it. He had offered Mlle. de La Vallière two hundred thousand livres, but she had indignantly rejected the offer before even she had any design on the king's affections. Perceiving later what a powerful rival he had, Fouquet endeavoured to become the confidant of her whom he could not possess, and thus but further exasperated the king.

Louis, in the first feeling of indignation, had been tempted to have Fouquet arrested in the middle of the very fête which was being held in his honour; but afterwards made use of an unnecessary dissimulation, almost as though the monarch, already all-powerful, was afraid of the party which Fouquet had gathered together.

He was the Attorney-General for parliament, an office which entitled him to the privilege of being tried by the combined chambers; but after so many princes, marshals and dukes had been tried by commissioners, it should have been surely possible to treat a magistrate in the same way, since it was thought wise to make use of unusual methods, such as without being unjust always leave behind them the flavour of injustice.

Colbert persuaded him to sell his office by a dishonourable trick. He was offered as much as 1,800,000 livres, which would be worth 3,500,000 to-day; and by a misunderstanding, he sold it for only 1,400,000 francs. The exorbitant amounts paid for seats in parliament, amounts which were later much reduced, prove that that body still commanded a considerable respect even in its decadence. The Duke de Guise, Grand Chamberlain to the king, had sold that office of the crown to the Duke de Bouillon for a mere 800,000 livres.

It was the Fronde and the civil war in Paris which so raised the price of judicial offices, while it was one of the greatest defects and misfortunes of a government long involved in debt, that France should be the only country where judicial offices were sold; it was, nevertheless, the result of the leaven of sedition and in itself an insult to the throne, that the office of the King's Attorney should cost more than the chief preferments of the crown.

Despite the fact that he had squandered state funds and appropriated them to his own use, Fouquet had, none the less, a certain greatness of soul. His depredations had all been used for public display and private liberality. In 1661 he handed over the price of his office to the royal treasury, but the magnanimous action did not save him. He who could have been arrested in Paris by a common police officer and two guards was cunningly lured to Nantes. The king paid him great attentions immediately before his downfall. I do not know why the majority of princes should have the custom of deceiving with false kindness those of their subjects of whom they wish to rid themselves. Duplicity at such a time is the opposite of greatness. It is never a virtue and only becomes a worthy expedient when it is entirely necessary. Louis XIV. appeared to belie his usual character; but he had been told that Fouquet was making great fortifications at Belle-Isle, and that he probably possessed too many allies, both within and without the kingdom. But it was plain enough, when he was arrested and taken to the Bastille and Vincennes, that his party was nothing more than a few courtiers and greedy women, who were in receipt of pensions from him, and who forgot him immediately that he was no longer in a position to bestow them. Other friends remained, however, proving that he was worthy of them. The celebrated Mme. de Sévigné, Pellisson, Gourville, Mlle. Scudéri and several men of letters stoutly defended him, and by their zeal succeeded in saving his life.

The following verses of Hénault, the translator of Lucretius, against Colbert, Fouquet's persecutor, are well known:

> Base sordid minister, poor slave misplac'd,
> Who groan'st beneath the weight of state affairs,
> Devoted sacrifice to public cares,
> Vain phantom, with a weary title grac'd;
>
> The dangerous point of envied greatness see;
> Of fallen Fouquet behold the sad remains,
> And while his fall rewards thy secret pains,
> Dread a more dismal fate prepared for thee

Those pangs he suffers thou one day may'st feel,
Thy giddy station dread, the court and fortune's wheel;
Against him cease thy prince's ire to feed.

From power's steep summit few unhurt descend;
Thyself, perhaps, shall soon his mercy need,
Then seek not all his rigour to extend.

M. Colbert, on hearing of this libellous sonnet, asked if the king was offended by it. He was told that he was not. "Then neither am I," replied the minister.

One must never be deceived by such well-considered replies, or by public declarations which are belied by the speaker's actions.

Colbert appeared to be moderate, but in reality he sought Fouquet's death with extraordinary ferocity. A man may be a good minister and yet vindictive. It is a pity that Colbert could not be as magnanimous as he was wary.

One of the most implacable of Fouquet's enemies was Michel Le Tellier, then Secretary of State and his rival in favour. He it was who afterwards became chancellor. To read his funeral oration and then compare it with his conduct, one can but conclude that a funeral oration is nothing more than a piece of declamatory oratory. The chancellor, Séguier, president of the commission, was, however, of all Fouquet's judges the one who sought his death with the greatest fury, and who treated him with the greatest harshness.

It must be admitted that to bring an action against Fouquet was in itself to disparage the memory of Cardinal Mazarin. None had embezzled state funds with a freer hand, and, as a sovereign power, he had appropriated to himself several sources of state revenue. He had traded in army munitions in his own name and reaped good profits. "By means of *lettres-de-cachet*," said Fouquet in his defence, "he imposed enormous taxes on the various districts, a thing which had never been done before except by him and for his own profit, and which, according to the ordinances, is punishable by death." It was thus that the cardinal had amassed immense wealth, which he himself no longer enjoyed.

I have heard the late M. de Caumartin, comptroller of finance, relate that in his youth, some years after the cardinal's death, he had been to Mazarin's palace, where his heir, the Duke, and the Duchess Hortense were living, and that he saw there a huge inlaid cupboard occupying the whole of one wall of his study. The keys had long since been lost, and the drawers had remained unopened. Amazed at such indifference, M. de Caumartin suggested to the Duchess de Mazarin that they might perhaps find some curios in the cupboard. It was thereupon opened, and found to be completely filled with doubloons, tokens and gold medallions. For more than a week Mme. de Mazarin threw handfuls of them out of the windows to people in the streets.

The fact that Cardinal Mazarin had abused his despotic power was no justification for Fouquet, but the irregularity of the proceedings taken against him, the length of the trial, the obvious and disgusting animosity of Chancellor Séguier towards him, the very passage of time which calms down the anger of the public, replacing it by pity for the wretch concerned, and finally the representations, always more powerful in favour of an unfortunate man than are the steps taken against him—all this, I repeat, was the means of saving his life. The trial dragged on for three years, from 1661 to 1664. Of the twenty-two judges who presided, not more than nine voted for the death penalty; the remaining thirteen, some of whom had accepted presents from Gourville, voted for perpetual banishment.

The king commuted the sentence to a less severe one. Such harsh treatment was consistent neither with the ancient laws of the realm nor with those of humanity. What most revolted the minds of citizens was that the chancellor exiled one of the judges, named Roquesante, who was chiefly responsible for inclining the court of justice to mercy. Fouquet was imprisoned in the Castle of Pignerol, and all historians agree in saying that he died there in 1680, but Gourville asserts in his *Memoirs* that he was released from prison some time before his death. The Countess de Vaux, his daughter-in-law, had already acquainted me with this fact; yet his family believe the contrary. Thus no one can be certain where this unfortunate man died, he whose least actions had been imposing at the time of his greatness.

Guénégaud, the Secretary of State, who had sold his office to Colbert, was also prosecuted by the Chamber of Justice, and was deprived of the greater part of his fortune. One of the most singular sentences of that court was that passed on a bishop of Avranches, who was fined twelve thousand francs. His name was Boislève; he was the brother of a tax-farmer, with whom he had shared bribes.

Saint-Evremond, who had been attached to Fouquet, was

involved in his downfall. Colbert, searching everywhere for proofs against the man he wished to ruin, seized upon some papers entrusted to Mme. du Plessis - Bellière, and found among them an autograph letter of Saint-Evremond relating to the Peace of the Pyrenees. The facetious document was read to the king and was judged treasonable. Colbert, scorning to avenge himself on an unknown man like Hénault, persecuted in Saint-Evremond a friend of Fouquet, whom he hated, and a wit whom he feared. The king went to the extreme length of punishing an innocent piece of raillery directed long ago at Cardinal Mazarin, for whom he felt no regret, and whom the whole court had insulted, slandered and denounced with impunity for several years. Of the thousand libels written against that minister, the least virulent alone was punished, and that only after his death.

Saint-Evremond, who found a retreat in England, lived and died as a free man and a philosopher. His friend, the Marquis de Miremond, told me some time ago in London that there was another reason for his disgrace, one which Saint-Evremond would never reveal. When Louis XIV. gave him permission to return to his native land at the close of his life, the philosopher disdained to regard such permission as a concession; he showed that one's country is where one can live, and as such he breathed the native air of London.

The new Minister of Finance, under the simple title of Comptroller-General, justified the severity of his prosecutions by restoring an order which his predecessors had sadly troubled, and working ceaselessly for the good of the state.

The court became the centre of pleasures, and a model for all other courts. The king prided himself on giving entertainments which should put those of Vaux in the shade.

Nature herself seemed to take a delight in producing at this moment in France men of the first rank in every art, and in bringing together at Versailles the most handsome and well-favoured men and women that ever graced a court. Above all his courtiers Louis rose supreme by the grace of his figure and the majestic nobility of his countenance. The sound of his voice, at once dignified and charming, won the hearts of those whom his presence had intimidated. His bearing was such as befitted himself and his rank alone, and would have been ridiculous in any other. The awe which he inspired in those who spoke with him secretly flattered the consciousness of his own superiority. The old officer who became confused and faltered in his speech when asking a favour, finally breaking off with "Sire, I have never trembled thus before your enemies," had no difficulty in obtaining what he asked.

Court society had not yet, however, perfected its taste. Anne of Austria, the queen-mother, was beginning to prefer retirement; the reigning queen hardly knew any French; generosity was as yet her only merit.

The king's sister-in-law, an English princess, brought to the court the charms of pleasant and vivacious conversation soon rendered more solid by the reading of good books, and a taste as sure as it was fastidious. She perfected her knowledge of the language, which at the time of her marriage she still wrote but ill. She inspired a new spirit of emulation and introduced a charm and gentility of manners into the court such as the rest of Europe had scarcely conceived. *Madame* had all the wit of her brother Charles II., set off by the charms of her sex, and by the gift and desire to please. A certain gallantry pervaded the court of Louis XIV. which propriety rendered but more piquant. That of the court of Charles II. was more conspicuous but also degraded by its coarseness.

At first *Madame* and the king frequently indulged in such intimate coquetries and secret familiarities as were denoted by certain little attentions oft repeated. The king sent verses to her; and she replied to them. It happened that the same man was at once the confidant of the king and *Madame* in this ingenious correspondence. This was the Marquis de Dangeau. The king engaged him to write for him, and the princess employed him to reply to the king. He thus served both without letting either suspect that he was employed by the other, and this was one of the causes of his success.

The knowledge of the affair threw the royal family into alarm, and the king replaced this over-free correspondence with a respect and friendship which were never altered.

When *Madame* afterwards engaged Racine and Corneille upon the tragedy of *Bérénice*, she was thinking not only of the king's breach with the High Constable Colonne, but of the restraint she had herself imposed upon his fondness for her, for fear it should become dangerous. Louis XIV. is adequately described in these two lines of Racine's *Bérénice*:

> His birth howe'er obscure, his race unknown,
> The world in him its sovereign chief would own.

These diversions made way for the ardent and obstinate passion which he entertained for Mlle. de La Vallière, a maid of honour of *Madame*. With her he enjoyed the rare felicity of being loved for himself alone. For two years she was the secret object of all the gay entertainments and fêtes given by the king. One of the king's young gentlemen-in-waiting, named Belloc, composed some verses which were mingled with the dance and performed both before the queen and before *Madame*—verses which gave mysterious utterance to the secret of their hearts, which soon ceased to be a secret.

All the public entertainments given by the king were paid by way of homage to his mistress. In 1662, a tournament was held, opposite the Tuileries, in an immense enclosure, which still retains the name of *Place du Carrousel* (i.e. *Tournament Square*). There were five troops of horse. The king headed the Romans; his brother, the Persians; the Prince de Condé, the Turks; his brother the Duke d'Enghien, the Indians; the Duke de Guise, the Americans. This last was Balafré's grandson. He was famous everywhere for the fatal daring with which he had attempted to capture Naples. In everything he was remarkable—for his imprisonment, his duels, his romantic love affairs, his prodigality and his adventures. He seemed to belong to another age. Seeing him pass with the great Condé, people cried: "There go the heroes of history and fable."

Forgetful of their sorrows for the time being, the queen-mother, the reigning queen, and the Queen of England, Charles I.'s widow, were seated under a canopy watching the show. The Count de Sault, son of the Duke de Lesdiguières, gained the prize and received it at the hands of the queen-mother. These entertainments brought into vogue more than ever the taste for devices and emblems which the tournaments had formerly brought into fashion and which now survived them.

An antiquary of the name of Douvrier devised at this time for Louis XIV. the emblem of a sun darting its rays on to a globe, with the words: *Nec Pluribus Impar*. The idea was partly copied from a Spanish device made for Philip II., and more suited to that king, who possessed the finest parts of the New World and so much territory in the Old, than to a young King of France whose expectations were as yet unrealised. The device had a wonderful success, and the king's coat of arms, the crown furniture, tapestries and statuary were all ornamented with it, but the king never wore it at his tournaments. Louis XIV. was unjustly censured for the pompousness of this device, as though he had chosen it himself, and its signification was perhaps more justly criticised. The device does not illustrate the meaning of the motto, nor does the motto convey a sense sufficiently distinctive and precise. For what may be explained in several ways is not worth explaining in any. Devices, the remnants of ancient chivalry, are well suited to fêtes, and are agreeable when the allusions are appropriate, novel and witty. But it is better to be without them than to tolerate poor or vulgar ones, such as that of Louis XII., which was the emblem of a hog, with the words: "Meddle and smart for it." Devices bear the same relation to inscriptions as masquerades to stately ceremonies.

The fête of Versailles, held in 1664, surpassed the tournament fête by its remarkable character, its splendour, and by pleasures that charmed the mind, which, mingling with the magnificence of the entertainments, added a style and refinement with which no fête had hitherto been embellished. Versailles had become a delightful abode, but had not yet acquired that magnificence which it was afterwards to know.

(1664) On the fifth of May the king proceeded to Versailles with the court, which comprised six hundred people, all of whose expenses were defrayed, as well as those of their suites, as also were the expenses of those who were engaged in preparing the entertainment. Nothing was wanting at these fêtes save monuments specially erected in their honour, such as those raised by the Greeks and Romans; but the speed with which theatres, amphitheatres and porticos, ornamented with as much magnificence as taste, were erected, was a marvel, which added to the illusion and which, transformed afterwards in a thousand ways, still further enhanced the charm of the spectacle.

The proceedings began with a kind of tournament. Those who were to take part appeared on the first day as if for a review; they were preceded by heralds-at-arms, pages and equerries, who carried their devices and shields; and on these shields were written, in letters of gold, verses composed by Perigni and Benserade. The latter, especially, had a remarkable talent for such polite verses, in which he made delicate and pointed allusions to people's characters, to personages of antiquity or of the legends which were being represented, and to the love-affairs that animated the court. The king impersonated Roger; all the crown diamonds sparkled on his dress and on the horse that he was riding. Stationed beneath triumphal arches the queens and three hundred ladies watched his entrance.

All eyes were fixed on the king, but he observed none but those of Mlle. de La Vallière. The fête was for her alone; and she enjoyed it lost amid the crowd.

The procession was followed by a golden chariot, eighteen feet high, fifteen feet broad and twenty-four feet long, representing the chariot of the sun. The four ages, of gold, silver, brass and iron; the heavenly signs, the seasons, the hours, followed this chariot on foot. All of them bore their characteristic emblems. Shepherds followed, carrying the barricades, which were placed in position to the fanfare of trumpets, followed at intervals by the playing of musettes and violins. Several personages who followed the chariot of Apollo approached the queens and recited verses suited to the occasion, the season, the king and the ladies. When the courses were finished and night fell, four thousand great torches illuminated the space where the entertainments were given. The tables were served by two hundred persons, representing the seasons, Fauns, Sylvans and Dryads, together with shepherds, vintagers and reapers. Pan and Diana advanced on a moving mountain and, descending, placed on the tables the most delicious fruits that field and forest could produce. Behind the tables, a theatre shaped in a semi-circle, filled with performers, rose suddenly to view. The arcades surrounding the tables and the theatre were adorned with five hundred green and silver candelabra filled with candles, and a gold balustrade encircled this vast enclosure.

These fêtes, surpassing those invented in any novel, lasted seven days. Four times did the king carry off the prize for the games, and then allowed the other knights to compete for the prizes he had won and afterwards abandoned.

La Princesse d'Élide, though not one of the best comedies of Molière, proved one of the pleasantest diversions of these fêtes: it pleased by an infinite number of delicate allegories of contemporary fashions, and by allusions which add much to the amusement of such fêtes, but which are lost for posterity. The court was still infatuated with the delusions of judicial astrology; more than one prince imagined with arrogant superstition that nature honoured him to the point of inscribing his destiny in the stars. Victor Amadeus, Duke of Savoy, father of the Duchess of Burgundy, had an astrologer attendant upon him even after his abdication. Molière had the temerity to attack this delusion in *Les Amants Magnifiques*, given at another fête in 1670.

There was also a court jester, as in *La Princesse d'Élide*. These wretches were still greatly in fashion. They were a relic of barbarism, which lasted longer in Germany than anywhere else. The need of amusement, the difficulty of obtaining agreeable and honourable entertainments in an age of ignorance and bad taste, were responsible for the invention of this melancholy pleasure, degrading to the human mind. The fool who attended Louis XIV. at that time had belonged to the Prince de Condé; his name was Angeli. The Count de Grammont said that of all the fools who engaged themselves in the prince's service, Angeli was the only one who had made his fortune. The buffoon was not lacking in wit. It was he who said "that he did not go to hear sermons preached because he did not like the *bawling* and did not understand the arguments."

(1664) Molière's farce entitled *Le Mariage Forcé* was also played at this fête. But what was truly admirable was the first performance of the first three acts of *Tartuffe*. The king wished to see this masterpiece before it was even finished. He afterwards defended it against those false bigots who wished to move heaven and earth to suppress it, and it will continue to live, as I have already said elsewhere, so long as there is good taste and a hypocrite in France.

The greater part of such brilliant ceremonies usually appeals only to sight and hearing. Mere pomp and show last but for a day; but when masterpieces of art, such as *Tartuffe*, enrich such fêtes, they leave behind them an enduring memory.

One still calls to mind certain features of the allegories of Benserade, which enlivened the ballets of that period. I shall quote only the following lines addressed to the king representing the sun:

> With you, I doubt we must not prate
> Of Daphne's scorn and Phaeton's fate;
>   He too aspiring, she inhuman,
> In snares like these you cannot fall,
> For who will dream that e'er you shall
>   Be fool'd by man or shunn'd by woman?

The chief glory of these amusements, which brought taste, polite manners and talents to such perfection in France, was that they did not for a moment detach the monarch from his incessant labours. Without such toil he could but have held a court, he could not have reigned: and had the magnificent pleasures of the court outraged the miseries of the people, they would only have been detestable; but the same man who gave these entertainments had given the people bread during the famine of 1662. He had bought up corn, which he sold to the rich at a low price, and which he gave free to poor families at the gate of the Louvre; he had remitted three millions of taxes to the people; no part of the internal administration was neglected, and his government was respected abroad. The King of Spain was obliged to allow him precedence; the Pope was forced to give him satisfaction; Dunkirk was acquired by France by a treaty honourable to the purchaser and ignominious to the seller; in short, all measures adopted after he had taken up the reins of government were either honourable or useful; thereafter, it was fitting that he should give such fêtes.

In 1664, the arrival of Chigi, the legate *a latere*, Pope Alexander VII.'s nephew, in the midst of all these rejoicings at Versailles, to give satisfaction to the king for the outrages committed by the Pope's guards, provided a new spectacle at court. Such great ceremonies are as so many fêtes to the public. The honours accorded to Chigi made the satisfaction that he rendered still more striking. Seated on a dais, he received the homage of the higher courts, of the corporations of towns, and of the clergy. He entered Paris to the firing of cannon, with the great Condé on his right-hand side, and that prince's son on his left; and attended by all this pomp, he came to humble himself, Rome and the Pope, before a king who had not so much as drawn a sword. After being received in audience, he dined with Louis XIV., everyone being occupied in treating him with magnificence and in procuring amusements for him. The Doge of Genoa was afterwards treated, albeit with fewer honours, with the same desire to please, which the king combined with his regal dignity.

All this conferred an air of grandeur on the court of Louis XIV., which eclipsed that of any other court in Europe. He desired that the glory which emanated from his own person should be reflected by all who surrounded him, so that all the nobles should be honoured but no one powerful, not even his brother or *Monsieur le Prince*. It was with this object in view that he passed judgment in favour of the peers in their long-standing feud with the presidents of parliament. The latter claimed the prerogative of speaking before the peers and had assumed possession of this right. Louis decided at an extraordinary council that when the king was present at a meeting of the High Chamber in its judicial capacity peers should speak before the presidents, as though owing this prerogative directly to his presence; and in the case of assemblies which are not judicial bodies he allowed the old custom to hold good.

For the purpose of distinguishing his chief courtiers, blue cassocks had been devised, embroidered in gold and silver. Permission to wear them was a great favour for men who were swayed by vanity. They were in nearly as great demand as the collar of the order of Saint-Louis. It may be mentioned, since it is here a question of small details, that cassocks were at that time worn over a doublet ornamented with ribbons, and over this cassock a shoulder-belt was fastened, from which hung the sword. A kind of lace neck-band was also worn, and a hat adorned with two rows of feathers. This fashion, which lasted until 1684, prevailed throughout the whole of Europe, with the exception of Spain and Poland. Already nearly every country took a pride in imitating the court of Louis XIV.

He introduced into his household a system which still obtains, regulated the ranks and offices, and created new posts in attendance on his person, such as the Grand Master of the Wardrobe. He restored the tables instituted by Francis I. and increased their number. Twelve of these were set apart for officers who dined in the royal presence, and were laid with as much nicety and profusion as those of many sovereigns: he desired all foreigners to be invited, and his consideration was extended to them during the whole of his reign. He was responsible for another attention still more subtle and refined. When the pavilions of Marli were built in 1679 all the ladies found a complete toilet set in their apartments; nothing that was essential to ease and luxury was forgotten: anyone who was fresh from travel could give meals in his own private room, and they were served with the same care as those of his master. Such small matters only acquire value when they are accompanied by great ones. Splendour and generosity characterised everything that he did. He made a present of two hundred thousand francs to the daughters of his ministers on their marriage.

What gave him the greatest glory in Europe was his liberality, which was unprecedented. The idea was suggested to him by a conversation with the Duke de Saint-Aignan, who related to him how Cardinal Richelieu had sent presents to certain foreign scholars who had written in his praise. The king did not wait to be praised, but sure of his desert he bade his ministers, Lyonne and Colbert, make a choice of a number of Frenchmen and foreigners upon whom he wished to confer marks of his generosity. Having written to foreign countries and acquired as much information as he could on so delicate a matter, where it was a question of making a selection among contemporaries, Lyonne first made a list of sixty persons; some of them received presents, and others annuities, according to their station, needs and merits.

(1663) Allacci, the librarian of the Vatican; Count Graiani, Secretary of State to the Duke of Modena; the illustrious Viviani, mathematician to the Grand Duke of Florence; Vossius, historiographer of the United Provinces; the celebrated mathematician, Huygens; a Dutch resident in Sweden, who was none other than Heinsius: finally, even certain professors of Altdorf and Helmstadt, towns almost unknown to the French—all these were astonished to receive letters from M. Colbert, in which he informed them that while the king was not their sovereign, yet he begged them to accept him as their patron. The tone of these letters was varied according to the importance of the person addressed, and they were all accompanied either by liberal gifts or by annuities.

Among the French singled out for these honours were Racine, Quinault and Fléchier, afterwards Bishop of Nîmes, and still quite young; they all received gifts. It is true that Chapelain and Cotin received annuities, but it was Chapelain whom the minister Colbert had particularly consulted. These two men, whose poetry has been so decried, were not without merit. Chapelain was extremely well-read, and what is more surprising, he had taste and was one of the most enlightened of critics. True, such talent is far removed from genius. Science and intelligence may guide an artist, but they cannot in any way create him. No one in France enjoyed so great a reputation during their lives as Ronsard and Chapelain. The fact is that Ronsard lived in a time of barbarism and the nation had scarcely emerged from this state during the life of Chapelain. Costar, the schoolfellow of Balzac and Voiture, called Chapelain the first of the heroic poets.

Boileau was not included in this generous scheme; as yet he had only written satires, and, as is well known, his satires attacked the very scholars whom the minister consulted. Some years afterwards the king honoured him without consulting anyone.

So liberal were the gifts distributed in foreign countries that Viviani had a house built in Florence with the money he had received from Louis XIV. Over the portals he inscribed in gold letters the words: *Aedes a Deo datae*—an allusion to the cognomen of Heaven-born which the public voice had bestowed on the prince from his birth.

It may easily be imagined what effect this extraordinary lavishness had upon the rest of Europe; and when one considers all the notable things achieved by the king soon afterwards, the most severe and particular of critics must acquiesce in the extravagant praises showered upon him. Nor were the French the only people to eulogise him. Twelve panegyrics on Louis XIV. were delivered in various towns in Italy—marks of respect which were prompted neither by hope nor fear, and which were brought to the king's notice by the Marquis Zampieri.

He did not cease to bestow his patronage upon literature and the arts. Proofs of this will be found in the special gift of about four thousand louis made to Racine, in the fortunes of Boileau, Quinault and especially Lulli, and of all those artists who dedicated their works to him. He also gave a thousand louis to Benserade for the engraving of the copper-plates for his *Metamorphoses* of Ovid, translated into rondeaus —a misplaced liberality which betokened only the sovereign's generosity. He was rewarding Benserade for the trivial merit of his ballets.

Several writers have ascribed this patronage of the arts and the magnificence of Louis XIV. solely to Colbert; but the only credit that can be attributed to him in the matter was that of encouraging his master's magnanimity and judgment. That minister, who had a wonderful talent for financial affairs, commerce, navigation, and the maintenance of order, did not possess the king's insight and nobility of soul; he lent himself eagerly to the plan, but was far from inspiring in Louis what was nature's gift.

In view of this it is difficult to see upon what grounds certain writers have reproached that monarch with avarice. A prince, who has estates entirely detached from the revenues of the state, may be miserly just as any other man; but a King of France, who is, in reality, but the distributor of his subjects' wealth, can scarcely be afflicted with this vice. He may be lacking in consideration and in the desire to reward merit, but these are things for which Louis XIV. cannot be reproached.

At the very time when he began to encourage talent by his patronage, Count Bussy-Rabutin was severely punished for the use he made of his. He was thrown into the Bastille in 1665, the pretext of his imprisonment being his book, *Les Amours des Gaules*. The real cause, however, was the ballad in which the king was too much compromised, and which was now brought to light again to ruin Bussy-Rabutin to whom it was attributed:

> Beyond expression sure this is,
> When Deodatus fondly kisses
> That beak so delicate and dear,
> Replete with charms from ear to ear.

His works were not of sufficient value to make up for the mischief that they did. His use of language was pure, and he had talent, but he was also too conceited and used his talents but to make fresh enemies. Louis XIV. would have acted generously had he pardoned him: as it was he avenged a personal injury while appearing to yield to the opinion of society. Count Bussy-Rabutin was released at the end of eighteen months; but he was deprived of his post, and disgraced for the remainder of his life, vainly professing a devotion to Louis XIV. which neither the king nor anyone else believed sincere.

CHAPTER XXVI

FURTHER CHARACTERISTICS AND ANECDOTES

To the glory, the pleasures, the grandeur and the gallantry that characterised the first years of his reign, Louis XIV. wished to add the delights of friendship, but it is no easy matter for a king to choose well. Of the two men to whom he showed the greatest confidence, one deceived him shamefully, and the other abused his kindness. The first was the Marquis de Vardes, the king's confidant in his love affair with Mme. de La Vallière. It is known that court intrigues determined the marquis to bring about the ruin of Mme. de La Vallière, whose position could not but arouse jealousy, but whose character had done nothing to earn her enemies. It is likewise known that, in concert with the Count de Guiche and the Countess de Soissons, he was bold enough to send a forged letter to the queen in the name of her father, the King of Spain. This letter informed the queen of matters of which she had better have been ignorant, which could only disturb the peace of the royal household. Not content with this treachery, he contrived that suspicion should fall on the most honourable members of the court, the Duke and Duchess de Navailles.

In 1665 these two innocent people were sacrificed to the resentment of the monarch who had been deceived. Vardes' blackguardly conduct was but too well known, and yet, guilty as he was, he received punishment scarcely more severe than that meted out to the innocent persons he had accused, who were obliged to resign their positions and leave the court.

The other favourite was the Count, afterwards Duke de Lauzun, at times the rival of the king's brief passions, at others his go-between, and afterwards so notorious for his efforts to contract a public marriage with *Mademoiselle*, and his success in afterwards marrying her secretly in spite of his promise to his master.

Deceived in him, the king declared that he had looked for friends and found nothing but intriguers. That disillusioned knowledge of men, which men acquire too late, caused him also to say: "Every time I fill a vacant post, I make a hundred people discontented, and one ungrateful."

During the war of 1667, pleasures, the decorations of royal

palaces and of Paris in general, and the policing of the realm were all alike continued.

Until 1670 the king made a practice of dancing in the ballet. He was then thirty-two. At a performance of the tragedy, *Britannicus*, at Saint-Germain, he was struck by the following lines:

> His chief desert in trifling feats to place,
> To drive the chariot foremost in the race,
> In low pursuits to win th' ignoble prize,
> Himself expos'd a show to vulgar eyes.

From that time he danced no more in public; the poet reformed the monarch. His love for the Duchess de La Vallière still continued, though interrupted by frequent infidelities, which did not cause her much anxiety. Few indeed were the women who could resist him, but he always returned to the one who, by the sweetness and goodness of her character, by a deep and real passion, even be it said by the charms of habit, had made him her subject without the aid of art; nevertheless from 1669 onwards she perceived that Mme. de Montespan was growing in favour; with her customary gentleness she competed against her rival; she had long to endure the bitterness of witnessing her rival's triumph, without so much as a complaint; in her distress she could still find some happiness in being respected by the king, whom she could never cease to love, and in seeing him without being loved in return.

At last in 1675 she found succour in that last resort of sensitive souls who can be subjected but by deep and ardent emotions. God alone, she thought, could succeed to the place in her heart vacated by her lover. Her conversion was as famous as her tenderness of heart. She became a Carmelite in Paris, and remained steadfast to her vows. Wearing a hair shirt, walking barefoot and fasting strictly, chanting at dead of night with the choir in a strange tongue, all these hardships were powerless to wound the delicacy of a woman accustomed to a life of abundant luxury, ease and pleasure. In such austerity she lived from 1675 to 1710, known only under the name of Louise, Sister of Mercy. A king who thus punished a guilty woman would be a tyrant; yet in such a manner many women have been punished for the crime of having loved. There is hardly an example of a politician having taken this rigorous course, yet political crimes would seem to demand a greater expiation than the indiscretions of love;

but those who rule the souls of men have influence only upon the weak.

When Sister Louise was told of the death of the Duke de Vermandois, a son whom she had had by the king, she said: "I must mourn his birth still more than I do his death." One daughter remained to her who, of all the king's children, bore the closest resemblance to her father: she married Prince Armand de Conti, nephew of the great Condé.

Meanwhile, the Marquise de Montespan enjoyed the royal favour with an arrogance and pomp in marked contrast to the former modesty of Mme. de La Vallière.

While these two ladies were still disputing the first place in the king's affections, the whole court was engaged in amorous intrigue. Even Louvois was concerned. Among the various mistresses of this minister, whose grim character seemed so ill-suited for love, there was a Mme. Dufresnoi, the wife of one of his clerks, for whom he afterwards used his influence to obtain a post in the queen's household. She was made a lady of the bedchamber, and was in personal attendance on the queen. The king, in thus favouring the passions of his ministers, endeavoured to justify his own.

It is a significant instance of the force of prejudice and habit, that while all married women were permitted to have lovers, the granddaughter of Henry IV. was not permitted to have a husband. *Mademoiselle*, after refusing so many sovereigns and even entertaining hopes of marrying Louis XIV., was now resolved, at the age of forty-four, to make the fortune of a private gentleman. She obtained permission to marry *Peguilin*, Count de Lauzun. of the House of Caumont, the last man to captain one of the two companies of halberdiers which no longer exist, and the first for whom the king created the post of Colonel-General of Dragoons. There had been abundant instances of princesses marrying private gentlemen; the Roman emperors used to give their daughters as the wives of senators; the daughters of the Asiatic potentates, more powerful and despotic than any King of France, are only married to their father's slaves.

Mademoiselle made over all her wealth, estimated at some twenty millions, to the Count de Lauzun, including four duchies, the sovereignty of Dombes, the province of Eu and the palace of Orleans, known as the Luxembourg. (1669) For herself she kept nothing, enchanted by the vain idea of bestowing a greater fortune on the man she loved than ever king bestowed upon his favourite subject. The contract was drawn up; for a day Lauzun was Duke de Montpensier. Nothing was lacking but the signature. All was prepared, when the king, urged by the protests of princes, ministers and the enemies of an over-fortunate man, retracted his promise and forbade the marriage. He had written to foreign courts announcing it; he now wrote to inform them that it would not take place. He was blamed for having consented to it; he was blamed for having prevented it. He grieved at making *Mademoiselle* unhappy; but notwithstanding such compunction at breaking his word, in November of 1670 he imprisoned Lauzun in the Castle of Pignerol for having secretly married the princess, whom a few months previously he had been willing should marry her in public; and he was thus incarcerated for ten long years.

There is more than one kingdom in which the monarch does not possess this power, and those who do possess it are more beloved if they omit to use it. Does a citizen who has done nothing to offend the laws of the state deserve to be punished so severely by the monarch who represents the state? Is there not an immeasurable difference between offending one's sovereign and betraying him? Should a king, then, treat a man more harshly than the law?

Those who have recorded that Mme. de Montespan, after opposing the marriage, was so incensed against the Count de Lauzun, who violently abused her, that she persuaded Louis XIV. to avenge her in this way, do that monarch less than justice. It would have been to add baseness to tyranny, to sacrifice a gallant man to a woman's anger, a favourite, who, deprived by him of the greatest fortune, was guilty of no other crime than that of complaining too freely of Mme. de Montespan. The reader must excuse such reflections, which are prompted by a consideration for the rights of humanity. But at the same time justice demands that Louis XIV. should not be accused of perpetrating so cruel a wrong, since during the whole of his reign he committed no act of such a nature. It is enough that he punished a clandestine marriage with such severity, an innocent liaison which he would have done better to overlook. It was proper for him to withdraw his favour, but to punish with imprisonment was excessive.

Those who have doubted this secret marriage have but to read with care the *Memoirs of Mademoiselle*. The *Memoirs* reveal things which she leaves unsaid. It is to be noted that the princess, who had complained so bitterly to the king of the breaking off of her marriage, did not dare to complain of her husband's imprisonment. She admits that people believed her married; she does not say that she was not, and were there nothing more than these words: "*I cannot, must not change my affections for him,*" they would be conclusive.

Lauzun and Fouquet were amazed to find themselves in the same prison; Fouquet, especially, who, from the height of his power and glory had observed Peguilin from afar in the crowd as a penniless provincial nobleman, thought him mad when the latter related to him that he had become the king's favourite and had received his consent to marry the granddaughter of Henri IV., with all the property and titles of the House of Montpensier.

Having languished ten years in prison, he was at length released, but this was only after Mme. de Montespan had persuaded *Mademoiselle* to give the sovereignty of Dombes and the province of Eu to the child Duke of Maine, who came into their possession after the princess's death. She only made this deed of gift in the hope that Lauzun would be acknowledged as her husband; but she was mistaken; the king only allowed her to give to her secret and unfortunate husband the territories of Saint-Fargeau and Thiers, with other considerable rentals, which Lauzun found inadequate. She was reduced to be his wife in secret and to be ridiculed in public. Unhappy at court, she was equally unhappy at home, the usual consequence of the passions; she died in 1693.

The Count de Lauzun himself journeyed to England in 1668. Fated always to meet with extraordinary adventures, he escorted King James II.'s wife and infant son to France. He was made a duke, commanded in Ireland with little success, and returned more renowned for his adventures than for his personal repute. In our own time he has died forgotten at a great age, as always happens to those who have figured in great events but have not done great things.

Meanwhile, from the beginning of the intrigues of which we have just spoken, Mme. de Montespan was all-powerful. Athénais de Mortemar, wife of the Marquis de Montespan, her elder sister, the Marquise de Thianges, and her younger sister, for whom she obtained the Abbey of Fontevrault, were the most beautiful women of their time, and all three were, in addition, remarkably gifted and accomplished. The Duke de Vivonne, their brother, the Marshal of France, was one of the best read of courtiers and endowed with the nicest taste. The king once said to him, "But what is the use of reading?" The Duke de Vivonne, who was a stout man of florid countenance, replied: "Reading does to the mind what your partridges do to my cheeks."

These four persons pleased all alike by a particular manner of conversation, a mixture of pleasantry, innocence and subtlety, which became known as the wit of the Mortemars. Each wrote with a sprightliness and grace which was all her own. Hence it will be seen how ridiculous is the tale which I still hear repeated, that Mme. de Montespan was obliged to have her letters to the king written by Mme. Scarron and that it was by this means that the latter became her rival, and a successful one.

Mme. Scarron, afterwards Mme. de Maintenon, had, indeed, more enriched her mind by reading; her conversation was more charming, more insinuating. There are letters of hers in which art lends its aid to nature, and the style is elegance itself. But Mme. de Montespan had no need of borrowed wit from anyone, and she reigned for a long time the favourite before Mme. de Maintenon was ever presented to her.

Her triumph was most apparent in the voyage which the king made to Flanders in 1670. The ruin of the Dutch was planned on this voyage in the midst of pleasures; it was a continuous triumphant procession, attended by the utmost magnificence.

The king conducted all military expeditions on horseback, but now for the first time he rode in a carriage with glass windows; post-chaises had not yet been invented. The queen, her sister-in-law, and the Marquise de Montespan accompanied him in this gorgeous carriage, followed by many others, and when Mme. de Montespan rode alone, her carriage was escorted by four life-guardsmen. The Dauphin and *Mademoiselle* arrived later, each with their courts; it was before the fatal proposal of her marriage; she shared all these triumphs undisturbed, and had the pleasure of seeing her lover, the king's favourite, at the head of his company of guards. The finest court furniture was brought with them to towns where they passed the night. In each town they found prepared a masked or fancy-dress ball, or a display of fireworks. The whole of his military household accompanied the king's retinue, and his domestic household either preceded or followed him. The tables were dressed just as at Saint-Germain. With this pomp the court visited all the conquered towns. The principal ladies of Brussels and of Ghent came to see such magnificence. The king invited them to his table, and made them presents with many flattering compliments. All officers in garrison towns received gifts. On some days as many as fifteen hundred gold louis were spent in such liberality.

All honours, all professions of allegiance were paid to Mme. de Montespan, excepting that which was due to the queen's position. But this lady did not know all that was going on. The king knew how to distinguish affairs of state from affairs of the heart.

Entrusted with the sole responsibility of bringing about the union of the two kings and the destruction of Holland, *Madame* embarked at Dunkirk in the fleet of her brother, Charles II., King of England, and accompanied by members of the French Court. She took with her Mlle. de Keroualle, who afterwards became the Duchess of Portsmouth, and whose beauty equalled that of Mme. de Montespan. She held later in England a position similar to that of Mme. de Montespan in France, but with greater honour. Charles was ruled by her until the last moment of his life; and though often unfaithful he remained ever subject to her charms. Never did woman preserve her beauty for so long; we have seen her at the age of nearly seventy years, with a figure still dignified and charming, untouched by the flight of years.

Madame visited her brother at Canterbury and returned in triumph. She enjoyed her triumph but for a short time, for a sudden and tragic death carried her off at the age of twenty-six on the 30th of June, 1670. The court was thrown into grief, and consternation was still further increased by the manner of her death. The princess was believed to have been poisoned. Montagu, the English ambassador, was convinced of it; the court did not doubt it, and the whole of Europe spoke of it. One of the old servants of her husband's household told me the name of the person who (according to him) had administered the poison. "The man," he told me, "was not wealthy, but immediately afterwards he retired to Normandy, where he bought an estate, and there lived in affluence for a long time. The poison," he added, "was powdered glass sprinkled over some strawberries in the place of sugar." The court and town thought that *Madame* had been poisoned with a glass of chicory water, after drinking which she was seized with frightful pains, soon followed by the convulsions of death. But human malice and the love of the extraordinary were the sole reasons for this general persuasion. The glass of water could not have been poisoned, since Mme. de la Fayette and another person drank the remainder without experiencing the slightest discomfort. Powdered diamonds are no more a poison than powdered coral. Madame had long suffered from an abscess in the liver. She was in a very bad state of health and had also been delivered of a still-born child. Her husband, whom everyone in Europe believed guilty, was not accused either before or after the event of any guilty act, and it is rare to find a criminal who has committed but a single crime. Mankind would indeed be unhappy were it as common to commit atrocious crimes as to believe them.

It was suggested that the Chevalier de Lorraine, a favourite of *Monsieur*, was impelled to this horrible revenge in order to avenge the exile and imprisonment which his disgraceful behaviour towards the princess had brought upon him. The fact is neglected that the Chevalier de Lorraine was then in Rome, and that it is more than a little difficult for a twenty-year-old Knight of Malta, in Rome, to buy the death of a great princess in Paris.

It is only too true that the weak and indiscreet conduct of the Viscount de Turenne was primarily responsible for these detestable rumours which people still take pleasure in retailing. At the age of sixty he was the lover and the dupe of Mme. de Coetquen, as he had been of Mme. de Longueville. He revealed to this lady the state secret which was withheld from *Monsieur*, the king's brother. Mme. de Coetquen told it to her lover, the Chevalier de Lorraine, and he made it known to *Monsieur*. The household of this prince was a prey to the bitterest jealousies and reproaches. The trouble started before *Madame's* voyage: its bitterness was redoubled on her return. The outbursts of *Monsieur* and the quarrels between his favourites and the friends of *Madame* threw the whole household into confusion and distress shortly before her death. *Madame*, in gentle and moving tones, reproached the Marquise de Coetquen for the unhappiness of which she was the cause. Falling on her knees beside the bed, her face bathed in tears, the marquise could but reply with these lines from Rotrou's *Venceslas*:

J'allais . . . j'étais . . . l'amour a sur moi tant d'empire,
Je me confonds, *Madame*, et ne vous puis rien dire.

Act IV. Sc. iv.

The Chevalier de Lorraine, the cause of these dissensions, was at first imprisoned by the king in Pierre-Encise, and the Count de Marsan, of the House of Lorraine, and the Marquis, afterwards Marshal, Villeroi, were exiled. The natural death of the unfortunate princess was regarded as the mournful result of these quarrels.

What confirmed the public in their suspicion that she had been poisoned was that at about this time the crime became common in France. During the horrors of civil war this cowardly method of revenge was quite unknown, but by a remarkable fatality it infected France at the time when her manners were being softened by glory and luxury, just as it crept into ancient Rome in the halcyon days of the republic.

Two Italians, one of whom bore the name of Exili, had laboured for many years with a German apothecary, named Glaser, to find what is known as the "philosopher's stone." The two Italians lost the little that they had, and attempted to regain by crime what they had lost by their folly. They sold poisons secretly. The confessional, the most powerful curb of human depravity, but which has been abused by those who think they may commit crimes for which they intend afterwards to atone—the confessional, I repeat, was the means of bringing to the knowledge of the Grand Penitentiary of Paris that several persons had met their death by poison, and he informed the government; the two suspected Italians were thrown into the Bastille, and one of them died there. Exili remained in prison for some time without being convicted, and from the depths of his prison spread abroad in Paris those dark secrets which cost the civil lieutenant d'Aubrai and his family their lives, and which at length brought about the foundation of the chamber of poisons, known as *la chambre ardente*.

Love was the prime motive of these horrible crimes. The Marquis de Brinvilliers, son-in-law of the civil lieutenant d'Aubrai, offered a lodging to Sainte-Croix, a captain in his regiment, and a man who proved too handsome. His wife gave him to fear the consequences of such an action, but he persisted in allowing this young man to live in the same house with her, young, pretty and susceptible as she was. The inevitable occurred; they fell in love with each other. The civil lieutenant, father of the marquis, was at once severe and foolish enough to apply for a *lettre de cachet*, by which the captain was sent to the Bastille, when he should but have been sent back to his regiment. Sainte-Croix was unfortunately placed in the same cell as Exili; and the Italian taught him a method of revenge the terrible consequences of which are but too well known. The marquise did not attempt the life of her husband, who had judged with indulgence a love of which he himself had been the cause; but the frenzy of revenge led her to poison his father, his two brothers and his sister. In the midst of these crimes she remained, however, extremely devout; she went often to confession, and when arrested at Liège, a general confession written in her own hand was discovered, which served to prove not so much her guilt as her audacity. It is not true that she had experimented with these poisons in the hospitals, as people said, and as is recorded in *Causes célèbres*, the work of a briefless barrister, written for the vulgar; but, like Sainte-Croix himself, she certainly had secret dealings with persons afterwards accused of similar crimes. She was burnt in 1676, after having her head cut off. Nevertheless, from 1670, when Exili first began to deal in poisons, until 1680, Paris was infected with such crimes. It is known that even Renautier, the comptroller-general of the clergy, and a friend of this woman, was accused some time afterwards of having made use of her secrets and that it cost him half his fortune to suppress the accusations.

La Voisin, La Vigoureux, a priest of the name of Le Sage, and others traded in the secrets of Exili, under the pretext of amusing inquisitive but weak-minded people by calling up spirits. The crime was thought to be more widespread than it really was. The *chambre ardente* was established at the Arsenal, close to the Bastille, in 1680. The highest in the land were summoned before this tribunal, including, among others, two nieces of Cardinal Mazarin, the Duchess de Bouillon, and the Countess de Soissons, the mother of Prince Eugene.

The Duchess de Bouillon was only summoned by a special writ, and accused of nothing more than an absurd inquisitiveness, only too common at that time, but lying, nevertheless, outside the jurisdiction of a legal tribunal. The ancient practice of consulting soothsayers, of having horoscopes cast, of seeking love-philtres, still prevailed among the people and even among the principal persons of the realm.

We have already told how, at the birth of Louis XIV., the

astrologer, Morin, was brought into the very bedchamber of the queen-mother, to cast the horoscope of the heir to the throne. We have even seen the Duke of Orleans, the regent of the kingdom, interested in that form of charlatanry which so beguiled the ancient world; and all the philosophy of the famous Count de Boulainvilliers could never cure him of this delusion. It was thus excusable in the Duchess de Bouillon and all the ladies who had similar weaknesses. The priest Le Sage, La Voisin and La Vigoureux made a regular income out of the curiosity of ignorant people, numerous then as now. They foretold the future, and called up the devil. Had they stopped there, both they and the *chambre ardente* would have made themselves nothing more than ridiculous.

La Reynie, one of the presidents of this chamber, was so ill-advised as to ask the Duchess de Bouillon if she had ever seen the devil; she replied that she saw him at that moment, that he was ugly and villainous-looking in the extreme, and that he was disguised as a councillor of state. The examination was abruptly cut short.

The affair of the Countess de Soissons and Marshal de Luxembourg was more serious. Le Sage, La Voisin, La Vigoureux, with other accomplices, were in prison, accused of having sold poisons known as *inheritance powders*; everyone who had been to consult them was prosecuted; the Countess de Soissons was among the number. The king condescended to tell this princess that if she felt herself to be guilty he would advise her to go into retirement. She replied that she was perfectly innocent, but she did not care to be examined in a court of justice. She therefore retired to Brussels, where she died at the end of 1708, while her son, Prince Eugene, was avenging her cause by one victory after another, and everywhere triumphing over Louis XIV.

Another illustrious person was arraigned before the *chambre ardente*: this was François Henri de Montmorenci-Boutteville, duke, peer and marshal of France, who united the great name of Montmorenci with that of the Imperial House of Luxembourg, and who had already gained fame throughout Europe by deeds worthy of a great captain. One of his secretaries, named Bonard, wishing to recover some important papers which had been lost, applied to the priest Le Sage to find them for him. Le Sage insisted that he should first confess himself, and then for nine days go

to three different churches and recite three psalms. But in
spite of the confession and the psalms the papers were not
recovered; they were in the possession of a girl named Dupin.
In the presence of Le Sage, Bonard performed a kind of
exorcism in the name of Marshal Luxembourg; but the girl
Dupin would not surrender them. In desperation Bonard
procured a fresh power of attorney from the marshal, and
between the text of the document and the signature there
were found two lines in a different handwriting by which
the marshal gave himself to the devil.

Le Sage, Bonard, La Voisin, La Vigoureux and more than
forty other accused persons having been imprisoned in the
Bastille, Le Sage deposed that the marshal had applied to
the devil and himself in order to bring about the death of
the girl Dupin, who had refused to surrender the papers;
his accomplices added that they had killed Dupin by
his orders, had quartered her body and thrown it into
the river.

The accusations were as improbable as they were atrocious.
The marshal should have appeared before the court of peers;
parliament and the peers should have insisted upon their
right to try him; but they did not do so. The accused gave
himself up in person, and was imprisoned in the Bastille;
this step alone was sufficient to prove his innocence of the
alleged assassination.

(1679) The Secretary of State, Louvois, who had no
liking for him, had him confined in a sort of dungeon six and
a half feet in length where he fell very ill. He was examined
on the second day, after which five whole weeks passed
without his case being advanced; this, a cruel injustice to
any man, was yet more reprehensible in the case of a peer
of the realm. He wished to write to the Marquis de Louvois
to complain of his treatment, but was not allowed to do so;
finally, he was again examined. He was asked if he had not
sent bottles of poisoned wine to the girl Dupin's brother
and his mistress.

It seemed preposterous that a marshal of France who had
been in command of armies, should have wished to poison
a wretched tradesman and his mistress with no possible hope
of gain from so foul a crime.

He was finally confronted with Le Sage and another priest
named Avaux, with whom he was accused of having practised
sorcery to bring about the death of more than one person.

All his misfortunes came from having once consulted Le Sage and asking him to draw up certain horoscopes.

Among the horrible imputations made during the trial was that of Le Sage, who said that the marshal, Duke of Luxembourg, had made a pact with the devil, by which his son was to marry the daughter of the Marquis de Louvois. The accused replied: "When Matthieu de Montmorenci married the widow of *Louis the Fat*, he did not invoke the devil, but applied to the States-General, who declared that if the young king was to obtain the support of the Montmorencis such a marriage would have to take place."

This was the reply of a proud, not a guilty man. The trial lasted fourteen months; no verdict was returned either for or against him. La Voisin, La Vigoureux and her brother, the priest, also named Vigoureux, were burnt together with Le Sage in the *Place de la Grève*. Marshal Luxembourg retired into the country for a few days and then returned to court to take up his duties as captain of the guards; he did not see Louvois, and the king said nothing to him of all that had passed.

In our own time we have seen how he was afterwards placed in command of armies, without having to solicit such a post, and with what brilliant victories he silenced his enemies.

It may be imagined what frightful rumours were spread abroad in Paris by these accusations. The punishment of the stake which was the fate of Voisin and her accomplices put an end at once to such researches and such crimes. The abominable practice was confined only to a few individuals and did not corrupt the wholesome morals of the nation; but it left in the minds of men a morbid tendency to see in natural deaths the result of violence.

What had been thought of the unhappy fate of Henrietta of England was later thought of her daughter, Maria Louisa, who was married in 1679 to Charles II., King of Spain. The young princess set out with reluctance for Madrid. *Mademoiselle* had often said to *Monsieur*, the king's brother: "Do not take your daughter so often to the court, or she will be too unhappy in any other place." The young princess wished to marry *Monseigneur*, the Dauphin. "I am making you the Queen of Spain," the king said to her, "could I do more for my own daughter?" "Ah!" she replied, "you could do more tor your niece." She passed away in 1689 at the same age as her mother. Common opinion had it that Charles II.'s Austrian council wanted to get her out of the way, because she loved her country and might prevent her husband from declaring for the Allies against France. What was believed to be a counter-poison was even sent to her from Versailles —an uncertain precaution, since what may cure one evil may aggravate another, and there is no general antidote; the so-called counter-poison arrived after her death. Those who have read the Memoirs compiled by the Marquis de Dangeau will find that Louis is reported to have said at supper: "The Queen of Spain has died from eating a poisoned eel pie; the Countess de Pernits and the chamber-maids Zapata and Nina, who ate some of the pie after her, have also been poisoned."

On reading this strange incident in these manuscript Memoirs, said to have been carefully compiled by a courtier who hardly quitted Louis XIV. for forty years, I resolved not to remain in doubt; I enquired from some of the old servants of the king if it were true that that monarch, always so reserved in speech, had ever uttered such imprudent words. They all assured me that nothing was farther from the truth. I asked the Duchess de Saint-Pierre on her arrival from Spain, if it were true that those three persons had died with the queen; she gave me positive proof that all three had for many years survived their mistress. Finally, I learnt that these Memoirs of the Marquis de Dangeau, regarded as a valuable record, are nothing more than superficial accounts, often written by one of his servants; and I will wager that such may often be perceived from the style, the fatuities and errors with which the work abounds. After these melancholy reflections to which the death of Henrietta of England had led us, we must return to the events at court which followed her death.

The Princess Palatine succeeded her a year afterwards and became the mother of the Duke of Orleans, regent of the kingdom. She was obliged to renounce her Calvinistic faith in order to marry *Monsieur*; but she continued to cherish a secret reverence for her former religion, such as can hardly be effaced from a heart on which it was imprinted in early childhood.

The misfortune of one of the queen's maids-of-honour in 1675 gave rise to new arrangements at court. The unfortunate occurrence is known by a sonnet of Nesnault's entitled *The Abortion*, which has been often quoted:

> O thou! who diest imperfect and unborn,
> Sad compound of creation and decay,
> Embryo unform'd, denied the light of day,
> Of blank and being the reproach and scorn,
> Produc'd by guilty love's impetuous tide,
> By guilty honour in its turn destroy'd.

The dangers to which young girls were exposed at an intriguing and voluptuous court brought about the substitution of twelve matrons of the palace for the twelve maids-of-honour who adorned the queen's court; and the households of succeeding queens have always thus been constituted. Such an arrangement made the court both more numerous and more magnificent, by attracting the husbands and relatives of these ladies, which augmented the society of the court and added to its luxury.

The Princess of Bavaria, the wife of *Monseigneur*, from the very beginning gave added radiance and vivacity to the court. The Marquise de Montespan had always attracted principal attention, but at length she ceased to charm, and her haughty outbursts of sorrow could not recapture a heart that was wearying of her. She still maintained, however, a great position at court, being mistress of the royal wardrobe, and even a position with regard to the king, on account of her children, the remembrance of past habit, and her influence.

All outward signs of respect and friendship were accorded her, but could not console her; and the king, grieved at causing her such violent sorrow, and yet attracted by other tastes, already found in the conversation of Mme. de Maintenon a sweetness which he no longer enjoyed in that of his former mistress. He felt himself torn between Mme. de Montespan whom he could not abandon, Mlle. de Fontange whom he loved, and Mme. de Maintenon whose conversation had become indispensable to him in the distressed state of his mind. These three rivals for his favour kept the whole court in a ferment. It reflects no little credit on Louis XIV. that he allowed none of these intrigues to influence affairs of state, and that love, while destroying the harmony of his court, never disturbed for a moment that of his government. Nothing, I think, proves better that Louis XIV. possessed a soul as great as it was sensitive of affection.

I would even maintain that such court intrigues, foreign as they are to the business of the state, have no rightful place in history, were it not for the fact that the great age of Louis XIV. makes everything of interest, and the veil that covers these mysteries has been raised so many times by other historians, who for the most part have defiled them.

CHAPTER XXVII

FURTHER CHARACTERISTICS AND ANECDOTES (*continued*)

THE youth, the beauty of Mlle. de Fontange, a son whom she bore to the king in 1680, the title of duchess which was conferred upon her, all contributed to remove Mme. de Maintenon from the premier position for which she hardly dared to hope, yet which she afterwards obtained; the Duchess de Fontange and her son, however, died in 1681.

No longer troubled by an open rival, the Marquise de Montespan ceased to waste her energies in angry murmurings. When a man has left his youth behind he nearly always needs the companionship of a woman of easy temper; the burden of affairs makes such a consolation all the more necessary. The new favourite, Mme. de Maintenon, conscious that her latent influence was daily increasing, bore herself with that art natural to women and not displeasing to men.

She wrote on one occasion to her cousin, Mme. de Frontenac, in whom she placed an entire confidence: "I send him away always sad at heart yet never despairing." During this period when she was rapidly growing in favour and Mme. de Montespan was nearing her fall, the two rivals saw each other every day, sometimes with a secret bitterness, at others indulging in brief confidences, driven by the necessity of mutual conversation, and the irksomeness of continual restraint. Each one agreed to write Memoirs of what happened at court from her own personal knowledge, but the work did not proceed very far. In the last years of her life Mme. de Montespan used to delight in reading parts of these Memoirs to her friends. Religious observances, which played so great a part in all such secret intrigues, strengthened still further the position of Mme. de Maintenon and weakened that of Mme. de Montespan. The king reproached himself for his attachment to a married woman and was more than ever conscious of this scruple as he felt his passion diminish. This embarrassing situation lasted until 1685, a year memorable for the repeal of the Edict of Nantes. What different scenes were then witnessed! On the one hand the despair and flight of part of the nation; on the other renewed fêtes at Versailles; Trianon and Marli built; nature tortured into fresh shapes in these haunts of luxury and gardens where art itself seemed exhausted. The marriage of the great Condé's grandson with Mlle. de Nantes, daughter of the king and Mme. de Montespan, was the last triumph of this mistress, who from that time retired from court.

Some time afterwards the king married two other children whom he had had by her; Mlle. de Blois to the Duke of Chartres, since become regent of the kingdom; and the Duke of Maine to Louise Bénédicte de Bourbon, granddaughter of the great Condé and sister of *Monsieur le Duc*, a princess famous for her wit and her taste in the arts. Those who have but a faint knowledge of the Palais-Royal and Sceaux know the falsity of the popular rumours concerning these marriages in one history and another.

(1685) Before the celebration of the marriage of *Monsieur le Duc* with Mlle. de Nantes, the Marquis de Seignelai gave for the occasion an entertainment to the king, worthy of that monarch, in the gardens of Sceaux, which had been laid out by Le Nôtre with as much taste as those of Versailles. An *Idyll of Peace*, written by Racine, was there performed. Another fête was held at Versailles, and after the marriage the king made a wonderful display of magnificence, the idea of which had been given by Cardinal Mazarin in 1656. Four stalls were set up in the Marli *salon* filled with the richest and rarest wares that the skilled workmen of Paris could produce: the stalls were covered with magnificent decorations, representing the four seasons of the year. Mme. de Montespan was in charge of one with *Monseigneur*. Her rival, Mme. de Maintenon, presided over another with the Duke of Maine. The newly-married couples had each their own—*Monsieur le Duc* with Mme. de Thiange, and *Madame la Duchesse*, whose extreme youth did not permit her to preside over one with another man, was with the Duchess de Chevreuse. The ladies and gentlemen who had been invited drew lots for jewels with which the stalls were decked. In this way the king made presents to the whole court in a manner worthy of a king. Cardinal Mazarin's lottery was neither so ingenious nor so striking. Such lotteries had formerly been popularised by the Roman emperors, but not one of them blended magnificence with such a show of gallantry.

After the marriage of her daughter Mme. de Montespan no longer appeared at court. She continued to live in Paris with a considerable retinue. She had a large income which would cease on her death and, in addition, the king conferred on her a monthly pension of one thousand golden louis. Every year she went to take the waters, and there arranged the marriages of girls in the neighbourhood to whom she presented dowries. She was no longer of an age when the imagination affected by vivid impressions turns towards the Carmelites. She died at Bourbon in 1707.

One year after the marriage of Mlle. de Nantes with *Monsieur le Duc,* the Prince de Condé died at Fontainebleau at the age of sixty-six, from an illness which was aggravated by an attempt which he made to visit *Madame la Duchesse* who was sick of the smallpox. It may be judged from such eagerness, which actually cost him his life, whether he was disgusted at the marriage of his grandson with the daughter of the king and Mme. de Montespan, as was stated in all those lying gazettes with which Holland was overrun at the time. A *History of the Prince de Condé,* culled from the same dens of ignorance and imposture, also relates that the king took delight in humiliating that prince on every opportunity, and that at the marriage of the Princess de Conti, daughter of Mme. de La Vallière, the Secretary of State denied him the title of *high and puissant seigneur,* as though that were ever the title given to princes of the blood. Is it possible that the author of the *History of Louis XIV.,* an inhabitant of Avignon, who based his work partly on these wretched memoirs, could be so ignorant of the world and the customs of the French Court as to repeat such falsehoods?

Meanwhile, after the marriage of *Madame la Duchesse* and the total eclipse of her mother, Mme. de Maintenon, triumphant, gained such an influence and inspired so great an affection and regard in Louis XIV. that on the advice of Father de La Chaise he married her secretly in January 1686, in a small chapel at the end of the apartments afterwards occupied by the Duke of Burgundy. There was no contract, no stipulations. The Archbishop of Paris, Harlai de Chanvalon, pronounced the benediction; the king's confessor was present, and Montchevreuil and Bontems, first valets of the chamber, were the only witnesses. This event can no longer be passed over in silence; it is mentioned by every writer, although names, place and dates have all been confused. Louis XIV. was then in his forty-eighth year and the lady whom he married fifty-two. This prince, covered with glory, wished to alleviate the toils of government with the innocent delights of private life; the marriage involved him in nothing unworthy of his rank. There was always a doubt at court as to whether Mme. de Maintenon were really married to him; she was respected as the king's favourite, but not treated as a queen.

The rise of this lady appears a very remarkable one in France, although, of course, the history of Europe furnishes many examples of even greater and more brilliant careers, which had still humbler origins. The Marquise of San Sebastian, wife of Victor Amadeus, King of Sardinia, was of no higher birth than Mme. de Maintenon; Catherine, Empress of Russia, was of much lower origin, and the first wife of James II., King of England, was also of inferior lineage according to European prejudices, even if those prejudices be not held in the rest of the world.

Mme. de Maintenon came of an old family, being the granddaughter of Theodore Agrippa d'Aubigné, gentleman of the chamber to Henri IV. Her father, Constant d'Aubigné, wishing to found a settlement in Carolina, had petitioned the English, and was accordingly imprisoned in the Castle of Trompette, from which he was released by the daughter of the governor, Cardillac, a Bordeaux nobleman. In 1627, Constant d'Aubigné married his preserver and took her with him to Carolina. On their return to France some years later they were both imprisoned at Niort in Poitou by orders of the court. In this prison at Niort was born, in 1635, Françoise d'Aubigné, who was destined to experience the extremes of fortune in all her moods. Taken at the age of three to America, left by the negligence of a servant on a river bank and narrowly escaping death from a poisonous snake, brought back an orphan to France at the age of eleven, and brought up with great harshness by Mme. de Neuillant, mother of the Duchess de Navailles, who was related to her, she was fortunate to marry, in 1651, Paul Scarron, who lodged close to her home in the rue d'Enfer. Scarron came of an old parliamentary family, distinguished by several great alliances; but his writing of burlesques lowered his reputation while it brought him troops of friends. Nevertheless, it was a piece of good fortune for Mlle. d'Aubigné to marry such a man, even although he was ill-favoured by nature, impotent and of very moderate means. Before her marriage she renounced the Calvinist religion, a faith which she had inherited from her ancestors. Her beauty and her wit soon brought her into notice, and she was eagerly sought after by the highest society in Paris; this period of her youth was undoubtedly the happiest in her life. After her husband's death, which occurred in 1660, she applied many times to the king for a small pension of fifteen hundred livres which Scarron had been receiving. At last, after several years, the king granted her a pension of two thousand, with these words: "Madame, I have kept you waiting a long time, but you have so many friends, that I wished to be alone in recompensing you."

This incident was related to me by Cardinal de Fleury, who often delighted in telling it, because he said Louis XIV. had paid him the same compliment on presenting him with the bishopric of Fréjus.

However, the actual letters of Mme. de Maintenon show that she owed this trivial help which secured her from privation to Mme. de Montespan. She was remembered some years later, when it became necessary to provide for the secret education of the Duke of Maine, a son borne to the king in 1670 by the Marquise de Montespan. But it was certainly not until 1672 that she was chosen to direct this secret education; she says in one of her letters: "If the children are the king's, I am quite willing; but I should not without some scruples take charge of those belonging to Mme. de Montespan; it is for the king to command; that is my last word." Mme. de Montespan had only two children in 1672— the Duke of Maine and the Count of Vexin. The dates of Mme. de Maintenon's letters, given as 1670, in which she speaks of the two children, one of whom was not yet born, are thus evidently false. Nearly all the dates of the letters which have been printed are wrong. Such inaccuracy would cast strong suspicions on the authenticity of the letters, were there not in addition a character of naturalness and truth such as is almost impossible to counterfeit.

It is of no great importance to know in what year the lady was entrusted with the care of Louis XIV.'s natural children but attention to such details serves to show with what care the principal events of this history have been recorded.

The Duke of Maine was born with a deformed foot. The chief physician, d'Aquin, who had the king's confidence, thought it good to send the child to take the waters of Barège. A person of trust was looked for who could take charge of the child. The king bethought himself of Mme. Scarron and M. de Louvois went secretly to Paris to propose the voyage. From that time she was entrusted with the education of the Duke of Maine, and was appointed to that post by the king, not, as it has been said, by Mme. de Montespan. She wrote personally to the king, and her letters pleased him greatly. This was the beginning of her fortune; her own merit did the rest.

The king, who could not at first feel at his ease with her, passed from dislike to trust and from trust to love. Those of her letters which have been preserved constitute a more valuable record than one would think; they reveal that mingling of religion and intrigue, of dignity and frailty so often to be found in the human heart, and which was in the heart of Louis XIV. Mme. de Maintenon seems filled at once with ambition and piety, neither striving for the mastery. Her confessor, Gobelin, approved both alike; he was both spiritual director and a courtier; his penitent, become ungrateful towards Mme. de Montespan, always conceals her fault. Her confessor fosters the self-deception, and in good faith she brings religion to the help of her faded charms, in order to supplant the benefactress who has become her rival.

This strange bargaining between love and conscience on the part of the king, of ambition and piety on the part of his new mistress, seems to have lasted from 1681 to 1686, the year of their marriage.

Her rise meant for her retirement. Shut up in her apartments, which were on the same floor as those of the king, she was restricted to the company of two or three ladies, confined like herself; even these she saw rarely. The king visited her every day after dinner, before and after supper, and stayed with her until midnight. He transacted affairs there with his ministers, while Mme. de Maintenon occupied herself in reading, or some needlework, never anxious to join in the discussion of state affairs, often, indeed, seeming to pay no attention to them, avoiding the slightest appear-

ance of intrigue or plot; much more occupied in pleasing
him who was her ruler, than in seeking to rule herself, and
husbanding her influence by exercising it seldom and with
great tact. She did not take advantage of her position to
secure preferments and important posts for her own family.
Her brother, the Count d'Aubigné, an old lieutenant-general,
was not even a marshal of France. The blue riband, and a
few secret shares in the general tax-farming of the realm,
were all his fortune; he once said to Marshal Vivonne, Mme.
de Montespan's brother, that "he had received his marshal's
baton in ready cash."

The Marquis de Villette, her nephew or cousin, was but a
commander of a squadron in the navy. Mme. de Caylus,
daughter of the Marquis de Villette, received but a modest
pension from Louis XIV. on her marriage. When marrying
her niece, d'Aubigné, to the son of the first Marshal de
Noailles, Mme. de Maintenon gave her but two hundred
thousand francs; the king supplied the rest. She herself
possessed only the property of Maintenon, which she had
bought with the bounties given her by the king. She was
eager that the public should pardon her rise to favour in
consideration of her disinterestedness. The second wife of the
Marquis de Villette, afterwards Lady Bolingbroke, could
never obtain anything from her. I have often heard her say
that she used to reproach her cousin for the little she did
for her family, and that she once said to her in anger: "You
take a pleasure in your own parsimony, while your family
is a victim of it." But Mme. de Maintenon forgot everything
in her fear of offending the sensibilities of Louis XIV.

She dared not even support Cardinal de Noailles against
Le Tellier. She had a great friendship for Racine; but the
friendship did not give her sufficient courage to protect him
against a passing displeasure of the king. Touched one day
by the eloquence with which he had spoken to her of the
poverty of the people in 1698, a poverty which was, as usual,
exaggerated, but which afterwards reached a deplorable
height, she persuaded her friend to draw up a memoir
describing the evil and suggesting a remedy. The king read
it, and on his showing some annoyance at its contents, she
was weak enough to reveal the author and, moreover, say
nothing in his defence. Racine, of a still weaker nature, was
consumed by a grief which hurried him to his grave.

The same dominant trait in her character which prevented

her from doing anyone a service also debarred her from doing anyone any harm. The Abbé de Choisi relates that Louvois had thrown himself at the feet of Louis XIV., begging him not to marry Scarron's widow. If the Abbé de Choisi knew of this occurrence, then Mme. de Maintenon must also have been aware of it; yet she not only forgave the minister, but appeased the king in those outbursts of anger which the blunt manners of the Marquis de Louvois sometimes excited in his master.

Thus, in marrying Mme. de Maintenon, Louis XIV. was merely providing himself with an agreeable and docile companion. The only public distinction which betrayed her secret rise in fortune was that at mass she occupied one of those small rostrums or gilded latticed seats which are usually set apart for the king and queen. Otherwise no outward show of greatness was vouchsafed her. The passion which she had inspired in the king, and which had led to her marriage, gradually developed into a deep and genuine affection, which age and familiarity but served to strengthen. At court and in the royal circle she had already acquired the reputation of a foundress, having established a seminary at Noisi, where several young ladies of quality had been gathered together, and the king had already assigned the revenues from the Abbey of Saint-Denys to this budding community. Saint-Cyr was built at one end of the park at Versailles in 1686. She gave this institution its form, drew up the rules with Godet Desmarets, Bishop of Chartres, and was herself the Superior of the convent. She often went there to spend a few hours, and to say that boredom alone persuaded her to spend her time in this way is but to repeat her own words. One has only to read her letters to Mme. de La Maisonfort, to which reference will be made in the chapter on Quietism:

"O! that I could tell you of my trials! That I could reveal to you the boredom which assails the great, and the difficulty they have in finding something to occupy their time! Do you not see that I am dying of *ennui* in the midst of wealth such as you would find it difficult to imagine? I was once young and pretty: I tasted all the pleasures, was the centre of attraction. When I grew older I enjoyed for many years the conversation of a brilliant and witty society. I came to favour, and I protest to you, my dear girl, that all conditions of life make one sensible of a frightful emptiness."

Could anything discourage ambition it would surely be this letter. Mme. de Maintenon, whose only care was the monotony of her life with a great king, said one day to her brother, the Count d'Aubigné: "I cannot bear it any longer, I wish I were dead." His reply to her is well known: "You have then been promised the Almighty as a husband?"

On the king's death she retired altogether to Saint-Cyr. It is surprising that the king left her almost nothing: he simply recommended her to the care of the Duke of Orleans. She wanted nothing more than a pension of eighty thousand livres, which was only paid to her up to her death, which occurred on the 15th of April, 1710.

Undue care was taken to omit the name of Scarron from her epitaph: no stigma attaches to the name, and its omission thus only serves to suggest a stigma which does not exist.

From the time that the king began to lead a more retired life with Mme. de Maintenon, the court became less animated and more serious; moreover, the alarming illness which he had experienced in 1686 also induced him to forgo the pleasures of those gay fêtes which up till that time had been held almost every year. He fell ill of an abscess in the large intestine. The science of surgery, which made greater progress in France during this reign than in all the rest of Europe, was not yet well acquainted with this malady: Cardinal Richelieu had died of it for want of proper treatment. The king's danger was felt throughout the whole of France. Crowds flocked to the churches to pray for their king's recovery, their faces streaming with tears. We ourselves have beheld an almost similar manifestation of universal sympathy when his successor lay at death's door at Metz in 1744. These two epochs will ever be a lesson to kings as to what they owe to a nation which can show such devotion.

From the time Louis XIV. felt the first attacks of this illness, his chief surgeon, Félix, searched the hospitals for patients who were in the same danger: he consulted the best surgeons, and, with their help, made new instruments to shorten the operation and render it less painful. The king bore the operation without a murmur. On the very day of the operation he had his ministers working at his bedside, and that the news of his danger might not affect any European court, he gave an audience to the ambassadors on the very next morning. His generosity in rewarding Félix was equal to his fortitude of spirit; he gave him land then valued at more than fifty thousand crowns.

From that time the king no longer went to the theatre. The Princess of Bavaria, grown melancholy and attacked by a lingering illness which carried her off in 1690, denied herself all pleasures and obstinately shut herself up in her apartment. She was fond of literature, and had even composed verses; but in her melancholy she desired only solitude.

It was the convent of Saint-Cyr that reawakened a love of intellectual pursuits. Mme. de Maintenon begged Racine, who had forsaken the theatre for Jansenism and the court, to write a tragedy which could be performed by her pupils. She desired a subject taken from the Bible, and the result was *Esther*. This piece, first performed at Saint-Cyr, was afterwards given several times at Versailles before the king during the winter of 1689. Prelates and Jesuits were alike eager to obtain permission to see this singular play. It is remarkable that this piece should have had such a universal success, and that two years later *Athalie*, played by the same children, should have completely failed. The contrary happened when these plays were performed at Paris long after the author's death, and when the original partiality was forgotten. *Athalie*, performed in 1717, was received as was its due, with raptures, while in 1721 *Esther* had but a cold reception and was not performed again. But by that time there were no longer flattering courtiers to recognise Mme. de Maintenon in Esther or malicious ones to see Mme. de Montespan in Vashti, M. de Louvois in Aman, and above all, the Huguenots persecuted by that minister, in the expulsion of the Hebrews. An unbiased public saw but an adventure devoid of interest as it was of truth; a mad king, who has lived six months with his wife without knowing, without even enquiring, who she is; a minister so absurd a monster as to bid the king destroy a whole nation, old men, women, children, for the lack of an obeisance; the same minister is fool enough to publish an order for killing every Jew within eleven months, apparently in order to give them time either to escape or to defend themselves; the imbecile king for no reason signs the absurd command, and again for no reason has his favourite unceremoniously hanged; all this, without plot, without action, without interest, greatly displeased everyone who had either sense or taste. But despite the puerility of the subject, thirty lines of *Esther* are worth more than many tragedies which have had great success.

These ingenious entertainments were renewed for the education of Adelaide of Savoy, Duchess of Burgundy, who came to France at the age of eleven.

It is one of the contradictions of our code of manners that while on the one hand a certain ignominy has remained attached to the public performance of plays, their representation in private has been regarded as the noblest and worthiest pastime of royal persons.

A little theatre was erected in Mme. de Maintenon's apartment. The Duchess of Burgundy and the Duke of Orleans performed there in company with those persons of the court who had most talent for it. The famous actor, Baron, instructed them in their parts and performed with them. The majority of Duché's tragedies, one of the king's gentlemen-in-waiting, were composed for this theatre; and the Abbé Genest, chaplain to the Duchess of Orleans, wrote plays for the Duchess of Maine, which were performed by the princess and her court.

These both trained the mind and enlivened society.

Not one of those who have been too ready to censure Louis XIV. can deny that until the Battle of Blenheim he was the only monarch at once powerful, magnificent, and great in every department. For while there have been heroes such as John Sobieski and certain Kings of Sweden who eclipsed him as warriors, no one has surpassed him as a monarch. It must ever be confessed that he not only bore his misfortunes, but overcame them. He had defects and made great errors, but had those who condemn him been in his place, would they have equalled his achievements?

The Duchess of Burgundy grew in grace and virtue. The praise bestowed on her sister in Spain aroused in her a spirit of rivalry which redoubled her powers of pleasing. She was not a perfect beauty, but she had a look like that of her son, afterwards Louis XV., a grand air and a noble figure. These natural advantages were heightened by wit and still more so by her extreme desire to win the good wishes of everyone. Like Henrietta of England, she was at once the idol and the model of the court, but yet with higher rank; she stood on the steps of the throne, and France expected from the Duke of Burgundy a government such as the sages of old conceived, whose austerity would be assuaged by the charms of this princess, which promised to be more appreciated than the philosophy of her husband. Everyone knows how ill-fated were these expectations. It was the destiny of Louis XIV. to see the whole of his family die before their time; his wife at forty-five and his only son at fifty; but a year later we witnessed the spectacle of his grandson the Dauphin, Duke of Burgundy, his wife, and their eldest son, the Duke of Brittany, being carried to the same tomb at Saint-Denys in the month of April 1712, while the youngest of their children, who afterwards ascended the throne, lay in his cradle at death's door. The Duke of Berri, brother of the Duke of Burgundy, followed them two years later, and his daughter was carried at the same time from her cradle to her coffin.

These years of desolation left such a deep impression on people's hearts that during the minority of Louis XV. I have met many people who could not speak of the late king's bereavement without tears in their eyes. Of all men, the one most to be pitied in the midst of these sudden deaths was he who, it seemed, was soon to inherit the kingdom.

The same suspicions that had arisen on the deaths of *Madame* and Maria Louisa, Queen of Spain, were now revived with extraordinary vehemence. The extreme sorrow of the public might almost have excused the calumny had it been excusable. There must have been a spirit of madness in the air for people to think that anyone could have foully caused the death of so many royal personages while leaving unharmed the only one who could avenge them. The Dauphin, Duke of Burgundy, his wife and son had died of an infectious purple fever. In less than a month more than five hundred people succumbed to this malady in Paris alone. The Duke of Bourbon, grandson of the Prince de Condé, the Duke de La Trimouille, Mme. de la Vrillière and Mme. de Listenai were all attacked at court. The Marquis de Gondrin, son of the Duke d'Antin, died of it in two days. His wife, afterwards Countess of Toulouse, was at death's door. The epidemic spread over the whole of France. In Lorraine, it carried off the elder children of Francis, Duke of Lorraine, destined one day to become emperor and restore the fortunes of the House of Austria.

It was enough, however, for a physician, named Boudin, a man of pleasure, as bluff as he was ignorant, to have said these words, "We cannot understand such diseases," to allow slander a free rein.

Philip, Duke of Orleans, nephew of Louis XIV., had a laboratory where he studied chemistry and many other sciences; this was irrefutable proof. The public outcry was terrible; one must have been a witness of it to believe it. Various pamphlets and some wretched histories of Louis XIV. would perpetuate these suspicions, if enlightened men did not take care to destroy them. I venture to say that, struck as I have been by the injustice of men in every age, I have sought widely in order to arrive at the truth. The Marquis de Cadillac has more than once related to me the following incident: he was one of the most honourable men in the kingdom, an intimate friend of this suspected prince, of whose conduct later he had much to complain. In the midst of all this public outcry the Marquis de Cadillac visited him in his palace to find him stretched on the floor, weeping bitterly, and overcome with despair. His chemist, Homberg, had gone to the Bastille to give himself up; but they had no orders to receive him, and he was refused admittance. In his extreme anguish the prince, incredible as it may seem, demanded that he himself should be put in prison; he wished to have his innocence established by judicial procedure; his mother also demanded this cruel justification. The secret warrant was being hurried on, but it was not yet signed, and at this emotional crisis the Marquis de Cadillac alone maintained sufficient composure to perceive the consequences of so desperate a step. He persuaded the prince's mother to object to the shameful warrant. The monarch, who granted it, and his nephew, who demanded it, were equally to be pitied.

CHAPTER XXVIII

FURTHER ANECDOTES (*continued*)

LOUIS XIV. concealed his sorrows in public; people saw no difference in him, but in private the shock of so many misfortunes overcame him, and he was convulsed with grief. He suffered all these family losses at the conclusion of a disastrous war, before he was even assured of peace, and at a time when his whole kingdom was plunged in misery. Yet he was not seen for one moment to be overcome by his misfortunes.

The remainder of his life was sad. The disorganisation of state finances, which he was unable to repair, estranged many hearts. The complete confidence he placed in the Jesuit, Le Tellier, a turbulent spirit, stirred them to rebellion. It is remarkable that the people who forgave him all his mistresses could not forgive this one confessor. In the minds of the majority of his subjects he lost during the last three years of his life all the prestige of the great and memorable things he had accomplished.

With the loss of nearly all his children, his affection redoubled for his legitimised sons, the Duke of Maine and the Count of Toulouse, and he proclaimed them and their descendants, in default of princes of the blood royal, heirs to the throne by an edict which was passed in 1714 without protest. He thus tempered by a natural law the rigour of the conventional laws, which deprive children born out of wedlock of all rights to the paternal succession. Kings, however, dispense with this law. He thought himself justified in doing for his own flesh and blood what he had done on behalf of several of his subjects: especially was he justified in doing for two of his children what he had persuaded parliament to pass unopposed for the princes of the House of Lorraine. A year later, in 1715, he decreed that the rank of his illegitimate sons should be equal to that of princes of the blood royal. The lawsuit which the princes of the blood afterwards instituted against the legitimised princes is well known. The latter preserved, however, for themselves and their children the honours accorded by Louis XIV. As to the position of their descendants, that will depend upon their age, their merit, and their fortune.

On his return from Marli towards the middle of the month of August 1715, Louis XIV. was attacked by the illness which ended his life. His legs swelled, and signs of gangrene began to show themselves. The Earl of Stair, the English ambassador, wagered, after the fashion of his country, that the king would not outlive the month of September. The Duke of Orleans, on the journey from Marli, had been left completely to himself, but now the whole court gathered round his person. During the last days of the king's illness, a quack physician gave him a cordial which revived him. He managed to eat, and the quack assured him that he would recover. On hearing this news the crowd of people that had gathered round the Duke of Orleans diminished immediately. "If the king eats another mouthful," said the Duke of Orleans, "we shall have no one left." But the illness was mortal. Arrangements were made for granting the absolute regency to the Duke of Orleans. In his will, ratified by parliament, the king had only given him very limited powers; or rather he had only made him president of the council of regency, in which he would have nothing more than the casting vote. Nevertheless, he said to him: "I have conserved to you all the rights to which your birth entitles you." He had overlooked the fundamental law which during a minority confers unlimited powers on the heir presumptive to the throne. This supreme power, which is liable to be abused, is dangerous; but a divided authority is no less so. He imagined that having been obeyed so unhesitatingly during his life, he would be so after his death, and forgot that the will of his own father had been broken.

(1 September, 1715) There is no one who does not know with what greatness of soul he perceived death approaching, saying to Mme. de Maintenon, "I had thought that it was more difficult to die," and to his servants, "Why do you weep? did you think me immortal?"—quietly giving his orders concerning many things, even the preparations for his own funeral. Whoever has many to witness his death dies always with a high heart.

During his last illness Louis XIII. had set to music the *De Profundis*, which was to be sung at his funeral. The fortitude with which Louis XIV. met his end was unattended by the pomp which had characterised his whole life. His courage even led him to the length of confessing his own faults, and his successor always kept written at the head of his bed the remarkable words which that monarch spoke to him, clasping him in his arms on the bed; these words are far other than those commonly reported in all the histories, and I give here an exact copy of them:

"You will soon be the monarch of a great kingdom. What I most strongly enjoin upon you is never to forget your obligations to God. Remember that you owe all that you are to Him. Endeavour to preserve peace with your neighbours. I have been too fond of war; do not imitate me in that, neither in my too great extravagance. Take counsel in all things and always seek to know the best and follow it. Let your first thoughts be devoted to helping your people, and do what I have had the misfortune not to be able to do myself. . . ."

This speech is very different from the narrow-mindedness attributed to him in certain memoirs.

He has been accused of wearing certain relics during the last years of his life. His own sentiments were exalted, but his confessor, who was of a different cast of mind, had persuaded him to adopt such unseemly habits, now quite gone out of fashion, in order to bring him more completely under his influence; moreover, these relics, which he was foolish enough to wear, had been given to him by Mme. de Maintenon.

Though the life and death of Louis XIV. were alike glorious, he was not mourned as he deserved. The love of novelty, the advent of a minority, during which everyone thought to make his fortune, the disputes over the *Constitution*, which embittered men's minds, all led to the news of his death being received with a feeling of even less than indifference. The same people who, in 1686, had implored Heaven with tears to bring about the recovery of their king, were now seen to follow his funeral procession with very different feelings. It is related that when quite young his mother said to him one day: "My son, imitate your grandfather and not your father." The king having asked her why: "Because," she said, "people wept at the death of Henri IV., but laughed at that of Louis XIII."

Though he has been accused of being narrow-minded, of being too harsh in his zeal against Jansenism, too arrogant with foreigners in his triumphs, too weak in his dealings with certain women, and too severe in personal matters; of having lightly undertaken wars, of burning the Palatinate, and of persecuting the reformers—nevertheless, his great qualities and noble deeds when placed in the balance eclipse all his faults. Time, which modifies men's opinions, has put the seal upon his reputation, and, in spite of all that has been written against him, his name is never uttered without respect, nor without recalling to the mind an age which will be forever memorable. If we consider this prince in his private life, we observe him indeed too full of his own greatness, but affable, allowing his mother no part in the government but performing all the duties of a son, and observing all outward appearances of propriety towards his wife; a good father, a good master, always dignified in public, laborious in his study, punctilious in business matters, just in thought, a good speaker, and agreeable though aloof.

I have remarked elsewhere that he never uttered those words which have been imputed to him, when the first gentleman-in-waiting and the grand master of the wardrobe were disputing the honour of attending on him, "What matters it which of my valets waits on me?" Such a rude speech could never come from a man so refined and considerate as he was, and is scarcely consistent with what he said one day to the Duke de La Rochefoucauld on the subject of his debts: "Why not speak to your friends?"—a very different expression, which in itself was worth much, and which was accompanied by a gift of fifty thousand crowns.

It is not even true that he wrote to the Duke de La Rochefoucauld: "I compliment you as your friend on the office of Grand Master of the Wardrobe, which I confer on you as your king." Historians have exhibited this letter as to his credit. They do not perceive how indelicate, how ill-bred it is to tell a person whose master one is, that one is his master. It would be suitable were a king writing to a subject who had rebelled; it is what Henri IV. might have said to the Duke de Mayenne before they were completely reconciled. Rose, the secretary of the council, wrote this letter, but the king had too much good taste to send it. It was this good taste which made him alter the pretentious inscriptions which the academician, Charpentier, placed on Lebrun's pictures in the gallery of Versailles: *The unbelievable passage of the Rhine : The marvellous capture of Valenciennes,* and so on. The king thought that *The capture of Valenciennes : The passage of the Rhine* would say yet more. Charpentier was quite right in embellishing these records of his country with inscriptions in our own tongue; it was excessive adulation and not the use of the vulgar tongue that spoilt his work.

Certain replies and witticisms of Louis XIV. have been preserved which are of very little account. It is said that when he decided to suppress Calvinism in France, he exclaimed: "My grandfather loved the Huguenots and did not fear them; my father loved them not at all, but feared them; as for myself, I neither love nor fear them."

In 1658, on giving the office of First President of the Parliament of Paris to M. de Lamoignon, at that time Master of Requests, he said to him: "Did I know a better man or a more worthy subject, I would have chosen him." He made use of nearly the same expressions to Cardinal de Noailles, on making him Archbishop of Paris. What constitutes the merit of these words is that they were true and that they stimulated the practice of virtue.

It is said that an imprudent preacher one day addressed him personally at Versailles, an audacious act which would have been impermissible if done to a private individual, far more so to a king. It is alleged that Louis XIV. contented himself with saying to him: "My father, I certainly like to take my share of a sermon, but I do not like to have it forced upon me." Whether he uttered these words or not, they may serve as a lesson.

He always expressed himself in a noble manner and with precision, striving to speak and act in public as behoved a sovereign. When the Duke of Anjou was departing to reign in Spain, he said to him, to show the unity which was henceforth to join the two nations: "The Pyrenees no longer exist."

Assuredly nothing reveals his character so well as the following memoir, the whole of which was written entirely by his own hand:

"Kings are often compelled to do things against their inclination, which offend their natural sense of right. They must take delight in pleasing people, and must often punish and thus lose the goodwill of persons whom they would naturally wish well. The interests of the state must come first. In any affair of importance, where it is possible to do better they should force themselves to do so, so that they may not have to reproach themselves afterwards; but I have been prevented by certain private interests, which have turned aside the regard I should have had for the greatness, the good and the power of the state. Vexed questions often present themselves; delicate problems which it is difficult to unravel, and on which one has but vague ideas. So long as one is in that condition it is permissible to remain undecided; but so soon as one makes up his mind about anything and believes he sees the better course, it must be taken. By so doing I have often been successful in what I have undertaken. The errors I have made and which have caused me infinite sorrow, have occurred as a result of easy-going and because I have allowed myself to be too much led by the advice of others. Nothing is so dangerous as weakness of whatever kind. In order to rule others, one must lift oneself above them, and, after hearing all sides, one must rely on his own judgment, which must be arrived at without prejudice, always taking care not to order or perform anything that is unworthy of oneself, of the character one bears, or of the dignity of the state. Well-intentioned princes who have some knowledge of their duties either through experience or study, and who take great pains to make themselves competent, find so many different things by which they can make themselves known, that they must pay special attention to each and general application to all. One must be on one's guard against oneself, beware of one's predilections, and always watch over one's temper. A king's profession is a great, noble and gratifying one, if he feels himself to be worthy of properly performing all the duties which he undertakes; but it is not free from troubles, fatigue and anxiety. Suspense is sometimes disheartening, and after taking a reasonable time to consider a question, one has to make up one's mind, and take the course that seems the best.

"A king works for himself, when he has the state in mind; the welfare of the one enhances the glory of the other: when the state is prosperous, exalted and powerful, he who is the cause of it is rendered glorious by it, and as compared with his subjects must still derive greater enjoyment from all that is most agreeable in life. If he commit an error, he must retrieve his mistake as soon as ever possible, nor should any consideration prevent him from so doing, not even for the sake of doing a kindness.

"In 1671, a man died who had the post of secretary of state, in charge of the foreign department. He was a capable man, but not without defects; he left no suitable man to occupy this post, which is a very important one.

"For some time I was in doubt as to whom I should appoint to this office, and after careful consideration I decided that a man who had had long experience in embassies would best fill the post.

"I ordered him to be sent for; my choice was approved by everyone, which does not always happen; and when he arrived, I appointed him to the post. I only knew of him by reputation, and by the fact that he had executed satisfactorily the commissions with which I had entrusted him; but the post I had given him proved too big and involved for him. I had not made the most of my opportunities, as I might have done, merely through being easy-going and

good-natured. At length, I was compelled to order his resignation, since everything that passed through his hands lost
the dignity and authority essential in carrying out the orders
of a King of France. Had I made up my mind to remove
him sooner, I should have escaped the inconveniences which
have since occurred and I should not have to blame myself
for my kindness to him which was prejudicial to the state.
I have stated this in detail in order to give an example of
what I have mentioned above."

This valuable memoir, hitherto unpublished, is a witness
to posterity of the integrity and magnanimity of his mind.
It might even be said that he judges himself too severely,
that no blame was attached to him for appointing M. de
Pomponne, since his choice of that minister was determined
by his services and reputation, and was confirmed by universal approval; and if he blamed himself for his choice of
M. de Pomponne, who at least had the good fortune to serve
his country in her time of great glory, what would he not
have to reproach himself with as regards M. de Chamillart,
whose ministry was so ill-fated and so universally condemned?

He wrote several memoirs in this vein, either for his own
benefit or for the instruction of the Dauphin, the Duke of
Burgundy. These reflections were set down after the events.
He would have approached more nearly the perfection to
which he was worthy of aspiring, had he been able to frame
a philosophy superior to ordinary politics and prejudices;
a philosophy such as in the course of centuries has been
practised by so few sovereigns, and which one can pardon
kings for not being acquainted with, since so many private
individuals are ignorant of it.

The following are some of the precepts he gave to his
grandson, Philip V., on his departure for Spain. They were
written in haste, with a carelessness that lays bare the mind
of the writer more surely than a studied speech.

"Love the Spanish and all your subjects attached to your
crown and person. Do not favour those who flatter you most;
esteem those who for the common good risk your displeasure.
It is in them you find your true friends.

"Make your subjects happy, and with this end in view, do
not make war until you are forced to do so, and have carefully
considered and weighed the reasons in your council.

"Endeavour to restore your finances; keep a watch on the
Indies and on your fleets; give thought to trade and continue

in a close union with France, nothing being so advantageous to our two powers as such a union which nothing can resist.

"If you are compelled to make war, put yourself at the head of your armies.

"Contrive to restore order in your armies everywhere, and begin with those in Flanders.

"Never put pleasure before duty; but prepare for yourself a kind of programme which will allow you some hours of liberty and amusement.

"There are few more innocent amusements than hunting and the pleasures of a country house, provided you do not spend too much on it.

"Give your undivided attention to affairs when you are consulted; listen carefully to the opening of any business, but reserve your decision.

"When you have acquired more knowledge, remember that it is you who have to decide; but no matter how experienced you are, always listen to every opinion and argument of your council, before making that decision.

"Do all that is possible to become well acquainted with the most important people, so that you may make use of them at the opportune moment.

"Always endeavour to have Spaniards for your viceroys and governors.

"Treat everyone with good humour; never say unpleasant things to anyone; but honour people of distinction and merit.

"Show your gratitude towards the late king and towards all those who were responsible for choosing you to succeed him.

"Place great trust in Cardinal Porto Carrero and show your gratitude to him for the way in which he has behaved.

"I think that you should do a great deal for the ambassador who has been so successful in his solicitations on your behalf, and who was the first to kneel to you as one of your subjects.

"Do not forget Bedmar; he is an accomplished man and able to serve you well.

"Put complete faith in the Duke d'Harcourt; he is a clever and honest man, and will only advise you with regard to your own duties.

"Keep all the French in order.

"Treat your own servants well, but do not be too familiar with them, and trust them still less. Employ them so long as they serve you well, dismiss them for the slightest fault, and never uphold them against the Spaniards.

"Have as little to do with the dowager queen as you may. See to it that she leaves Madrid, but does not leave Spain. Wherever she may be, keep a watch on her doings and prevent her from meddling with any of your affairs. Suspect those who have too much intercourse with her.

"Keep always an affection towards your family. Remember their sorrow at parting with you. Carry on constant correspondence with them on all matters both great and small. Ask us for anything you are in want of or desire to have, and which you lack; we will ask the same of you.

"Never forget that you are a Frenchman and what may befall you. When you have got children who will ensure the Spanish succession, visit your kingdoms, go to Naples and Sicily; go on to Milan, and come back through Flanders; that will give you an opportunity of seeing us again; in the meanwhile, visit Catalonia, Aragon and other parts. See what must be done for Ceuta.

"Throw money to the people when you are in Spain, and especially when you enter Madrid.

"Do not appear surprised at the extraordinary people you will find there. Do not scoff at them. Every country has its peculiar manners, and you will soon become accustomed to what at first sight seems so astonishing.

"Avoid as much as you can granting favours to those who lay out money to obtain them. Give opportunely and freely, and hardly ever accept presents, unless they be quite trifling. If it happen that you cannot avoid accepting them, requite the donors with more generous gifts after the lapse of a few days.

"Have a casket in which you can put any special thing, and let no one have the key but yourself.

"I conclude with the most important advice I can give you. See to it that you are the ruler. You must be master; never have a favourite nor a prime minister. Consult your council and listen to what they have to say, but decide for yourself. God, who has made you a king, will give you the necessary wisdom, so long as your intentions are good."

The mind of Louis XIV. was rather precise and dignified than witty; and indeed one does not expect a king to say notable things, but to do them. What is necessary to every man in office is never to let anyone leave his presence discontented, and to make himself agreeable to all who approach him. One may not be able to confer benefits at every moment, but one can always say pleasant things. Louis made a successful practice of doing so.

Between him and his court there existed a continual intercourse in which was seen on the one side all the graciousness of a majesty which never debased itself, and on the other all the delicacy of an eager desire to serve and please which never approached servility. He was considerate and polite, especially to women, and his example enhanced those qualities in his courtiers; he never missed an opportunity of saying things to men which at once flattered their self-esteem, stimulated rivalry, and remained long in their memory.

One day, the Duchess of Burgundy, who was still quite young, seeing at supper a very ugly officer, joked long and loudly about his ugliness. "I think, Madame," said the king in a still louder voice, "that he is one of the handsomest men in my kingdom, for he is one of the bravest."

A staff officer, rather brusque in his manners, which had not become softened even at the court of Louis XIV., had lost an arm in battle; the king had compensated him for the loss of an arm so far as one can compensate anyone for such a loss, but the officer complained, "I would that I had lost the other one as well, when I should no longer be able to serve your majesty." "I should be very sorry for you and for myself," the king replied, and followed up his words by bestowing some favours on him. He was so averse to saying disagreeable things, which are like fatal arrows in the mouth of a prince, that he would not even allow himself the most innocent and mildest of jests, while ordinary individuals perpetrate every day the cruellest and most bitter ones.

He delighted and was skilled in ingenious pursuits, such as improvisations and the composing of pleasing songs; and sometimes he also improvised little parodies on airs such as the following:

> Here's Phil, my younger brother,
> With Chancellor Serrant;
> He seldom makes a pother,
> He likes the wise Boifranc
> Much better than the other;

and the following, which he composed one day when dismissing his council:

> The Council in vain at his elbow appears
> When his bitch comes across; from all business he'll fly,
> Nought else he minds or sees or hears,
> When once the hounds are in full cry.

These trifles at least serve to show that such exercises of the wits formed one of the pleasures of the court, that he entered into such pleasures and that he knew how to live in private as a man, as well as sustain the part of monarch in the theatre of the world.

Although his letter to the Archbishop of Rheims, concerning the Marquis de Barbesieux, is written in an extremely careless manner, it does more honour to his character than the cleverest thoughts could have done to his wit. He had conferred on that young man the post of Secretary of State for War, which his father, the Marquis de Louvois, had held before him. Soon dissatisfied with the conduct of his new secretary of state, he wished to remonstrate with him without humiliating him too much. To this end he appealed to his uncle, the Archbishop of Rheims, and begged him to admonish his nephew. In his letter he is like a master who knows all, or like a father speaking of his son.

"I know," he said, "what I owe to the memory of M. de Louvois; but if your nephew does not mend his ways I shall be compelled to take measures. I shall be sorry to do so, but it will be necessary. He has talents, but does not make good use of them. He gives too many supper parties to the princes, instead of working: he neglects his duty for pleasure; he keeps officers waiting too long in his antechamber; is arrogant in his speech with them and sometimes harsh."

That is what I remember of the letter, which I once saw in the original. It plainly shows that Louis XIV. was not ruled by his ministers, as has been thought, and that he knew how to control his ministers.

He was fond of praise, and it is desirable that a king should be so, since then he strives to deserve it. But Louis XIV. did not always welcome it when it was inordinate.

When the French Academy, which always gave him a list of the subjects proposed for prizes, named the following: *Of all the king's virtues, which is the one that is the most estimable?* the king blushed, and preferred not to have such a subject discussed. He tolerated the prologues of Quinault, but it was when he was at the height of his glory, at a time when the nation in their intoxication overlooked his own. Virgil and Horace, out of gratitude, and Ovid, with contemptible weakness, lavished much higher praises on Augustus, and, when one recalls to mind the proscriptions, much less deserved.

Had Corneille said to one of the courtiers in Cardinal Richelieu's apartment: "Tell his reverence the cardinal that I know more about poetry than he does," the minister would never have forgiven him; yet that is what Boileau said aloud to the king in a dispute which arose over some verses which the king thought good, and of which Boileau disapproved. "He is right," said the king, "he does know more about it than I do." The Duke of Vendôme had a boon companion, Villiers, one of those men of pleasure who make a merit of cynical licence. He lodged him in his apartment at Versailles, and he was commonly known as Villiers-Vendôme. Villiers loudly disapproved of Louis XIV.'s tastes in music, painting, architecture and gardens. Did the king plant a grove, furnish an apartment, or erect a fountain, Villiers found everything badly arranged, and expressed his opinion in no measured terms. "It is strange," said the king, "that Villiers should have singled out my house, in order to come and mock at everything that I do there."

Meeting him one day in the gardens: "Well," he said to him, showing him one of his latest contrivances, "this, I suppose, does not happen to please you?" "No," replied Villiers. "Nevertheless," replied the king, "there are many people who are far from displeased with it." "That may well be," retorted Villiers, "each to his own taste." Laughingly the king replied: "One cannot please everyone."

One day, when Louis XIV. was playing backgammon, a dispute arose over a move. A discussion ensued, and the courtiers remained silent. Count Grammont arrived on the scene. "Give us your decision," said the king to him. "Sire, it is you who are in the wrong," said the count. "And how can you say so, when you do not know what move I made?" "Well, sire, do you not see that had there been any doubt at all about it, all these gentlemen would have decided in your favour?"

The Duke d'Antin made himself conspicuous in that age by his remarkable gift, not for saying flattering things, but for performing them. The king went to pass the night at Petit Bourg, and remarked what a pity it was that a large avenue of trees hid the view of the river. The duke had them cut down during the night. The king on awakening was astonished at no longer seeing the trees of which he had disapproved. "It is because your majesty disapproved of them that you no longer see them," replied the duke.

We have also related elsewhere how the same man, having observed that the king took a dislike to a somewhat extensive wood bordering the canal at Fontainebleau, took the opportunity when he was out walking, and all being ready, gave orders for the wood to be felled, and the whole of it was immediately cut down. These are the acts of a clever courtier, not of a flatterer.

Louis XIV. has been accused of intolerable pride, because the base of his statue in the *Place des Victoires* is encircled with slaves in chains. But it was not he who erected that statue, nor the one in the *Place de Vendôme*. That in the *Place des Victoires* commemorates the greatness of soul of the first Marshal La Feuillade and his gratitude towards his sovereign. It cost him five hundred thousand livres, which would be worth a million to-day, and the town added as much again to have it erected. It is evident therefore that it was as much a mistake to ascribe the pompousness of that statue to Louis XIV., as to assume that the marshal's magnanimity was nothing else than vanity and flattery.

People could talk of nothing but the four slaves; but they represent vices repressed as much as nations conquered—the abolition of the duel and the suppression of the heresy; inscriptions also witness to this effect. They also record the union of the seas, the Peace of Nimeguen, and betoken acts of service rather than warlike exploits. Moreover, it is a time-honoured practice for sculptors to carve figures of slaves at the base of the statues of kings. It would be better still to represent there free and happy citizens; but, after all, slaves are to be seen at the base of the statues of the beloved Henri IV. and Louis XIII. in Paris; also at Leghorn beneath the statue of Ferdinand de' Medici, who certainly enslaved no nation, and in Berlin, under the statue of an Elector who repulsed the Swedes, but gained no conquests.

France's neighbours and even the French themselves have very unjustly made Louis XIV. responsible for this practice. The inscription: *Viro immortali, To the immortal man*, has been deemed idolatrous, as if that word signified aught else but the immortality of his glory. Viviani's inscription over his house in Florence: *Aedes a deo datae, A house bestowed by a god*, would seem much more idolatrous; yet it is only an allusion to the title of *Heaven-sent* and to Virgil's lines, *Deus nobis haec otia fecit (Ecl. I. v. 6)*.

With regard to the statue in the *Place de Vendôme*, it

was the city which erected it. The Latin inscriptions which occupy the four sides of the base are more grossly flattering than those on the statue in the *Place des Victoires*. There one reads that it was only against his will that Louis XIV. ever took up arms. On his death-bed he most solemnly refuted this extravagant compliment with words which will be remembered long after such inscriptions are forgotten, inscriptions which were merely the despicable work of certain men of letters.

The king had intended that the buildings surrounding this square should be constructed for his public library. The square was very large; it had at first three sides, forming the three fronts of an immense palace, whose walls were already built, when in 1701 the city was forced by the hardness of the times to build houses for private individuals on the ruins of the half-completed palace. The Louvre has consequently not been finished; and the fountain and obelisk which Colbert wished to have built opposite to the gate of Perrault exist only on paper; the beautiful gate of Saint-Gervais is thus left in gloom; and the greater part of the monuments of Paris leave much to be desired.

The nation would rather that Louis XIV. had preferred his Louvre and capital to the palace of Versailles, which the Duke de Créqui called a worthless favourite. Posterity gratefully admires the great things he did for the public; but criticism tempers our admiration when we see what defects there are in the splendour of Louis XIV.'s country house.

It follows from what we have related, that in everything this monarch loved grandeur and glory. A prince who, having accomplished as great things as he, could yet be of plain and simple habits, would be the first among kings, and Louis XIV. the second.

If he repented on his death-bed of having lightly gone to war, it must be owned that he did not judge by events; for of all his wars the most legitimate and necessary, namely, the war of 1701, was the only one unsuccessful.

By his marriage he had, besides *Monseigneur*, two sons and three daughters who died in infancy. He was more fortunate in his amours; only two of his natural children died in infancy; eight others survived and were legitimised, and five of them had issue. There was also a young girl, in attendance on Mme. de Montespan, an unacknowledged daughter, whom he married to a gentleman of the name of La Queue, who lived near Versailles.

There was every reason to suspect that one of the nuns at the convent of Moret was his daughter. She was very dark-skinned and resembled him in many ways beside. The king endowed her with twenty thousand crowns when placing her in this convent, and the belief she entertained that she was of high birth made her so haughty that her superiors complained of it. When on a journey to Fontainebleau Mme. de Maintenon visited the convent of Moret, and with the idea of instilling more modesty in this nun, she did what she could to dissuade her from the notion which was responsible for her haughtiness.

"Madame," that person said to her, "that a lady of your quality should take the trouble to come here especially to tell me that I am not the king's daughter, convinces me that I am." This anecdote is still related at the convent of Moret.

The description of so many details may be repellent to a philosopher; but curiosity, a failing that is common to all men, almost ceases to be so when it has for its object times and men who attract the notice of posterity.

CHAPTER XXIX

INTERNAL GOVERNMENT. JUSTICE. TRADE. POLICE. LAWS. MILITARY DISCIPLINE. NAVAL AFFAIRS, ETC.

ONE owes this much justice to public men who have benefited their own age, to consider the point from which they started in order to perceive more clearly the changes they wrought in their country. Posterity owes them eternal gratitude for the examples they gave, even though such examples have been surpassed. Such lawful glory is their only reward. It is certain that the love of such glory inspired Louis XIV., at the time of his taking the government into his own hands, in his desire to improve his kingdom, beautify his court and perfect the arts.

Not only did he impose upon himself the duty of regularly transacting affairs with each of his ministers, but any well-known man could obtain a private audience with him and any citizen was free to present petitions and projects to him.

The petitions were first received by a master of requests who wrote his recommendations in the margin; and they were then despatched to the ministerial offices. Projects were examined in council if they were thought worthy of such attention, and their authors were on more than one occasion admitted to discuss their proposals with the ministers in the king's presence. There was thus a channel between the throne and the nation which existed notwithstanding the absolute power of the monarch.

Louis XIV. trained and inured himself to work; work which was the more arduous to him as he was new to it and the allurement of pleasures might easily distract him. He wrote the first despatches to his ambassadors. The more important letters were often revised by his own hand, and he made it a habit to read every document which bore his name.

Colbert had scarcely restored the finances of the country after the fall of Fouquet, when the king rescinded all the taxes owing for the years 1647 to 1658—in particular, three millions of poll-taxes. Certain burdensome duties were removed by payment of five hundred thousand crowns a year. The Abbé de Choisi seemed thus much misinformed or very prejudiced when he said that the receipts had not decreased. They were undoubtedly decreased by such abatements and increased as a result of better methods of collection.

It was due to the efforts of the first president of Bellièvre, assisted by the benefactions of the Duchess d'Aiguillon and a few citizens, that the general hospital was founded. The king enlarged it and had others built in all the principal towns of the kingdom.

The great highways hitherto impassable were no longer neglected and became gradually what they are to-day under Louis XV.—the admiration of foreigners. Leaving Paris in any direction one may now travel from fifty to sixty miles to various places near at hand on well-paved roads bordered by trees. The roads constructed by the ancient Romans were more lasting, but not so wide and beautiful.

Colbert's genius was chiefly directed to commerce, which was as yet undeveloped and whose fundamental principles were as yet unknown. The English, and to a still greater extent the Dutch, carried nearly all the trade of France in their ships. The Dutch especially loaded up in our ports with French produce and distributed it throughout Europe.

In 1662 the king took steps to exempt his subjects from a tax known as *freight duty,* which was payable by all foreign ships; and allowed the French every facility for transporting their own goods themselves at lower charges. It was then that maritime trade sprang up. The council of commerce which is still in existence was established, and the king presided over it every fortnight. Dunkirk and Marseilles were declared free ports, a privilege which soon attracted the trade of the Levant to Marseilles and that of the North to Dunkirk.

A West India company was formed in 1664 and an East India company was established in the same year. Previous to this the luxury of France had been entirely dependent upon the industry of Holland. The supporters of the old system of economy, timid, ignorant and narrow-minded, vainly declaimed against a system of commerce by which money, which is imperishable, was continually being exchanged for perishable goods. They did not reflect that these wares from the Indies, which had become indispensable, would have been much dearer if bought from a foreign country. It is true that more money is sent to the East Indies than is received from them, and that Europe is thus impoverished. But the bullion itself comes from Peru and Mexico, being the price paid for our wares at Cadiz, and more of this money remains in France than is absorbed by the East Indies.

The king gave more than six millions of present-day money to the company; and urged wealthy people to interest themselves in it. The queens, princes and all the court provided two millions in the currency of the time, and the higher courts furnished twelve hundred thousand livres; financiers, two millions; the company of merchants, six hundred and fifty thousand livres. Thus the whole nation supported their ruler.

This company exists to the present day; for although the Dutch took Pondicherry in 1694 with the result that trade with the Indies declined from that time, it received a fresh impetus under the regency of the Duke of Orleans. Pondicherry then became the rival of Batavia, and this Indian company, founded under extremely adverse conditions by the great Colbert, re-established in our time by remarkable efforts, was for some years one of the principal resources of the kingdom. In 1669 the king also formed a Northern company; he contributed to its funds as to the Indian company. It was then clearly shown that there is nothing derogatory in trade, since the most influential houses took an interest in such establishments, following the example of their monarch.

The West India company was no less encouraged than the others, the king supplying a tenth part of the total funds.

He gave thirty francs for every ton exported and forty for every ton imported. All who built ships in national ports received five livres for every ton of carrying capacity.

One cannot be too much astonished that the Abbé de Choisi should have condemned these institutions in his *Memoirs*, which must not be relied upon. We perceive to-day all that Colbert in his capacity as minister did for the good of the nation, but it was not perceived at the time; he worked for ungrateful people. Paris resented his interference in suppressing certain revenues of the town hall acquired very cheaply since 1656, and the fall in the value of bank-notes, which had been lavishly poured out under the preceding ministry, much more than it appreciated what he had done for the common good. There were more merchants than good citizens. Few persons had any views on the public welfare. It is well known how private interests blind the eyes and cramp the mind; I am speaking not only of the interests of a merchant, but those of a company. those of a town. The rude answer given by a merchant, named Haxon, when consulted by Colbert, was still widely quoted in my youth: "You found the carriage overturned on one side and you have upset it on the other"; and this anecdote is to be found in Moreri. It was left for the spirit of philosophy, introduced at a very late period into France, to amend the prejudices of the people, before complete justice could be at length accorded to the memory of that great man. He had the same exactitude as the Duke de Sulli and possessed much wider views. The one could merely organise, the other could build up great institutions. After the Peace of Vervins, the only difficulty Sulli had to overcome was the maintenance of a rigid and strict economy; Colbert was obliged to provide at a moment vast resources for the wars of 1667 and 1672. Henri IV. assisted Sulli with his economy reforms, while the extravagance of Louis XIV. continually thwarted Colbert's efforts.

Nevertheless, there is little that was not either re-established or created in his time. In 1665, visible proof of a liberal circulation was forthcoming when the interest on the loans of the king and private individuals was reduced to five per cent. He wanted to enrich France and increase her population. People in the country were encouraged to marry by exempting those who had done so by the age of twenty from paying poll-tax for a period of five years; and every head of a family of ten children was exempt for the remainder of his life, since he gave more to the state by the product of his children's work than he would have done by paying taxes. Such a law should never have been repealed.

Each year of this ministry, from 1663 to 1672, was marked by the establishment of some manufacture. Fine stuffs, which had hitherto come from England and Holland, were now manufactured at Abbeville. The king advanced to the manufacturer two thousand livres for each loom at work, in addition to considerable grants. In the year 1669 there were 44,200 wool looms at work in the kingdom. Fine silk manufactures produced more than fifty millions in the currency of the time, and not only were the profits much greater than the outlay on the necessary silk, but the growing of mulberry trees enabled the manufacturers to dispense with foreign silk for the weaving of their material.

In 1666 glass began to be made as fine as that of Venice, which had hitherto supplied the whole of Europe, and soon French glass attained a splendour and beauty which have never been surpassed elsewhere. The carpets of Turkey and Persia were excelled at *La Savonnerie*. The tapestries of Flanders yielded to those of *Les Gobelins*. At that time more than eight hundred workmen were employed in the vast Gobelin works, and three hundred of them were actually lodged there; the finest painters directed the work, which was executed either from their designs or copied from those of the old Italian masters. It was in the precincts of the Gobelins that inlaid work was also produced—a delightful kind of mosaic work—and the art of marquetry was brought to perfection.

Besides the fine tapestry factory at *Les Gobelins* another was established at Beauvais. The first manufacturer in the town employed six hundred workmen, and the king made him a present of sixty thousand livres. Sixteen hundred girls were employed in making lace; thirty of the best operatives in Venice were engaged, and two hundred from Flanders;

and they were presented with thirty-six thousand livres to encourage them.

The manufactures of Sedan cloth and of Aubusson tapestry, which had deteriorated and dwindled, were again set going. Rich stuffs, in which silk was interwoven with gold and silver, were made at Lyons and Tours, with a fresh outburst of industry.

It is well known that the ministry bought from England the secret of that ingenious machine by which stockings can be made ten times more quickly than with the needle. Tin, steel, fine crockery-ware, morocco leather, which had always been brought from foreign countries, were now worked in France. But certain Calvinists, who possessed secrets of tin and steel smelting, carried them away with them in 1686, and shared them and many others with foreign nations.

Every year the king bought about eight hundred thousand livres' worth of works of art, manufactured in his kingdom, and gave them away as presents.

The city of Paris was very far from being what it is to-day. The streets were unlighted, unsafe and dirty. It was necessary to find money for the constant cleaning of the streets, for lighting them every night with five thousand lamps, completely paving the whole city, building two new gates and repairing the old ones, keeping the permanent guard, both foot and mounted, to ensure the safety of the citizens. The king charged himself with everything, drawing upon funds for such necessary expenses. In 1667 he appointed a magistrate whose sole duty was to superintend the police. Most of the large cities of Europe have imitated these examples long afterwards, but none has equalled them. There is no city paved like Paris, and Rome is not even illuminated.

In every sphere matters tended to become so perfect that the second-lieutenant of police in Paris earned a reputation in the performance of his duties which placed him on a level with those who did honour to their age; he was a man capable of anything. He was afterwards in the ministry, and would have made a good general in the army. The position of second-lieutenant of police was beneath his birth and capabilities; yet in filling that post he earned much greater reputation than when occupying an uneasy and transient office in the ministry towards the end of his life.

It should be here pointed out that M. d'Argenson was not by any means the only member of ancient chivalry who performed the office of a magistrate. France is almost the only country in Europe where the old nobility has so often donned the robe. Nearly all other countries, swayed by a relic of Gothic barbarism, are unaware of the greatness of this profession.

From 1661 the king was ceaseless in his building at the Louvre, Saint-Germain and Versailles. Following his example private individuals erected thousands of dwellings in Paris as magnificent as they were comfortable. Their number increased to such an extent that in the environs of the *Palais-Royal* and *St. Sulpice* two new towns sprang up in Paris, both vastly superior to the old. It was about this time that those magnificent spring carriages with mirrors were invented, so that a citizen of Paris could ride through the streets of that great city in greater luxury than the first Roman triumvirs along the road to the Capitol. Inaugurated in Paris, the custom soon spread throughout the whole of Europe, and, become general, it is no longer a luxury.

Louis XIV. took delight in architecture, gardens, and sculpture, his delight being for all that was grand and imposing. From 1664 the Comptroller-General Colbert, who was in charge of buildings, a duty properly belonging to the ministry of arts, devoted himself to the carrying out of his master's plans. The Louvre must first be finished, and François Mansard, one of the greatest French architects of all time, was chosen to construct the immense buildings that had been projected. He declined to proceed, unless he were allowed to alter certain parts already built which appeared to him defective. These doubts he cast on the scheme, to alter which would have entailed too great an expense, were the cause of his services being dispensed with. The cavalier Bernini was summoned from Rome, famous already for the colonnade surrounding the parvis of St. Peter's, the equestrian statue of Constantine, and the Navonna fountain. An equipage was provided for his journey. He was brought to Paris as a man come to do honour to France. He received, in addition to the five louis a day for the eight months he remained, a present of fifty thousand crowns and a pension of two thousand, and five hundred for his son. This generosity of Louis XIV. towards Bernini was yet greater than the munificence accorded to Raphael by Francis I. In gratitude Bernini afterwards cast at home the equestrian statue of the king which now stands at Versailles. But once arrived in Paris with so much pomp as the only man worthy to work for Louis XIV., he was not a little astonished to see the design of the façade of the Louvre on the Saint-Germain-l'Auxerrois side, which when finished shortly afterwards became one of the most imposing architectural monuments to be found in the world. Claude Perrault was the draughtsman, and it was executed by Louis Levau and Dorbay. He invented machines for conveying the stone blocks, fifty-two feet long, which form the pediment of this majestic building.

Men sometimes seek very far afield for what they have at home. Not a Roman palace has an entrance comparable to that of the Louvre, for which we are indebted to that Perrault upon whom Boileau dared to try to pour ridicule. In the opinion of travellers, those famous *vineyards* are not comparable to the *Château de Maisons*, which was built at such small cost by François Mansard. Bernini was magnificently remunerated, but did not deserve his rewards: he merely drew up plans which were never executed.

After building the Louvre, the completion of which is greatly to be desired, founding a town at Versailles close to the palace which cost so many millions, building Trianon, Marli, and beautifying so many other buildings, the king had completed building the Observatory, begun in 1666, at the time that he founded the Academy of Sciences. But the work glorious for its utility, its vastness and the difficulties of its construction, was the Languedoc canal, which connected the two seas, and finds an outlet in the port of Cette, built for that purpose. All these undertakings were begun after 1664 and were continued uninterruptedly until 1681. The founding of the Invalides and its chapel, the finest in Paris, the building of Saint-Cyr, the last of the edifices to be erected by that monarch, would alone suffice to hallow his memory. Four thousand soldiers and a large number of officers, who find consolation in their old age and relief for their wounds and needs in the former of those great institutions; two hundred and fifty girls of noble birth who receive in the latter an education worthy of their high position, are so many witnesses to the glory of Louis XIV.

The institution of Saint-Cyr will be surpassed by the one which Louis XV. is about to found for the education of five hundred noblemen, but so far from causing Saint-Cyr to be forgotten, it will remind one of it; the art of doing good is thus brought to perfection.

Louis XIV. resolved at the same time to do greater things, of more general utility as they were more difficult of accomplishment, and one of these was the remodelling of the laws. He instructed the chancellor Séguier, Lamoignon, Talon, Bignon and, above all, the state councillor, Pussort, to set to work. He was sometimes present at their meetings. The year 1667 marked the epoch of his earliest statutes as it did his earliest conquests. The civil code appeared first to be followed by the law of rivers and forests, and later statutes concerning every kind of manufacture; the criminal code, the laws of commerce and the marine laws were passed in annual succession. A new kind of justice was even introduced in favour of the negroes in French colonies, a people who had not hitherto possessed the rights of mankind.

A sovereign need not possess a profound knowledge of jurisprudence; but the king was well versed in the principal laws; he entered into their spirit, and knew when either to enforce or modify them as occasion demanded. He often passed judgment on his subjects' law-suits, not only in the council of the state secretaries, but in that one bearing the name of the *council of the parties*. Two judgments of his have become famous, in which he decided against himself.

The first case, which was tried in 1680, was an action between himself and certain private individuals in Paris who had erected buildings on his land. He gave judgment that the houses should remain to them with the land belonging to him, which he made over to them.

The other one concerned a Persian, named Roupli, whose merchandise had been seized by the clerks of his farms in 1687. His decision was that all should be returned to him, and he added a present of three thousand crowns. Roupli carried back to his own country his admiration and gratitude. When the Persian ambassador, Mehemet Rixabeg, came afterwards to Paris, it was discovered that he had long known of that action by the fame which it had spread abroad.

The suppression of duelling was one of the greatest services rendered to the country. Formerly such duels had been sanctioned by kings, even by parliament and by the Church, and though forbidden since the days of Henri IV., the pernicious practice was more prevalent than ever. The famous combat of the La Frettes in 1663, when eight combatants were engaged, determined Louis XIV. to pardon such duels no longer. His well-timed severity gradually reformed the nation and even neighbouring nations, who conformed to our wise customs after having copied our bad ones. At the present day the number of duels in Europe is a hundred times less than in the time of Louis XIII.

Legislator of his people, he was no less so of his armies. It is astonishing that before his time the troops had no uniform dress. It was he who in the first year of his administration decreed that each regiment should be distinguished by the colour of their uniform, or by different badges—a regulation which was soon adopted by all other nations. It was he who organised the brigadiers and gave the king's household troops the status they hold at the present day. He formed a company of musketeers from Cardinal Mazarin's guards and fixed the number of men for the two companies at five hundred, whom he furnished with the uniform they still wear to-day.

During this reign the post of High Constable was abolished, and after the death of the Duke of Épernon there were no more colonels-general of infantry; they were too much the master; he resolved to be the only master, and deserved to be so. Marshal Grammont, a mere colonel in the French guards under the Duke d'Épernon, and taking his orders from this brigadier-general, now only took them from the king, and was the first to bear the title of colonel of the guards; Louis himself appointed these colonels to the head of their regiments, presenting them with his own hands a gold gorget with a pike, and afterwards a spontoon, when the use of pikes was abolished. In the king's regiment, which is of his creation, he founded the grenadiers, at first to the number of four to each company; afterwards, he formed a company of grenadiers in each infantry regiment, and provided the French guards with two of them; at the present day there is one in every infantry battalion in the army. He greatly enlarged the corps of dragoons and gave them a brigadier-general. Nor must be forgotten the institution of breeding-studs in 1667. Heretofore, they had been absolutely neglected, and they were of great assistance in providing mounts for the cavalry; an important resource which has since been too much neglected.

The use of the bayonet attached to the end of the musket originated with him. Before his time they were sometimes employed, but only a few of the regiments fought with this weapon. There was no regular practice and no drill, all being left to the will of the general. Pikes were considered to be the most formidable weapon. The Fusiliers, founded in 1671, were the first regiment to employ bayonets and to be drilled in the use of that weapon.

The use to which artillery is put at the present day is entirely due to him. He established schools at Douai, and later at Metz and at Strasburg, and the artillery regiment found itself at last provided with officers who were nearly all capable of efficiently conducting a siege. All the magazines in the country were well stocked and eight thousand hundred-weights of powder were distributed amongst them every year. He formed a regiment of bombardiers and hussars; before his time hussars were only to be found among the enemy.

In 1688 he established thirty militia regiments, furnished and equipped by the communes. These regiments were trained for war, but they did not neglect the tilling of the land.

Companies of cadets were maintained at most of the frontier towns; they were taught mathematics, drawing, and all manner of drill, and carried out the duties of soldiers. This system was pursued for ten years. At length the difficulties in the way of training insubordinate youths proved too great; but the corps of engineers, formed by the king and for which he drew up regulations which still obtain, will last for ever. Under Louis XIV. the art of fortifying towns was brought to perfection by Marshal Vauban and his pupils, whose works surpassed those of Count Pagan. He constructed or rebuilt one hundred and fifty fortresses.

For the maintenance of military discipline, he created inspectors-general, and afterwards superintendents, who reported on the condition of the troops, and their reports showed whether the commissaries had carried out their duties.

He founded the Order of Saint Louis, and this honourable distinction was often more sought after than wealth itself. The Hôtel des Invalides crowned the efforts he made to be worthy of the faithful service of his subjects.

It was by such efforts that, from the year 1672, he possessed one hundred and eighty thousand regular troops, and increasing his forces proportionately to the increase in the number and power of his enemies he had at length as many as four hundred and fifty thousand men under arms, including the marines.

Before that time no such powerful armies had been seen. His enemies were able to put in the field armies almost as large, but to do so their forces were compelled to be united. He showed what France could do unaided, and had always, if not great success, at any rate great resources.

He was the first to give displays of war manœuvres and mimic warfare in times of peace. In 1698 seventy thousand troops were mustered at Compiègne. They performed all the operations of a campaign, the display being intended for the benefit of his three grandsons. The luxurious accompaniments of this military school made of it a sumptuous fête.

He was as assiduous in his efforts to secure the sovereignty of the seas as he had been to form numerous and well-trained armies upon land, even before war was declared. He began by repairing the few ships that Cardinal Mazarin had left to rot in the ports. Others were bought from Holland and Sweden, and in the third year of his government he despatched his maritime forces in an attempt to take Jijeli on the coast of Africa. In 1665 the Duke of Beaufort began to clear the seas of pirates, and two years later France had sixty warships in her ports. This was only a beginning, but while in the midst of making new regulations and fresh efforts, he was already conscious of his strength, and would not allow his ships to dip their flag to the English. It was in vain that King Charles II.'s council insisted on this right, which the English had acquired long since by reason of their power and labours. Louis XIV. wrote to his ambassador, Count d'Estrades, in these terms: "The King of England and his chancellor may see what forces I possess, but they cannot see my heart. I care for nothing apart from my honour."

He only said what he was determined to uphold, and in fact the English surrendered their claims and submitted to a natural right and Louis XIV.'s firmness. Equal conditions obtained between the two nations on the seas. But while insisting upon equality with England, Louis maintained his superiority over Spain. By reason of the formal precedence conceded in 1662, he compelled the Spanish admirals to dip their flag to his ships.

Meanwhile the work of establishing a navy capable of upholding such arrogant sentiments progressed everywhere. The town and port of Rochefort were built at the mouth of the Charente. Seamen of all classes were enrolled, some of whom were placed on merchant vessels and others distributed among the royal fleets. In a short time sixty thousand were enrolled.

Building commissions were set up in the ports so that ships might be constructed on the best possible lines. Five naval arsenals were built at Brest, Rochefort, Toulon, Dunkirk and Hâvre-de-Grâce. In 1672, there were 60 ships of the line and 40 frigates. In 1681, there were 198 ships of war, counting the auxiliaries and 30 galleys in the port of Toulon, either armed or about to be so; 11,000 of the regular troops served on the ships, and 3000 on the galleys. 166,000 men of all classes were enrolled for the various services of the navy. During the succeeding years there were a thousand noblemen or young gentlemen in this service, carrying out the duties of soldiers on board ship, and learning everything in harbour to do with the art of navigation and tactics; they were the marine guards, having the same rank at sea as the cadets on land. They had been formed in 1672, but in small numbers; they have since proved themselves a school which has produced the finest ships' officers in the navy.

As yet no officer in the marine corps had been made a Marshal of France, a proof that this vital part of France's forces had been neglected. Jean d'Estrées was made the first marshal in 1681. It seems that one of Louis XIV.'s great objects was to stir up rivalry for this honour in all classes, without which there is no initiative.

The French fleets held the advantage in every naval battle fought until the engagement of La Hogue in 1692, when Count de Tourville, obeying the orders of the court, attacked with forty ships a fleet of ninety English and Dutch ships; he was forced to yield to superior numbers and lost fourteen ships of the first class, which ran aground and were burnt in order to prevent them falling into the enemy's hands. In spite of this set-back the naval forces still held their own; but they deteriorated during the war of the succession. Subsequently Cardinal Fleury neglected to repair their losses during the leisure of a prosperous peace—the very time in which to re-establish them.

The naval forces greatly assisted in protecting trade. The colonies of Martinique, San Domingo and Canada, hitherto languishing, now flourished, and with unhoped-for success; for from 1635 to 1665 these settlements had been a burden upon the nation.

In 1664, the king established a colony at Cayenne and soon afterwards another in Madagascar. He sought by every means to redress the folly and misfortunes which France had brought upon herself by ignoring the sea, while her neighbours were founding empires at the ends of the world.

It will be seen by this cursory glance what great changes Louis XIV. brought about in the state; and that such changes were useful since they are still in force. His ministers vied with each other in their eagerness to assist him. The details, indeed the whole execution of such schemes was doubtless due to them, but his was the general organisation. There can be no shadow of doubt that the magistrates would never have reformed the laws, the finances of the country would not have been put on a sound basis, nor discipline introduced into the army, nor a regular police force instituted throughout the kingdom; there would have been no fleets, no encouragement accorded to the arts; all these things would never have been peacefully and steadily accomplished in such a short period and under so many different ministers, had there not been a ruler to conceive of such great schemes, and with a will strong enough to carry them out.

His own glory was indissolubly connected with the welfare of France, and never did he look upon his kingdom as a noble regards his land, from which he extracts as much as he can that he may live in luxury. Every king who loves glory loves the public weal; he had no longer a Colbert nor a Louvois, when about 1698 he commanded each comptroller to present a detailed description of his province for the instruction of the Duke of Burgundy. By this means it was possible to have an exact record of the whole kingdom and a correct census of the population. The work was of the greatest utility, although not every comptroller had the ability and industry of M. de Lamoignon of Baville. Had the comptroller of every province carried out the king's intent so well as the magistrate of Languedoc with regard to the numbering of the population, this collection of records would have been one of the finest achievements of the age. Some of them are well done, but a general scheme was lacking since the same orders were not issued to each comptroller. It is to be wished that each one had given in separate columns a statement of the number of inhabitants of each estate, such as nobles, citizens, labourers, artisans, workmen, cattle of all kinds, fertile, mediocre, and poor land, all clergy, both orthodox and secular, their revenues, and those of the towns and communes.

In most of the records submitted all these details are confused; the matter is not well thought out and inexact; one must search, often with great difficulty, for the needed information such as a minister should have ready to hand and be able to take in at a glance so as to ascertain with ease the forces, needs and resources at his disposal. The scheme was excellent, and had it been methodically carried out would have been of the greatest utility.

The foregoing is a general account of what Louis XIV. did or attempted to do in order to make his country more flourishing. It seems to me that one can hardly view all his works and efforts without some sense of gratitude, nor without being stirred by the love for the public weal which inspired them. Let the reader picture to himself the condition to-day, and he will agree that Louis XIV. did more good for his country than twenty of his predecessors together; and what he accomplished fell far short of what he might have done. The war which ended with the Peace of Ryswick began the ruin of that flourishing trade established by his minister Colbert, and the war of the succession completed it.

Had he devoted the immense sums which were spent on the aqueducts and works at Maintenon for conveying water to Versailles—works which were interrupted and rendered useless—to beautifying Paris and completing the Louvre; had he expended on Paris a fifth part of the money spent in transforming nature at Versailles, Paris would be in its entire length and breadth as beautiful as the quarter embracing the Tuileries and the Pont-Royal; it would have become the most magnificent city in the world.

It is a great thing to have reformed the laws, but justice has not been powerful enough to suppress knavery entirely. It was thought to make the administration of justice uniform; it is so in criminal cases, in commercial cases and in judicial procedure; it might also be so in the laws which govern the fortunes of private citizens.

It is in the highest degree undesirable that the same tribunal should have to give decisions on more than a hundred different customs. Territorial rights, doubtful, burdensome or merely troublesome to the community, still survive as relics of a feudal government which no longer exists; they are the rubbish from the ruins of a gothic edifice.

We do not claim that the different classes of the nation should all be subject to the same law. It is obvious that the customs of the nobility, clergy, magistrates and husband-men must all be different, but it is surely desirable that each class should be subject to the same law throughout the king-dom; that what is just or right in Champagne should not be deemed unjust or wrong in Normandy. Uniformity in every branch of administration is a virtue; but the difficulties that beset its achievement are enough to frighten the boldest statesman. It is to be regretted that Louis XIV. did not dispense more readily with the dangerous expedient of em-ploying tax-farmers, an expedient to which he was driven by the continual advance drawings he made on his revenues, as will be seen in the chapter on finance.

Had he not thought that his mere wish would suffice to compel a million men to change their religion, France would not have lost so many citizens. Nevertheless, this country, in spite of the shocks and losses she has sustained, is still one of the most flourishing in the world, since all the good that Louis XIV. did for her still bears fruit, and the mischief which it was difficult not to do in stormy times has been remedied. Posterity, which passes judgment on kings, and whose judgment they should continually have before them, will acknowledge, weighing the greatness and defects of that monarch, that though too highly praised during his lifctime, he will deserve to be so for ever, and that he was worthy of the statue raised to him at Montpellier, bearing a Latin inscription whose meaning is *To Louis the Great after his death*. A statesman, Don Ustariz, who is the author of works on the finance and trade of Spain, called Louis XIV. *a marvel of a man.*

All these changes that we have mentioned in the govern-ment and all classes of the nation inevitably produced a great change in customs and manners. The spirit of faction, strife and rebellion which had possessed the people since the time of Francis II., was transformed into a rivalry to serve their king. With the great landowning nobles no longer living on their estates, and the governors of the provinces no longer having important posts at their command, each man desired to earn his sovereign's favour alone: and the state became a perfect whole with all its powers centralised.

It was by such means that the court was freed from the intrigues and conspiracies which had troubled the state for so many years. There was but a single plot under the rule of Louis XIV. which was instigated in 1674 by La Truaumont,

a Norman nobleman, ruined by debauchery and debts, and
aided and abetted by a man of the House of Rohan, master
of the hounds of France, of great courage but little discretion.

The arrogance and severity of the Marquis de Louvois
had irritated him to such a point that on leaving him one
day he entered M. Caumartin's house, quite beside himself,
and throwing himself on a couch, exclaimed: "Either
Louvois dies . . . or I do." Caumartin thought that this outburst was only a passing fit of anger, but the next day, when
the same young man having asked him if he thought the
people of Normandy were satisfied with the government,
he perceived signs of dangerous plans. "The times of the
Fronde have passed away," he told him; "believe me, you
will ruin yourself, and no one will regret you." The chevalier
did not believe him, and threw himself headlong into the
conspiracy of La Truaumont. The only other person to
enter into the plot was a chevalier of Préaux, a nephew of
La Truaumont, who, beguiled by his uncle, won over his
mistress, the Marquise de Villiers. Their object and hope
was not and could not have been to raise a new party
in the kingdom; they merely aimed at selling and delivering
Quillebeuf into the hands of the Dutch and letting the
enemy into Normandy. It was rather a base and poorly
contrived piece of treachery than a conspiracy. The torture
of all the guilty parties was the only result of this senseless
and useless crime, which to-day is practically forgotten.

The only risings in the provinces were feeble disorders
on the part of the populace, which were easily suppressed.
Even the Huguenots remained quiet until their houses of
worship were pulled down. In a word, the king succeeded
in transforming a hitherto turbulent people into a peace-
loving nation, who were dangerous only to their foes, after
having been their own enemies for more than a hundred
years. They acquired softer manners without impairing
their courage.

The houses which all the great nobles built or bought in
Paris, and their wives who lived there in fitting style, formed
schools of gentility, which gradually drew the youth of the
city away from the tavern life which was for so long the
fashion, and which only encouraged reckless debauchery.
Manners depend upon such little things that the custom of
riding on horseback in Paris tended to produce frequent
brawls, which ceased when the practice was discontinued.

Propriety, due in large part to the ladies who gathered circles of society in their *salons*, made wits more agreeable, and reading in the long run made them more profound. Treason and great crimes, such as bring no disgrace upon men in times of sedition and intrigue, were now hardly known. The enormities of the Brinvilliers and the Voisins were merely passing storms in an otherwise clear sky, and it would be as unreasonable to condemn a nation for the notorious crimes of a few individuals, as it would be to canonise a people for the reforms of a La Trappe.

Hitherto all the various professions could be recognised by their characteristic failings. The military and the youths who intended to take up the profession of arms were of a hot - headed nature; men of law displayed a forbidding gravity, to which their custom of always going about in their robes, even at court, contributed not a little. It was the same with university graduates and with physicians. Merchants still wore their short robes at their assemblies and when they waited upon ministers, and the greatest merchants were as yet but unmannerly men; but the houses, theatres, and public promenades, where everyone began to meet in order to partake of more refined pleasures, gradually gave to all citizens almost the same outward appearance. It is noticeable at the present day, even behind a counter, how good manners have invaded all stations of life. The provinces in time also experienced the effects of these changes.

We have finally come to enjoy luxury only in taste and convenience. The crowd of pages and liveried servants has disappeared, to allow greater freedom in the interior of the home. Empty pomp and outward show have been left to nations who know only how to display their magnificence in public and are ignorant of the art of living. The extreme ease which obtains in the intercourse of society, affable manners, simple living and the culture of the mind, have combined to make Paris a city which, as regards the harmonious life of the people, is probably vastly superior to Rome and Athens during the period of their greatest splendour.

These ever-present advantages, always at the service of every science, every art, taste or need; so many things of real utility combined with so many others merely pleasant and coupled with the freedom peculiar to Parisians, all these attractions induce a large number of foreigners to travel or take up their residence in this, as it were, birthplace of society. The few natives who leave their country are those who, on account of their talents, are called elsewhere, and are an honour to their native land; or they are the scum of the nation who endeavour to profit by the consideration which the name of France inspires; or they may be emigrants who place their religion even before their country, and depart elsewhere to meet with misfortune or success, following the example of their forefathers who were expelled from France by that irreparable insult to the memory of the great Henri IV.—the revocation of his perpetual law of the Edict of Nantes; or finally they are officers dissatisfied with the ministry, culprits who have escaped the vigorous laws of a justice which is at times ill-administered, a thing which happens in every country in the world.

People complain at no longer seeing that pride of bearing at court. There are certainly no longer petty autocrats, as at the time of the Fronde, under Louis XIII., and in earlier ages; but true greatness has come to light in that host of nobles so long compelled in former times to demean themselves by serving over-powerful subjects. To-day one sees gentlemen, citizens who would formerly have considered themselves honoured to be servants of these noblemen, now become their equals and very often their superiors in the military service.

The more that services rendered are accounted above titles of nobility, the more flourishing is the condition of the state.

The age of Louis XIV. has been compared with that of Augustus. It is not that their power and individual events are comparable; Rome and Augustus were ten times more considered in the world than Louis XIV. and Paris, but it must be remembered that Athens was the equal of the Roman Empire in all things whose value is not dependent upon might and power.

We must also bear in mind that there is nothing in the world to-day to compare with ancient Rome and Augustus, yet Europe taken as a whole is vastly superior to the whole of the Roman Empire. In the time of Augustus there was but a single nation, while at the present day there are several nations, all civilised, warlike, and enlightened, who cultivate arts unknown to the Greeks and Romans; and of these nations, there is none that has shone more brilliantly in every sphere for nearly a century, than the nation moulded to a great extent by Louis XIV.

CHAPTER XXX

FINANCE AND PUBLIC ADMINISTRATION

IF Colbert's administration be compared with all preceding administrations, posterity will cherish the memory of that man, whose body the maddened populace wished to tear in pieces after his death. The French certainly owe their industries and trade to him, and consequently that wealth whose sources are sometimes diminished in time of war, but which always become again abundant in time of peace. Nevertheless, in 1702, people were so ungrateful as to charge Colbert with the general depression which was beginning to make itself felt in every department of the state. About that time a certain Bois-Guillebert, a lieutenant-general in the bailiwick of Rouen, published a work entitled *Description of France* in two small volumes, in which he claimed that everything had been on the decline since 1660. This was exactly contrary to the truth. France had never been in such a flourishing state as from the death of Cardinal Mazarin to the war of 1689, and even during that war the body of the state, though beginning to feel distress, was sustained by the vigour which Colbert had infused into every limb. The author of the *Description* maintained that since 1660 the landed property of the kingdom had diminished in value by fifteen hundred millions. Nothing was more false nor more improbable. However, these captious arguments convinced those who wished to be so that the absurd paradox was true. The same thing happens in England, where at her most flourishing periods there are hundreds of pamphlets published proving that the state is ruined. It was, however, easier in France than elsewhere to discredit the ministry of finance in the minds of the people. This ministry is the most hated for the simple reason that taxes are always hated: moreover, as many prejudices and as much ignorance prevailed in general in financial matters as in philosophy.

Instruction has been so long delayed that even in our days, in 1718, one hears parliament in a body tell the Duke of Orleans that "the intrinsic value of the silver mark is twenty-five livres"; as if there were any real and intrinsic value other than that of weight and standard; and the Duke of

Orleans, though an extremely well-educated man, had not sufficient intelligence to refute this mistake of parliament.

Colbert brought both knowledge and genius to the administration of the finance department. Like the Duke de Sulli, he began by putting a stop to fraudulent practices and pilferings which were enormous. The collecting of taxes was simplified as far as possible, and by exercising an economy which was little short of miraculous, he increased the king's treasury and at the same time reduced the poll-tax. It will be seen from the memorable decree of 1664, that a sum of one million in contemporary currency of the period was annually devoted to the encouragement of manufactures and maritime trade. So little did he neglect agriculture, which had hitherto been abandoned to the rapacity of tax-farmers, that when English merchants offered to his brother, M. Colbert de Crossi, French ambassador in London, in 1667, to supply France with Irish cattle and salted provisions for the colonies, the comptroller-general replied that for the last four years they had been re-selling them to foreign countries.

To succeed in establishing such an admirable system of administration it was necessary to create a court of justice and bring about certain sweeping reforms. He was obliged to cancel more than eight millions of municipal stock, acquired at an extremely low price, the holders receiving the same price that they themselves had paid. Such various changes required decrees. Since the time of Francis I. parliament had had the right to examine them. It was proposed to have them registered simply by the chamber of accounts; but the old method of procedure prevailed; and in 1664 the king himself went to parliament to supervise the passing of his decrees.

He never forgot the Fronde, the proscription of a cardinal, his first minister, and the other decrees authorising the seizure of the royal funds, and the plundering of the goods and money of citizens attached to the crown. All these abuses having begun by protestations against decrees concerning state revenues, in 1667 the king decreed that parliament should make no protest after the lapse of a week, having once recorded their allegiance. The edict was renewed in 1673, and accordingly, during the whole course of his administration, he suffered no protest from any judicial court, except in the fateful year of 1709, when the parliament of Paris vainly protested against the injury which the minister of finance did to the state by varying the price of gold and silver.

Nearly all citizens were convinced that had parliament, knowing the causes of such things, confined itself to bringing to the close attention of the king, the misfortunes and the needs of the people, the dangers of taxation and the still greater danger of such taxes being sold to farmers who both deceived the king and oppressed the people, the right of making remonstrances would have become an inviolable resource of the state, a check on the rapacity of financiers, and a perpetual warning to ministers. But the strange abuses of so wholesome a remedy had so exasperated Louis XIV. that he saw nothing but the abuses and condemned the remedy. His indignation reached such a pitch that in 1669, on 13 August, he again attended parliament in person for the purpose of revoking the privileges of nobility, previously granted to all higher courts in 1664, during his minority.

But in spite of this decree, registered in the presence of the king, the custom has remained of allowing all whose fathers have held a judicial office in a higher court for twenty years, or who had died in office, to enjoy such privileges of nobility.

In thus humbling a body of magistrates, he desired to encourage both the nobles who defend the country and the farmers who supply it with food. Already in a decree of 1666 he had granted an annuity of two thousand francs, worth at the present day nearly four thousand, to every gentleman who had twelve children, and a thousand francs to those who had ten. Half of this gratuity was guaranteed to all the inhabitants of towns who were exempted from paying poll-tax, and, of those who were taxable, every father of a family who had or who had had ten children was free from all taxes.

It is true that Colbert did not do all that he could have done, still less all that he wished to do. Men's minds were not yet sufficiently enlightened, and in a great kingdom there are always great abuses. The arbitrary poll-tax, the multiplicity of dues, the custom duties payable from one province to another, which make the people of one part of France strangers and even enemies to another, the different standards of weight from town to town, and twenty other ills in the body politic, could not be cured.

The greatest mistake attributed to that minister is that

of not daring to encourage the export of wheat. No wheat had been exported to foreign countries for many years. Its cultivation had been neglected during the stormy period of Richelieu's ministry, and it was still more neglected during the civil wars of the Fronde. In 1661 famine completed the desolation of the land, which nature, however, aided by labour, is always ready to repair. In that disastrous year the parliament of Paris passed a decree which, while in principle appearing just, proved nearly as fatal in its consequences as all the decrees wrung from that body during the civil wars. Merchants were forbidden, under the severest penalties, from entering into any association for the marketing of wheat, and individuals were prohibited from hoarding it. What was good in a time of temporary famine became harmful in the long run, and discouraged all farming whatsoever. To have annulled such a decree at a critical and unfavourable moment would have meant a revolution among the lowest class.

The minister was reduced to the necessity of buying dearly from foreign countries the very wheat which the French had formerly sold to them in years of plenty. The people had food, but at great cost to the state; the order which Colbert had introduced into the country finances, however, rendered this loss a light one.

The fear of another famine closed all French ports to the exportation of wheat. Each provincial comptroller, moreover, prided himself on opposing the passage of wheat from his own to a neighbouring province. Even in prosperous times wheat could only be sold by permission of the council. This fatal regulation appeared justified by past experience. Every member of the council feared that any trading in wheat would compel them once more to repurchase that necessary commodity at a high cost from other nations, which the self-interest and shortsightedness of the growers would incline to sell very cheaply.

Thus the peasant farmer, still more timorous than the council, feared to be ruined if he raised a commodity from which he could hope to obtain no great profit, and the land was consequently not so well tilled as it should have been. The fact that all the other departments of the administration were in a flourishing state prevented Colbert from applying a remedy to the defect in the principal department of all.

It is the only blot on his ministry, and it is a great one;

but what excuses it and proves how unpopular is the task of eradicating such prejudices inherent in French administration and how difficult is the task of doing right, is the fact that this defect, though apparent to all intelligent citizens, was not remedied by any minister for fully a hundred years, until the memorable epoch of 1764, when a more enlightened comptroller-general relieved France from profound distress by restoring to her free trade in wheat, with restrictions almost identical with those commonly in use in England.

About 1672, in order to provide for the expenses of wars, buildings and entertainments, Colbert was obliged to renew what he had at first intended to abolish for ever, namely, the farming of taxes, government stocks, sale of new offices, increase of pledges on crown property, in a word, everything which maintains the state for a certain length of time, but encumbers it for centuries.

He went beyond the limits he had prescribed for himself: for from all his writings which remain one can perceive that he was convinced that the wealth of a nation lies in the number of its inhabitants, in the cultivation of the land, in industry and trade; and it is thus obvious that the king, possessing very few estates of his own and being only the trustee for the property of his subjects, really became rich only by taxes which are easily collected and equally distributed.

Colbert was so afraid of delivering the state into the hands of tax-farmers that a short time after the dissolution of the Court of Justice, which he had had instituted against them, he sanctioned a decree of the council which ordained the death penalty against anyone who should advance money on new taxes. By this comminatory decree, which was never printed, he sought to intimidate the cupidity of business men. But soon afterwards he was obliged to utilise their services without even repealing the decree; the king was urgent, and prompt measures were necessary.

This expedient, brought to France from Italy by Catherine de' Medici, had so corrupted the government by its fatal facility, that, after having been suppressed during the prosperous reign of Henri IV., it reappeared during the whole of Louis XIII.'s reign, and infected especially the latter years of Louis XIV.

In short, while Sulli enriched the state by wise economy,

being supported by a king as parsimonious as he was brave, a soldier king who rode at the head of his army, and a father to his people; Colbert sustained the state in spite of the extravagance of a pompous master who was lavish of everything that would make his reign more brilliant.

It is recorded that on Colbert's death, when the king proposed to appoint Le Pelletier Minister of Finance, Le Tellier said to him: "Sire, he is not fitted for that post." "Why?" asked the king. "He is not hard-hearted enough," replied Le Tellier. "But," replied the king, "I have no wish that my people should be treated harshly." The new minister was certainly well-meaning and just, but in 1688, when the country was again plunged into war and had to contend against the League of Augsburg, that is to say, against nearly the whole of Europe, he found himself saddled with a burden which even Colbert found too heavy, and his first resource was the easy and fatal expedient of borrowing and creating government stocks. In the next place he proposed to cut down luxuries, which, in a kingdom full of manufactures, is to cut down industry and the circulation of money, and which only a nation that obtains its luxuries from abroad should do.

Orders were given that all solid silver ornaments, which were to be seen in large numbers of the houses of great noblemen—a sure sign of affluence—were to be delivered up to the Mint. The king set the example, and parted with all his silver tables, candelabra, fine solid silver couches, and all his other furniture, which were masterpieces of carving from the hands of Ballin, an artist unique of his kind, and all executed from designs by Lebrun. They had cost ten millions; they produced three. The wrought silver ornaments of private individuals yielded three more millions. The resource was slight.

Then the ministry committed one of those huge blunders which has only been lately rectified; it altered the currency, changed the standards of the new coinage, giving a value to the crown out of all proportion to that of the quarter; the result was that as quarters were increased in value and crowns diminished, all quarters passed over into foreign countries; there they were coined as crowns, and thus a profit was made by sending them back again to France. A country must indeed be sound at heart to be still powerful after having sustained such blows so often. Ignorance was as yet rife; finance, like physics, was still a science based on idle conjecture. Tax-farmers were so many charlatans who cheated the ministry, and they cost eighty millions to the state. It takes twenty years of toil and drudgery to repair such losses.

By 1691 and 1692 the state finances were consequently considerably disorganised. Those who attributed the reduction in the sources of wealth to the extravagance of Louis XIV. on his palaces, the arts, and his entertainments, were unaware that expenditure which encourages industry, so far from impoverishing, actually enriches a state. It is war that evitably impoverishes the public treasure, unless it be replenished with the spoils of a defeated enemy. But I know of no nation that has enriched itself by its victories since the ancient Romans. Italy in the sixteenth century owed her riches to her trade. Holland would never have existed long as a power had she confined herself to capturing the Spanish silver fleet, without drawing the means of her subsistence from the East Indies. England has always impoverished herself by war even when defeating the French fleets; and trade alone has enriched her. The Algerians, who have practically nothing save what they gain from piracy, are a very wretched people.

Among the European nations a few years of war place the victor in almost as desperate a situation as the vanquished. War is a gulf in which all channels of prosperity are swallowed up. Ready money, the source of all prosperity and all misfortune, raised with so much trouble in the provinces, finds its way into the coffers of a hundred contractors and a hundred of their partisans, who advance the capital and purchase by such advances the right of plundering the nation in the sovereign's name. Private individuals, upon this looking upon the government as their enemy, conceal their money, and a deficient circulation weakens the resources of the kingdom.

No hasty remedy can take the place of a settled and stable economic scheme, established long since. The poll-tax was instituted in 1695. It was abolished at the Peace of Ryswick and immediately restored. In 1696, Pontchartrain, the comptroller-general, sold letters of nobility for two thousand crowns apiece; five hundred individuals bought them, but the resource was temporary while the disgrace was permanent. All nobles, both old and new, were forced to register their coats-of-arms and to pay for the permission to seal their letters with their heraldic arms. Special and illegal tax-gatherers dealt with this affair and advanced money. The ministry almost without exception employed such petty expedients in a country which could have furnished greater ones.

The ministry did not venture to levy the *dixième* (that is, a tenth part of the individual's total income) until 1710. But this tax, following in the wake of so many other oppressive taxes, was so much resented that it was not vigorously enforced. The government derived no more than twenty-five millions yearly from it at forty francs to the mark.

Colbert had made slight changes in the cash value of the currency. It is better not to change it at all. Gold and silver, the bases of exchange, should be invariable standards. He had only increased the cash value of the silver mark from twenty-six francs to twenty-seven or twenty-eight, and during the last years of Louis XIV. his successors raised the imaginary value of this coin to forty livres; a fatal proceeding by which the king was relieved for a moment only to be ruined the next; for instead of receiving one silver mark he now received little more than half. A man owing twenty-six livres in 1668 would pay one mark, and in 1710 a man owing forty livres would pay very much the same amount, i.e. one mark. The lowered values unsettled what little trade there remained as much as the increased values had done.

A paper currency would have proved an adequate expedient, but such paper money should be introduced in a time of prosperity, and can then hold its own in difficult times.

In 1706 the minister Chamillart began to use a certain kind of paper money for payments; notes were issued from the Mint in exchange for used coin, and notes known as *billets de subsistance et d'ustensiles* were also given to persons in payment for the billeting of troops; but as this paper money was refused by the king's treasury, it was discredited almost as soon as it appeared. The government was reduced to continue borrowing heavily and pledging four years of crown revenue in advance.

What were known as extraordinary measures were continually being adopted; ridiculous offices were created which were always bought by those eager to avoid payment of the poll-tax; for this tax being considered degrading in France, and all men being vain by nature, the bait of freeing them from this ignominy will always dupe them; and the high wages attached to such newly-created posts tempt people to buy them in difficult times, not stopping to think they will be abolished in more prosperous days.

Thus in 1707 the posts of overseers of the king's vine-dressers and wine-brokers were instituted, and these produced 180,000 livres. The offices of royal recorders and of sub-deputies to the comptrollers of provinces were created; likewise king's councillor comptrollers for the superintendence of the storing of timber, superintendents of police, officers of royal barbers and wig-makers, controller-overseers of fresh butter-making, tasters of salted butter. We smile at such follies now; but they were wept for them.

The comptroller-general, Desmarets, a nephew of the illustrious Colbert, who succeeded Chamillart in 1708, was unable to remedy an evil which everything tended to make incurable.

Nature conspired with misfortune to crush the state. The bitter winter of 1709 compelled the king to remit nine millions of poll-tax to the people at a time when he could not pay his troops. The scarcity of food was such that it cost forty-five millions to feed the army. The expenditure of the year 1709 amounted to two hundred and twenty-one millions, and the ordinary revenue of the king did not produce forty-nine. It was consequently necessary to ruin the state to preserve it from its enemies. Disorder increased to such an extent and so little was done to check it, that long after peace was signed at the beginning of 1715, the king was obliged to pledge thirty-two millions of notes, in exchange for eight millions in cash, and at his death he left two thousand six hundred million livres of debts, at twenty livres to the mark, to which the currency was at that time reduced, and which amounts to about four thousand five hundred million livres in our currency of 1760.

It is astonishing but nevertheless true that this enormous debt would not have been an impossible burden to bear had trade been in a flourishing condition, paper money honoured, and had there existed solid companies as security for the money, as in Sweden, England, Venice and Holland; for when a powerful state is in debt to no one but itself, confidence and the circulation of money are sufficient to remove it, but France at that time was far from possessing sufficient resources to set such a huge complicated machine in motion, whose very weight was crushing her.

In the course of his reign Louis XIV. spent eighteen milliards, which amounts on an average to a yearly expenditure of three hundred and thirty millions, compensation being made for the rise and fall in the value of money.

Under the great Colbert's administration the ordinary revenues of the crown only amounted to one hundred and seventeen millions at twenty-seven livres, and afterwards twenty-eight livres, to the silver mark. Thus the whole of the surplus expenditure was provided by extraordinary measures. Colbert, the greatest enemy of this baneful expedient, was obliged to make use of it, in order to obtain the money promptly. During the war of 1672 he borrowed eight hundred millions in present-day currency. Scarcely any of the old crown lands were left to the king. They have been declared the inalienable property of the crown by every parliament in the kingdom, and yet they have nearly all of them been transferred. At the present day the king's revenue is vested in that of his subjects: it is a perpetual interchange of debts and payments.

The king owes his subjects annually more millions in cash in the form of dividends on municipal stock, than any king has ever received from crown lands.

To gain an idea of this enormous increase in taxes, debts, wealth, circulation of money, and at the same time of disorganisation and misery, which France and other countries have experienced, one has only to consider that on the death of Francis I. the state was in debt to the extent of about thirty thousand livres for perpetual municipal stock, and that at the present day the debt amounts to more than forty-five millions.

Those who have sought to compare the revenue of Louis XIV. and Louis XV. have found that, with regard to the fixed and current revenue alone, Louis XIV. was much more wealthy in 1683, at the time of Colbert's death, with one hundred and seventeen millions of revenue than his successor in 1730 with nearly two hundred millions, and this is entirely borne out by a consideration merely of the fixed and ordinary revenues of the crown, since one hundred and seventeen millions in specie at twenty-eight livres to the mark are worth more than two hundred millions at forty-nine livres, which was the amount of the king's revenue in 1730; moreover, one must take into account the losses caused by the borrowings of the crown; the king's revenues, however—

that is to say, the state revenues—were afterwards increased, and an understanding of finance affairs was so far improved that during the disastrous war of 1741 the country was never for a moment insolvent. The expedient of establishing sinking-funds has been resorted to in imitation of the English; it has become necessary to adopt some part of their financial system as also of their philosophy; and were it possible to introduce into an essentially monarchic state those circulating notes, which at least double the wealth of England, the government of France would attain to the last degree of perfection, but a perfection perhaps too near abuse under a monarchical system.

In 1683 there was a silver coinage to the value of about five hundred millions in the kingdom; and in 1730 about twelve hundred millions according to present-day reckoning. But under Cardinal Fleury's ministry the metallic currency was nearly double of that during Colbert's administration. It would therefore appear that France was only about a sixth part richer in circulating wealth after Colbert's death. True, she has a much greater wealth of manufactured gold and silver wares for purposes of utility and luxury. In 1690, there were only a hundred millions' worth of such articles in present-day currency, but by the year 1730 they were worth as much as the coinage in circulation. Nothing shows more plainly how trade, whose sources were first opened by Colbert, has grown when once the channels necessarily closed in time of war have again been opened. The industries of the country have been perfected, despite the emigration of so many skilled workmen driven from their country by the revocation of the Edict of Nantes, and these industries are daily increasing. The nation is capable of accomplishing as great and even greater things than were achieved under Louis XIV., because initiative and commerce always become invigorated when they are encouraged.

To see the affluence of private individuals, the enormous number of comfortable houses in Paris and in the provinces, the quantity of carriages, the commodities and refinements known under the general name of luxury, one would think that there was twenty times as much wealth as formerly; but all this is rather the product of ingenious labour than of great wealth. It costs but little more to-day to be housed comfortably than it did to be housed wretchedly under Henri IV.

A beautiful mirror of French manufacture now decks our houses at far less cost than the little mirrors we formerly bought from Venice. Our beautiful and ornamental stuffs are much cheaper than those formerly imported from abroad, and also of better quality.

In fact, it is not gold and silver that ensure the comforts of life, but industrial initiative. A people who possessed nothing beside those precious metals would be very wretched; a people who lacked those metals, but successfully cultivated all the products of the land, would indeed be rich. France possesses this advantage, together with a larger quantity of precious metals than it is necessary to put into circulation.

As skilled labour was brought to greater perfection in the towns, it spread into the country districts as well. Complaints will always be raised about the conditions of the tillers of the land. They are heard in every country in the world and are nearly always the murmurings of the idle rich, who condemn the government much more than they sympathise with the people. It is true that in almost every country, if those who pass their days in rustic toil had the leisure to complain, they would rebel against the exactions which deprive them of a part of their livelihood. They would express their detestation of being compelled to pay taxes which they have not imposed upon themselves and to carry the burden of the state without sharing in the advantages enjoyed by other citizens. It is not within the province of history to enquire how much the people should contribute to the state without being oppressed, or to mark the precise point, always a difficult matter, between the just carrying out of laws and their abuse, between taxation and robbery; but history should point out how impossible it is for a town to flourish unless the surrounding country is also flourishing; for it is undoubtedly the country which feeds the towns. On certain days one hears, in every town in France, reproaches made by those whose profession permits them to declaim in public against the various kinds of commodities which come under the name of luxuries. It is obvious that such luxuries can only be supplied by the skilled labour of the workers in the fields, and is always dearly paid for.

More vines were planted and were better cultivated; new wines unknown before were produced, such as those of Champagne, which were given the colour, body and strength of those of Burgundy, and big profits are repeated from their sale in foreign countries; this increase in the production of wines led also to the making of brandies. Extraordinary developments were made in the cultivation of gardens, vegetables and fruits, and the provision trade with the American colonies was largely augmented as a result; the complaints which have ever been raised of the misery of the countryside now ceased to have any ground for justification

Besides, in these vague complaints no distinction is made between growers, peasant farmers and labourers. The last live simply by the work of their hands; and thus it is in all countries of the world, where the majority must exist by manual toil. But there is hardly a kingdom in the world where the husbandman and farmer live under more comfortable conditions than in certain provinces of France; England alone can dispute the claim. The proportionate poll-tax, substituted in place of the arbitrary one in certain provinces, has still further helped to consolidate the prosperity of those farmers in possession of ploughs, vineyards and gardens. The farm-labourer, the workman, work because forced to do so by necessity; it is the lot of man. The greater number of such men are bound to be poor, but they need not be wretched.

The middle classes enriched themselves by industry. Ministers and courtiers became less wealthy, since while the amount of money in circulation had increased by nearly a half, salaries and pensions remained the same, and the price of food and commodities had almost doubled; in every country in Europe the same thing happened. Titles and fees remained everywhere on the old footing. An elector, receiving the investiture of his states, pays only what his predecessors paid at the time of the Emperor Charles IV. in the fourteenth century, and no more than a single crown is due to the Emperor's secretary for his services in that ceremony.

What is still more extraordinary is that while everything has increased, the sum total of the currency, the quantity of gold and silver bullion, the price of commodities, nevertheless the soldier's pay has remained the same as it was two hundred years ago; foot-soldiers receive five sous in cash just as they did in the time of Henri IV. Not one of all these ignorant men, who sell their lives so cheaply, is aware that, taking into account the raising of the currency and the high prices of food and commodities, he is receiving about two-thirds less than the soldiers of Henri IV. If he knew it and demanded an increase of two-thirds of his pay, he would have to be given it; in that event every European power would maintain but one-third of its present troops, the forces would remain in the same proportion, and agriculture and manufactures would profit by it.

It should further be observed that, owing to the increasing profits of trade and the decrease in real value of all high official appointments, there is less wealth than formerly among the great and more among the middle class; the result has been to lessen the distance between classes. Formerly the poor had no other alternative but to serve the great; to-day industry has opened a thousand paths that were unknown a century ago. Thus, however state finances may be administered, France possesses an incalculable treasure in the labours of nearly twenty millions of inhabitants.

CHAPTER XXXI

SCIENCE

This happy age, which saw the birth of a revolution in the human mind, gave at its commencement no signs of such a destiny; to begin with philosophy, there seemed no likelihood in the time of Louis XIII. that it would extricate itself from the chaos in which it was plunged. The Inquisition in Italy, Spain and Portugal had linked philosophical errors with religious dogmas; the civil wars in France and the Calvinist disputes were not more calculated to elevate human reason than was the fanaticism in England at the time of Cromwell. No sooner did a canon of Thorn resuscitate the ancient planetary system of the Chaldeans, so long buried in oblivion, than its truth was condemned at Rome; and the Brotherhood of the Holy Office, composed of seven cardinals, having pronounced the movement of the earth, without which there can be no true science of astronomy, not merely heretical, but absurd, and the great Galileo having asked forgiveness, at the age of seventy, for having spoken the truth, there seemed no likelihood that truth could be established upon earth.

Chancellor Bacon had pointed out the way from afar;

Galileo had discovered the laws of falling bodies; Torricelli was on the point of discovering the weight of the air surrounding us, and various experiments had been made at Magdeburg. Ignoring these few attempts, the schools persisted in their folly, and the world in its ignorance. Then came Descartes; he did the opposite to what he should have done; instead of studying Nature, he sought to interpret her. He was the greatest geometrician of his age; but geometry leaves the mind where it finds it. Descartes' geometry was too much given to flights of fancy. He who was the foremost among mathematicians wrote scarcely anything else but philosophic romances. A man who scorned to make experiments, who never quoted Galileo, who thought to build without materials, could erect but an imaginary structure.

All that was romantic in his book succeeded, while the scraps of truth intermingled in these new extravagances were at first contested. But at length this modicum of truth prevailed, thanks to the system he had introduced. Before him no one had had a thread in the labyrinth; he at least provided one which others made use of, when he himself had gone astray. It was much to destroy the delusions of Peripateticism, though it was by the introduction of others. Each strove for mastery; each fell in due season, leaving reason to raise itself on their ruins. About 1655, Cardinal Leopold de' Medici had founded a society for making experiments in Florence, under the name of *del Cimento*. In that country of the arts it was already felt that one could only understand anything of the vast edifice of Nature by examining it piece by piece. After Galileo's death, and from the time of Torricelli, this Academy rendered great services.

In England under Cromwell's sombre rule, a few philosophers met together for the purpose of seeking truth in peace, while elsewhere fanaticism suppressed all truth. Recalled to the throne of his forefathers by a repentant and fickle nation, Charles II. presented letters patent to this budding academy; but this was the government's only gift. The Royal Society, or rather the Free Society of London, worked for the honour of working. We owe to this body the discoveries on the nature of light, the principle of gravitation, the aberrations of fixed stars, astronomical geometry, and a hundred other discoveries, which would justify one in calling this age the *Age of the English*, as well as the *Age of Louis XIV*.

In 1666 M. Colbert, jealous of this new glory, and anxious

that France should share it, at the request of several scholars obtained permission from Louis XIV. to found an Academy of Science. Like the English society and the French Academy, it was a free institution until 1699. By offering liberal annuities, Colbert attracted Domenico Cassini from Italy, Huygens from Holland and Roemer from Denmark. Roemer determined the velocity of the solar rays; Huygens discovered the ring and one of the satellites of Saturn, and Cassini the other four. We owe to Huygens, if not the original invention of pendulum clocks, at any rate the correct principles underlying the regularity of their movements, principles which he deduced from a wonderful geometrical system.

By the rejection of every system a certain amount of knowledge in every branch of true physics was gradually acquired. People were astonished to see a system of chemistry which did not profess either to search for the philosopher's stone or to prolong life beyond the natural limits; a system of astronomy which did not predict future events, and a system of medicine which was independent of the phases of the moon. Putrefaction was no longer thought to breed spontaneously insects and plants.

There was an end of miracles when Nature was better understood and she was studied in all her productions.

Geography was astonishingly developed. The observatory built by Louis XIV.'s orders was hardly finished, when, in 1669, Domenico Cassini and Picard set to work to determine the meridian line. In 1683 it was continued as far as Roussillon. This was the most glorious achievement of astronomy and was sufficient in itself to immortalise the age.

In 1672 scientists were sent to Cayenne to make some useful observations. On this voyage there was first originated the notion of the oblateness of the earth's sphere, which was afterwards proved by the great Newton; this led the way for those more famous voyages which have since rendered Louis XV.'s reign illustrious.

In 1700 Tournefort was sent out to the Levant, the object of his voyage being to collect plants for the royal garden, hitherto neglected, but now restored to its proper state in which it has become worthy of the curiosity of Europe. The royal library, already numerous, was enriched by more than thirty thousand volumes under Louis XIV., and this example has been so well followed in our days that it now contains more than one hundred and eighty thousand volumes. The law school, which had been closed for a century, was reopened. Chairs were founded in every university in France for the teaching of French law. It seemed right that others should not be taught, and that the admirable Roman laws, embodied with those of the country, should form the whole jurisprudence of the nation.

The publishing of journals originated during this reign. It is well known that the *Journal des Savants*, first issued in 1665, was the forerunner of all similar works, which at the present day circulate all over Europe, and into which, as into the most useful things, too many abuses have crept.

The *Academy of Belles-Lettres*, first formed in 1663 by some members of the French Academy for the purpose of having medallions struck to commemorate and hand down to posterity the achievements of Louis XIV., became useful to the public when it was no longer solely occupied with its monarch, and began to undertake researches into antiquity, and exercise a judicious criticism on ideas and events. It did very much for history what the Academy of Sciences did for physics; it dissipated error.

The spirit of learning and criticism which spread from place to place imperceptibly destroyed much of the prevalent superstition. To this dawn of reason was due the king's declaration in 1672, which forbade tribunals hearing simple accusations of sorcery. No one would have dared to do this in the reign of Henri IV. or Louis XIII., and while people have still been tried for sorcery since 1672, judges have as a usual rule only condemned the accused as blasphemers, or in certain cases as poisoners in addition.

It had hitherto been very common to try sorcerers by throwing them bound into the water; if they floated, they were judged guilty. Many of the judges in the provinces had ordered such trials, and they long continued among the common people. Every shepherd was a sorcerer, and amulets and charmed rings were worn in the towns. Hazel twigs were definitely thought to have the power of revealing the sources of springs, treasures and thieves, and in more than one province of Germany the belief in their efficacy is still strong. There was hardly a person who did not have his horoscope cast. People spoke of nothing but magic secrets; almost everything was illusion. Solemn treatises were written on these subjects by scholars and magistrates, among whom was to be found a group of demonologists. There were tests by which real magicians could be distinguished, and those really possessed, from impostors; in short, up to that period hardly anything had been adopted from antiquity save its errors.

Superstitious notions were so deeply rooted in men's minds that even as late as 1680 people were alarmed at comets. Scientists hardly dared to controvert this universal dread. Jacques Bernouilli, one of the greatest mathematicians in Europe, when questioned about these comets by prejudiced persons, replied that a comet's head could not be a sign of divine wrath, because the head remains unchanged, but that the tail might certainly mean such a thing.

Yet in point of fact neither the head nor the tail remains unchanged. It was left to Bayle to write his famous book against popular superstition, a book which, read in the light of human reason of to-day, seems less caustic than when it first appeared.

One would not think that sovereigns would be under any obligation to philosophers. Yet it is true that the philosophic spirit which has penetrated practically every class of society save the lowest, has done much to promote the rights of sovereigns. Disputes which would once have produced excommunications, interdicts and schisms, have had no such effect. It has been said that the peoples would be happy could they have philosophers for kings, but it is also true to say that kings are so much the happier when many of their subjects are philosophers.

It must be admitted that this spirit of reason, which is beginning to control education in the large towns, was powerless to prevent the frenzied acts of the fanatics of the Cevennes or to prevent the populace of Paris from rioting before a tomb at Saint-Medard, or to settle disputes as bitter as they were frivolous between men who should have known better; but before this century such disputes would have brought about disturbances in the state; the greatest citizens would have believed in the miracles of Saint-Medard, and fanaticism, so far from being confined to the regions of the Cevennes, would have spread to the towns.

All branches of science and literature were utilised in this century, and so many writers contributed to extend the enlightenment of the human spirit that those who would have been accounted marvellous in former ages, were now lost in the crowd. Their individual glory is slight on account of their number, but the glory of their age is all the greater.

CHAPTER XXXII

LITERATURE AND THE ARTS

THE philosophy of reason did not make such great progress in France as in England and in Florence, and while the Academy of Sciences contributed greatly to the enlightenment of the human mind, it did not place France in front of other nations. All the great discoveries and the great truths originated elsewhere.

But in rhetoric, poetry, culture, didactic or merely amusing books, the French were the legislators of Europe. There was no longer taste in Italy. True rhetoric was everywhere unknown, religion ridiculously expounded in the pulpit and cases absurdly argued in the courts.

Preachers quoted Virgil and Ovid; barristers, St. Augustine and St. Jerome. The genius had not yet been found to give to the French language the turn of phrase, the numbers, the propriety of style and the dignity it afterwards possessed. A few verses of Malherbe showed only that it was capable of grandeur and force; but this was all. Men of talent who could write excellently in Latin, such as President de Thou and a certain chancellor de L'Hospital, wrote but indifferently in their own language, which proved to be a refractory medium in their hands. French was as yet but noteworthy for a certain simple directness which had constituted the sole merit of Joinville, Amyot, Marot, Montaigne, Regnier and the *Satire Ménippée*. This *naiveté* was very near to carelessness and coarseness.

Jean de Lingendes, Bishop of Mâcon, unknown to-day, since he omitted to publish his works, was the first orator to speak in the grand style. His sermons and funeral orations, though stained with the rust of his time, were a model of later orators, who imitated and surpassed him. The funeral oration on Charles Emmanuel, Duke of Savoy, surnamed "the Great" by his countrymen, delivered by Lingendes in 1630, contained such grand flights of eloquence, that long afterwards Fléchier took the whole of the exordium, as well as the text and several considerable passages, to embellish his famous funeral oration on the Vicomte de Turenne.

At this period Balzac gave number and harmony to prose. It is true that his letters were bombastic effusions; he wrote thus to the first Cardinal de Retz: "You have just grasped the sceptre of kings and the rose-coloured livery." Speaking of the perfumed waters, he wrote thus to Boisrobert, from Rome: "I am curing myself by swimming in my chamber in the midst of perfumes." With all these faults, he charmed the ear. Rhetoric has such power on men that Balzac was praised in his day for having discovered that small, neglected, but necessary branch of art which consists in the harmonious choice of words, even although he often employed it out of place.

Voiture gave some idea of the airy charm of the epistolary style, which is not the best since it consists of nothing more than wit. His two volumes of letters are a jumble of conceits containing not a single instructive letter, not one which comes from the heart, not one that paints the manners of the time and the characters of men; they show not so much the use of wit as its abuse.

The language gradually became more refined and took on a permanent form. The change was due to the French Academy, and above all to Vaugelas. His *Translation of Quintius Curtius*, which appeared in 1646, was the first good book to be written in a pure form, and there are few of its expressions and idioms which have become obsolete.

Olivier Patru, who followed him closely, did much to rule and purify the language, and though not considered to be deeply versed in the law, he displayed a conciseness, clarity, propriety and elegance of diction in his speeches, such as had never before been known at the Bar.

One of the works which most contributed to form the taste of the nation and give it a spirit of nicety and precision was the little collection of *Maxims* by François, Duke de La Rochefoucauld. Although there is but one real truth expressed in this book, namely, that "self-love is the mainspring of every action," yet the thought is presented under so many various aspects, that it is nearly always striking. It is not so much a book as materials to embellish a book. The little collection was read with eagerness; and it accustomed people to think and to express their thoughts in a vivid, concise and elegant manner. It was a merit which no other writer had had before in Europe, since the revival of letters.

The first book of genius, however, to appear in prose, was the collection of *Provincial Letters*, in 1656. Every variety of style is to be found there. After the lapse of a century,

there is not a single word which has undergone that altera-
tion of meaning which so often changes a living language.
To this work must be ascribed the moment when the language became fixed. The Bishop of Lucon, son of the celebrated Bussi, told me that when he asked the Bishop of
Meaux what book he would rather have written had he not
written his own, Bossuet replied: "*The Provincial Letters.*"
They have lost much of their pertinence now that the
Jesuits have been suppressed and the objects of their disputes
come into contempt.

The good taste which distinguishes this book from beginning to end, and the vigour of the final letters, did not at
first reform the loose, slovenly, incorrect and disconnected
style which for long afterwards characterised the writings
and speeches of nearly all authors, preachers and barristers.

One of the first to display a reasoned eloquence in the
pulpit was Bourdaloue, about 1668. It was a new departure.
After him came other pulpit orators, such as Massillon,
Bishop of Clermont, who brought to their addresses greater
elegance and finer and more penetrating descriptions of the
manners of the age; but not one of them eclipsed him. His
style was vigorous rather than florid, without any touch of
fancy, so that it seemed that he was more inclined to con-
vince people than to touch their hearts, and he never sought
to please.

One may sometimes wish that in banishing bad taste from
the pulpit which it degraded, he had also done away with
the practice of preaching from a text. For, to speak at some
length on a quotation of a line or two, to strain oneself to
keep the whole of the sermon centred on those two lines,
seems a work unworthy of the solemn office of a minister.
The text becomes a sort of device, or rather enigma, which
is unravelled by the sermon. The Greeks and the Romans
were ignorant of such a practice. It was introduced during
the decadence of letters, and course of time has hallowed it.

The custom of dividing all subjects under two or three
headings, some of which, such as a question of morals,
require no division, and others, such as matters of controversy, require many more, remains a tiresome custom,
which Bourdaloue found in common use and with which
he himself complied.

He had been preceded by Bossuet, afterwards Bishop of
Meaux. Bossuet, who became so great a man, was affianced

in his youth to Mlle. Desvieux, a girl of remarkably fine character. His talent for theology, and that remarkable gift of eloquence which characterised it, showed themselves at such an early age that his parents and friends persuaded him to give himself to the Church alone. Mlle. Desvieux herself urged him to this course, preferring the glory that he was sure to obtain to the happiness of living with him. He had preached when quite young in 1662 before the king and queen-mother, long before Bourdaloue was known. His sermons, aided by a noble and impressive delivery, the first to be heard at court that approached the sublime manner, met with such great success that the king wrote to his father, the comptroller of Soissons, to congratulate him on possessing such a son.

However, on Bourdaloue's appearance, Bossuet was no longer considered the foremost preacher. He was already himself given to the composition of funeral orations, a kind of oratory which requires an imagination and majestic dignity which approaches poetry, from which art, indeed, something must always be borrowed, though with discretion, when one aspires to the sublime. The funeral oration on the queen-mother, which he delivered in 1667, brought him the bishopric of Condon; but the oration was not worthy of him, and, like his sermons, was not printed. The funeral panegyric on the Queen of England, widow of Charles I., which he delivered in 1669, appears in every detail a masterpiece. The subjects of such pieces of rhetoric are happy in proportion to the misfortunes which the dead experienced. They may be compared to tragedies where it is the misfortunes of the principal characters that interest us most. The funeral panegyric of *Madame*, carried off in the flower of life, who actually breathed her last in his arms, gained the greatest and rarest of triumphs, that of drawing tears from the eyes of courtiers. He was obliged to stop after the words: "O ill-fated, horrible night! when suddenly, like a clap of thunder, echoed the dire news: *Madame* is dying. *Madame* is dead. . . ." The listeners burst into sobs, and the orator's voice was lost amidst the sighs and weeping of the congregation.

The French were the only people who succeeded in this kind of oratory. Some time afterwards, the same man introduced a new style, which could hardly have succeeded save in his own hands. He applied the art of oratory to history itself, a literary genre which would seem incapable of admitting it. His *Discourse on Universal History*, written for the Dauphin's education, has neither precedent nor imitators. While the system which he adopts to reconcile the Jewish chronology with that of other nations has met with certain opposition among scholars, his style has met with nothing but admiration. The lofty vigour with which he describes the manners and customs, the government, the rise and fall of great empires, is astonishing, as are the vigorous, true and lively strokes with which he paints and passes judgment on the nations.

Nearly all the works which added lustre to this age were of a kind unknown to the ancients. *Télémaque* is of the number. Fénelon, the pupil and friend of Bossuet, and afterwards against his will his rival and enemy, wrote this singular book, which resembles now a novel and now a poem, and in which a modulated prose takes the place of verse. Apparently his aim was to treat the novel as Bossuet had treated history, lending it a fresh dignity and charm and, above all, drawing from fiction a moral beneficial to mankind, and hitherto entirely overlooked in nearly all fictitious compositions. It has been thought that he wrote the book to serve as an exercise for the instruction of the Duke of Burgundy and other French princes, whose tutor he was, in the same way as Bossuet had written his *Universal History* for the education of *Monseigneur*. But his nephew, the Marquis de Fénelon, who inherited the graces of that celebrated man and who was killed at the Battle of Raucoux, assured me to the contrary. It would certainly have been unseemly for a priest to have taught the loves of Calypso and Eucharis as his first lessons to the royal princes.

This work was not written until he had retired to his archbishopric of Cambrai. Full of classical learning and endowed with a lively and sensitive imagination, he invented a style which could belong to none other than himself, and which flowed easily and fluently. I have seen the original manuscript, and there are not ten erasures in it. He wrote it in three months, in the midst of his unfortunate disputes on Quietism, little suspecting how superior such recreation was to his more learned occupation. It is said that a servant stole a copy of the manuscript and had it printed. If that is so, the Archbishop of Cambrai owes the great reputation he has in Europe to that dishonest act, but to that act

was also due the loss of any hope of favour at court
for ever.

People pretend to discern in *Télémaque* a veiled criticism
of Louis XIV.'s government. Sesostris, displaying too much
pomp in the hour of triumph, Idomeneus revelling in luxury
at Salentini and forgetting the necessities of life, were thought
to represent the king, although after all it is impossible for
anyone to indulge in superfluous luxury except by a super-
abundance of the products of the needful arts.

In the eyes of malcontents the Marquis de Louvois seemed
represented under the name of Protesilas, vain, harsh and
proud, an enemy of the great captains who served the state
but not the minister.

The Allies who had united against Louis XIV. in the war
of 1688, and later caused his throne to totter in the war of
1701, joyfully recognised him in the character Idomeneus,
whose arrogance disgusted all his neighbours. These allusions
made a profound impression, aided, as they were, by a
harmonious style, which insinuates in so delicate a manner
the advantages of peace and moderation. Foreigners and
even the French themselves, weary of so many wars, saw
with malicious relief a satire in a book written for the purpose
of inculcating virtue. Innumerable editions were brought
out. I have myself seen forty in the English language. It is
true that after the death of that monarch, who had been so
feared, so envied, so respected by all, and so hated by a few,
when human malice had at length surfeited its appetite for
those alleged allusions which cast a slur upon his conduct,
the critics of a sterner taste treated *Télémaque* with some
severity. They blamed its wearisomeness, its details, its too
little connected adventures, and its oft-repeated and little-
varied descriptions of country life, but this book has always
been considered one of the finest monuments of a brilliant age.

The *Characters* of La Bruyère may be regarded as a production of a unique kind. No examples of such a work are to
be found in the classics any more than of *Télémaque*. The
public were struck by a style at once rapid, terse and vigorous, by picturesque expressions, in a word, by a totally new
use of the language which did not, however, break its rules;
and the numerous allusions contained in the work crowned
its success. When La Bruyère showed the manuscript of
his work to M. de Malezieu, the latter said to him: "Here
is something which will bring you many readers and many

enemies." When the generation that was attacked in this book had passed away, its reputation declined. Nevertheless, as there are some books which belong to all time and to all countries, it is probable that it will never be forgotten. *Télémaque* had some imitators; the *Characters* of La Bruyère had many more. It is easier to write short descriptions of things that strike us, than to compose a lengthy work of imagination which is both pleasing and instructive.

The delicate art of introducing charm into a philosophical work was as yet an innovation; of which the first example was *La Pluralité des Mondes* of Fontenelle, and a dangerous one, since the true dress of philosophy is method, clarity and, above all, truth. The fact that this work is partly based on the chimerical hypothesis of Descartes' vortices is sufficient to preclude it from being ranked among the classics by posterity.

Among these literary novelties mention should be made of the works of Bayle, who compiled a kind of dictionary of logic. It was the first work of its kind in which one may learn how to think. One must abandon to the fate of all second-rate books the articles in this collection which contain such unimportant facts as are alike unworthy of Bayle, of a serious reader and of posterity. For the rest, in thus counting Bayle among the authors who gave lustre to the age of Louis XIV., though he was a refugee in Holland, I am but conforming to a decree of the parliament of Toulouse, which proclaimed the validity of his will in France despite the rigour of the laws, and expressly stated "that such a man could not be regarded as a foreigner."

This is no time to expatiate upon the large number of good books which were produced in this age; we shall only dwell on those works which are characterised by new or remarkable genius, and which distinguish this age from others. The eloquence of Bossuet and Bourdaloue, for example, was not and could not be that of a new Cicero, it was of a new order and excellence. If there is anything to approach the Roman orator it is the three memorials composed by Pellisson for Fouquet. They are in the same manner as some of Cicero's orations, a medley of legal matters and state affairs, judiciously treated with an art that never obtrudes and diffused with passages of touching eloquence.

Historians there were, but no Livy. The style of the *Conspiracy of Venice* is comparable to that of Sallust.

It is obvious that the Abbé of Saint-Réal had taken that writer for his model, and it is possible that he has surpassed him. All the other writings which we have just mentioned seem of a new creation. It is that above all which distinguishes this illustrious age; for, as for scholars and commentators, the sixteenth and seventeenth centuries had produced them in shoals; but true genius in any genre had not yet been developed.

Who would think that such masterpieces of prose would probably never have been written, had they not been preceded by poetry? Yet such is the progress of the human spirit in every nation, verses were everywhere the earliest children of genius and the first masters of eloquence.

Nations do not differ from the individual. Plato and Cicero began by writing poetry. People knew by heart the few fine stanzas of Malherbe, when it was not possible to quote a noble and sublime passage of prose, and in all probability if Pierre Corneille had not lived the genius of prose-writers would not have been developed.

Corneille is the more highly to be admired in that when he began to compose his tragedies he had but wretched models to guide him; that these models were admired made it still more difficult for him to choose the right path, and to dishearten him still further they were approved by Cardinal Richelieu, the patron of men of letters, though not of good taste. He remunerated such wretched scribblers as are customarily importunate, and, with an arrogance of mind which well became him in other affairs, he was inclined to disdain those in whom he perceived with a certain envy signs of real genius, such as will never bow the knee to idle patronage. It is rare indeed that a powerful man, himself an artist, is seen to give his protection to the artists who best deserve it.

Corneille had to contend with his age, his rivals, and Cardinal Richelieu. I do not propose to repeat here what has been written about *The Cid*; I shall merely remark that the Academy, in passing judgment between Corneille and Scudéri, was over-mindful of Cardinal Richelieu's good favour when it censured the love of Chimène. To love her father's murderer and yet seek to revenge that murder was admirable. To have made her master her love would have been to break one of the fundamental laws of the tragic art, which is chiefly concerned with conflicts of the heart, but at that time the art was itself unknown to all except the author.

The Cid was not the only work of Corneille which Cardinal

Richelieu sought to depreciate. The Abbé d'Aubignac tells us that that minister disapproved also of *Polyeucte*.

The Cid was after all a highly embellished imitation of *Guillem de Castro*, and in several passages a translation. *Cinna*, which followed it, was unique. I knew an old servant of the house of Condé, who told me that the great Condé, at the age of twenty, being present at the first performance of *Cinna*, shed tears at these words of Augustus:

> I am the world's great master and my own;
> I am, I will be. Memory and time
> Shall this last, greatest victory record.
> I triumph over wrath too justly rous'd,
> And latest age the conquest shall applaud
> Cinna, let us be friends; 'tis I who ask it.

They were the tears of a hero. The great Corneille causing the great Condé to weep with admiration constitutes a truly commemorative epoch in the history of the human spirit.

The number of plays unworthy of his genius which he composed years later did not prevent the nation from regarding him as a great man, just as the faults of Homer have never prevented his being sublime. It is the privilege of true genius, and especially of the genius who opens up a new avenue of thought, to make mistakes with impunity.

Corneille had formed himself alone; but Louis XIV., Colbert, Sophocles and Euripides all contributed to form Racine. An ode which he composed at the age of eighteen on the occasion of the king's marriage brought him a present which he had not expected, and this decided him to become a poet. His reputation was steadily increased, while that of Corneille has suffered a slight eclipse. The reason is that Racine in all his works after *Alexandre* is always elegant, always correct, always true; he speaks to the heart; and Corneille not infrequently fails in all these respects. Racine was far in advance of both the Greeks and Corneille in his knowledge of the passions, and carried the music of his verse and the elegance of his style to the highest perfection attainable. These men taught the nation to think, to feel, and to express their thoughts. Their audiences, whom they alone had enlightened, at length became relentless critics of the very men who had instructed them.

In the time of Cardinal Richelieu there were few persons in France competent to detect the faults of *The Cid*; yet in 1702, when *Athalie*, a masterpiece of the theatre, was performed at the house of the Duchess of Burgundy, the courtiers thought themselves sufficiently qualified to condemn it. Time has avenged the author; but the great man died without enjoying the success of his finest work. A numerous party long took pride in being prejudiced against Racine. Mme. de Sévigné, the first letter-writer of her age, who had no rival in the sprightly recounting of trifles, always thought that Racine *would not go far*.

She judged him like coffee, of which she said: "People will soon grow tired of it." Reputations can ripen by the passage of time alone.

By the singular good-fortune of the age Molière was the contemporary of Corneille and Racine. It is not true to say that when Molière appeared he found the stage entirely lacking in good comedies. Corneille himself had presented *Le Menteur* (*The Liar*), a play of character and intrigue, borrowed like *The Cid* from the Spanish theatre; and Molière had written but two of his great masterpieces, when Quinault presented to the public *La Mère Coquette* (*The Mother as Coquette*), a comedy of both character and intrigue, and indeed a model of intrigue. It appeared in 1664; and was the first comedy in which those who were afterwards known as *Marquises* were caricatured. The majority of the great lords at the Court of Louis XIV. were eager to imitate the grand air, the majesty and dignity of their masters. Those who were in a lower position copied the haughty manners of their betters, until at last there were many who carried this air of superiority and overweening conceit to the highest point of absurdity.

The failing lasted long. Molière attacked it often and contributed to rid the public of such self-important mediocrities, as well as of the affectation of the *précieuses* (*affected young women*), the pedantry of the *femmes savantes* (*learned ladies*), and the robe and Latin jargon of the doctors. Molière was, one may say, the legislator over the good manners of society. I am speaking here only of the service he rendered to his age; his other merits are sufficiently well known.

Such an age was worthy of the consideration of future ages; an age in which the heroes of Corneille and Racine, the characters of Molière, the symphonies of Lulli, all of them novelties to the nation, and (since we are here concerned only with the arts) the eloquence of Bossuet and Bourdaloue, were appreciated by Louis XIV., by *Madame* noted for her good taste, by such men as Condé, Turenne, Colbert and a host of eminent men in every department of life. There will never again be such an era in which a Duke de La Rochefoucauld, the author of the *Maxims*, after discoursing with a Pascal and an Arnauld, goes to the theatre to witness a play of Corneille.

Boileau attained to the level of these great men, not with his early satires, for posterity will not give a second glance to the *Embarras de Paris*, and to the names of the Cassaignes and Cotins, but by the exquisite epistles with which he has instructed posterity, and especially by the *Art Poétique*, in which Corneille could have found much to learn.

La Fontaine, far less chaste in style, and far less faultless in his language, but unique in the simplicity and grace which are typical of his work, placed himself by the simplest of writings almost on a level with these sublime writers.

As the originator of a wholly new style, rendered but more difficult by its apparent ease, Quinault was worthy to be placed among his illustrious contemporaries. It is well known how unjustly Boileau sought to disparage him.

Boileau had never sacrificed on the altar of the Graces; and all his life he attempted, though in vain, to belittle a man whose true worth was recognised by them alone. The sincerest praise that we can give a poet is to remember his verses: whole scenes from Quinault are known by heart, a tribute which no Italian opera could obtain. French music has retained a simplicity which is no longer appreciated by other nations; but the natural and beautiful simplicity, which is so frequently and charmingly shown in Quinault, still delights everyone in Europe who is conversant with our language and possesses a cultured taste.

Were a poem like *Armide* or *Atys* to be discovered in antiquity, with what idolatry would it be received! But Quinault was a modern.

All these great men were known and protected by Louis XIV., with the exception of La Fontaine. His excessive simplicity of life, which was carried to the length of personal negligence, caused him to be slighted by a court whose favours he did not seek; but he was welcomed by the Duke of Burgundy and received kindnesses from that prince in his old age. Despite his genius, he was almost as artless as the heroes of his fables. A priest of the Oratory, named Pouget, took great credit to himself for having treated that man of such guileless character, as though he were speaking to the Marquise de Brinvilliers or La Voisin. His tales are all borrowed from Poggio, Ariosto and the Queen of Navarre. If desire be dangerous, pleasantries do not make it so. His admirable fable of the *Animals afflicted with the Plague*, who accuse themselves of their misdeeds, might be applied to La Fontaine himself. All is pardoned to the lions, wolves and bears, and an innocent animal is sacrificed for having eaten a blade or two of grass.

In the company of these men of genius, who will be the delight and instruction of future ages, there sprang up a host of schools of pretty wits who produced innumerable elegant works of minor importance, that contribute to the amusement of cultured people, just as there have been many pleasing painters whom one would not put beside such painters as Poussin, Lesueur, Lebrun, Lemoine and Vanloo.

But towards the end of Louis XIV.'s reign two men rose above the crowd of mediocre talents and acquired great reputations. The one was La Motte Houdar, a man of a wise and generous rather than of a lofty spirit, a careful and methodical prose-writer, but often lacking favour and grace in his poetry, and even that correctness which it is only permissible to sacrifice for the sublime. At first he wrote fine stanzas rather than fine odes. His talent deteriorated soon afterwards; but many beautiful fragments which remain to us in more than one genre, will place him for ever above the rank of authors that may be ignored. He proved that in the art of letters a writer of the second rank may yet do good service.

The other was Rousseau, a man of less intellect, less delicacy and less ease than La Motte, but with a greater talent for the art of versifying. His odes were imitations of La Motte, but they excelled in elegance, in variety, and in fancy. His psalms equalled in grace and harmony the sacred songs of Racine. His epigrams are more highly finished than those of Marot. He was far less successful in opera, which requires delicacy of feeling, in comedies, in which humour is indispensable, and in moral epistles, which must delineate the truth; for he lacked all those qualities. Thus he failed in those branches which were foreign to him.

He would have corrupted the French language if others had imitated the *Marotic* style which he employed in serious works. But fortunately his adulteration of the purity of our language with the outworn forms of two centuries earlier proved only a passing phase. Some of his epistles are rather strained imitations of Boileau, but are not based on sufficiently clear ideas or acknowledged truths: *"Truth alone can please."*

This genius degenerated considerably in foreign countries, whether age and misfortunes had impaired his talents, or whether, his principal merit consisting in the choice of words and happy turns of phrase, a merit more rare and necessary in a great writer than might be thought, he was no longer within reach of the same assistance. Far from his native country, he might count among his misfortunes the lack of any severe critics.

His continued ill-fortune was the outcome of an ungovernable self-pride, too near inclined to jealousy and spite. His fate cannot but be a striking lesson to every man of talent; but he is to be considered here only as a writer who contributed not a little to the honour of letters.

Scarcely any great genius arose after the halcyon days of these great writers, and towards the time of the death of Louis XIV. Nature herself seemed to be reposing.

The path was difficult at the beginning of the age because no one had yet trodden it; it is difficult to-day because it has been beaten flat. The great men of the past age taught us how to think and speak; they told us things which we knew not. Those who succeed them can hardly say anything that is not known already. In short, a kind of distaste has arisen from a very surfeit of masterpieces.

Thus the age of Louis XIV. suffered the same fate as those of Leo X., Augustus and Alexander. The ground which in those illustrious periods produced so many fruits of genius had been long prepared. Both moral and physical causes have been searched in vain to provide reason for this slow fecundity, followed by a long period of sterility. The true reason is that among the nations who cultivate the fine arts many years must elapse before the language and taste become purified. Once these first steps have been made men of genius begin to appear; rivalry and public favour incite fresh efforts and stimulate all talents. Each artist seizes upon the natural beauties which are proper to his particular genre. Any man who thoroughly examines the theory of the arts of pure genius must know, if he has anything of talent himself, that the prime beauties, the great natural opportunities which are suited to the nation for which the author is working are few in number. The subjects available and their

appropriate elaboration have much narrower limits than
might be thought. The Abbé Dubos, a man of great judgment, who wrote a treatise on poetry and painting about
the year 1714, was of the opinion that in the whole of French
history there was but a single subject for an epic poem, the
destruction of the League by Henri-Quatre. He should have
added that since embellishments of the epic theme, such as
were well suited to the Greeks, the Romans and the Italians
of the fifteenth and sixteenth centuries, are prohibited among
the French, and the gods of fable, oracles, invulnerable
heroes, monsters, sorceries, metamorphoses and romantic
adventures no longer held to be fit subjects, the beauties
appropriate to the epic poem are confined within a very
narrow circle. If, therefore, it happens that any artist seizes
upon the only embellishments suited to the times, the subject
and the nation, and who carries out what others have
attempted, those who come after him will find the ground
already occupied.

It is the same with the art of tragedy. It is a mistake to
believe that the great tragic passions and emotions can be
infinitely varied in new and striking ways. Everything has
its limits.

High comedy has no less its own. In human nature there
are at the most a dozen characters that are really comic
and that are marked by striking qualities. The Abbé Dubos,
lacking talent, believes that men of talent can discover a
whole host of new characters; but nature would first have
to make them. He imagines that the little differences that
distinguish one man from another can be as successfully
treated as the fundamental qualities. It is true that there
are numberless shades of differences, but the number of
brilliant colours is small; and it is these primary colours of
which a great artist does not fail to make use.

The eloquence of the pulpit, and especially funeral orations,
provide a case in point. Moral truths once eloquently expressed, descriptions of human misery and human weaknesses,
of the vanity of greatness and the ravages of death, once
painted by able fingers, and all becomes commonplace. One
is reduced to imitating them or going astray. An adequate
number of fables having once been written by a La Fontaine, any additions to them can but point the same moral
and relate almost the same adventures. Genius can thus
flourish but in a single age and must then degenerate.

The other branches of literature whose subject-matter is, as it were, being continually renewed, such as history and natural science, which require only hard work, judgment and common sense, can more easily maintain their position; and the plastic arts such as painting and sculpture can avoid degeneration when those in power, like Louis XIV., take care to employ only the best artists. For in painting and in sculpture, the same subjects can be treated a hundred times; artists still paint the Holy Family, though Raphael expended all the genius of his art on this subject; but one would not be permitted to treat again the themes of *Cinna, Andromaque, L'Art Poétique* and *Tartuffe*.

It must be noted that, the past age having enlightened the present, it has become so easy to write mediocre stuff that we have been flooded out with books and, what is worse, with serious though useless books; but among this multitude of mediocre writing an evil becomes a necessity in a city at once large, wealthy and idle, in which one party of citizens being continually occupied in entertaining the other, there have appeared, from time to time, excellent works of history, of reflection or of that light literature which is the recreation of all sorts of minds.

Of all the nations, France has produced the greatest number of such works. Its language has become the language of Europe; everything has contributed to this end; the great writers of the age of Louis XIV., and their successors the exiled Calvinist ministers, who brought their eloquence and logic into foreign countries; above all, a Bayle, who, writing his works in Holland, has had them read by every nation; a Rapin de Thoyras, who has written in French the only good history of England; a Saint-Evremond, whose acquaintance was sought by every person of the Court of London: the Duchess de Mazarin, to please whom was everyone's ambition; Mme. d'Olbreuse, later Duchess von Zell, who carried with her into Germany all the graces of her country. The social spirit is the natural heritage of the French; it is a merit and a pleasure of which other nations have felt the need. The French language is of all languages that which expresses with the greatest ease, exactness and delicacy all subjects of conversation which can arise among gentlefolk; and it thus contributes throughout all Europe to one of the most agreeable diversions of life.

CHAPTER XXXIII

THE ARTS (*continued*)

THE arts which do not solely depend upon the intellect had made but little progress in France before the period which is known as the age of Louis XIV. Music was in its infancy; a few languishing songs, some airs for the violin, the guitar and the lute, composed for the most part in Spain, were all that we possessed. Lulli's style and technique were astonishing. He was the first in France to write bass counter-point, middle parts and figures. At first some difficulty was experienced in playing his compositions, which now seem so easy and simple. At the present day there are a thousand people who know music, for one who knew it in the time of Louis XIII.; and the art has been perfected by this spread of knowledge. To-day, there is no great town which has not its public concerts: yet at that time Paris itself had none; the king's twenty-four violins comprised the sum total of French music.

The familiarity with music and its dependent arts has so increased that towards the end of Louis XIV.'s reign the practice of dancing figures to music was instituted, so that at the present day it may be truly said that people dance at sight.

There were several very great architects during the regency of Marie de' Medici. She had the Palace of Luxembourg built in the Tuscan style, in honour of her country and for the adornment of our own. The same de Brosse, whose gate of Saint-Gervais is still standing, built a palace for this queen, which she never occupied. Cardinal Richelieu, with all his greatness of mind, was far from having as good taste in such matters as she. The cardinal's palace, which is now the Palais-Royal, is indeed a proof of this. We had great hopes when we saw the fine façade of the Louvre being built, which is such as to make one long to see the palace completed. Many citizens built themselves magnificent houses, more distinguished for the exquisite taste of the interior rather than of the exterior, and gratifying the luxury of private individuals even more than adorning the city.

Colbert, the Mæcenas of all the arts, founded an Academy of Architecture in 1671. A Vitruvius is not enough, one must have an Augustus to employ him.

Municipal officials should also have an ardour for the arts, an ardour which must be enlightened. Had there been two or three mayors like President Turgot, the city of Paris would not be disgraced by such a badly built and badly situated town hall, by such a small and badly laid-out square, famous only for its gibbets and its bonfires; by the narrowness of the streets in the busiest quarters—in short, by this relic of barbarism in the midst of splendour and in the very home of all the arts.

Painting began with Poussin in the reign of Louis XIII. No account need be taken of the indifferent painters who preceded him. Since his time every age has had its great painters, though not in that profusion which is one of Italy's glories; but without stopping to dwell upon Lesueur, who owned no master, or Lebrun, who rivalled the Italians in design and execution, we have had more than thirty painters who have bequeathed works of art very worthy of regard. Foreigners are beginning to take them from us. The galleries and apartments of one great king I have seen filled with nothing else but French pictures, whose value we should perhaps be loath to recognise. In France I have seen a picture of Santerre refused for twelve thousand livres. There is scarcely to be found in Europe a larger painting than the ceiling of Lemoine at Versailles, and I know not whether there are any more beautiful. Since then we have had Vanloo, considered even in foreign countries as the finest painter of his time.

Not only did Colbert organise the Academy of Painting as it is to-day, but in 1667 he persuaded Louis XIV. to establish one in Rome. A palace was purchased in that capital for the residence of the director, and pupils who have won prizes at the Paris Academy are sent there to study, the expenses of their journey and board being defrayed by the king; they there copy ancient works of art, and study the works of Raphael and Michael Angelo. The desire to imitate both ancient and modern Rome is in itself a noble homage to the eternal city, and the homage has still been rendered even since the enormous collections of Italian paintings amassed by the king and the Duke of Orleans, and the masterpieces of sculpture which France has produced, have enabled us to dispense with the necessity of seeking masters abroad.

It is chiefly in sculpture that we have excelled, and in the art of casting colossal equestrian figures in a single mould.

Should posterity discover one day fragments of such works of art as the baths of Apollo, buried under ruins, or exposed to the ravages of the weather in the thickets of Versailles; or the tomb of Cardinal Richelieu in the Sorbonne chapel, too little noticed by the public; or the equestrian statue of Louis XIV. made in Paris to grace the city of Bordeaux; or the Mercury which Louis XV. presented to the King of Prussia; and many other works of art equal to those that I have mentioned, one cannot but think that these productions of our time would find a place among the finest of Greek antiquity.

We have equalled the ancients in our medallions. Warin was the first to raise this art from mediocrity towards the end of the reign of Louis XIII. Those dies and stamps now arranged in historical order in the corridors of the Louvre gallery are a marvellous sight. They are worth about two millions, and the greater part of them are masterpieces.

The art of engraving precious stones was no less successfully cultivated. That of reproducing pictures, and of perpetuating them by means of copper plates, and thus handing down to posterity all kinds of representations of nature and of art, was still in a very imperfect state in France previous to this age. It is one of the most pleasing and useful of arts. We owe its discovery to the Florentines, who invented it towards the middle of the fifteenth century, and it has made even greater progress in France than in the country of its origin, because a greater number of works of that class were produced there. Collections of royal engravings often formed the most magnificent gift of the king to ambassadors. The chasing of gold and silver, which requires a knowledge of designing, and good taste, was brought to the highest degree of perfection to which it is possible for the skill of man to attain.

Now that we have surveyed all the arts which contribute to the pleasures of the people and the glory of the state, we cannot pass over in silence the most useful of all the arts, and one in which the French excelled all other nations in the world; I mean the art of surgery, whose progress was so rapid and far-famed in this age, that people came to Paris from the ends of Europe for any cure or operation that required exceptional skill. Not only was France almost the only country in which first-rate surgeons were to be found, but it was in that country alone that the requisite instru-

ments were properly made; France provided all her neighbours with them, and I have heard from the mouth of the
celebrated Cheseldon, the greatest surgeon in London, that
it was he who first began to make in London, in 1715, the
instruments of his art. Medicine, which helped to improve
surgery, did not reach a higher degree of perfection in France
than in England, or under the famous Boerhaave in Holland;
medicine indeed, like natural science, was perfected by making
use of the discoveries of our neighbours.

The foregoing is, on the whole, a faithful account of the
progress of the human spirit in France during that age which
began in the time of Cardinal Richelieu, and ended in our
days. It will be with difficulty surpassed, and, if in some ways
it be eclipsed, it will remain the model of more fortunate
ages, to which it will have given birth.

CHAPTER XXXIV

THE USEFUL ARTS AND SCIENCES IN EUROPE DURING THE REIGN OF LOUIS XIV

WE have sufficiently intimated throughout the whole of
this history that the national disasters which fill it, and
which followed one another almost without a break, are in
the long run erased from the register of time. The details
and devices of politics sink into oblivion; but sound laws,
institutions, and achievements in the sciences and the arts
remain for ever.

The crowd of foreigners who travel to Rome to-day, not
as pilgrims, but as men of taste, find few traces of Gergory VII.
or Boniface VIII.; they admire the temples built by men
like Bramante and Michael Angelo, the pictures of Raphael
and the sculpture of Bernini; if they are men of intelligence,
they read Ariosto and Tasso and honour the ashes of Galileo.
In England Cromwell's name is but spoken of now and then;
people no longer discuss the Wars of the *White Rose*, but
they will study Newton for years at a time, and no one is
surprised to read in his epitaph that *he was the glory of the
human race*, though one would be much surprised to find
in England the memory of any statesman accorded such
an honour.

I would gladly have it in my power to do justice to all
the great men who, like Newton, gave lustre to their country
during the last hundred years. I have called that period the
age of Louis XIV., not only because that monarch gave
greater encouragement to the arts than all his fellow-kings
together, but also because in his lifetime he outlived three
generations of the kings of Europe. I have set the limits of
this epoch at some years before Louis XIV. and some years
after him; for it was during this space of time that the human
spirit has made most progress.

From 1660 to the present day the English have made
greater progress in all the arts than in all preceding ages.
I will not here repeat what I have said elsewhere of Milton.
It is true that some critics disapprove of his fantastic
descriptions, his paradise of fools, his alabaster walls which
encircle the earthly paradise; his devils, who transform
themselves from giants into pigmies that they may take
less room in council, seated in a vast hall of gold erected
in hell; his cannons fired from heaven, his mountains hurled
at the heads of foes; his angels on horseback, angels who
are cut in two and their dissevered bodies as quickly joined
together again. His long descriptions and repetitions are
considered tedious; it is said that he has equalled neither
Ovid nor Hesiod in his long description of the way in
which the earth, the animals and mankind were created. His
dissertations on astronomy are condemned as too dry and
the creations of his fancy as being extravagant, rather than
marvellous, and more disgusting than impressive; such is a
long passage upon chaos; the love of Sin and Death and the
children of their incest; and Death, "who turns up his nose
to scent across the immensity of chaos the change that has
come over the earth, like a crow scenting a corpse"—Death,
who smells out the odour of the Fall, who strikes with his
petrifying hammer on cold and dry; and cold and dry with
hot and moist, transformed into four fine army generals,
lead into battle their embryonic atoms like light-armed
infantry. Criticism indeed exhausts itself, but never praise.
Milton remains at once the glory and wonder of England;
he is compared to Homer, whose defects are as great, and
he is preferred to Dante, whose conceptions are yet more
fantastic.

Among the large number of pleasing poets who graced
the reign of Charles II., such as Waller, the Earl of Dorset

and the Earl of Rochester, the Duke of Buckingham and many others, we must single out Dryden, who distinguished himself in every branch of poetry; his works are full of details both brilliant and true to nature, lively, vigorous, bold and passionate, merits in which none of his own nation equals him nor any of the ancients surpass him. If Pope, who succeeded him, had not written late in life his *Essay on Man*, he could not be compared to Dryden.

No other nation has treated moral subjects in poetry with greater depth and vigour than the English; there lies, it seems to me, the greatest merit of her poets.

There is another kind of elegant writing which requires at once a mind more cultured and more universal; such was Addison's; he achieved immortal fame with his *Cato*, the only English tragedy written from beginning to end in an elegant and lofty style, and his other moral and critical works breathe a perfect taste; in all he wrote, sound sense appears adorned by a lively fancy, and his manner of writing is an excellent model for any country. Dean Swift left several passages whose like is not to be found among the writers of antiquity—a Rabelais made perfect.

The English have hardly any examples of funeral orations; it is not their custom to praise their kings and queens in churches; but pulpit oratory, which was in London coarse before the reign of Charles II., suddenly improved. Bishop Burnet admits in his *Memoirs* that it was brought about by imitating the French. Perhaps they have surpassed their masters; their sermons are less formal, less pretentious and less declamatory than those of the French.

It is, moreover, remarkable that this insular people, separated from the rest of the world and so lately cultured, should have acquired at least as much knowledge of antiquity as the Italians have been able to gather in Rome, which was for so long the meeting-place of the nations. Marsham penetrated the mysteries of ancient Egypt. No Persian had such a knowledge of the Zoroastrian religion as the scholar Hyde. The Turks were unacquainted with the history of Mahomet and the preceding centuries, and its interpretation was left to the Englishman Sale, who turned his travels in Arabia to such good profit.

There is no other country in the world where the Christian religion has been so vigorously attacked and so ably defended as in England. From Henry VIII. to Cromwell men argued and fought, like that ancient breed of gladiators who descended into the arena sword in hand and a bandage on their eyes. A few slight differences in creed and dogma were sufficient to cause frightful wars, but from the Restoration to the present day when every Christian tenet has been almost annually attacked, such disputes have not aroused the least disturbance; science has taken the place of fire and sword to silence every argument.

It is above all in philosophy that the English have become the teachers of other nations. It is no mere question of ingenious systems. The false myths of the Greeks should have disappeared long ago and modern myths should never have appeared at all. Roger Bacon broke fresh ground by declaring that Nature must be studied in a new way, that experiments must be made; Boyle devoted his life to making them. This is no place for a dissertation on physics; it is enough to say that after three thousand years of fruitless research, Newton was the first to find and demonstrate the great natural law by which all elements of matter are mutually attracted, the law by which all the stars are held in their courses. He was indeed the first to see the light; before him it was unknown.

His principles of mathematics, which include a system of physics at once new and true, are based on the discovery of the calculus, incorrectly called *infinitesimal*, a supreme effort of geometry, and one which he made at the age of twenty-four. It was a great philosopher, the learned Halley, who said of him "that it is not permitted to any mortal to approach nearer to divinity."

A host of expert geometricians and physicists were enlightened by his discoveries and inspired by his genius. Bradley discovered the aberration of the light of fixed stars, distant at least twelve billion leagues from our small globe.

Halley, whom I have quoted above, though but an astronomer, received the command of one of the king's ships in 1698. It was on this ship that he determined the position of the stars of the Antarctic Pole, and noted the variations of the compass in all parts of the known globe. The voyage of the Argonauts was in comparison but the crossing of a bark from one side of a river to the other. Yet Halley's voyage has been hardly spoken of in Europe.

The indifference we display towards great events become too familiar, and our admiration of the ancient Greeks for trivial ones, is yet another proof of the wonderful superiority of our age over that of the ancients. Boileau in France and Sir William Temple in England obstinately refused to acknowledge such a superiority; they were eager to disparage their own age, in order to place themselves above it: but the dispute between the ancients and the moderns has been at last decided, at any rate in the field of philosophy. There is not a single ancient philosopher whose works are taught to-day to the youth of any enlightened nation.

Locke alone should serve as a good example of the advantage of our age over the most illustrious ages of Greece. From Plato to Locke there is indeed nothing; no one in that interval developed the operations of the human mind, and a man who knew the whole of Plato and only Plato, would know little and that not well.

Plato was indeed an eloquent Greek; his *Apologia of Socrates* stands a service rendered to philosophers of every nation; he should be respected, as having represented ill-fortuned virtue in so honourable a light and its persecutors in one so odious. It was long thought that ethics so admirable could not be associated with metaphysics so false; he was almost made a Father of the Church for his *Ternaire*, which no one has ever understood. But what would be thought to-day of a philosopher who should tell us that one substance is the same as *any other*; that the world is a figure of twelve pentagons; that fire is a pyramid which is connected with the earth by numbers? Would it be thought convincing to prove the immortality and transmigration of the soul by saying that sleep is born of wakefulness and wakefulness of sleep, the living from the dead and the dead from the living? Such reasonings as these have been admired for many centuries, and still more fantastic ideas have since been employed in the education of mankind.

Locke alone has developed the *human understanding* in a book where there is naught but truths, a book made perfect by the fact that these truths are stated clearly.

To complete our review of the superiority of the past century over all others, we may cast our eyes towards Germany and the North. Hevelius of Danzig was the first astronomer to study deeply the planet of the moon; no man before him surveyed the heavens with greater care: and of all the great men that the age produced, none showed more plainly why it should be justly called the age of Louis XIV. A magnificent library that he possessed was destroyed by fire; upon which the King of France bestowed on the astronomer of Danzig a present which more than compensated him for the loss.

Mercator of Holstein was the forerunner of Newton in geometry; and the Bernouillis in Switzerland were worthy pupils of that great man. Leibnitz was for some time regarded as his rival.

The celebrated Leibnitz was born at Leipzig; and died, full of learning, in the town of Hanover; like Newton, worshipping a god, and seeking counsel of no man. He was perhaps the most universal genius in Europe: a historian assiduous in research; a sagacious lawyer, enlightening the study of law with science, foreign to that subject though it seem; a metaphysician sufficiently open-minded to endeavour to reconcile theology with metaphysics; even a Latin poet, and finally a mathematician of sufficient calibre to dispute with the great Newton the invention of the infinitesimal calculus, so that for some time the issue remained uncertain.

It was the golden age of geometry; mathematicians frequently challenged one another, that is to say, they sent each other problems to be solved, almost as the ancient kings of Asia and Egypt are reported to have sent each other riddles to divine. The problems propounded by the geometricians were more difficult than the ancient riddles; and in Germany, England, Italy and France, not one of them was left unsolved. Never was intercourse between philosophers more universal; Leibnitz did much to encourage it. A republic of letters was being gradually established in Europe, in spite of different religions. Every science, every art, was mutually assisted in this way, and it was the academies which formed this republic. Italy and Russia were allied by literature. The Englishman, the German and the Frenchman went to Leyden to study. The celebrated physician Boerhaave was consulted both by the Pope and by the Czar. His greatest pupils attracted the notice of foreigners and thus became to some extent the physicians of the nation; true scholars in every branch drew closer the bonds of this great fellowship of intellect, spread everywhere and everywhere independent. This intercourse still obtains, and is indeed one of the consolations for those ills which political ambition scatters throughout the earth.

Italy throughout this century preserved her ancient glory, though she produced no new Tassos nor Raphaels; it is enough to have produced them once. Men like Chiabrera, and later Zappi and Filicaia, showed that refinement is still a characteristic of that nation. Maffei's *Merope* and the dramatic works of Metastasio are worthy monuments of the age.

The study of true physics, founded by Galileo, was still pursued despite the opposition of an ancient and too hallowed philosophy. Men like Cassini, Viviani, Manfredi, Bianchini, Zanotti and many others spread the same light in Italy which was already lighting other countries; and, while admitting that the chief rays of this beacon came from England, let it be said that Italian teachers at least did not hide their eyes from the gleam.

All branches of literature were cultivated in this ancient home of the arts, and with as great success save in those subjects where a liberty of thought unknown to Italy gives wider scope. This age, above all, was better acquainted with antiquity than all preceding ages. Italy provided more such monuments than all the rest of Europe, and every fresh excavation has but extended the boundaries of knowledge.

We owe this progress to a few learned men, a few geniuses scattered in small numbers in various parts of Europe, nearly all of them unhonoured for many years and often persecuted; they enlightened and consoled the world when it was devastated by war. The names of all those who thus gave lustre to Germany, England and Italy may be found elsewhere. A foreigner is perhaps little able to appreciate the merits of all these illustrious men. It is enough, here, if we have shown that during the past century mankind, from one end of Europe to the other, has been more enlightened than in all preceding ages.

CHAPTER XXXV

ECCLESIASTICAL AFFAIRS—MEMORABLE CONTROVERSIES

OF the three estates of the nation the Church is the least numerous, and it is only in France that the clergy has come to form a separate estate. It is an astonishing thing, but nevertheless true; and as I have said before, nothing shows more plainly the force of custom. The clergy, once recognised as a separate estate, has ever demanded the most careful and discriminating control on the part of the sovereign. To maintain friendly relations with the See at Rome and at the same time to uphold the liberties of the Gallican Church; to secure obedience from the bishops as his subjects without interfering with the rights of the episcopacy; to subject them in many matters to the secular tribunal and allow them to remain judges in others; to force them to contribute to the needs of the state without damaging their prerogatives: all this required a blending of diplomacy and resolution which Louis XIV. hardly ever failed to display.

Decency and order were gradually restored in the French clergy which civil war and the licentiousness of the times had dissipated. The king no longer allowed any layman to possess a benefice under the name of a hired cleric (known as a *confidentiaire*), nor anyone who was not a priest to acquire a bishopric, like Cardinal Mazarin, who was appointed to the bishopric of Metz without even being a sub-deacon, and the Duke de Verneuil who, though a layman, had also possessed it.

The sum annually paid to the king by the French clergy and the conquered towns amounted to about two million five hundred thousand livres; and later, the value of gold having increased, they assisted the state to the amount of about four millions every year by means of taxes known as *the tenth*, a special subsidy and free gifts. The word and privilege of *free gift* are a survival of the ancient custom by which all nobles holding fiefs gave *free gifts* to their kings to supply the needs of state. Bishops and abbés, being held lord of fiefs by a long-established abuse, were only obliged to provide soldiers in times of feudal anarchy. Kings possessed at that time nothing but their estates, like other nobles. But while all else changed, the clergy remained the same, and preserved the custom of assisting the state by free gifts.

To that ancient custom, which is preserved by a society that often meets and which cannot but be lost by a society which never does so, one must add the immunity always claimed by the Church, and this maxim, that her property belongs to the poor; not that she claims to owe nothing to the state from whom she receives everything, for the state in time of need ranks as first among the poor; but she alleges her right to give only voluntary aid, and Louis XIV. always demanded this aid in such a way that he could not be refused.

People are astonished that the clergy in France and Europe are taxed so little; they are thought to own a third of the kingdom. If they possessed as much as that, they ought certainly to pay a third of the taxes, which would amount in an average year to more than fifty millions, excluding indirect taxes, which every subject has to pay; but the vaguest notions and opinions prevail in regard to these matters.

Of all the Catholic churches, that of France has undoubtedly amassed the least wealth. Not only is there no bishop who has obtained possession, like the Bishop of Rome, of a considerable sovereignty, but there is no abbot like the Abbé Monte Cassiano and the German abbots, who enjoy almost regal prerogatives. As a general rule bishops in France do not receive a large income. Those of the Bishops of Strasburg and Cambrai are the largest, but that is because they originally belonged to Germany and the German Church was much richer than the Empire.

In his *History of Naples* Giannone asserts that the ecclesiastics receive two-thirds of the revenue of the country. France was never troubled with such an infamous abuse. It is said that the Church owns a third of the kingdom, just as one says at random that there are a million inhabitants in Paris. If people would only take the trouble to calculate the revenues of bishops, they would find from the value of the leases fifty years ago that the annual revenues of all the bishoprics put together were at that time computed at not more than four millions, and those of the commendatory abbeys did not exceed four million five hundred thousand livres. It is true that the declared value of the leases was a third less than their real value, and if the increase in value of land property be taken into consideration the total revenue of all consistorial benefices cannot now be less than sixteen millions. Nor should it be forgotten that of this money a considerable sum is sent annually to Rome, which never returns, and which must be set down as a dead loss. The king is indeed extremely liberal towards the Holy See; in the course of a generation the state is deprived of more than four hundred thousand silver marks, which, in course of time, would impoverish the kingdom, did not commerce more than repair the loss.

To those benefices that pay their first year's income to Rome must be added the rectories, convents, collegiate churches, religious houses, and other livings of every kind; but we shall not be far from the truth in putting their annual income throughout the whole kingdom at fifty millions.

Those who have investigated this matter at once with impartiality and care have been unable to estimate the revenues from all branches of the secular and canonical Gallican Church at more than ninety millions. It is not an exorbitant sum for the maintenance of ninety thousand persons belonging to religious orders and about one hundred and sixty thousand priests, according to the reckoning of 1700. More than a third of these ninety thousand monks, moreover, live on the proceeds of offertories and masses. Many cloistered monks cost their monastery less than two hundred livres a year, while there are monastic priests who enjoy an income of two hundred thousand livres. It is this flagrant disproportion that is so striking and that gives rise to so many complaints. We pity a country parson whose arduous labours only procure him a definite pittance of three hundred livres, with perhaps from four to five hundred livres from offerings, while an idle monk, once he has become an abbé but no less idle, enjoys an immense revenue and receives princely tithes from those who are subject to him. These abuses are practised to a much greater extent in Flanders, Spain, and especially the Catholic states of Germany, where princes are sometimes seen as monks.

Abuses take the place of laws in nearly every country, and it may well be asked: If the wisest men should meet together to frame the laws, what state would continue to exist in its present form?

The clergy of France still observe the onerous custom of paying a free gift to the king of several millions, over a stretch of some years. They borrow the money; and, after paying interest due, refund the capital to their creditors; they thus pay twice over. It would be more advantageous to the state and to the clergy in general, and certainly more logical, for the clergy to subscribe to the nation's needs by contributions in proportion to the value of each benefice. But it is difficult for men to renounce old customs. It was due to this same attitude that the clergy, though assembling every five years, never acquired a hall of assembly or so much as a single piece of furniture.

It is obvious that, though paying out less, they might have rendered the king much greater assistance, and could

well have built a palace in Paris that would have added a
new ornament to that capital.

During the minority of Louis XIV. the morals of the
French clergy were not as yet fully purged of the vices introduced by the *Ligue*. During the youth of Louis XIII., and
at the last meeting of parliament in 1614, the most numerous
part of the nation, known as the third estate, who form
indeed the basis of the state, vainly petitioned parliament
to lay down as a fundamental law, "that no spiritual power
can deprive kings of their sacred rights, which they hold
from God alone, and that it shall be deemed a crime of high
treason to teach that kings may be deposed or put to death."
Such was the substance in so many words of the nation's
demand. It was made at a time when the blood of Henri-
Quatre was still smoking. Nevertheless, Cardinal Duperron,
a bishop of France, and born within its boundaries, vehemently opposed the demand on the ground it was not for
the third estate to propose laws which might affect the
Church. Why did he not do to the clergy what the third
estate wished to do to parliament? On the contrary, he was
so far from doing so that in his rage he actually declared
"that the power of the Pope was absolute, plenary, direct
in regard to spiritual affairs, and indirect in regard to temporal,
and that he had power to order the clergy to excommunicate
those who asserted that the Pope could not dethrone kings."
The nobility was won over, the people was silenced. Parliament renewed its ancient decrees, declaring the crown independent and the king's person sacred. The ecclesiastical
assembly, while admitting that the king's person was sacred,
persisted in maintaining that the crown was dependent. It
was the same spirit which had once deposed *Louis le Débon-
naire,* and it was so powerful now that the court, weakening,
was forced to imprison the printer who had published the
decree of parliament under the title of *Fundamental law.*
Parliament, it was said, was acting thus in order to keep the
peace; but it was punishing those who were supplying the
crown with weapons of defence. Such scenes were never
witnessed at Vienna; the fact was that while France feared
Rome, Rome in her turn feared the House of Austria.

The cause that failed was so far the cause of every king
that James I. of England wrote a book against Cardinal
Duperron, and it is that monarch's finest work. It was also
the people's cause, whose tranquillity demands that its

sovereigns shall not be dependent on a foreign power. Reason gradually prevailed, and Louis XIV. had no trouble in making its voice heard, supported as it was by all the authority of his power.

Antonio Perez, once first minister in Spain, commended three things to Henri-Quatre, *Roma, Consejo, Pielago,* that is, Rome, the council, and the ocean: but Louis XIV. was so supreme in the last two departments, that he could well neglect the first. He was careful to preserve the custom of appealing to parliament against ecclesiastical laws in all cases where such laws affected the royal jurisdiction. The clergy often complained of it, but sometimes praised it; for if on the one hand such appeals uphold the rights of the state against episcopal authority, on the other they affirm that authority by defending the privileges of the Gallican Church against the claims of the Court of Rome; so that the bishops looked upon parliaments as at once their enemies and defenders; and the government took care that in spite of religious quarrels the limits of the land were passed, easy as it were to overstep them. The power of corporate bodies and societies is like the interests of commercial towns; it is for the legislator to adjust them.

THE LIBERTIES OF THE GALLICAN CHURCH

The word *liberties* implies subjection. Liberties and prerogatives are so many exemptions from a general bondage. One should therefore speak of the rights and not the liberties of the Gallican Church. These rights are those of all the early churches. The bishops of Rome never had the least jurisdiction over the Christian societies of the Eastern Empire; but they encroached everywhere among the ruins of the Western Empire. The Gallican Church was long the only one to dispute with the See of Rome those ancient rights which each bishop had bestowed upon himself, when after the first Council of Nicæa the ecclesiastical and purely spiritual administration was modelled on the civil government, and each bishop had his own diocese just as each imperial province had its own. Certainly no gospel directs that a bishop of the city of Rome may send legates *a latere* to France with powers to judge, reform, distribute, and raise money among the people:

To order French prelates to go to Rome and plead;

To levy taxes on the benefices of the kingdom under such names as festivals, spoliations, inheritances, first-year fruits, incompatibilities, orders, ninths, tenths, annates and so on;

To excommunicate the king's officials and prevent them from carrying out the duties of their office;

To legitimise the succession of bastards;

To annul the wills of those who died without bequeathing a certain part of their property to the Church;

To allow French ecclesiastics to sign away their landed property;

To appoint judges to enquire into the lawfulness of marriages.

Finally, it was calculated that there were more than seventy abuses against which royal parliaments had always maintained the natural liberty of the nation and the dignity of the crown.

Whatever influence the Jesuits may have had under Louis XIV., and whatever restraint that monarch may have put on the remonstrances of parliament after he took up the reins of government himself, nevertheless not one of all the parliaments called during his reign ever lost an opportunity of opposing the claims of the Court of Rome; and the king approved of such vigilance, since here the inherent rights of the nation were at one with those of its monarch.

At once the most important and most delicate affair of this kind was the king's right of ward, known as the *régale* or *droit du roi*. By this right French kings may, during the period that a see is vacant, nominate to all the *simple* livings of the dioceses, and may use the revenues of the bishopric as they see fit. At the present day this is an especial prerogative of the kings of France; but each state has its special rights. The kings of Portugal enjoy a third of the revenues of bishoprics in their kingdom. The Emperor has the right to the first offerings and has always nominated the principal livings as they become vacant. The kings of Naples and Sicily have still greater privileges. The prerogatives of Rome are for the most part founded on usage rather than on original claims.

The Merovingian kings used to confer on their sole authority bishopric and all other livings. In 742 Carloman made Archbishop of Mayence that same Boniface who afterwards out of gratitude anointed Pepin. There still remain many signs of the power possessed by kings to confer important posts; and the more important they are, the more necessary is it that they should be dependent on the head of the state. The rivalry of a foreign bishop might well seem dangerous, and that the right of nomination should be reserved to this foreign bishop was often thought still more so. More than once it caused a civil war. Since kings bestowed bishoprics, it seemed right that they should preserve the slight privilege of disposing of the revenue and nominating to a few *simple* livings during the short period that elapses between the death of a bishop and the taking by his successor of the oath of fealty. Several bishops of towns annexed to the crown under the third dynasty, that of the Capets, determined not to acknowledge this privilege, which certain nobles had been too weak to make respected. The popes sided with the bishops, and their claims were long left undecided. In 1608 the parliament of Henri IV. decreed that the *droit du roi* should be established throughout the kingdoms; the clergy complained, whereupon the king, who managed both the bishops and Rome itself, raised the question in his council and took care not to settle it.

Both Cardinal Richelieu and Cardinal Mazarin obliged the council to pass decrees by which bishops who declared themselves exempt were compelled to set forth their claims. Nothing was decided until 1673, and until that time the king hardly dared bestow a single benefice in any diocese south of the Loire during the vacancy of a see.

Finally, in 1673, the Chancellor Étienne d'Aligre ratified a decree by which all the bishoprics of the kingdom were subjected to the *droit du roi*. Two bishops, unfortunately the two most virtuous men in the kingdom, obstinately refused to submit; they were Pavillon, Bishop of Aleth, and Caulet, Bishop of Pamiers. At first they defended themselves with plausible reasons; upon which equally strong arguments were brought to bear against them. When lengthy disputes occur between enlightened men there is every probability that the question is far from clear; it was indeed very obscure, but it was evident that it was neither in the interests of religion nor of law and order to prevent a king from carrying out in two dioceses what he did in all the others. The two bishops remained, however, inflexible. Neither had sworn the oath of fealty, and the king considered himself entitled to appoint canons to the livings of their churches.

The two prelates excommunicated those who were thus

appointed by the *droit du roi*. Both were suspected of Jansenism. Pope Innocent X. was unfriendly towards them; but when they declared against the claims of the king they were supported by Odescalchi, Innocent XI. This Pope, virtuous and obstinate as they, wholeheartedly took their part.

At first the king contented himself with banishing the principal incumbents of these bishops. He showed greater moderation than two men who prided themselves on their saintliness. The Bishop of Aleth, respected on account of great age, was allowed to die in peace. The Bishop of Pamiers remained alone and unshaken. He redoubled his excommunications and persisted in refusing to take the oath of fealty, convinced that such an oath subordinates the Church too much to the monarchy. The king seized his temporal possessions, but the Pope and the Jansenists compensated him. Finally he was deprived of his revenues and died in 1680, convinced that he had upheld God's cause against the king. His death did not end the dispute; certain canons appointed by the king came to take possession of their livings, but were driven out of the church by monks claiming to be canons and grand vicars, and excommunicated. Montpezat, Archbishop of the Province of Toulouse, before whom this case came for trial, vainly pronounced sentences against these pretended grand vicars; they appealed to Rome, according to the custom of taking to the Court of Rome ecclesiastical cases judged by archbishops of France—a custom inconsistent with the liberty of the Gallican Church; but all man-made governments are inconsistent. Parliament issued decrees. A monk named Cerle, who was one of these grand vicars, violated both the judgment of the provincial archbishop and the decrees of parliament. The latter tribunal sentenced him by default to be beheaded and dragged on a hurdle. He was executed in effigy, but from his hiding-place he hurled insults at the archbishop and the king; and the Pope defended him. The pontiff did more; convinced, like the Bishop of Pamiers, that the *droit du roi* constituted an ecclesiastical abuse, and that the king had no right in the diocese of Pamiers, he annulled the decrees of the Archbishop of Toulouse, and excommunicated not merely the new grand vicars appointed by that prelate, but also the canons appointed by the king and their supporters.

The king summoned a convocation of the clergy, composed of thirty-five bishops and as many deputies of the second degree. For the first time the Jansenists took the side of the people, and being an enemy of the king, the Pope favoured them though far from liking them. He regarded it as a matter of honour to resist that monarch on every opportunity; and afterwards in 1689 he even joined the Allies against King James, since Louis XIV. was protecting that prince; it was indeed said at the time that in order to put an end to the quarrels between Europe and the Church, King James must become a Huguenot and the Pope a Catholic.

Meanwhile the ecclesiastical convocations of 1681 and 1682 unanimously declared for the king. There was yet another minor dispute which was becoming serious; the election of a prior in one of the suburbs of Paris set the king and the Pope by the ears. The Roman pontiff had annulled a decree of the Archbishop of Paris and rescinded his nomination to this priory. Parliament judged the measures adopted by Rome to be improper. The Pope issued a bull ordering the Inquisition to burn the decree of parliament, and parliament in turn ordered the suppression of the bull. Such struggles have long been the usual and inevitable results of that old-established compromise between a natural liberty by which a nation governs itself at home, and subjection to a foreign power.

The ecclesiastical convocation took up a position which shows that wise men can maintain their dignity while yielding to their sovereign, without the intervention of another power. They agreed to the extension of the *droit du roi* throughout the kingdom; but this was as much a concession on the part of the clergy, who moderated their claims out of gratitude to their protector, as a formal admission of the absolute rights of the crown.

Convocation justified itself towards the Pope by a letter in which occurs a passage which of itself might well serve as a perpetual rule for all disputes; it reads "that it is better to sacrifice part of one's rights than to disturb the peace." The king, the Gallican Church, and the two chambers of parliament were content. The Jansenists wrote libels: but the Pope was obdurate; he annulled the resolutions of convocation in a pastoral letter and ordered the bishops to retract. It was enough to separate the Church of France from the Church of Rome for ever. Under Cardinal Richelieu and Mazarin the idea of creating a patriarch had been discussed. The desire of every magistrate was to cease paying annates to Rome: Rome was no longer to have power to appoint incumbents to the livings in Brittany during six months of the year; French bishops were no longer to be designated bishops *by permission of the Holy See*. Had he wished, the king had only to say the word; he was master of convocation, and he had the nation behind him. Rome had lost everything through the obduracy of a virtuous pontiff, who of all the popes of that age alone could not understand and adapt himself to the times; but old-established barriers are not broken down without violent shocks. Wider interests were necessary, greater passions and ardours had to be inflamed before any sudden rupture with Rome should take place, and it was extremely difficult to bring about such a secession while efforts were being made to uproot Calvinism. It was thought to be a bold stroke to publish the four famous decisions of the same ecclesiastical convocation, in 1682, the chief points of which were:

1. God gave no power either direct or indirect to Peter and his successors over temporal matters.
2. The Gallican Church agrees with the council of Constantius, which proclaims that General Councils are superior to the Pope in spiritual affairs.
3. The rules, customs and practices established throughout the French Church and kingdom must remain unalterable.
4. The decisions of the Pope in matters of faith are only absolute when the Church has accepted them.

Every tribunal and every theological body registered these four propositions in their entirety, and an edict was issued forbidding the teaching of anything contrary to them. This resolute attitude was regarded in Rome as an attempt at rebellion, and by every Protestant in Europe as a feeble effort towards liberty by a Church once free, which was only breaking four links of its fetters.

The four precepts were at first enthusiastically taken up by the nation, but afterwards with declining zeal. Towards the end of Louis XIV.'s reign they began to be regarded as doubtful, and Cardinal de Fleury afterwards rescinded part of them at an ecclesiastical convocation, without causing the least disturbance by his disavowal, since by then the enthusiasm of the people had died down and the ministry of

Cardinal Fleury was alike undistinguished in all it did. They have since been upheld with great vigour.

Meanwhile Innocent XI. became more embittered; he refused to issue bulls to all bishops and all commendatory abbés appointed by the king; so that on his death in 1689 there were twenty-nine dioceses in France without bishops. These prelates did not omit to receive their revenues; but they dared not undergo consecration nor carry out their episcopal duties. The idea of creating a patriarch was revived. The dispute over the rights of ambassadors in Rome, which provoked further irritation, made people think that the time had come at last to establish in France a *Catholic-Apostolic* Church, which should in no wise be *Roman*. The attorney-general de Harlai and the solicitor-general Talon, made it sufficiently understood, when they appealed in 1687 against the bull opposing the franchise of ambassadors and exclaimed against the obstinacy of the Pope in leaving so many churches without pastors; but the king would never consent to such a step, which was more easy of accomplishment than its daring character appeared to imply.

The cause of Innocent XI. became, however, the cause of the Holy See. The four propositions of the French clergy attacked the phantom of infallibility (which is maintained at Rome, though not believed) and the real power attaching to the phantom. Alexander VIII. and Innocent XI. followed the example of the haughty Odescalchi, but with less obstinacy; they confirmed the sentence pronounced against the ecclesiastical convocation; they refused to issue bulls to the bishops; in short, they did too much, because Louis XIV. had not done enough. The bishops, tired of being appointed by the king alone and of finding themselves without duties to perform, asked the Court of France for permission to make peace with the Court of Rome.

The king, weary of the strife, consented. Each of the bishops wrote separately to say that he "was grievously distressed by the proceedings of the convocation"; each declared in his letter that he did not accept as decisions what had been decided there, nor as decrees what had there been enacted. Innocent XI. (Pignatelli), more conciliating than Odescalchi, was satisfied with these overtures. The four propositions continued, none the less, to be taught in France from time to time; but such weapons rusted when they were no longer fought with, and the dispute was glossed

over without being settled, as nearly always happens in a
state which holds no settled and invariable principles on
such matters. Thus in France we are sometimes rebelling
against Rome, sometimes submitting to her, according to
the dispositions of those who are in power and the particular
interests of those by whom the leaders of the state are ruled.

Louis XIV. had no other ecclesiastical quarrel with Rome
and suffered no interference from the clergy in temporal
matters.

Under his rule the clergy attained to a respectability and
decorum unknown during the barbarous ages of the two
earlier dynasties, during the still more barbarous epoch of
feudal rule, a decorum absolutely unknown during the civil
wars and the disorders of Louis XIII.'s reign, and above all
during the Fronde, with a few exceptions such as must always
be the case with vices as with the predominating virtues.

For the first time people's eyes began to be opened to the
superstitions always associated with religion. Despite the
parliament of Aix and the Carmelites, people were still
allowed to be told that Lazarus and Magdalene had never
journeyed into Provence. The Benedictines could no longer
make people believe that Denys the Areopagite had ruled
the Church of Paris. Pretended saints, false miracles, false
relics, began to be discredited, sound reason such as was
already enlightening the philosophers began to spread
everywhere, though slowly and with difficulty.

The Bishop of Châlons-sur-Marne, Gaston Louis de
Noailles, brother of the cardinal, was sufficiently enlightened
to seize and have taken away in 1702 a relic that had been
preserved with precious care for several centuries in the
church of Notre-Dame, and adored as the navel of Jesus
Christ. All Châlons murmured against the bishop. Presidents,
councillors, the king's followers, treasurers of France, merchants, leading men, canons, pastors, all drew up a judicial
decree, unanimously protesting against the bishop's violent
act, demanding the return of the sacred navel, and pointing
to the fact that the robe of Jesus Christ was preserved at
Argenteuil; his handkerchief at Turin and at Laon; one of
the nails of the Cross at Saint-Denys, and many another
relic which, preserved and despised, does so much harm to
religion which we revere. But the bishop's sober firmness at
length prevailed over the credulity of the people.

Various other superstitions connected with customs once

laudable still exist. The Protestants have triumphed over them, but they are obliged to admit that there is no Catholic Church where such abuses are less common and more despised than in France.

The truly philosophical spirit, which took root only towards the middle of the period, succeeded in suppressing neither the old nor the new theological disputes, which were outside its province. We shall now speak of these dissensions which are a disgrace to human reason.

CHAPTER XXXVI

CALVINISM IN THE TIME OF LOUIS XIV

It is undeniably a terrible reproach that the Christian church should have been perpetually torn with strife, and that blood should have been shed for so many centuries by men who proclaimed the god of peace. Paganism knew no such fury. It covered the world in darkness, but shed hardly a drop of blood save that of beasts; and while the Jews and pagans sometimes devoted human victims, such sacrifices, horrible as they were, did not give rise to any civil wars. The religion of the pagans was wholly comprised in a code of morals and their ceremonies—morals which are common to men at all times and at all places, and feasts, which were merely outward signs of rejoicing, and could not disturb the human race.

The spirit of dogma bred the madness of religious wars in the minds of men. I have long sought the reason why this spirit of dogma, which divided the schools of heathen antiquity without causing the least disturbance, should have caused such great and horrible ones among ourselves. Fanaticism alone is not the cause; for the gymnosophists and the Brahmins, the most fanatical of men, never did any harm to any save themselves. Should not one trace the origin of this new plague that has come to ravage the earth to that inborn rebellion of the republican spirit, which animated the early Church, against authority that hates resistance of any kind? The secret assemblies that first defied the laws of a few Roman emperors in caves and crypts gradually created a state within the state; it was like a republic hidden within the heart of the Empire. Constantine drew it from underground to place it, so to speak, level with the throne. Soon the authority attached to the large sees found itself in opposition with the popular spirit which had till then pervaded all Christian societies. Often when the bishop of a metropolitan see expressed a certain opinion, a suffragan bishop, priest, or deacon would hold a different view. Mankind resents in secret all authority, the more so since every authority endeavours to increase its powers. And when to resist that authority a pretext is found which may well be deemed sacred, revolt soon becomes a duty. Thus some become persecutors and others rebels, while all alike bear witness to God of the justice of their cause.

We have seen how, following the controversies of a priest, Arius, with a certain bishop, the mania for ruling over the souls of men distracted the world. To surrender one's conscience to the will of God, to be ordered to believe under pain of death to the body and eternal torments for the soul, such with certain men was the highest point to which they reached in their tyranny over the mind; and to resist such menaces was in others the last effort of natural liberty. Those who have perused my *Essay on Manners and Customs* will remember that from the time of Theodosius there was a perpetual struggle between the secular and ecclesiastical jurisdictions; and since Charlemagne repeated conflicts have taken place between the large fief-holders and their sovereigns, bishops often in rebellion against their kings, and popes at variance with kings and bishops.

There were but few disputes in the Latin Church during the first centuries. The constant invasions of the barbarians hardly allowed time for reflection; and there were few doctrines sufficiently developed to fix the universal faith. In the age of Charlemagne nearly the whole of the West renounced the worship of images. A Bishop of Turin, Claude by name, vehemently forbade them and upheld several doctrines which are still to-day the foundation of the Protestant religion. These beliefs persisted in the valleys of Piedmont, the Dauphiny, Provence and Languedoc; they broke out in the twelfth century, and soon afterwards produced the war of the Albigenses; then invading the University of Prague they stirred up the Hussite wars. There was only an interval of about one hundred years between the end of the disturbances that arose from the cinders of John Hus and Jerome of Prague and those which arose with the sale of indulgences. The ancient doctrines accepted by the Vaudois, the Albigenses and the Hussites, revived and newly expounded by Luther and Zwingli, were eagerly received in Germany as a pretext for seizing much of the property of which the bishops and abbés had possessed themselves, and for resisting their emperors who were then making rapid strides towards an absolute despotism. The doctrines triumphed also in Sweden and Denmark, countries where the people lived free under their kings.

The English, endowed by nature with a spirit of independence, adopted them, modified them and formed from them a religion all their own. Presbyterianism established itself in Scotland at an unhappy time—a kind of republicanism whose pedantry and austerity were even more intolerable than the severity of the climate and the tyranny of the bishops which had caused such complaints. It only ceased to be dangerous in Scotland when held in check by reason, laws and force. The Reformation spread to Poland and made great progress there in those few towns where the people enjoyed the rights of liberty. The largest and richest section of the Swiss republic accepted it without a qualm. It was on the point of being established in Venice for the same reasons; and would have taken root there had not Venice been so near to Rome; and also, perhaps, had the government not feared democracy, a state to which the people naturally aspire in every republic, and which was then indeed the main theme of almost every Protestant preacher. The Dutch only adopted this religion when they had shaken off the yoke of Spain; and Geneva in becoming Calvinist became entirely republican.

The House of Austria banished the new religions from its states as far as possible. They scarcely affected Spain. In Savoy they were exterminated by fire and sword—Savoy, the country in which they had originated. The inhabitants of the valleys of Piedmont experienced in 1655 what the people of Merindol and Cabrières had experienced in France under Francis I. The Duke of Savoy, as an absolute monarch, exterminated the sect so soon as it seemed dangerous; there remain to-day but a few feeble offshoots forgotten among the rocks that conceal them. Under the firm rule of Francis I. and Henry II. Lutherans and Calvinists caused no great disturbances in France; but as soon as the government became weak and divided religious quarrels broke out with violence. Condé and Coligni, turned Calvinist since the Guises were Catholics, rivalled each other in overthrowing the state. The fickleness and impetuosity of the nation, the mania for novelty and fanaticism, transformed for a space of forty years the most cultured people into a nation of barbarians.

Henri IV., brought up in a religion he loved, though not madly devoted to any, could not, despite his victories and his virtues, reign without renouncing Calvinism; become a Catholic, he was not so ungrateful as to wish to exterminate a sect, so long the enemy of kings, but to which he owed in part his crown; nor, had he wished to do so, had he the power. He cherished, protected and restricted it.

At that period the Huguenots in France comprised about a twelfth part of the nation. Among them were to be found many powerful lords, and whole towns might be found Protestant. They made war on kings; and it had been necessary to grant them towns where they could dwell in safety; Henri III. had granted them fourteen in the Dauphiny alone; Montauban, Nîmes in Languedoc; Saumur, and, above all, La Rochelle, which formed a separate republic, owing its power to the trade and support of England. At length Henri IV. seemed to be satisfying his own desires, his policy, even his duty, in granting to that sect the famous Edict of Nantes in 1598. The Edict was not at bottom more than a confirmation of the privileges which French Protestants had obtained from previous kings by force of arms, and which Henri-Quatre, once secure on the throne, allowed them out of sheer goodwill.

By the Edict of Nantes, which the name of Henri IV. rendered more famous than all others, every fief-holding noble of the high court of justice might practise freely in his castle the so-called reformed religion, every noble not a member of the High Court might admit thirty people to his chapel. The full exercise of the religion was authorised in all places immediately under the jurisdiction of parliament.

Calvinists might print, without having to make application to their superiors, any of their books in towns where their religion was permitted.

They were declared capable of holding every office and dignity in the state; and the decree was borne out by the fact that the king made dukes and peers of the nobles de La Trimouille and de Rosni.

A special chamber was created in the parliament of Paris, composed of a president and sixteen councillors, to judge all lawsuits in which reformers were concerned, not only throughout the immense jurisdiction of Paris, but also in those of Normandy and Brittany. It was called *the Chamber of the Edict*. It is true that only a single Calvinist was ever legally admitted among the councillors of this tribunal. Nevertheless, as it was intended to prevent the annoyance of which that sect complained, and men always take a pride in fulfilling a duty which brings them distinction, the chamber, though composed of Catholics, rendered the most impartial justice to the Huguenots on the latter's own avowal.

The Huguenots had a kind of parliament in little at Castres, independent of the parliament of Toulouse. At Grenoble and Bordeaux there were chambers half Catholic and half Calvinist. Their churches convoked synods just like the Gallican Church. These and many other privileges brought the Calvinists together on equal footing with the rest of the nation. It was in truth bringing enemies together, but the authority, the goodness, the skill of that great king kept them in harmony throughout his life.

After the deplorable death of Henri IV., which can never be regarded save with horror, during the weakness of a minority and a divided court, it was difficult for the republican spirit of the reformers to refrain from abusing their privileges and for the court, weak as it was, not to endeavour to restrict them. The Huguenots had already established little societies in France, imitating the example of the Germans. The delegates from such *circles* were often seditious, and many of the nobles in the party had great ambitions. The Duke de Bouillon, and especially the Duke de Rohan, the most trusted leader of the Huguenots, soon stirred into revolt the revolutionary doctrines of the preachers and the blind impetuosity of the people. In 1615 the general assembly of the party had the temerity to present a document to the court in which, among other insolent demands, they asked that reforms should be made in the king's council. In 1616 they resorted to arms in certain places, and the boldness of the Huguenots combining with the dissensions of the court, hostility towards the favourites and the unrest of the nation, all was in a state of prolonged disturbance. It was a period of revolt, intrigues, alarms, calls to arms, peaces hastily made and as soon broken; a period which made the celebrated Cardinal Bentivoglio, at that time nuncio in France, declare he had seen nothing but storms.

In the year 1621 the reformed Church of France offered Lesdiguières, afterwards High Constable, the generalship of their armies and one hundred thousand crowns a month. But Lesdiguières, more far-sighted in his ambition than they in their disputes, and knowing them from having led them, preferred to fight against rather than to command them, and as an answer to their offers became a Catholic. The Huguenots thereupon appealed to the Marshal Duke de Bouillon, who replied that he was too old; they finally conferred the ill-fated post on the Duke de Rohan, who, jointly with his brother, Soubise, dared to make war upon the King of France.

In the same year Louis XIII. was conducted from province to province by the High Constable de Luines. More than fifty towns submitted to him, with scarcely any resistance; but he was checked at Montauban, and had to suffer the shame of retreat: La Rochelle was besieged in vain, by its own efforts and with the help of England it resisted all attempts at capture; and the Duke de Rohan, guilty of high treason, negotiated for peace with his king, almost as one sovereign with another.

After this peace and the death of the High Constable de Luines, the renewal of the war was inevitable, and Rochelle, which was still leagued with England and the French Calvinists against its sovereign, was again besieged. A woman (the Duke de Rohan's mother) defended the town for a whole year against the royal army, the activities of Cardinal Richelieu, and the undaunted leadership of Louis XIII., who braved death more than once during the siege. The town suffered all the extremities of hunger, and its surrender was only due to the dam, about five hundred feet in length, which Richelieu ordered to be built in imitation of that erected by Alexander before Tyre in ancient times. It prevented supplies landing from the sea, and thus brought about the defeat of the people of Rochelle. Guiton, the mayor, who had sworn to bury himself beneath the ruins of Rochelle, after having surrendered at discretion, had the temerity to appear before Cardinal Richelieu with his guards. The mayors of the chief Huguenot towns indeed possessed them. Guiton, however, was now deprived of his property, and the town of its rights. The Duke de Rohan, leader of the heretic rebels, still carried on the war for his party; and deserted by the English, though Protestants, he leagued himself with the Spanish, though they were Catholics. But Richelieu's firm measures forced the Huguenots, who were beaten on all sides, to submit.

All the edicts hitherto enacted in their favour had been in the nature of treaties with their kings. Richelieu desired that the one he now decreed should be called the *Edict of Grace*. The king now spoke as a sovereign who forgave. Permission to practise the new religion in Rochelle was removed as also on the Isle of Ré, in Oléron, Privas and Pamiers; but the Edict of Nantes remained in force, and was still regarded by the Calvinists as their fundamental law.

It seems strange that the despotic and fearless Cardinal Richelieu should not have repealed this famous edict; he had at that time another scheme, more difficult of fulfilment perhaps, but not less suited to his wide ambition and lofty hopes. He sought the glory of mastering men's minds; enlightened himself, he believed, that by his power and his statecraft he could do this. His scheme was to win over certain of the preachers, to whom the Protestants gave the name of *ministers*, and who are now known as *pastors*; to make them first acknowledge that the Catholic religion was not a crime in the eyes of God, then gradually to lead them on, granting a few points of minor importance, and making it appear to the Court of Rome that he had conceded nothing. He counted on dazzling a certain number of the reformers, winning over others with presents and favours, and finally appeared to have united them to the Church, leaving time to do the rest and envisaging only the glory of having either accomplished or prepared the way for the great work and of making believe that he had carried it out. The famous Capuchin friar, Joseph, on the one hand, and on the other two ministers who had been won over, were the prime movers in this affair. But it seems that Cardinal Richelieu presumed too much and that it is more difficult to reconcile theologians than to dam the ocean.

Richelieu, rebuffed, determined to crush the Calvinists, but other matters intervened. He had to contend at the same time with the nobles of the kingdom, the royal household, the whole House of Austria, and often with Louis XIII. himself. He died at length prematurely, and in the midst of all these turmoils, leaving all his schemes incomplete and his name powerful and feared, rather than revered and loved.

Nevertheless, after the taking of Rochelle and the Edict of Grace, the civil wars came to an end, yielding place to controversy, alone. Everywhere those bulky books were printed which are now no longer read. The clergy, and especially the Jesuits, sought to convert the Huguenots. The reforming ministers made efforts to bring over some of the Catholics to their opinions. The king's council would be engaged in issuing decrees about a village cemetery over which the partisans of the two religions were wrangling, about a place of worship built on property formerly belonging to the Church, about schools, about the prerogatives of owners of castles, about burials, about bells; and rarely did the Protestants win their case. After the ravages and havoc of war, all that remained were these petty disturbances. The Huguenots no longer possessed a leader when the Duke de Rohan ceased to hold that office and the House of Bouillon no longer retained Sedan. They even claimed it as a merit to remain peaceful in the midst of the factions of the Fronde and the civil wars, stirred up by princes, parliaments and bishops, who claimed to serve the king against Cardinal Mazarin.

Hardly a single religious dispute arose during the lifetime of the minister. He did not hesitate to confer the post of Comptroller-General of Finance on a Calvinist and a foreigner, named Hervart.

Reformers were freely admitted as tax-farmers, sub-tax-farmers, and to all subordinate posts.

Colbert, who restored the industries of the nation and who may be regarded as the founder of its trade, employed many Huguenots in the industries connected with the arts, in manufactures and in the navy. All such useful occupations gradually moderated their ruling passion for controversy; and the glory surrounding Louis XIV. for fifty years, his power, his stable and vigorous government, banished all idea of resistance from the reforming party as from all others in the state. The magnificent entertainments of a gay court also contributed to throw ridicule on the prudery of the Huguenots. In proportion as good taste prevailed, the psalms of Marot and Beza could not but inspire an unconscious feeling of repugnance; made to charm the Court of Francis II., they were only suited to the populace of Louis XIV. Rational philosophy, which was beginning to make some strides towards the middle of the century, was inevitably bound in time to make reasonable men disgusted with polemical disputes.

But while reason was by slow degrees penetrating men's minds, the spirit of controversy was itself the means of maintaining the peace of the state; for the fame of the Jansenists beginning at that time to spread abroad, they divided the votes of those who delight in such subtleties; they wrote against Jesuits and Huguenots alike; the latter replied to Jansenists and Jesuits; and the Lutherans of the province of Alsace wrote against them all. A battle of pens between so many parties, whilst the state was occupied with important matters and the government was all-powerful, could only end by becoming in a few years the occupation of idle people, and fell sooner or later into insignificance.

Louis XIV. was urged into action against the reformers by the incessant protests of the clergy, by the insinuations of the Jesuits, by the Court of Rome, and, finally, by the chancellor Le Tellier and his son Louvois, who were both Colbert's enemies and wished to bring about the downfall of the Protestants as rebels, since Colbert favoured them as useful subjects. Louis XIV., moreover, by no means familiar with their doctrine, not unreasonably regarded them as former rebels, who had been with difficulty suppressed. He first applied himself to the task of gradually undermining at all points the foundations of their religion; on the least pretext they were deprived of a house of worship; they were forbidden to marry Catholics, an action perhaps hardly wise, since it ignored the power of a sex with which the court was but too well acquainted. The commissioners and bishops endeavoured in the most plausible manner to deprive the Huguenots of their own children.

In 1681 Colbert issued orders that no person of the reformed religion should be employed in the tax-farming administration. They were excluded as far as possible from the societies of arts and crafts. While the king thus restricted their powers he did not make their bondage unduly burdensome. Decrees were issued forbidding any violence towards them. Severity was modified by an insinuating clemency and harshness only existed in the formalities of justice.

A means which is often efficacious in bringing about conversion was utilised to a large extent: money was employed, but not sufficient use was made of this expedient. Pellisson was entrusted with these secret transactions: that Pellisson,

who had long been himself a Calvinist, and who was noted
for his works, his eloquent style, his devotion to the comptroller, Fouquet, whose chief secretary, favourite and victim
he had been. He had the good fortune to become enlightened
and change his religion at a time when such a change could
bring him both promotion and wealth. He donned the clerical
robe, acquired benefices and a post as master of requests.
About the year 1677, the king entrusted him with the
revenue of the abbeys of Saint-Germain-des-Prés and Cluny,
together with one-third of the revenues of dependent livings,
to be distributed among those who wished to be converted.
Cardinal Lecamus, Bishop of Grenoble, had already used
this method. Placed in charge of his department, Pellisson
distributed the money in the provinces. He attempted to
bring about many conversions by the expenditure of petty
sums. Such money, distributed among the poor, swelled the
quarterly list which Pellisson presented to the king, making
him believe that people were everywhere submitting to his
power or to his favours.

In 1681, encouraged by such small successes, which time
would have added to, the council made so bold as to issue
a proclamation by which children were to renounce their
religion at the age of seven, and following upon this decree,
many children in the provinces were arrested in order to
compel them to abjure their faith and soldiers were quartered
at the homes of their parents.

It was this inconsiderate haste of the chancellor, Le
Tellier, and his son, Louvois, that was responsible for many
families quitting the provinces of Poitou, Saintonge and the
neighbouring districts in 1681. Foreign countries hastened
to profit by it.

The King of England and the King of Denmark, and
especially the city of Amsterdam, invited the French Calvinists to take refuge in their countries, and guaranteed them
a living. Amsterdam even promised to build a thousand
houses for the fugitives.

The council, perceiving the dangerous consequences of a
too hasty misuse of authority, thought to remedy the affair
by the same authority. They knew how necessary artisans
were in a country where trade was flourishing, and sailors
at a time when a powerful navy was being formed. Consequently orders were issued forbidding any person employed in
these professions to leave the country on pain of the galleys.

It was discovered that some of the Calvinist families were selling their estates. A proclamation was accordingly issued confiscating all such property in the event of the vendor leaving the kingdom within a year. Severity was now redoubled against the ministers themselves. Their places of worship were closed on the slightest pretext. All the revenues left in trust to consistories were appropriated for hospitals throughout the kingdom.

Masters of Calvinist schools were forbidden to receive boarders. Ministers were subjected to the poll-tax; Protestant mayors were deprived of their noble rank. Any officers of the king's household and the king's secretaries who were Protestants were ordered to resign from their posts. No persons of the reformed religion were any longer allowed to become notaries, barristers, or even to exercise the profession of solicitors.

The clergy were earnestly charged to obtain converts, and Protestant pastors were prohibited from so doing, under pain of perpetual banishment. All these decrees were publicly solicited by the clergy of France. After all, they were children of the house who did not wish to share their home with strangers forcibly obtruded on them.

Pellisson continued to buy converts; but Mme. Hervart, widow of the comptroller-general of finance, inspired by the religious zeal for which women have at all times been noted, despatched as much money to prevent conversions as Pellisson had to make them.

Finally, in 1682, the Huguenots were bold enough openly to break the law in certain districts. They held meetings in Vivarais and the Dauphiny close to the spots where their churches had been pulled down. They were attacked; and they defended themselves. It was but a faint spark from the late civil war. Two or three hundred unfortunate beings, without leaders, position or even definite plans, were dispersed in a quarter of an hour; and their defeat was followed by heavy punishments. The grandson of the pastor Chamier, who had drawn up the Edict of Nantes, was broken on the wheel by the orders of the Commissioner of the Dauphiny. He is regarded as one of the most illustrious martyrs of the sect, and the name of Chamier has for long been held in veneration among the Protestants.

In 1683, the Commissioner of Languedoc had the preacher Chomel broken alive upon the wheel. Three others were condemned to the same punishment and then to be hanged; but they saved themselves by flight and were executed in effigy only.

These measures inspired terror but at the same time increased obstinacy. It is known only too well that the greater the sufferings men endure for their religion the more they cling to it.

The king was now persuaded that, having sent missionaries throughout the provinces, it was now necessary to despatch dragoons. Such violent measures would appear ill-timed; they were the outcome of the spirit then dominant at court, that everything must bow before the name of Louis XIV. They did not stop to consider that the Huguenots were no longer those of Jarnac, Moncontour and Coutras; that the fury of the civil wars was extinguished; that the long-drawn-out disorder was dying of inanition; that everything has its appointed time in the lives of men; that while the fathers had rebelled against Louis XII. their children were loyal to Louis XIV. In England, Holland and Germany several sects, who had been at each other's throats in the previous century, were now living peacefully together in the same towns. All went to prove that an absolute monarch can be equally well served by Catholics and Protestants. The Lutherans of Alsace provided eloquent testimony to this. Christina would seem to have been right in saying in one of her letters with reference to these violent measures and the subsequent emigrations: "I look upon France as a sick person, whose arms and legs have been cut off in order to treat him for a disorder of which he would have been completely cured by the exercise of gentleness and patience."

Louis XIV., who on seizing Strasburg in 1681 had protected Lutheranism, might have tolerated Calvinism in his own dominions; time, indeed, would have abolished it, as it diminishes each day the number of Lutherans in Alsace. Was it likely that in coercing a great number of his subjects he would not lose a still greater number, who, in spite of edicts and guards, would take to flight, rather than submit to a violence which they regarded as a horrible persecution? And why wish to force more than a million persons to hate a name that was beloved and precious, to which Protestants and Catholics, French people and foreigners alike had already joined the name of *Great*? Even from the point of view of policy alone, it appeared wise to protect the Calvinists and

play them off against the incessant claims of the Court of
Rome. It was at this very time that the king publicly broke
off relations with Innocent XI., the enemy of France. But
Louis XIV., while reconciling the interests of his religion
with those of his own greatness, wished at the same time
to humiliate the Pope and crush the Calvinists.

He foresaw in the two undertakings a blaze of glory such
as he was always greedy of. The bishops, several of the commissioners, every member of the council, persuaded him that
his soldiers had only to show themselves to finish what his
good deeds and missions had begun. He thought to use nothing
more than *authority*: but those to whom the authority was
entrusted actually exercised an excessive severity.

Towards the end of 1684 and the beginning of 1685, when
Louis XIV., who still maintained a powerful army, stood in
no fear of any of his neighbours, troops were sent into all
towns and castles where Protestants were in large numbers;
and as it was the dragoons, who were badly disciplined at
that time, who committed the worst excesses, this massacre
become known as the "dragonnade."

The frontiers were with all precautions watched so as
to stop the flight of those whom it was desired to reunite to
the Church. It was in the nature of a hunt made in a vast
enclosure.

A bishop, commissioner, sub - delegate priest or any
authorised person marched at the head of the soldiers. The
principal Calvinist families were assembled, especially those
who were thought the weakest. They renounced their religion
in the name of their fellow-believers, and those who obstinately
clung to their faith were handed over to the soldiers, who had
every licence of action, short of killing them; in spite of this
provision several of them were so maltreated that they died.
In foreign lands the children of refugees still utter bitter cries
over this persecution of their fathers, and compare it to the
most horrible persecutions suffered by the early Church.

The contrast was indeed strange between the stern and
pitiless orders and the luxurious court from which they
emanated, the refinement of its manners, the elegance and
charm of its society. The Marquis de Louvois showed the
inexorable nature of his character in this affair; the same
spirit was recognisable which had wished to engulf Holland
in the waves and which afterwards laid the Palatinate in
ashes. There are still extant certain letters of his written in

1685, couched in these terms: "His Majesty wishes to enforce the severest measures against those who will not embrace his religion, and those who wish to achieve the senseless glory of being the last to be converted must be driven to the last extremity."

Paris was not exposed to such disturbances; the cries of the victims would have made themselves heard too near the throne. Monarchs may think little of making their subjects wretched, but they are distressed to hear their outcry.

(1685) While places of worship were everywhere being demolished and people were being forced to renounce their religion at the point of the sword, the Edict of Nantes was at length revoked in the month of October 1685, and the ruin of the edifice, already undermined in every part, was completed.

The legislative chamber of the Edict had already been abolished. Calvinist councillors in parliament were ordered to resign their posts. The council issued decree after decree for the purpose of uprooting the remnants of the proscribed religion. Seemingly the most deadly was the decree ordering the abduction of the children of avowed reformers and the placing of them in charge of their nearest Catholic relations; an order so violently offending all natural ties that it was never carried out.

This famous edict which revoked the Edict of Nantes seems indeed to have provoked a result wholly contrary to the purpose in view. It was desired to reunite the Calvinists throughout the kingdom with the Church. Gourville, an extremely prudent man, when consulted by Louvois, proposed, so it was said, to arrest all ministers and only release those who, secretly bribed with sums of money, should publicly abjure their religion and thus assist the cause of reunion more than the efforts of missionaries and soldiers. Instead of following this prudent counsel, the edict ordered all ministers refusing to be converted to leave the kingdom within fourteen days. They were blind indeed if they thought that in driving away the shepherds they would prevent a large number of their flocks from following them. It was to presume too much upon their power and show very little knowledge of men, to imagine that so many embittered souls whose imaginations were inflamed with the idea of martyrdom, especially in the southern provinces of France, would not risk everything in order to go among strangers and proclaim their loyalty and the glory of their exile to nations envious of Louis XIV., who welcomed the crowds of fugitives with open arms.

The old chancellor Le Tellier, on signing the edict, exclaimed joyfully: "*Nunc dimittis servum, Domine, quia viderunt oculi mei salutare tuum.*" He little knew that he was putting his signature to one of the greatest calamities of France.

His son, Louvois, was likewise mistaken if he thought that an order issued by him was sufficient to defend all frontiers against those who considered flight a duty. Ingenuity when applied to evading the law is always stronger than authority. It was only necessary to bribe a few guards and the crowds of fugitives passed unmolested. In the course of three years nearly fifty thousand families left the kingdom and were afterwards followed by still more. They brought with them to foreign countries their arts, their manufactures and their wealth. Nearly the whole of the north of Germany, a pastoral country possessing no industries, assumed a new aspect under the influence of these invading multitudes. They filled whole towns. They manufactured cloths, laces, hats, stockings, all of which had previously been brought from France. A whole quarter of London was populated with French silk operatives; others brought to that city the perfected art of glass-cutting, an art that was henceforth lost to France. In Germany one may still frequently find traces of the gold first spread throughout the country by the refugees. In this way France lost about five hundred thousand of her inhabitants, enormous sums of money, and, what was worst of all, arts and crafts on which her enemies grew wealthy. Holland secured excellent officers and soldiers. The Prince of Orange and the Duke of Savoy formed regiments wholly composed of refugees. The very sovereigns of Savoy and Piedmont, who had practised such cruelties upon the reformers of their own countries, hired those of France; and it was certainly through no religious zeal that the Prince of Orange enlisted them. Some of them emigrated as far as the Cape of Good Hope, where they established settlements. The nephew of the celebrated lieutenant-general in the navy, Duquesne, founded a little colony at this distant spot; but it did not prosper, and most of those who set sail for it perished. There are still, however, some survivors of this colony close

to the Hottentots. The French have thus been scattered
farther abroad than the Jews.

It was to no purpose that the prisons and galleys were
filled with those who were captured in the act of flight.
What could be done with so many wretches, whom tortures
only served to strengthen in their belief? What was the use of
sending lawyers and infirm old men to the galleys? Some
hundreds of them were transported to America. Finally, the
council came to the conclusion that if emigration were no
longer prohibited, men would be no longer incited by the
secret pleasure of disobedience, and the number of desertions
would diminish. But the council was again mistaken, and
after having opened the avenues of escape it unavailingly
closed them for a second time.

In 1685 Calvinists were forbidden to employ Catholic
servants for fear their masters should convert them; in the
following year a further edict was issued ordering them to
dismiss their Huguenot servants, so that they might be
arrested as vagabonds. There was no consistency in the way
in which these people were persecuted, except in the determination to crush them so as to convert them.

All their places of worship destroyed, and their ministers
exiled, it became a question of retaining in the Roman Church
all those who had been either persuaded or intimidated into
being converted. There remained more than four hundred
thousand of them in the kingdom. They were forced to go to
mass and to communicate. Some, who spat out the consecrated wafer after they had received it, were condemned
to be burnt alive. The bodies of those who refused to receive
the last sacraments were drawn on a hurdle and thrown
on dung-heaps.

All persecutions produce converts when their blows are
struck whilst enthusiasm is at white heat. The Calvinists
assembled everywhere to sing their psalms, in spite of the
penalty of death decreed against all who should hold meetings.
The death penalty was also pronounced against ministers
who should re-enter the country, and a reward of five thousand five hundred livres was offered to anyone who informed
against them. Several of those who returned met their deaths
on the scaffold or on the rack.

Though seemingly crushed, the sect still lived on. Its
members vainly hoped during the war of 1689 that King
William, having dethroned his Catholic father-in-law, would

give his support to Calvinism in France: and during the war of 1701 rebellion and fanaticism broke out in Languedoc and the neighbouring districts.

The rebellion was fomented by means of prophecies. They have been in every age a means of deluding the simple and inflaming the fanatical. If by chance but one of the hundred events which impostors dare to predict come to pass, all the others are forgotten, and it is regarded as a token of God's favour and evidence of a prodigy. If a prediction is not fulfilled, it is explained away and a new meaning given to it; enthusiasts accept it and the fools believe.

The minister Jurieu was one of the most fiery of the prophets. He began by setting himself up to be greater than certain of the popular prophets of the time, such as Cottenus, a certain Christine, Justus Velsius, and Drabitius, whom he regarded as inspired by God. Later, he put himself almost on a level with the author of the Apocalypse and St. Paul; his adherents, or rather his enemies, had a medallion struck in Holland with this inscription: *Jurius propheta*. He predicted the deliverance of the people of God for eight years. He established a school of prophecy in the mountains of the Dauphiny, Vivarais and the Cevennes, districts peculiarly adapted for the acceptance of predictions, peopled by ignorant and hot-headed people, rendered fanatical by the hot climate and still more so by their preachers.

The first of these schools of prophecy was established in a glass-works, situated on a mountain in the Dauphiny, called Peira; an old Huguenot, named De Serre, foretold the ruin of Babylon and the restoration of Jerusalem. He taught children the words of the Scripture which say: "When three or four are gathered together in my name, there am I in the midst of them; and with a grain of faith you shall move mountains." Finally he received the Spirit; it was conferred on him by being breathed into his mouth, just as it is said in St. Matthew that Jesus breathed on his disciples before his death; he was beside himself, had convulsions, spoke in a strange voice, became motionless, deranged, his hair on end, according to the ancient usage of all nations and all the rules of inspired madness as handed down from century to century. Children received the gift of prophecy in this way, and if unable to move mountains, it was because they had sufficient faith to receive the Spirit, but not enough to work miracles; thereupon they redoubled their fervour in order to obtain the supreme gift.

While the Cevennes was thus a school of religious enthusiasm certain ministers who called themselves Apostles returned secretly to preach to the people.

Claude Brousson, who came of a respectable family in Nîmes, an eloquent and extremely zealous man, held in high repute in foreign countries, returning in 1698 to his own land, was convicted not only of having discharged the duties of his ministry in spite of the edicts, but of having carried on ten years before a correspondence with enemies of the state. He had indeed conceived the plan of smuggling English and Savoyard troops into Languedoc. The project, written in his own hand, and addressed to the Duke of Schomberg, had been intercepted long before and was now in the possession of the commissioner of the province. Hunted from town to town, Brousson was arrested at Oléron and removed to the fortress of Montpellier. On being questioned by the commissioner and his judges, he replied that he was the apostle of Jesus Christ, that he had received the Holy Spirit, that he could not betray the headquarters of the faith, and that it was his duty to spread the bread of the world among his brothers. He was asked if the apostles had formulated schemes for stirring up provinces; he was shown his fatal document, and unanimously condemned by the judges to be broken alive on the wheel (1698). He died with the constancy of the early martyrs. The whole sect, so far from regarding him as a state criminal, looked upon him as nothing short of a saint, who had sealed his faith with his blood; and an account of *The Martyrdom of M. de Brousson* was published.

Upon this the number of prophets increased and the spirit of frenzy was redoubled. By an unlucky chance it happened in 1703 that an abbé of the house of Du Chaila, an inspector of missions, received an order from the court to shut up in a convent the two daughters of a nobleman who had been recently converted. Instead of conveying them to the convent he first took them to his castle. A crowd of Calvinists gathered, broke open the gates and released the two girls and some other prisoners. The rebels seized the Abbé du Chaila, offering him his life if he would embrace their religion. He refused. One of the prophets cried out: "Die then, the Holy Spirit condemns thee, thy sin be on thine own head," and he was shot dead. Immediately afterwards they seized the collectors of poll-tax and hanged them with their own scrolls round their necks. They proceeded to massacre all the priests they met. On being pursued they took refuge in the woods and mountains. Their numbers increased; their prophets and prophetesses, inspired by God, proclaimed the restoration of Jerusalem and the fall of Babylon. An abbé, La Bourlie, suddenly appeared in the midst of their wild retreat, bringing them money and arms.

He was the son of the Marquis de Guiscard, deputy-governor to the king, and one of the most enlightened men in the kingdom. The son was indeed unworthy of such a father. Having committed some crime, he had taken refuge in Holland and now proceeded to stir up the Cevennes to revolt. Afterwards he went to London, where he was arrested in 1711 for having betrayed the English ministry after having betrayed his own country. Brought before the council, he snatched from the table one of those long knives capable of inflicting a fatal wound, and stabbed the Chancellor, Robert Harley, afterwards Earl of Oxford; he was loaded with chains and thrown into prison, finally avoiding execution by taking his own life. Such was the man who, in the name of the English, the Dutch and the Duke of Savoy, came to encourage the fanatics and promise them powerful assistance.

(1703) A large portion of the country secretly befriended them. Their war-cry was: *No taxes and liberty of conscience;* and it won over the populace on every hand. In the eyes of the people such acts of madness vindicated the plans of Louis XIV. for exterminating Calvinism; but had the Edict of Nantes not been revoked such frenzies would never have been aroused.

The king first despatched Marshal Montrevel with a few troops. He made war on these wretches with a barbarity which surpassed their own. Prisoners were broken on the wheel and burnt; and soldiers who fell into the hands of the rebels were put to no less cruel deaths. Louis, obliged to wage war on numerous fronts, could send but few troops against them. It was difficult to surprise them among the well-nigh inaccessible rocks, or in the caves and woods which they reached by unfrequented paths and whence they suddenly descended like wild beasts. In one regular engagement they even held at bay a detachment of marine troops. Three marshals of France were successively engaged against them.

Marshal Villars succeeded Marshal Montrevel in 1704. Since it was still more difficult to find them than to defeat them, Marshal Villars, after making himself feared, proposed an amnesty. Some of the rebels accepted it, undeceived by promises of help from the Duke of Savoy who, imitating the example of so many other sovereigns, persecuted them in his own country but was willing to protect them against his enemies.

Jean Cavalier was the most famous of their leaders and the only one who merits separate mention. I saw him afterwards in Holland and in England. He was a slight, fair man, with a pleasant and refined expression. Among his followers he was known as David. From baker's apprentice he became, at the age of twenty-three, the leader of a fairly large body of followers, owing to his courage, and with the help of a prophetess, who declared that he was appointed by express command of the Holy Ghost. He was at the head of eight hundred men, whom he was forming into regiments when the amnesty was proposed. He asked for hostages, and was given them. Upon this, followed by one of his leaders, he came to Nîmes, where he negotiated with Marshal Villars.

(1704) He agreed to raise four regiments from the rebels, who would serve the king under four colonels, of whom he would be the first and the other three of whom he would appoint himself. The regiments were to be allowed to exercise their religion freely, like the foreign troops in the pay of France, though the practice could not be permitted elsewhere. These conditions had already been accepted when envoys arrived from Holland with offers of money and promises to prevent their being carried out. They succeeded in detaching Cavalier from the chief fanatics; but having given his word to Marshal Villars he was determined to keep it. He received a colonel's commission, and began to form his regiment with a hundred and thirty men who were personally devoted to him.

I have often heard Marshal Villars say that he asked this young man how it was that at his age he had such power over men so savage and unruly. He replied that when they disobeyed him his prophetess, who was called the *Great Marie*, immediately became inspired and condemned the defaulters to death: and they were killed without more ado. Later on, putting the same question to Cavalier, I received the same reply.

This remarkable agreement was made after the Battle of Blenheim. After having denounced Calvinism with so much dignity, Louis XIV. now made peace, under the name of an amnesty, with a baker's apprentice; and Marshal Villars presented him with a colonel's commission and an annuity of twelve hundred livres.

The new colonel went to Versailles, where he received orders from the minister of war. The king saw him and shrugged his shoulders. Watched by the ministry, Cavalier became alarmed and withdrew to Piedmont. From there he passed to Holland and to England. He took part in the war in Spain, where he commanded a regiment of French refugees at the Battle of Almanza. The deeds of this regiment serve to show what madness there is in civil wars and how religion adds to this fury. Cavalier's Calvinist soldiers happened to be opposed by a French regiment. As soon as they recognised their adversaries, both sides, without stopping to fire, fell upon each other with the bayonet. It has already been mentioned that the bayonet is used but little in actual fighting. The behaviour of the first line, composed of three ranks, after they have fired the first volley decides the fate of the battle; but on this occasion fury produced results hardly ever achieved by valour. Of the two regiments not three hundred men were left alive. Marshal Berwick often used to describe this engagement with astonishment.

Cavalier died a general and governor of the island of Jersey, with a great reputation for bravery, having preserved of his early madness only his courage, and having substituted discretion for that fanaticism which could no longer justify itself by example.

Marshal Villars was recalled from Languedoc and replaced by Marshal Berwick. The reverses sustained by the king's arms at that time gave encouragement to the fanatics of Languedoc who, looking to Heaven for help, received assistance from the Allies. Money was sent to them by way of Geneva. They were waiting for officers who were to be despatched from Holland and England. They had secret committees of information in every town in the province.

Among the most formidable of their conspiracies was that by which they planned to seize the person of the Duke of Berwick and the commissioner Baville in Nîmes, stir up revolt in Languedoc and the Dauphiny, and allow the enemy to enter those provinces. The secret was kept by more

than a thousand conspirators; but the indiscretion of one of
their number disclosed the whole plot. More than two hundred
persons perished on the scaffold. Marshal Berwick exterminated with fire and sword as many of the wretches as he
could find. Some died with swords in their hand, others on
the wheel or at the stake. Still others, more given to pro-
phesying than fighting, found their way to Holland, where
they were received by the French refugees as messengers
from another world. They marched in front of them, singing
psalms and strewing their path with twigs of trees. Several
of the prophets crossed to England; but finding the Episcopal
Church too like the Roman, they attempted to substitute
their own. Their belief was so strong that, confident with
sufficient faith they could perform miracles, they offered to
raise a dead man from the grave, allowing even the particular
body to be chosen by others. People are everywhere the same,
and the Presbyterians were capable of joining the ranks of
these fanatics against the Anglican clergy. Who would believe that one of the greatest European geometricians, Fatio
de Duillers, and such a learned man of letters as Daudé were
the leaders of these religious enthusiasts? Fanaticism makes
a confederate even of science and stifles reason.

The English Church treated these miracle workers as they
should ever be treated. They allowed them to disinter a
body in the churchyard of a cathedral. The place was surrounded by guards, and all was done in order. The proceedings
concluded with the prophets being pilloried.

Such extravagant fanaticism could scarcely succeed in
England, where philosophy was beginning to hold sway.
They disturbed Germany as little since the three religions,
Catholic, Evangelical and Protestant, were equally protected
under the Treaties of Westphalia. For political reasons the
United Provinces tolerated all religions in their state. In
short, at the end of the age, France alone suffered great
ecclesiastical disputes in spite of the advance of reason.
Slow in influencing the learned, reason was scarcely yet able
to guide scholars, still less ordinary citizens. It must first
be established in the minds of leaders, then gradually it
descends and, at length, rules the people who are unaware
of its existence, but who, perceiving the moderation of their
superiors, learn how to imitate them. It is one of the great
works of time, and the time was not yet come.

CHAPTER XXXVII

JANSENISM

CALVINISM inevitably stirred up civil wars and shook the foundations of states. Jansenism on the other hand gave rise but to theological disputes and wars of the pen; the reformers of the sixteenth century had severed all the bonds that bound men to the Roman Church, had treated as idolatry what the Church held as most sacred, had opened the gates of the monasteries, and removed their wealth to secular institutions, so that of necessity one of the two parties had to perish at the hands of the other. Indeed, the religion of Calvin had appeared in no country without exciting persecutions and religious wars. But the Jansenists made no attacks upon the Church, bore no grudge against its fundamental dogmas or its goods and wrote on abstract subjects as much against the reformers as against the papal bulls; they finally had no credit with any party, and saw their sect despised throughout nearly the whole of Europe, though several of its members had been highly esteemed, alike for their attainments and their morals.

At the very time that the Huguenots were attracting serious attention, Jansenism was disquieting France rather than disturbing her. Like so many others, the disputes originated abroad. About 1552 a certain doctor of Louvain, named Michel Bay, who was known as Baius, according to the pedantic custom of the times, presumed to advance certain propositions with regard to divine grace and predestination. The question, like nearly the whole of metaphysics, really lies in the perplexing labyrinth of fate and free will, in which all the ancients went astray, and in which mankind has no thread to guide it. That spirit of inquisitiveness implanted in mankind by God, that impulse necessary to our attainment of knowledge, is forever leading us beyond the object we have in view, like all the other faculties of the human mind, which, if they did not carry us too far, would perhaps never incite us far enough.

Men have thus disputed on all subjects, both known and unknown; but while the disputes of the ancient philosophers were always peaceable, those of theologians often end in bloodshed and are always violent.

The Franciscans, who no more understood these questions than did Michel Baius, thought the doctrine of free will to be in jeopardy and the doctrine of Scotus endangered. Hostile towards Baius, moreover, by reason of another quarrel of very similar nature, they denounced seventy-three of Baius's propositions to Pope Pius VI. It was the future Sixtus the Fifth, at that time grand master of the Franciscans, who drew up the bull of condemnation in 1567.

Either through fear of compromising himself, or through aversion to discussing such subtleties, or through indifference and scorn for the theses of Louvain, the Pope condemned the seventy-three propositions wholesale, as being schismatic, savouring of heresy, offensive, rash and suspicious, without specifying any particular one or going into any detail. The method resembles that of a supreme power, and leaves little room for dispute. The doctors of Louvain were much put aback on receiving the bull; there was one sentence especially in which the placing of a comma in one place or in another resulted in either tolerating or condemning certain of Michel Baius's opinions. The university sent a deputation to Rome to learn from the Holy Father where the comma should be placed. The only reply of the Court of Rome, which had other matters to attend to, was to send to these Flemings a copy of the bull in which there was no comma at all. It was deposited in the archives. Morillon, the grand vicar, argued that the Pope's bull should have been submitted to, *even if it contained errors*. Morillon's policy was the right one; for it is surely much better to submit to a hundred inaccurate bulls than to burn a hundred towns to the ground, as did the Huguenots and their adversaries. Baius was persuaded by Morillon and retracted peaceably.

Some years afterwards, Spain, as prolific in scholastic writers as she is destitute of philosophers, produced Molina the Jesuit, who believed that he had discovered exactly how God acts towards His creatures and how His creatures thwart Him. He postulated two orders, the natural and the supernatural, the predestination of grace and the predestination of glory, and the doctrines of prevenient and co-operative grace. He was the inventor of the system of concomitant aid of the middle science and of congruism. This middle science and congruism were certainly extraordinary concepts. By means of his middle science God ingeniously consults man's will, in order to discover what the man will

do when he is given the requisite grace; and then, according
to the usage which God divines will be made of free will, so
He makes His arrangements which determine the actions
of man; these arrangements were represented by Molina
as congruism.

The Spanish Dominicans, who understood this interpretation no more than the Jesuits, but who were jealous
of them, declared in writing that Molina's book *was the
forerunner of Antichrist.*

The Court of Rome took up the dispute, which was already
in the hands of the Grand Inquisitors, and very wisely
imposed silence on both parties, which neither of them
observed. Finally, the case was solemnly argued before
Clement VIII., and, to the disgrace of the human mind, all
Rome took sides in the dispute. A Jesuit named Achille
Gaillard assured the Pope that he knew of an infallible means
for bringing about peace within the Church; he gravely
proposed to accept the doctrine of general predestination
on condition that the Dominicans should admit the middle
science, and the two systems should then be reconciled as
best they could. The Dominicans refused to agree to Achille
Gaillard's proposals. Their celebrated member, Lernos,
upheld the doctrine of prevenient aid and its complement
of active virtue. Debates became even more numerous
without anyone understanding what was being talked about.

Clement VIII. died without having succeeded in bringing
the pros and cons of the argument to a clear issue. Paul V.
took up the case; but, as he himself was engaged in a still
more important controversy with the Venetian republic, he
put a stop to all the debates which are still known as *de
auxiliis.* The name, as vague in itself as the questions there
debated, was given them because the word means *help,* and
they were discussing in this dispute the question of the help
which God gives to weak-willed mankind. Paul V. finally
ordered both sides to keep the peace.

While the Jesuits were framing their middle science and
their congruism, Cornelius Jansenius, Bishop of Ypres, revived certain ideas of Baius in a large book on St. Augustine,
which was not printed until after his death; so that he became
the leader of a sect without even suspecting it. Scarcely
anyone read the book which caused so much disturbance;
but Duverger de Hauranne, Abbé of Saint-Cyran, a friend
of Jansenius, and a man as ardent in his religious beliefs as

he is vague and discursive in his writings, came to Paris and converted a few young doctors and old women. The Jesuits petitioned Rome to condemn Jansenius's book, as continuing the thesis of Baius, and this was done in 1641; but the theological faculty in Paris, and all who interested themselves in metaphysics, were divided on the subject. There is apparently little to be gained by believing with Jansenius that God ordains impossible things; such an attitude is neither philosophical nor comforting; but the secret pleasure of belonging to a party, the hatred incurred by the Jesuits, the desire to be conspicuous, and the restlessness of people's minds—all contributed to the formation of a new sect.

The faculty condemned five of Jansenius's propositions by a majority of votes. The five propositions were accurately copied from the book so far as their meaning was concerned, but the exact words were not used. Sixty doctors appealed to parliament against the ruling, and the legislative chamber, sitting in vacation, summoned the parties to appear.

They did not obey the summons; but Habert, a doctor belonging to one of the parties, stirred up the people against Jansenius, while the celebrated Arnauld, a disciple of Saint-Cyran, who was on the other side, defended Jansenism with all the force of his eloquence. He hated the Jesuits even more than he adored sacramental grace; and he was hated by them all the more because his father, who had practised as a barrister, had vehemently pleaded the case of the university against their establishment. His relatives had won considerable reputations for themselves in the legal and military professions. His genius and the circumstances in which he found himself led him to engage in a war of pens, and make himself the leader of a party, an ambition which puts all others in the shade. He waged war against the Jesuits and the Protestants until he was eighty years of age. One hundred and four volumes came from his pen, of which scarcely a single one now ranks with those master-works that are the glory of the age of Louis XIV. and the library of the nations. All his works were in great demand during his lifetime, both on account of the author's reputation and the warmth of the disputes. That ardour cooled, and his books were forgotten. The only works of his that have remained are those that belong solely to reason, his *Geometry*, the *Rational Grammar* and the *Logic*, in which he displayed great gifts.

No man was ever born with a more philosophic mind; but his philosophy was corrupted by the polemics which obsessed him, and which plunged for sixty years into the wretched controversies of the schoolmen and the evils arising from perversity, a spirit born to enlighten the minds of men.

The university was divided on the question of the five notorious propositions, as also were the bishops. Eighty-eight French bishops wrote in a body to Innocent, calling upon him to settle the matter, and eleven others wrote beseeching him to do nothing. Innocent X. passed judgment, and condemned each of the five propositions separately, but in every case without quoting the pages from which they were taken or the matter that preceded and followed them.

These omissions, which would not have been made the pettiest civil case before the tribunals, were made by the Sorbonne University, the Jansenists, the Jesuits and the sovereign pontiff himself. The basis of the five condemned propositions must obviously be in Jansenius. One has only to turn to the third volume, page 138 of the Paris edition of 1641, and read there word for word:

"All this clearly and evidently proves that there is nothing more certain and fundamental in the doctrine of St. Augustine than that certain of the commandments are impossible, not only for believers, ignorant people and hardened sinners, but also for the faithful and the righteous, notwithstanding their intentions and their efforts, according to the strength they may possess; and that they may lack grace, which alone can make these commandments possible." One may also read on page 165 "that according to St. Augustine, Jesus Christ did not die for all men."

Cardinal Mazarin ordered the Pope's bull to be unanimously accepted at a convocation of the clergy. He stood well with the Pope at the time: moreover he did not love the Jansenists and had reason to hate the factions.

Peace seemed to have returned to the Church of France; but the Jansenists wrote so many letters, St. Augustine was so often quoted, and the women were so much incited, that after the reception of the bull there were more Jansenists than ever.

A priest of Saint-Sulpice took it upon himself to refuse absolution to M. de Liancourt, because it was said that he did not believe that the five propositions were to be found in Jansenius and that he harboured heretics in his house. This was a fresh scandal, and a fresh subject for the pamphleteers. Doctor Arnauld distinguished himself in this controversy, maintaining in a fresh letter addressed to a duke and peer either real or imaginary that the condemned propositions of Jansenius were not in Jansenius, but that they were to be found in St. Augustine and several of the Fathers. He added that "St. Peter was a just man who lacked grace without which nothing is possible."

It is true that St. Augustine and St. Chrysostom had said the same thing; but the circumstances of the case which are all-important proved Arnauld to be at fault. It was said that he must have poured water into the Holy Father's wine, for there are always people to make fun of what others regard as serious. The faculty convened a meeting, at which Chancellor Séguier himself was present on behalf of the king. Arnauld was found guilty and dismissed from the Sorbonne (1654). The presence of the chancellor among the theologians had an air of tyranny which offended the public, and the trouble taken to fill the hall with a crowd of doctors and mendicant friars, little accustomed to such great numbers in such surroundings, led Pascal to say in his *Provincial Letters*, "that it was easier to find monks than reasons."

The majority of the monks did not for a moment admit congruism, the middle science and the irregular bestowal of grace which Molina postulated: but they believed in sufficient grace, to which the will may consent, yet never does consent; and an active grace which it can but does not resist; this they explained clearly enough by saying that one could resist this grace in a partial but not in a composite sense.

While these sublime matters may not seem to agree overmuch with human reason, the ideas of Arnauld and the Jansenists seemed to agree too much with pure Calvinism: this was precisely the basis of the dispute which separated the followers of Gomar from those of Arminius. The quarrel divided Holland just as Jansenism divided France; but in Holland it became a political faction rather than a dispute between men of leisure; it was responsible for the death of the Pensionary Barneveldt on the scaffold, a horrible crime still held in detestation by the Dutch now that their eyes are opened to the absurdity of such disputes, the horrors of persecution and to the happy necessity of tolerance, the resource of wise men who govern against the fickle enthusiasm of those who only argue. In France the controversy gave rise to nothing more than mandates, bulls, *lettres de cachet* and pamphlets; for there were more important disputes afoot.

Arnauld had merely been dismissed from the university. The petty persecution gained him a host of friends, but both he and the Jansenists had still the Church and Pope against them. One of the first acts of Alexander VII., the successor to Innocent X., was to renew the ecclesiastical condemnation of the five propositions. The French bishops who had already drawn up a formulary, now framed a new one, which concluded in these terms: " With heart and mouth I condemn the doctrine of the five propositions contained in the book of Cornelius Jansenius, the said doctrine not being that of St. Augustine, which Jansenius has wrongly interpreted."

It was necessary to subscribe to this formulary, which the bishops circulated among all suspected persons in their dioceses. It was desired that the nuns of Port-Royal of Paris and Port-Royal des Champs should sign it: since these two establishments were the sanctuaries of Jansenism, under the rule of Arnauld and Saint-Cyran.

A house had been established close to the monastery of Port-Royal des Champs, which formed the retreat of a few worthy but obstinate-minded scholars, linked to each other by their religious opinions; they were engaged in the teaching of young men specially selected. Racine, the poet who of all times and nations best understood the workings of the human heart, was brought up in this school. Pascal, first of the French satirists, for Boileau must be accounted second, was intimately connected with these famous and dangerous recluses. The formulary was presented to the nuns of Port-Royal of Paris and Port-Royal des Champs for their signature; they replied that they could not conscientiously admit, following the Pope and bishops, that the five propositions were contained in Jansenius's book, since they had not read it; that his real meaning had been misunderstood; and that while it was possible that the five propositions were false, Jansenius was not wrong.

Such obstinacy exasperated the court. The civil lieutenant, d'Aubrai (as yet there was no lieutenant of police), was despatched to Port-Royal des Champs to eject all the recluses who had taken refuge within its walls, and all their young pupils. The destruction of the two monasteries was threatened; but a miracle saved them.

Mlle. Perrier, a member of Port-Royal of Paris, and a

niece of the celebrated Pascal, had an inflammation in one of her eyes; the ceremony of kissing a thorn from the crown which had once been worn by Jesus Christ was performed at Port-Royal. This thorn had been for a long time past in the possession of Port-Royal, though it is difficult to understand how it had been preserved and brought from Jerusalem to the neighbourhood of Saint-Jacques. The sick girl kissed it, and was cured a few days later. The opportunity was not lost to declare and testify that she had been cured in a moment of an incurable lachrymal fistula. The girl died only in 1728. People who lived with her for many years have assured me that her cure was quite slow, which is very probable; but what is far from probable is that God, who does not perform miracles for the purpose of spreading our religion over nineteen-twentieths of the world, where that religion is either unknown or regarded with horror, would really have disturbed the course of nature on behalf of a young girl, in order to justify a dozen nuns who claimed that Cornelius Jansenius was not the author of a dozen lines attributed to him, or that he had written them in a different sense from that which was imputed to them.

The miracle made such a stir that the Jesuits were impelled to write against it. A certain priest, Annat, confessor to Louis XIV., published *The Spoil-sport of the Jansenists, on the occasion of a miracle said to have been performed at Port-Royal by a Catholic Doctor*. Annat was neither doctor nor *doctus*. He thought to prove that if a thorn had come from Judæa to cure the young girl Perrier, it was in order to prove to her that Jesus had died for *all* and not *the few*; everyone jeered at Father Annat. The Jesuits then decided to perform miracles themselves; but they had no popular success at all; only the miracles of the Jansenists were at that time in fashion. Some years afterwards they performed another miracle. Sister Gertrude was cured of an inflammation in the leg at Port-Royal: but this prodigy had no success; the time had gone by for such miracles, and moreover Sister Gertrude had no Pascal for an uncle.

The Jesuits, who had the support of popes and kings, were completely discredited in the minds of the people. They were forcibly reminded of former events, such as the assassination of Henri-Quatre, planned by Barrière and carried out by their proselyte Chatel, the torture of Father Guignard, their expulsion from France and Venice, the Gunpowder Plot, the bankruptcy of Seville. Every means was employed to make them hateful. Pascal went further; he made them ridiculous. His *Provincial Letters*, which now appeared, were models of eloquence and wit. The finest comedies of Molière have not more Attic salt than the first *Provincial Letters*; the last equal in sublimity anything Bossuet ever wrote.

It is true that the whole book rested on a false basis. The author skilfully ascribed to the whole of the society the extravagant ideas of a few Spanish and Flemish Jesuits. He could have unearthed as easily such ideas among the Dominican and Franciscan casuists; but the only victims he wanted were the Jesuits. In these letters he attempted to prove that they had formed a scheme to corrupt the morals of mankind—a scheme which no sect nor any society ever conceived or could conceive; but it mattered little whether his attack were well grounded: it was a question of attracting the public.

The Jesuits, who did not then possess a single good writer, could not blot out the ignominy they suffered from the best-written book which had yet appeared in France; very nearly the same thing happened to them in their disputes as happened to Cardinal Mazarin. Such men as Blot, Marigni and Barbançon had made all France laugh at his expense, at the time when he was master of France. These Jesuit fathers were now credited with having had the *Provincial Letters* burnt by a decree of the parliament of Provence; they made themselves no less ridiculed, and by this act became but more hated by the nation.

The principal nuns of the convent of Port-Royal of Paris were removed under a guard of two hundred men and distributed in various other convents; only those who signed the formulary being allowed to remain. All Paris took an interest in the removal of these nuns. Sister Perdreau and Sister Passart, who signed and persuaded others to sign, were the subjects of jests and ditties, with which the town was flooded by that class of idle men who always look upon the ribald side of everything, and who amused themselves, whilst the believers sighed, the rioters of the Fronde declaimed, and the government acted.

Persecution only served to strengthen the position of the Jansenists. Four prelates—Arnauld, Bishop of Angers, the doctor's brother; Buzanval of Beauvais; Pavillon of Aleth;

and Caulet of Pamiers, the same prelate who afterwards opposed Louis XIV. over the *droit du roi*—declared against the new formulary, which had been drawn up by Pope Alexander VII. himself, and was similar in all essential points to the first, which had been accepted in France by the bishops and even by parliament. Incensed by their attitude, Alexander VII. appointed nine French bishops to proceed in law against the four rebellious prelates. On this both parties concerned became more embittered.

When everyone, however, was on fire to know whether the five propositions were in Jansenius or not, Rospigliosi, who had succeeded to the papal throne under the name of Clement IX., conciliated all parties for some time. He persuaded the four bishops to sign the formulary *sincerely*, instead of *unconditionally*; he thus apparently allowed them to maintain their opinion, while condemning the five propositions, that they were not taken from Jansenius. The four bishops offered a few short explanations, and Italian urbanity succeeded in calming French vivacity. The substitution of one word for another brought about the peace which was called "the peace of Clement IX." and also "the peace of the Church," though it only concerned an obscure dispute, unknown or despised by the rest of the world. Since the time of Baius, popes have always seemed to aim at suppressing these controversies, in which no agreement is arrived at, and instead, to compel the two parties to teach the same moral system which all the world is agreed upon. Nothing could be wiser; but it was with men that they had to deal.

The Jansenists imprisoned in the Bastille were set at liberty by the government, among them being Saci, the author of a *Translation of the Testament*. The exiled nuns were brought back; they signed the formulary *sincerely* and thought they triumphed by using the word. Arnauld emerged from the retreat where he had taken refuge and was presented to the king, welcomed by the nuncio, and regarded by the public as a Father of the Church; he engaged himself henceforth to combat only against the Calvinists, for he had to be making war on someone. During this peaceful interval he wrote his book on *The Perpetuity of Faith*, in which he was aided by Nicole, and grave disputes arose over this book between the authors and the minister Claude, in which each side claimed the victory, as usually happens in such controversies.

The peace arranged by Clement IX. proved only a temporary truce, since the parties concerned were little disposed to be conciliated, all of them being of a turbulent nature. Secret conspiracies, intrigues and insults were constantly interchanged.

The Duchess de Longueville, sister of the great Condé, famous alike in the civil war and in her love-affairs, being now advanced in years and having no other occupation, became a "devout"; and since she hated the court, and breathed the very air of intrigue, she became a Jansenist. She had a house built at Port-Royal des Champs, where she sometimes retired with other recluses. It was at the time of the Jansenists' most brilliant successes. Men like Arnauld, Nicole, Le Maistre, Herman, Saci and many others who, though less renowned, were men of considerable merit and reputation, assembled at her house. They substituted for those sallies of wit, which the Duchess de Longueville had learnt at the Hôtel de Rambouillet, their sober conversations and that manly, vigorous and animated turn of mind which was the distinguishing feature of their books and speech. They contributed not a little to the spreading of good taste and true eloquence in France. But unfortunately they were still more anxious to spread abroad their own ideas. It would seem that they were in themselves a proof of the system of fatalism with which they were charged. It was as if they were obsessed by the invincible determination to draw persecutions upon themselves for a few chimerical ideas, when they might have enjoyed the greatest esteem and the happiest of existences by renouncing these vain disputes.

In 1679 the Jesuit faction, still exasperated by the *Provincial Letters*, stirred up all authorities against the party. Mme. de Longueville, no longer able to intrigue for the Fronde, intrigued for Jansenism. Meetings were held in Paris, sometimes at her house and sometimes at Arnauld's. The king, who had already determined to crush Calvinism, saw with displeasure the rise of a new sect. He threatened; and at length Arnauld, fearing enemies who would be armed with sovereign power, and deprived by death of the support of Mme. de Longueville, resolved to leave France for ever and retire to the Netherlands, where he lived unknown, without money, and even without servants. This was the man whose nephew had been a minister of the state and who himself might have been a cardinal. The pleasure of being able to

write freely was worth everything else to him. He lived till
1694 in retirement, forgotten by the world, his place of
retreat known only to his friends, for ever writing, for ever a
philosopher superior to misfortune, and to his last breath
setting the example of a pure, strong and unshakable soul.

His party continued to be persecuted in the Catholic
Netherlands, a country known as *in obedience*, where papal
bulls are sovereign laws. It was persecuted still more bitterly
in France.

The extraordinary part of the whole matter was that the
question, "whether the five propositions were really to be
found in Jansenius," still continued to be the only pretext
for carrying on the petty civil war. The distinction between
the *fact* and the *law* occupied all minds. At length, in 1701,
a theological problem known as *the supreme case of conscience*,
was propounded: "Should the sacraments be administered
to a man who had signed the formulary, but who believed
at the bottom of his heart that the Pope and even the Church
might be mistaken in the facts?" Forty doctors replied that
absolution could be administered to such a man.

Immediately the fight began again. The Pope and the
bishops argued that they should be believed on the question
of fact. Noailles, Archbishop of Paris, enjoined belief in the
law by divine faith, and in the *fact* by human faith. Others,
including Fénelon, Archbishop of Cambrai, who did not
agree with M. de Noailles, insisted upon divine faith for the
act. It would have been better, perhaps, had they taken the
trouble to quote the passages in question from the book;
but that they never did.

In 1705 Pope Clement XI. issued the bull *Vineam Domini*,
by which he ordained belief in the act, without explaining
whether it was by divine or human faith. It was a new thing
for the Church to ask for the signature of young women to
its bulls: yet this honour was now paid to the nuns of Port-
Royal des Champs, and Cardinal de Noailles was obliged to
present the bull to them to test them. They signed it, *without
detracting from the peace of Clement IX.*, and maintained a
respectful silence with regard to *the act*.

It is difficult to say which is the more remarkable—the
acknowledgment demanded from the nuns that five propositions were contained in a certain Latin book, or the
obstinate refusal of the nuns to admit it.

The king asked the Pope for a bull ordaining the suppression of their convent. Cardinal de Noailles deprived them of the sacraments, and their advocate was imprisoned in the Bastille. All the nuns were removed and placed in a less disobedient convent. In 1709 the lieutenant of police razed their residence to the ground, and finally, in 1711, the bodies buried in the church and cemetery were disinterred and removed elsewhere.

The disturbances did not subside with the destruction of the monastery. The Jansenists were still eager to hatch plots and the Jesuits to make themselves indispensable. Father Quesnel, a priest of the Oratory, and a friend of the celebrated Arnauld, whom he accompanied in retirement until the latter's death, had been engaged since 1671 on a book of pious reflections on the text of the New Testament. The book contains certain maxims which might be thought favourable to Jansenism; but they are interspersed with such a large number of sacred maxims full of that fervour which wins men's hearts, that the work was received with universal applause. Good may be found in almost everything, whereas evil has to be searched for. Praises of the book from the first confirmed these views when the author had brought his work to its final perfection. I even know for certain that the Abbé Renaudot, one of the most learned men in France, being in Rome during the first year of Clement XI.'s pontificate, and one day visiting the Pope, who was both the friend of scholars and one himself, found him reading Father Quesnel's book. "Here is an excellent book," said the Pope; "we have no one here in Rome who can write like this. I should like to have the author close to me." This was the same pope who afterwards condemned the book.

Nevertheless, Clement XI.'s praises and the censures which followed them must not be regarded as inconsistent. One may be very much impressed with the striking beauties of a work when one is reading it and only later condemn its hidden faults. One of the prelates who had most highly commended Quesnel's book in France was Cardinal de Noailles, Archbishop of Paris. He had extended his patronage to him, was Bishop of Châlons, and the book was dedicated to him. The cardinal, full of piety and knowledge, and one of the best-tempered and most peace-loving of men, patronised a few Jansenists without being one: and though bearing little love to the Jesuits, neither persecuted nor feared them.

The Jesuits attained a considerable reputation from the

time when Father de La Chaise ruled Louis XIV.'s conscience and became the real head of the Gallican Church. Father Quesnel, who feared them, had retired to Brussels with the learned Benedictine Gerberon, a priest of the name of Brigode, and several others of the same persuasion. Upon the death of the celebrated Arnauld, he had become the head of the party, and like his predecessor, enjoyed the pleasing distinction of setting up a secret empire outside the jurisdiction of sovereigns, an empire in which he ruled men's consciences and was the heart and soul of a faction composed of enlightened men. The Jesuits, who were more numerous and more powerful than his party, soon began to molest him in his solitude. They arraigned him in the court of Philip V., who still ruled the Netherlands, just as they had pursued his master, Arnauld, before Louis XIV. They obtained an order from the King of Spain for the arrest of these recluses. (1703) Quesnel was thrown into the prison of the Archbishop of Malines. A gentleman who thought that the Jansenists would make his fortune if he could rescue their leader, pierced one of the prison walls and effected Quesnel's escape, who fled to Amsterdam, where he died in 1719 in extreme old age, after having helped to found a few Jansenist churches in Holland, a feeble band which grow weaker every day.

All his papers were seized on his arrest, and all that characterises the formation of a definite party was there discovered. The copy of a former contract was found made between the Jansenists and Antoinette Bourignon, a celebrated visionary and a rich woman, who had bought in the name of her spiritual mentor the island of Nordstrand close to Holstein, for the purpose of there assembling a number of persons whom she wished to form into a sect of mystics.

Bourignon had printed at her own expense nineteen large volumes of pious thoughts, and expended half her wealth in procuring converts. She had succeeded only in making herself ridiculous and had, moreover, suffered the persecutions attending all such innovations. At length, despairing of establishing a following on her island, she had re-sold it to the Jansenists, who succeeded no better in establishing themselves there.

Among the manuscripts of Quesnel there was also discovered a scheme still more heinous had it not been so senseless. When, in 1684, Louis XIV. sent the Count d'Avaux to Holland with full authority to arrange a truce of twenty years with any powers that were willing to agree to it, the Jansenists, styling themselves the *disciples of St. Augustine,* imagined that they would be included in this truce, as though they were a formidable party, such as the Calvinists had long been. The fantastic idea was never realised; but peace proposals between the Jansenists and the King of France were drawn up in writing. There was certainly a desire in this project of making themselves more important than they really were, and this was sufficient for them to be regarded as criminals. From that it was an easy matter to make Louis XIV. believe that they were dangerous.

He was not wise enough to know that vain speculative ideas would fall of themselves if they were abandoned to their fate. It was giving them an importance which they did not possess to treat them as state affairs.

It was not difficult to make people believe that Father Quesnel's book was heretical after its author had been accused of treason. The Jesuits urged the king to demand from Rome in person the condemnation of the book. It would certainly be to condemn Cardinal Noailles, who had been its most zealous defender, and they flattered themselves, with good reason, that the Pope, Clement XI., would humble the Archbishop of Paris. It should be mentioned that Clement XI., as Cardinal Albani, had printed a book by his friend, Cardinal di Sfondrate, which was full of Molinist ideas, and that Mme. Noailles had denounced the book. It was natural to think that Albani, now become Pope, would treat the praises of Quesnel at least as harshly as had been his own of Sfondrate.

Public opinion made no mistake. About 1708, Pope Clement XI. issued a decree denouncing Quesnel's book. But temporal affairs now interfered to prevent the complete success of this spiritual matter which had been solicited. Clement XI., by acknowledging Archduke Charles as King of Spain, after having previously acknowledged Philip V., had incurred the displeasure of the court. Flaws were discovered in his decree; it was not sanctioned in France, and disputes were hushed until the death of Father de La Chaise, the king's confessor, an even-tempered man, with whom conciliation was always easy, and who recognised that in dealing with M. de Noailles he was dealing with the ally of Mme. de Maintenon.

The Jesuits had the right of appointing the king's confessor, as they had with nearly all Catholic princes. This was a prerogative they reaped from the canons of their order by which they renounced all ecclesiastical preferments. What their founder established out of humility of heart was become a powerful factor in their greatness. The older Louis XIV. grew the more important became the post of confessor. The post was given to Le Tellier, son of an attorney of Vire in Lower Normandy, a melancholy, fervent and obstinate man, who concealed his passions beneath a cold exterior; he did all the harm that is possible to do in such a post, where it is but too easy to urge what one desires oneself and ruin those that one hates; he had his own particular grievances to redress. The Jansenists had contrived to have one of his books on Chinese rites condemned at Rome. His personal relations with Cardinal Noailles were unhappy, and he had no tact in the management of affairs. He created dissension throughout the whole French Church. In 1711 he drew up certain letters and mandates to be signed by certain bishops. Letters containing accusations against Cardinal Noailles were sent them, to which they had only to append their signatures. Such tactics in secular affairs do not go unpunished; they were found out yet were none the less successful.

The king's conscience was pricked by his confessor, at the same time that his dignity was offended by the thought of a rebellious sect. It was in vain that Cardinal Noailles demanded that justice should be done in *these iniquitous mysteries*; the confessor persuaded him that he had employed human means to bring about divine results, and as he was actually defending the Pope's authority and the unity of the Church, the basic grounds of dispute were in his favour. The cardinal appealed to the Dauphin, the Duke of Burgundy; but he found him already biased by letters and friends of the Archbishop of Cambrai.

Human frailty enters every heart. Fénelon was not yet philosopher enough to forget that Cardinal Noailles had contributed to his condemnation and that Quesnel was now paying the debt of Mme. Guyon.

Mme. de Maintenon's influence could no longer help the cardinal. This episode alone should be sufficient to reveal the character of that lady, who had scarcely any feelings of her own and whose only care was to conform to those of the king. Three lines, written in her own hand to Cardinal Noailles.

give a complete illustration in miniature of her attitude to Father Le Tellier's intrigue, of the king's views, and of the crisis: "You are sufficiently acquainted with me to know what I think of this new revelation; but there are many reasons for my keeping silent. It is not for me to judge nor to condemn; I have only to keep silent and pray for the Church, for the king and for you. I have given your letter to the king, and he has read it; overcome with grief, I can tell you no more."

The cardinal archbishop, tyrannised over by a Jesuit, deprived the Jesuits of all authority to preach or to confess, except a few of the wisest and most moderate. His position gave him the dangerous right of forbidding Le Tellier to confess the king: but he dared not provoke his enemy to this extent. "I fear," he wrote to Mme. de Maintenon, "that I shall appear to be too submissive to the king in granting powers to one who least merits them. I pray that God may reveal to him the danger he runs in entrusting his soul to a man of such character."

In several collections of memoirs, Father Le Tellier is reported to have said that either he would lose his post or the cardinal his. Such were very probably his thoughts, but it is little likely that he expressed them.

When the minds of men have become embittered, opponents usually attempt to do each other as much harm as they can.

Certain partisans of Father Le Tellier, bishops who were hoping for the cardinal's hat, made use of the royal authority to kindle sparks that might have been extinguished. Instead of imitating the example of Rome, which had on various occasions imposed silence on both parties; instead of curbing the ambitions of a monk and guiding the cardinal; instead of forbidding such disputes like duels and compelling all priests like all nobles to be useful without being dangerous; in short, instead of crushing both parties by his sovereign power, supported by reason and every magistrate, Louis XIV. thought better to solicit in his name a declaration of war from Rome and call forth the famous bull *Unigenitus*, which filled the rest of his life with bitterness.

The Jesuit, Le Tellier, and his party forwarded one hundred and three propositions to Rome for condemnation. The Holy Office proscribed one hundred and one. The bull was issued in September 1715, and on its publication in France raised up practically the whole country against it. The king had demanded it to prevent a schism and it was near to causing one. The outcry was general, since among the hundred and one propositions there were certain ones which appeared to everyone to contain the most innocent meaning and to express the purest moral truth.

A large gathering of bishops was convened in Paris. Forty accepted the bull for the sake of peace; giving at the same time certain explanations to calm the scruples of the public. The absolute and unconditional acceptance was sent to the Pope and the modifications were published to appease the people. They hoped by this to satisfy at once the pontiff, the king, and the populace; but Cardinal de Noailles and seven other bishops of the assembly, who were of the same mind, would accept neither the bull nor its modifications. They wrote to the Pope asking his Holiness himself to make corrections.

They paid him this insult with all due respect; but the king would not hear of it; he would not allow the letter to appear, ordered the bishops back to their dioceses, and forbade the cardinal to remain at court. Such persecution gave the archbishop a new consideration in the public eye. Seven more bishops joined him. It created an actual rupture, not only in the episcopacy, but in the whole clergy and the religious orders. It was admitted on all sides that the question did not affect fundamental principles of religion; nevertheless, a civil war sprang up between the disputants, just as though the overthrow of Christianity was threatened, and both sides resorted to every political expedient as in the most secular affair.

Various methods were employed to induce the Sorbonne to accept the bull. The majority of the voters were not in favour of it, but, nevertheless, it was enrolled on the register. The ministry was scarcely able to keep up the supply of *lettres de cachet* for imprisoning or exiling the opponents of the bull.

The bull had been sanctioned by parliament in 1714, saving the ordinary rights of the crown, the liberties of the Gallican Church, and the power and jurisdiction of the bishops; but the public outcry was still heard protesting against submission. Cardinal di Bissi, one of the most ardent defenders of the bull, admitted in a letter that it would not have been received with greater indignation at Geneva than at Paris.

Men were especially violent against the Jesuit, Le Tellier. Nothing is more exasperating to our nation than the rise of a monk to power. His authority seems a violation of his vows: but if he abuse it, then he is held in horror. All the prisons had long been filled with citizens accused of Jansenism. Louis XIV., too ignorant of these matters, was made to believe that such was his duty as a most Christian king, and that he could only expiate his sins by persecuting heretics. The most disgraceful thing, however, was that copies of the examinations of these unfortunate people were laid before the Jesuit, Le Tellier. Never has justice been more basely betrayed; never has power been more shamefully and contemptibly used. These records of their tyranny were discovered in 1768 in Jesuit houses after they had at last reaped the reward of their excesses and had been banished from the kingdom by every parliament, by the votes of the nation, and, to crown all, by an edict of Louis XV.

In 1715 Le Tellier so far presumed on his authority as to propose at an assembly of the national council that Cardinal de Noailles should be deposed. Thus did a monk and a confessor make use of his king, his penitent and his religion to accomplish his vengeance.

In order to prepare this council, at which it was a question of deposing a man who had become the idol, not only of Paris, but of France, by the purity of his life, the gentleness of his character, and still more by persecutions, Louis XIV. was persuaded to order parliament to issue a decree by which every bishop who had not accepted the bull *absolutely and unconditionally* should be compelled to sign it or be prosecuted with the utmost rigour of the canon law. The chancellor Voisin, secretary of state for war, a man of an unfeeling and despotic nature, drew up the edict. D'Aguesseau, the attorney-general, better versed in the laws of the realm than the chancellor, and full of the fearless spirit of youth, refused absolutely to accept any responsibility for such a measure. The first president, de Mesme, remonstrated with the king on the consequences. The matter dragged on. The king was dying; and these wretched disputes disturbed and hastened his last moments. His pitiless confessor harassed his exhausted powers by continual exhortations to consummate a work which would reflect no credit on his memory. The king's servants twice indignantly refused him entrance to the royal chamber, and at last implored him not to speak to the king about the decree. Finally the king died and all was changed.

The Duke of Orleans, regent of the kingdom, having first reversed the whole form of Louis XIV.'s government, substituting councils for the offices of secretaries of state, created a council of conscience, with Cardinal de Noailles as president. The Jesuit, Le Tellier, was banished, execrated by the public, and little loved by his colleagues.

The bishops who opposed the bull appealed to a future council, though it should never be convened. The Sorbonne, the vicars of the diocese of Paris, and whole bands of monks made the same appeal, and finally Cardinal de Noailles made his appeal in 1717, but was not willing at first to make it public. It is said that his appeal was printed in spite of him. The Church of France remained split up into two parties, the *accepters* and the *refusers*, the former being the hundred bishops who had supported the Jesuits and Capuchins under Louis XIV., and the latter including fifteen bishops and the whole nation. The accepters drew their strength from Rome; the others from the universities, the parliaments and the people. Volume after volume was printed, letter after letter. Each side reproached the other with being schismatical or heretic.

Mailli, Archbishop of Rheims, a staunch and prominent adherent of Rome, had put his name to two documents which parliament ordered to be burnt by the common hangman. On learning this the archbishop had a *Te Deum* sung, to render thanks to God for an insult done to him by the schismatic. God rewarded him; he was made a cardinal. Languet, Bishop of Soissons, was subjected to the same treatment by parliament, and apprised that body "that it was not for him to judge them, even for a crime of high treason." He was condemned to pay a fine of ten thousand livres; but the regent was not willing for him to pay them, fearing, so he said, that he might also become a cardinal.

Rome burst forth into reproaches; the two parties wasted their energies in fruitless negotiations; they appealed and appealed again; and all for certain now-forgotten passages from the book of an octogenarian priest who lived upon charity in Amsterdam.

The senseless financial system of the country contributed more than one would think to bringing about peace in the Church. People threw themselves so actively into trade, and the lust for making money became such an obsession with the general public, who were fascinated by this novelty, that there was no one to listen to anyone who wished to discuss Jansenism and bulls. Paris thought as little about it as about the war that was being waged on the Spanish frontier. The incredibly large and rapid fortunes which were being made, the extreme lengths to which luxury and comfort were carried, it was these which put an end to ecclesiastical disputes: the pursuit of pleasure did what Louis XIV. had been unable to do.

The Duke of Orleans seized the opportunity to reunite the Church of France. His foreign policy was vitally interested; for he feared to see the united forces of Rome, Spain and one hundred bishops ranged against him.

It was necessary to persuade Cardinal de Noailles not only to accept the bull, which he considered scandalous, but to withdraw his appeal, which he considered legitimate. This was more than his benefactor, Louis XIV., had demanded of him in vain. The Duke of Orleans was to find the greatest opposition from Parliament, which had been banished to Pontoise; nevertheless, he succeeded in all he undertook. *A body of doctrine* was set up which the cardinal was at last prevailed upon to promise to accept. The Duke of Orleans himself, accompanied by princes and peers, was present at the grand council, to sanction the issue of an edict that enjoined the acceptance of the bull, the withdrawal of appeals, unity and peace. Parliament, chagrined that decrees which should legally have been submitted to them had been brought before the grand council, and threatened, moreover, with being transferred from Pontoise to Blois, sanctioned all that the grand council had sanctioned, saving the customary reservations, i.e. the maintenance of the liberties of the Gallican Church and the laws of the kingdom.

The cardinal archbishop, who had promised to retract when parliament should yield, was now called upon to keep his word, and his official withdrawal was published on 20 August, 1720.

Dubois, the new Archbishop of Cambrai and son of an apothecary of Brive-la-Gaillarde, afterwards cardinal and first minister, had the greatest hand in this affair, in which Louis XIV.'s power had failed. No one was ignorant of the conduct, character and habits of that minister. It was a case of the dissolute Dubois mastering the pious Noailles. It will be remembered how scornfully the Duke of Orleans and his minister spoke of the quarrels which they silenced, what ridicule they poured on the war of controversy. Yet their very contempt and ridicule were instruments of peace. The disputants grew weary of quarrelling over matters at which the whole world laughed.

From that time everything relating to Jansenism, Quietism, bulls, theological controversies and the like, perceptibly lost its interest. There remained but a few of the appellant bishops who still clung obstinately to their opinions.

A few well-known bishops and some of the lesser known clergy did indeed persist in their devotion to Jansenism, persuading themselves that God was about to destroy the world because a sheet of paper entitled a *Bull*, printed in Italy, had been received in France. Had they but thought for a moment what a small part of the map is taken up by France and Italy, and what insignificant figures provincial bishops and parish priests cut in the world, they would not have declared that God was about to annihilate the whole world out of love for them, which, as posterity can see, was far from being the case. Cardinal de Fleury was guilty of a different sort of folly—that of believing that such pious fanatics were a danger to the state.

He was also eager to please the Pope, Benedict XIII., who came of the ancient house of Orsini, but was himself an obstinate old monk, who believed that bulls emanated from God Himself.

Orsini and Fleury accordingly convened a little council at Embrun, for the purpose of passing sentence on Soanen, the Bishop of the village of Senez, eighty-one years of age, a former priest of the Oratory, and a Jansenist more stubborn than the Pope.

The president of the council was Tencin, Archbishop of Embrun, who was more concerned with obtaining the cardinal's hat than in upholding a bull. He had been prosecuted by the parliament of Paris for simony and was regarded by the public as an incestuous and cheating priest. But he had converted Law, the banker and comptroller-general, and thus had turned a Scotch Presbyterian into a French Catholic. The good work had brought the converter wealth and the Archbishopric of Embrun.

Soanen was regarded as a saint by all the province. The simoniac condemned the saint, forbade him to carry on his duties as bishop and priest, and consigned him to a Benedictine monastery among the mountains, in which place the prisoner constantly prayed for the converter's soul until his death at the age of ninety-four.

All France was roused to indignation against the council, the sentence and especially the president of the council, and talked of the matter for quite two whole days.

The enfeebled Jansenist party resorted to miracles; but even their miracles did not succeed. An aged priest of Rheims, named Rousse, who had died as they say in the odour of sanctity, cured toothache and sprains, but in vain; the Holy Sacrament was carried to the suburb of Saint-Antoine in Paris and after three months cured a woman, named Lafosse, of a hæmorrhage, though at the same time turning her blind; but the miracle was no more successful than the first.

At length some fanatics conceived the notion that a deacon, named Paris, brother of a councillor in parliament and buried in the cemetery of Saint-Médard, was about to perform miracles. Some votaries of the sect who went to pray upon his tomb were so carried away by their imagination that in their deranged state of mind they suffered slight convulsions. The tomb was immediately surrounded by people; crowds gathered there day and night. Some climbed on to the tomb, giving their bodies strange twitches which they regarded as miraculous signs. The secret instigators of the sect encouraged such frenzies. Prayers were recited in the vulgar tongue around the tomb: the air was full of accounts of deaf people who had heard a few words, of blind who had caught glimpses of something, of cripples who had walked upright for a few moments. The miracles were even attested before the courts by a whole host of witnesses who had almost seen them, since they had come there in the hope of doing so. The government allowed the epidemic to run its course for a whole month. But the crowds grew more numerous, miracles increased and it was necessary at last to close the cemetery and place a guard around it. Thereupon the same fanatics proceeded to work their miracles in their own houses. The tomb of the deacon, Paris, was in very truth the tomb of Jansenism in the minds of all sensible people. In less enlightened times such farcical proceedings would have had serious consequences. Apparently those who provoked them were unaware of the age in which they lived.

Superstition was so rife that Carré, a councillor of parliament, surnamed *Montgeron*, had the audacity to present to the king in 1736 a list of all these miracles, attested by a large number of witnesses. This madman, the spokesman and dupe of maniacs, said in his memorandum to the king, "that one could not help believing witnesses who died in support of their evidence." Should one day his writings be in existence while all other books are lost, posterity will look upon our age as an age of barbarism.

In France these absurdities were the dying strugglers of a sect which, no longer supported by men like Arnauld, Pascal and Nicole, and upheld only by convulsionaries, became degraded; one would hear little of such disputes which disgrace and harm the name of true religion, were it not for those few turbulent spirits who from time to time endeavour to fan the dying embers of a fire into a new conflagration. Should ever they succeed again, it will not be Molinism and Jansenism which will provide the ground of dispute. A thing that has been made to appear ridiculous can be no longer dangerous; the exact nature of the quarrel will be changed; but men are never at a loss for pretexts to harm each other, though they have no longer any cause.

Religion has still power to sharpen the dagger-point. In a nation there are always certain persons who have no intercourse with honest people, who are not of the age in which they live, who are untouched by the advance of reason, and who may still be affected by the scourge of fanaticism, like certain plagues which afflict only the lowest classes of society.

The Jesuits seemed involved in the downfall. Their blunted weapons found no enemies left to fight; their influence at court, which Le Tellier had abused, was lost to them; their *Journal de Trevoux* earned them neither the esteem nor the friendship of men of letters. The bishops, over whom they had tyrannised, made no distinction between them and the other religious orders; and the latter, who had suffered humiliation at their hands, now humbled them in their turn. On more than one occasion the parliaments gave them to understand what they thought of them, by proscribing certain of their writings which would otherwise have been forgotten. The university, which was beginning at that time to make important researches into literature and to offer an excellent education, attracted from them a large number of young men, and they looked forward to the time when men of genius should arise among them and circumstances should favour their return to power; but they were much deceived in their hopes; their downfall, the suppression of their order in France, their expulsion from Spain, from Portugal and Naples, finally proved how ill-advised Louis XIV. had been to put his confidence in them.

Those who are infatuated with such disputes would do well to cast an eye over the general history of the world; for if one takes into account the large number of nations, the variety of their manners and customs and the difference of their religions, it will be seen what an insignificant figure a Molinist or a Jansenist makes upon the earth. They would then blush for their mad attachment to a party that is swallowed up in the crowd and lost in the immensity of things.

CHAPTER XXXVIII

QUIETISM

In the midst of Calvinist factions and Jansenist disputes there arose yet another controversy in France over Quietism. It was an unfortunate result of the progress achieved by the human mind in the age of Louis XIV., that attempts were made to overstep the prescribed limits of human knowledge, or rather it was a proof that we had not yet made progress enough.

The dispute concerning Quietism is one of those extravagances of the mind, full of theological subtleties, such as would have left no trace on the mind of man were it not for the names of the two illustrious rivals who disputed it. A woman alike of no repute, of no real intelligence, possessing only a heated imagination, set at loggerheads the two greatest men in the Church at that time. Her name was Jeanne Bouvier de la Motte, her family coming from Montargis. She was married to the son of Guyon, the constructor of the Briare canal. Become a widow while still fairly young, possessing wealth, beauty and a mind fitted to shine in society, she became obsessed with what is called *spirituality*. Lacombe, a Barnabite from the district of Annecy, near Geneva, was her spiritual adviser. This man, whose mind held a vulgar medley of passion and religion and who died mad, plunged the soul of his penitent into mystical reveries to which she was already addicted. The desire to be a St. Teresa of France blinded her to the French and Spanish national characters. The ambition to have disciples, perhaps the strongest of all ambitions, took entire possession of her mind.

Her spiritual adviser, Lacombe, escorted her to his native place of Annecy in Savoy, where the titular Bishop of Geneva resided. It was in itself a highly improper thing for a monk to conduct a young widow away from her native country; but it has been a practice with nearly all founders of a sect to drag women along in their train. At first the young widow acquired a certain authority in Annecy by her lavish distribution of alms. She held conferences; she enjoined on her hearers complete self-denial, serenity of mind, the suppression of all its desires, the cult of the interior soul, pure and disinterested love, that is neither humiliated by fear, nor inspired by the hope of reward.

People of facile and credulous imaginations, especially women and youthful monks, who loved the word of God more than they knew when it came of a beautiful woman, were easily moved by such eloquent words, the only sure means of winning souls ready for conversion. She began to make proselytes. The Bishop of Annecy was authorised to expel her and her spiritual adviser from the country: and they repaired to Grenoble. There she distributed a small book, entitled *The Short Method*, and another one called *Torrents*, written with the same eloquence of style as her speeches; and in consequence she was again obliged to fly from Grenoble.

Flattering herself that she had now attained the rank of a father confessor, she had a vision and prophesied; afterwards communicating her prophecy to Father Lacombe. "All the powers of hell," she said, "will band themselves together to hinder the progress of the interior life and the receiving of Jesus Christ in the souls of men. The tumult will be so great that not one stone will be left upon another, and I foresee that there will be disturbances, wars and confusion throughout all the earth. Woman will become pregnant with the spirit and the dragon will rear himself upright in her path."

The prophecy was partly realised; hell did not array its forces; but on returning to Paris with her spiritual adviser, after having promulgated together the tenets of their religion

throughout 1687, the Archbishop of Harlai-Chanvalon procured an order from the king for the imprisonment of
Lacombe as a seducer, and for shutting up Mme. Guyon in
a convent as a lunatic requiring protection; but before this
blow fell Mme. Guyon had ensured means for her own protection. In the lately founded establishment of Saint-Cyr
she had a cousin, Mme. de La Maisonfort, a favourite of
Mme. de Maintenon, and she had gained the favour of the
Duchess de Chevreuse and the Duchess de Beauvilliers. All
her friends were loud in their complaints that the Archbishop
of Harlai, who was known to be inordinately fond of women,
should persecute a woman who spoke of nothing but the
love of God.

Mme. de Maintenon's all-powerful influence imposed silence
on the Archbishop of Paris, and gave Mme. Guyon her liberty.
She went to Versailles, gained admittance to Saint-Cyr,
attended certain religious gatherings held by Abbé Fénelon,
after making a third party at dinner with Mme. de Maintenon. The Princess d'Harcourt, the Duchesses de Chevreuse,
de Beauvilliers and de Charost were initiated into the
mysteries.

Abbé Fénelon, at that time tutor to the royal children,
was the most brilliant man at court. Nature had given him
a tender heart and a fancy at once gentle and abundant, and
his mind had been nurtured in the finest schools of literature.
Full of taste and charm, he preferred the pathetic and
sublime in theology to what is mournful and perplexing.
Added to these qualities was a kind of romantic strain which
led him, not to the ecstasies of Mme. Guyon, but to love of
spirituality, which was not far removed from the ideas
of that lady.

His imagination responded eagerly to candour and virtue,
as others are kindled by their passions. His dominant passion
was the love of God for Himself, and, seeing in Mme. Guyon
but a pure soul caught by the same passion as his own, he
had no hesitation in allying himself to her.

It was strange that he should be fascinated with the
revelation, prophecies and such-like gibberish of a woman
who was filled to excess with interior grace, for which she
had to find an outlet, and who emptied herself (as she put it)
of this superfluity of grace into the body of the chosen
disciple seated near her; but in his friendship and with his
mystical ideas, Fénelon was like a man in love; he condoned

all faults and continued to be attracted by the conformity of those essential feelings which had first charmed him.

Assured of his devotion and proud of such a disciple, whom she called her son, and relying even on Mme. de Maintenon, Mme. Guyon disseminated widely her ideas at Saint-Cyr. Godet, Bishop of Chartres, whose diocese included Saint-Cyr, became alarmed and complained of her conduct. The Archbishop of Paris once more threatened to take proceedings against her.

Mme. de Maintenon, who aimed only at making Saint-Cyr an abode of peace, who was fully aware that the king was opposed to all innovations, who had no need to acquire esteem by becoming the leader of a kind of sect, and who, in short, was only solicitous of her reputation and peace of mind, now broke off all connection with Mme. Guyon and forbade her to remain longer at Saint-Cyr.

Abbé Fénelon perceived the approaching storm, and feared to lose the high offices which he coveted. He advised his friend to place herself under the protection of the celebrated Bossuet, Bishop of Meaux, already regarded as a father of the Church. She yielded to the decisions of that prelate, received the sacrament at his hands, and gave him all her writings for examination.

With the consent of the king, the Bishop of Meaux co-opted for this task the Bishop of Châlons, afterwards Cardinal de Noailles, and Abbé Tronson, Superior of Saint-Sulpice. They met secretly in the village of Assi, near Paris. Chanvalon, Archbishop of Paris, annoyed that others should act as judges in his diocese, publicly censured the books under examination.

Mme. Guyon withdrew to the town of Meaux itself, consented to all that Bossuet demanded and promised to proselytise no more.

Meanwhile, in 1695, Fénelon was made Archbishop of Cambrai, and was consecrated by the Bishop of Meaux. It seemed that the affair, as yet merely ridiculous, had been hushed up, never to be reopened. But Mme. Guyon, accused of still spreading her doctrine after promising not to do so, was arrested by the king's orders in the same year, 1695, and imprisoned at Vincennes, as if she had been a danger to the state: but that she was far from being, and her pious meditations did not deserve the attention of the king. At Vincennes she composed a large volume of mystical verse, inferior even to her prose; she parodied popular operas, librettos, and was often heard singing:

> Pure, perfect love surmounts yon starry skies;
> We little know when first it takes its rise
> What pangs the subject heart will prove.
> Vincennes had never shock'd, nor tears bedimm'd these eyes,
> Had I ne'er felt this pure and perfect love.

Men's opinions are conditioned by time, place and circumstances. While Mme. Guyon was languishing in prison, she who had become the bride of Jesus Christ during one of her ecstasies, and who, from that time, no longer called upon the saints, saying that it was not meet for the mistress of the house to address herself to servants; at that very time, I say, petitions were being heard at Rome for the canonisation of Maria de Agreda, who had had more visions and revelations than all the mystics put together; and as a crowning example of life's innumerable contradictions, the Sorbonne was persecuting that very Agreda whom they wished to make a saint in Spain. The University of Salamanca condemned the Sorbonne and was condemned in turn. It is difficult to say which side displayed the greater stupidity and folly; but the greatest without doubt was to give to such extravagances the importance that is still sometimes accorded them.

Bossuet, long regarded as the mentor and master of Fénelon, become jealous of his disciple's reputation and influence, and, desiring still to preserve the power he had obtained over all his colleagues, demanded that the new Archbishop of Cambrai should also condemn Mme. Guyon and assent to his pastoral instructions. Fénelon was willing neither to sacrifice his opinions nor his friend. Compromises were suggested, promises were given, and each side complained that the other had broken his word. On his departure for his diocese, the Archbishop of Cambrai had his *Maxims of the Saints* printed in Paris, a work in which he thought he had refuted all the charges brought against his friend and developed the orthodox ideas of such as devote themselves to holy meditation, who conquer the senses and aspire to a state of perfection hardly dreamt of by ordinary men. The Bishop of Meaux and his friends rose up in arms against the book. They denounced it to the king, as though it were as dangerous as it was unintelligible. Bossuet, whose repute and learning the king respected, was consulted, and, falling on his knees before his sovereign, he asked his pardon for not having warned him sooner of the fatal heresy of the Archbishop of Cambrai.

Such zeal appeared far from sincere to the numerous friends of Fénelon. The courtiers saw in it a courtier's trick. It was scarcely credible that a man of Bossuet's nature should believe in his heart that the pious notion of loving God for Himself was a fatal *heresy*. It is possible that he was sincere in his hatred of such mystical devotion and still more so in his secret hate for Fénelon, and that, confusing one with the other, he honestly believed that he was doing right in bringing this accusation against his colleague and former friend, thinking, perhaps, that indictments that would bring disgrace upon a warrior can bring honour to a churchman, and that religious zeal can hallow base proceedings.

The king and Mme. de Maintenon consulted de La Chaise without delay; the confessor replied that the archbishop's book was excellent, that all the Jesuits were delighted with it and only the Jansenists disapproved of it. The Bishop of Meaux was not a Jansenist, but he was well versed in their finest works. The Jesuits had no liking for him, and were not loved by him.

Court and town were divided on the question, and all attention being turned to this dispute, the Jansenists had time to breathe. Bossuet wrote against Fénelon. Both sent their works to Pope Innocent XII. and submitted themselves to his decision. Circumstances appeared little favourable to Fénelon; Quietism, of which the Archbishop of Cambrai was accused, had just been vehemently condemned at Rome in the person of the Spaniard, Molinos, and it was Cardinal d'Estrées, French ambassador in Rome, who had pursued him. Cardinal d'Estrées, whom we have since witnessed in his old age more engrossed in the pleasures of society than in theology, had persecuted Molinos to please the enemies of that unfortunate priest. He had even persuaded the king to demand from Rome the condemnation which he easily obtained, so that Louis XIV. was, without knowing it, the most formidable enemy to the pure faith of the mystics.

Nothing is easier in such delicate questions to discover in a book upon which judgment is being passed passages resembling those in a book already banned. The Archbishop of Cambrai had on his side the Jesuits, the Duke de Beauvilliers, the Duke de Chevreuse and Cardinal Bouillon, lately

French ambassador at Rome; while the Archbishop of Meaux had his own great name and the principal French prelate. He presented to the king the signatures of several bishops and a large number of doctors who were all in arms against the *Maxims of the Saints*.

So great was Bossuet's authority, that Father de La Chaise dared not uphold the cause of the Archbishop of Cambrai in the presence of the king, his penitent, and Mme. de Maintenon entirely abandoned her friend. The king wrote to Pope Innocent XII. to say that the Archbishop of Cambrai's book had been represented to him as a pernicious work, that he had placed it in the hands of the nuncio, and urged his Holiness to pass sentence upon it.

It was claimed, even publicly stated in Rome (indeed the rumour has still its followers), that the Archbishop of Cambrai was only persecuted because he had opposed the proclamation of the king's secret marriage with Mme. de Maintenon. Those who invented these stories maintained that that lady had persuaded Father de La Chaise to urge the king to acknowledge her as queen; that the Jesuit had artfully transferred this perilous task to Abbé Fénelon, and that the tutor of the royal children had preferred the honour of France and of his pupils to his own position; and that he had then thrown himself on the mercy of Louis XIV. in order to avoid a situation whose singularity would do him more harm in the eyes of posterity than any rewards of conscience that he might derive during his own life.

It is quite true that while Fénelon had retained his post as tutor to the Duke of Burgundy after his appointment to the archbishopric of Cambrai, the king had heard in the meantime of his intimacy with Mme. Guyon and Mme. de Maintenon. He considered, moreover, that he was instilling into the mind of the Duke of Burgundy precepts of an excessively rigorous nature and principles of government and morals which might one day be construed as a condemnation of that air of grandeur and that eagerness of glory, of wars lightly undertaken and the popularity of entertainments and pleasures, which had characterised his reign.

He wished to hear what the new archbishop had to say upon political principles. Fénelon, full of his ideas, allowed the king to have a glimpse of some of the precepts which he afterwards developed in the passages of *Télémaque* which deal with government; precepts more fitting to Plato's

Republic than to the practical government of men. After the conversation, the king, it is said, declared that he had been conversing with the finest but also most fantastic intellect in his kingdom.

The Duke of Burgundy was informed of what the king had said, and he repeated it some time afterwards to M. de Malezieu, who taught him geometry. I heard it from M. de Malezieu himself; Cardinal de Fleury confirmed it.

After this conversation the king easily believed that Fénelon was as fanciful in matters of religion as in politics.

It is at any rate certain that the king had a personal spite against him. Godet des Marais, Bishop of Chartres, who ruled Mme. de Maintenon and Saint-Cyr with the despotism of an autocrat, poisoned the king's mind, who consequently took a principal part in that absurd dispute though understanding nothing. It had been doubtless easy to let it drop since it subsided in so short a time, but it caused such a disturbance at court, that he feared a conspiracy still more than heresy. That is the true cause of Fénelon's persecution.

The king gave orders to Cardinal de Bouillon, his ambassador at Rome at that time, in letters during the month of August 1697, to procure the condemnation of a man whom it was desired to convict as a heretic; and he wrote in his own hand to Pope Innocent XII. to urge him to decide.

The Council of the Holy Office appointed a Dominican, a Jesuit, a Benedictine, two Franciscan friars, a Feuillant and an Augustine friar to investigate the case. They were commonly known in Rome as counsellors. The cardinals and prelates usually leave the study of theological questions to these monks, so as to devote themselves to politics, intrigue or the pleasures of indolence.

The counsellors examined the thirty-seven propositions at thirty-seven meetings and, by a majority of votes, found them erroneous, whereupon the Pope, presiding at an assembly of cardinals, condemned them in a pastoral letter which was published and promulgated in Rome on 13 March, 1699.

The Bishop of Meaux had triumphed; but the Archbishop of Cambrai reaped a greater triumph from his defeat. He submitted himself unreservedly and unconditionally. He mounted his own pulpit at Cambrai to condemn his own book. He forbade his friends to defend it. This unique example of submission on the part of a scholar, who from the very fact of being persecuted could have formed a large party, the candour or the astuteness of the move won him all hearts, and made the name of him who had won the victory almost to be hated. Fénelon lived on in his diocese highly esteemed as an archbishop and a man of letters. His pleasant manners, displayed in his conversation as in his writings, gained him loving friends among all who met him. His persecution and his *Télémaque* won for him the veneration of Europe. The English, above all, who were fighting in the district that contained his diocese, were particularly anxious to show him their respect. The Duke of Marlborough took care that his estates were spared. He was always held in high esteem by his pupil, the Duke of Burgundy, and would have had a part in the government had the prince lived.

It was observed how difficult it was for him, in his philosophical and honourable retreat, to detach himself from a court like that of Louis XIV., though there are other courts which famous men have quitted without regret, but he always spoke of that court with a zest and interest that pierced the veil of his resignation. Several works on philosophy, theology and belles-lettres were written in his retreat. The Duke of Orleans, afterwards regent, consulted him on knotty questions such as interest all men, but which few men think about. He questioned him whether one could prove the existence of a God, if that God desired worship, what form of worship he approved, and whether He would be offended if one chose wrongly. He asked many questions of this nature, as a philosopher in search of truth, and the archbishop replied to him as a philosopher and a theologian.

Vanquished in the disputes of the schoolmen, it would perhaps have been more fitting had he refrained from taking any part in the quarrels concerning Jansenism; however, he again entered the lists. On a former occasion, Cardinal de Noailles had allied himself with the strongest side against him; the Archbishop of Cambrai now did the same, hoping to be recalled to court and be consulted; so reluctant is the human mind to disengage itself from mundane affairs when once they have allayed its restlessness. Nevertheless, his aspirations were as temperate as his writings, and towards the end of his life he disdained to be drawn into any dispute, imitating the example of Huet, Bishop of Avranches, one of the most learned men in Europe, who at the end of his days recognised the vanity of the majority of the sciences and of the human mind itself. The Archbishop of Cambrai (who would believe it!) wrote the following parody on one of Lulli's airs:

> When young I was exceeding wise,
> And pil'd up knowledge in a heap;
> Now nothing I prize,
> But trifles and toys,
> And creep to the grave without noise,
> Nor wish to look before I leap.

He composed these lines in the presence of his nephew the Marquis de Fénelon, afterwards ambassador at The Hague, and it was he who gave them to me, so that I can vouch for the truth of the matter. It would be of little importance in itself, did it not prove how differently, in the sad quietude of age, we often view things which had seemed so grand and interesting at an age when the mind, more active, was the plaything of its desires and its illusions.

These disputes, like many other controversies that arose from indolence, which long held the attention of all France, to-day have vanished. One marvels at the rancour and bitterness which they caused. The philosophic spirit, which is spreading farther every day, seems as if it would ensure the public peace; and even the fanatics who revolt against the philosophers are indebted to them for the security they enjoy and which they do their best to lose.

The dispute concerning Quietism, unhappily given such importance in the reign of Louis XIV., and to-day despised and quite forgotten, ruined Cardinal Bouillon at court. He was the nephew of the celebrated Turenne, to whom the king owed his safety during the civil war, and afterwards the aggrandisement of his kingdom.

Bound by friendship to the Archbishop of Cambrai and yet entrusted with the king's orders to proceed against him, he sought to reconcile the two duties. It is evident from his letters that he was never false to his ministerial office, though remaining faithful to his friend. Following the orders of the court, he urged the Pope to give his sentence; but at the same time he did all he could to bring about a reconciliation between the two parties.

An Italian priest named Giori, who was sent to spy upon him by the opposing faction, succeeded in worming himself into his confidence and then slandered him in his letters;

finally, a few miles on his journey he had the meanness to ask him for the loan of a thousand crowns, and having obtained the money made his escape. It was the letters of this wretch that were responsible for the ruin of Cardinal Bouillon at court. The king overwhelmed him with reproaches, as if he had betrayed the state, though all his despatches go to prove that he had comported himself with as much dignity as discretion.

He obeyed the king's orders in demanding the condemnation of certain pious but absurd precepts of the mystics, who are the alchemists of true religion; but he remained faithful to his friend in staving off the blows that were directed against the person of Fénelon. Even supposing that it was a matter of deep concern to the Church that God should not be loved for Himself alone, it was no such matter of deep concern that the Archbishop of Cambrai should be disgraced. But unfortunately the king wished Fénelon to be condemned, either through spite against him, which seemed beneath the dignity of such a king, or through surrender to the other party, which seems still more degrading to the dignity of the throne.

Whatever it was, on 16 March, 1699, he wrote a letter full of humiliating rebukes to Cardinal Bouillon. He declared that he desired the condemnation of the Archbishop of Cambrai; it is the letter of a man who had been annoyed. *Télémaque* was then creating a great stir throughout the whole of Europe, and the *Maxims of the Saints*, which the king had not read at all, were punished in place of the precepts to be found in *Télémaque*, which he had read.

Cardinal Bouillon was immediately recalled and set out from Rome, but learning a few miles on his journey that the dean of the cardinals was dead, he was obliged to return and claim the position which belonged to him by right, since though still young he was the senior of the cardinals.

The position of dean of the Sacred College in Rome carries with it great privileges, and as matters were regarded in those days, France welcomed the idea that it should be occupied by a Frenchman.

Moreover there was no lack of duty towards his king in taking possession of his property before setting out for Paris. Yet this step was an offence which the king never forgave. On arriving in France the cardinal was exiled, and his exile lasted ten whole years.

At length, wearying of so prolonged a period of disgrace, he decided in 1710 to quit France for ever, at the time when Louis XIV. was seemingly about to be crushed by the Allies and the kingdom was threatened on all sides.

His relatives, Prince Eugene and the Prince of Auvergne, received him on the frontiers of Flanders, where they were victorious. He sent back to the king the Cross of the Order of the Holy Ghost and his resignation of the post of grand almoner of France, addressing the following words to him: "I regain the liberty which is mine by right of descent from a foreign prince and as the son of a sovereign, trusting only in God and depending on my dignity as cardinal of the Holy Church and dean of the Sacred College. I shall strive to devote the remainder of my life to serving God and the Church in that place that is next to the highest."

He appeared to base his claim as an independent prince, not only on the axiom of lawyers who affirmed that *he who renounces all is no longer bound by anything* and that every man is free to choose his own place of abode, but upon the fact that he was actually born in Sedan when his father was still the ruler of Sedan; he regarded his status of an independent prince as unalterable, and as for his title of dean of the College of Cardinals, which he placed second to that of the Pope himself, he justified himself by the example of all his predecessors, who have taken undisputed precedence of kings at all ceremonies at Rome.

The French court and the parliament of Paris were governed by entirely different principles. D'Aguesseau, attorney-general and afterwards chancellor, accused him before the assembled chambers, who issued a writ for his arrest and confiscated all his property. He lived out the rest of his life in honourable poverty, and died a victim of Quietism, which he regarded with contempt, and of a friendship which he had nobly reconciled with duty.

It should be mentioned that when he left the Netherlands to go to Rome, the court were apparently apprehensive of his being made Pope. I have before me a letter of the king to Cardinal La Trimouille, dated 26 May, 1710, in which this fear is expressed. "Anything may be expected," he said, "from a subject who holds the idea that his fortune depends upon himself alone. It will be sufficient for Cardinal Bouillon to discover that his present position (with which he is at the moment dazzled) is in reality inferior to his birth and gifts, for him to think every road permissible by which he may arrive at the highest place in the Church, once he has gazed on that splendour from nearer at hand."

Thus a writ was issued against Cardinal Bouillon and orders given *that he should be put in the Conciergerie prison if it was possible to lay hands on him,* simply in the fear that he would ascend a throne which is regarded as the most exalted on earth by all who profess the Catholic religion; and that by joining Louis XIV.'s enemies he would take a greater revenge even than Prince Eugene, the arms of the Church being capable of effecting nothing by themselves, but much when allied with those of Austria.

CHAPTER XXXIX

DISPUTES CONCERNING CHINESE CEREMONIES: WITH THE RESULT OF PROSCRIBING CHRISTIANITY IN CHINA

OUR national spirit, with its restlessness, was not content with wrangling after seventeen centuries over points of our own religion, it must needs bring that of the Chinese into our quarrels. The controversy did not cause any great disturbances, but it typified more than any other that unquiet, contentious and quarrelsome spirit which seems the product of European civilisation.

A Jesuit, Matteo Ricci, at the end of the seventeenth century was one of the first missionaries in China. The Chinese were then and are still at a point in philosophy and literature which we reached about two centuries ago. The respect they entertain for their old teachers keeps them within certain limits which they dare not overstep. Progress in the sciences is the work of time and daring intellects; but ethics and the science of government being easier to understand than the sciences, and perfected among them long before the other arts, it has happened that the Chinese, having remained at the same point for more than two thousand years in the sciences, are mediocre in science, but the first nation in the world in ethics and the science of government, as they are the oldest.

After Ricci, many other Jesuits made their way into the vast empire, and under the mask of European knowledge they contrived to sow in secret the seeds of the Christian religion in the minds of the children of the people, whom they seized every opportunity of teaching. The Dominicans, who were among the missionaries, accused the Jesuits of tolerating idolatry whilst they were preaching Christianity. The question was delicate, as had their behaviour to be in China.

The laws and internal tranquillity of this vast empire are based on the most natural and sacred law of nature, the respect of children for their parents. To this is added the veneration they have for their first teachers of a moral code and especially for Confutzee, whom we call Confucius, a sage of ancient times, who taught them virtue nearly six centuries before the founding of Christianity.

On certain days every family meets together in private to pay honour to its ancestors, and the learned men in public to do honour to Confucius. They prostrate themselves on these occasions, which is their way of greeting their superiors, a custom which the Romans observed throughout the whole of Asia, and called *adoring*. They burn candles and perfumes. Twice a year state officials, known by the Portuguese as *mandarins*, slaughter animals in front of the hall dedicated to the memory of Confucius, and their flesh is afterwards eaten. Are these ceremonies idolatrous? Or are they merely civic? Do they regard Confucius and their ancestors as gods? Or are they merely invoked in the same way as our saints? Is it, in short, a political custom which the superstitious Chinese abuse? It was difficult for foreigners to unravel these mysteries in China; it was impossible to decide them in Europe.

In 1645, the Dominicans denounced these Chinese customs before the Inquisition in Rome, and acting on their statements, the Holy Office prohibited the Chinese ceremonies, until the Pope's will should be known.

The Jesuits defended the Chinese and their practices which, it seemed, in an empire so jealous of its customs, could not be forbidden without entirely blocking the path of the Christian religion; they set forth their reasons for taking up this attitude. In 1656, the Inquisition permitted their learned men to reverence Confucius and allowed the Chinese children to honour their parents, *protesting against superstition, if it existed*.

As the matter remained undecided and the missionaries

were in constant disagreement, the case was referred to Rome from time to time; meanwhile the Jesuits who were in Pekin made themselves so useful to the emperor, Kang-hi, in their capacity of mathematicians, that that prince, famed for his benevolence and virtues, at length allowed them to act as missionaries and to teach Christianity in public. It should be mentioned here that this despotic emperor, the grandson of the conqueror of China, was nevertheless bound by custom to the laws of the empire, by which he was unable on his own authority to sanction Christianity; he was obliged to bring his application before a tribunal, and himself drew up two petitions on behalf of the Jesuits. At length, in 1692, Christianity was permitted in China, solely owing to the indefatigable efforts and the diplomacy of the Jesuits.

There is in Paris an establishment set apart for foreign missions; some of the priests from this establishment were at that time in China. The Pope, who sends papal vicars into all countries known as *infidel nations*, appointed a priest, named Maigrot, from this house in Paris to act as papal vicar at the head of the Chinese mission, and gave him with the bishopric of Conon, a small Chinese province in Fukien. This Frenchman, become a bishop in China, not only declared the rites performed for the dead to be superstitious and idolatrous, but denounced the learned men as atheists; he was supported by all the extremists in France. The very men who were so vociferous in their outcries against Bayle, who were so loud in reproving him for saying that it was possible for a community of atheists to exist, who declared that such a state of society was inconceivable, calmly maintained that such a society was flourishing in China under the wisest of governments. The worst enemies with whom the Jesuits had to contend were not the mandarins and the people, but the missionary brethren. They urged at Rome that it was so inconsistent to say that the Chinese were atheists and at the same time idolaters. Learned men had been reproached for denying the existence of everything but matter, but if such were the case it would be difficult for them to invoke the soul of Confucius and their ancestors. One reproach would appear to destroy the other, unless it is claimed that such contradictions exist in China, as they often do in our own country; but one would have had to be very conversant with their tongue and customs to be able to distinguish this contradiction. The case of the Chinese Empire was prolonged for a considerable time at the courts of Rome; meanwhile the Jesuits were attacked on every side.

Father Lecomte, one of their learned missionaries, had written in his *Memoirs of China* that "this people has for two thousand years preserved the knowledge of the true God: has sacrificed to the Creator in the oldest temple in the world; China practised the purest moral code while Europe was yet steeped in error and corruption."

In another work I sought to show that this nation can be traced back, with an authentic history and through a series of twenty-six calculated eclipses of the sun, to before the date usually assigned to the Flood. Yet never have their savants possessed any other religion than the worship of a Supreme Being. Their religion was founded on justice. They could not know the laws God gave successively to Abraham and to Moses and, lastly, the perfect law of the Messiah, so long unknown to the western and northern nations. It is certain that the Gauls, Germany, England and the whole of the North were plunged in the most barbaric idolatry at a time when the courts of the vast Chinese Empire were developing their laws and customs, and acknowledging but one God, whose simple creed had never changed among them. Such plain truths should have justified the assertions of the Jesuit Lecomte. Yet, since it was possible to discover in his statements things that somewhat clashed with commonly accepted ideas, they were attacked by the Sorbonne.

In 1700, Abbé Boileau, brother of the great Boileau, not less critical and more inimical towards the Jesuits, denounced this eulogy of the Chinese as blasphemy. Abbé Boileau was a fervent and remarkable man, who wrote humorously on serious and daring subjects. He was the author of the book of the *Flagellants*, and of others of a like nature. He declared that he wrote them in Latin for fear that the bishops should condemn them, and his famous brother said of him that "had he not been a doctor of the Sorbonne, he would have been a doctor of Italian Comedy." He declaimed vehemently against the Jesuits and the Chinese, beginning his attack by saying "that the eulogy passed on those people had been like a violent blow to him, a Christian." The rest of the assembly was likewise shocked. Discussions followed; a doctor, named Lesage, suggested that they should send twelve of their most stalwart brethren to the spot to ascertain the facts. A stormy scene ensued, but in the end the Sorbonne declared the eulogy passed on the Chinese to be false, scandalous, rash, impious and heretical.

This dispute, as violent as it was puerile, embittered that which was raging about the ceremonies, and at last Pope Clement XI. sent a legate to China in the following year. He chose Thomas Maillard de Tournon, titular Patriarch of Antioch, who could not arrive before 1705. Until then the Court of Pekin was unaware that it was being judged at Rome and Paris. The situation could not have been more absurd had the republic of San Marino set itself up as mediator between the Grand Turk and the Persian Empire.

The Emperor Kang-hi received the Patriarch de Tournon with great kindness. But one may judge of his surprise when the legate's interpreters informed him that the Christians, who were preaching their religion in his dominions, were at variance with each other, and that the legate had come to put an end to a dispute of which the Court of Pekin had never heard. The legate gave him to understand that, with the exception of the Jesuits, all the missionaries condemned the ancient customs of the empire, and suspected even his Chinese Majesty and the learned men themselves of being atheists, only admitting the existence of a material heaven. He added that he would bring before him a learned Bishop of Conon, who would explain the whole matter, if his Majesty would deign to hear him. The monarch's astonishment was redoubled on learning that there were bishops within his empire. But that of the reader will be no less to learn that the indulgent monarch pushed courtesy so far as to allow the Bishop of Conon to come and speak against the religion and customs of his country and against his person. The Bishop of Conon was given an audience. He knew very little Chinese. The emperor first asked him to interpret the four characters painted in gold above his throne. Maigrot could read but two of them, yet he maintained that the words *King-tien*, which the emperor had himself written on his tablets, did not mean *Worship the Lord of Heaven!* The emperor patiently explained to him through the interpreters that that was the exact meaning of the words, and condescended to enter into a long discussion. He justified the honours paid to the dead, but the bishop was inflexible. One can easily imagine that the Jesuits had more influence at the court than he. The emperor, who might have punished him with death according to Chinese law, was content to banish him. He gave orders that all Europeans who wished to remain in the heart of the empire should henceforth take out letters patent and undergo an examination.

The legate, de Tournon, was ordered to leave the capital. As soon as he arrived at Nankin he issued a mandate condemning absolutely the Chinese rites of the dead and forbidding the use of the word which the emperor had used to mean *the God of Heaven*.

The legate was then banished to Macao, which has always belonged to China, though they allow the Portuguese to have a governor there. While the legate was shut up in Macao, he received the cardinal's hat from the Pope; but it only enabled him to die a cardinal in 1710. The enemies of the Jesuits attributed his death to them. They should have been satisfied with regarding them as the cause of his banishment.

Such differences among foreigners, who came to instruct the empire, threw discredit upon the religion that they preached. It was still more decried when the court, becoming better acquainted with the Europeans, learnt that not only were the missionaries divided, but that among the merchants who landed at Canton there were several sects sworn enemies of each other.

The Emperor Kang-hi died in 1724. This prince was a lover of all the European arts. The Jesuits sent out to him were the most enlightened of their order. They earned his affection by the services they rendered him and obtained from him, as we have seen, permission to practise and teach Christianity in public.

Young-tching, his fourth son, appointed by him to the throne, in preference to his elder brothers, succeeded, undisturbed by any complaints from the elders. Filial piety, which lies at the foundation of this empire, enjoins that under any circumstances it is a crime and a disgrace to murmur against the last wishes of a father.

The new emperor, Young-tching, surpassed his father in his regard for the laws and the public welfare. No emperor gave more encouragement to agriculture. He patronised this, the first of the useful arts, to the point of promoting to the rank of mandarin of the eighth order the husbandman in each province who should be judged by the magistrates of his canton to be the most diligent, the most industrious and the most honest man; not that the husbandman should then give up his work in which he had been successful, in order to carry out the duties of a magistrate of which he would know nothing; he remained a husbandman with the title of mandarin, and enjoyed the right of taking his seat at the table of the viceroy of the province. His name was also inscribed in letters of gold in a public hall. It is said that this regulation, so alien to our customs, and which perhaps condemns them, still obtains.

This prince ordained that no person throughout the whole empire should suffer the death penalty before an account of the criminal proceedings had been sent to him, and even presented three times. Two motives that led to this edict are as honourable as the edict itself. The one is the value that should be attached to human life; the other, the love that a king should have for his people.

He established large storehouses of rice in each province, so economically that they did not tax the resources of the people, and forever precluded the possibility of famine. Every province gave vent to their joy by fresh public shows and acknowledged their gratitude by erecting triumphal arches in his honour: but he exhorted them in an edict to discontinue such amusements, since they were ruinous to the economy he wished them to practise, and forbade them to build monuments to him. "If I grant favours," he said in a letter to the mandarins, "it is not because I seek vainglorious fame; I wish my people to be happy; I wish them to improve and perform all their duties. These are the only monuments I accept."

Such was this emperor, and it was he, unfortunately, who prohibited the Christian religion. The Jesuits had already erected several public churches and certain princes of the blood had even been baptised; alarm began to be felt at the spread of such fateful innovations within the empire. The misfortunes that had befallen Japan impressed people more than the purity of Christianity, too generally ignored, was capable of doing. It was known that at that very period disputes, which alienated the missionaries of the various orders from each other, had uprooted the Christian religion in Tung-yin; and these very disputes, which caused still more disturbance in China, set all tribunals against these men who had come to preach their doctrines, but who disagreed among themselves about their own doctrines,

Lastly, it was discovered that in Canton there were Dutch, Swedish, Danish and English who, though Christians, did not acknowledge themselves of the same religion as the Christians in Macao.

These considerations combined at length led the supreme tribunal of rites to prohibit the preaching of Christianity. The decree was issued on 10 January, 1724, but it inflicted no disgrace upon the missionaries, it exacted no severe penalties, and its expressions were not in the least offensive; the decree even suggested that the emperor should retain in Pekin those who might be useful in the teaching of mathematics. The emperor ratified the decree, and issued an edict ordering the missionaries to be sent back to Macao, attended by a mandarin, so that they should be safeguarded on the way and protected from all insults. These are the very words of the edict.

He retained some of them in attendance on his person, among them being the Jesuit Parennin, whose praises I have already sounded—a man renowned alike for his learning and for his wisdom, who spoke both Chinese and Tartar with fluency. He was indispensable, not only as an interpreter, but was an excellent mathematician. His reputation in France is principally based upon his erudite and instructive reports on Chinese science in his replies to the learned questions raised by one of our finest philosophers. This Jesuit had enjoyed the favour of the Emperor Kang-hi and still retained that of Young-tching. Could anyone have saved the Christian religion, it was he. With two other Jesuits he obtained audience of the emperor's brother, who was deputed to examine and report on the decree. Parennin gives a straightforward account of the reply that they received. The prince, who was inclined to favour them, declared: "Your actions puzzle me: I have read the accusations brought against you; your incessant disputes with the other Europeans concerning Chinese rites have done you infinite harm. What would you say if we came to Europe and behaved as you have done? In all honesty, would you tolerate it?" It was difficult to reply to such questions. However, they induced the prince to speak to the emperor on their behalf, and when they were admitted into the presence of the throne, the emperor informed them that he had finally decided to dismiss all those who styled themselves missionaries.

We have elsewhere quoted his words: "If you were

able to deceive my father, do not expect to do the same with me."

In spite of the judicious orders of the emperor, some of the Jesuits returned secretly to the provinces during the reign of the celebrated Young-tching's successor, and were condemned to death for having openly violated the laws of the empire. Not otherwise have Huguenot ministers been executed in France, when they have assembled people together against the orders of the king. As we have already remarked, this mania for proselytising is a disorder confined exclusively to our climes, and has always been unknown in Asia proper. The Eastern peoples have never sent missionaries into Europe, and it is only Western nations who have been eager to carry their opinions, like their commerce, to the extremities of the globe.

The Jesuits even brought about the deaths of several Chinese, noticeably of two princes of the blood who had befriended them. Must they not be accounted the most wretched of men to have come from one end of the world to the other in order to sow the seeds of discord in the imperial family and cause two princes to meet death on the scaffold! They thought to make their mission reverenced in Europe by claiming that God had declared for them, causing four crosses to appear against the clouds on the Chinese horizon. They had pictures of these crosses engraved in their *Instructive and Curious Letters*: but if God had wished China to become a Christian nation, would He have confined Himself to engraving crosses on the sky? Would He not have engraved them in the hearts of the Chinese?

THE END

INDEX

INDEX